Drew University Studies in Liturgy Series
General Editors: Kenneth E. Rowe and Robin A. Leaver

1. *Pulpit, Table, and Song: Essays in Celebration of Howard Hageman,* by Heather Murray Elkins and Edward C. Zaragoza
2. *St. James in the Streets: The Religious Processions of Loíza Aldea, Puerto Rico,* by Edward C. Zaragoza
3. *The Impact of the Liturgical Movement on American Lutheranism,* by Timothy C. J. Quill
4. *The Language of the Psalms in Worship: American Revisions of Watts's Psalter,* by Rochelle A. Stackhouse
5. *The Matter and Manner of Praise: The Controversial Evolution of Hymnody in the Church of England, 1760–1820,* by Thomas K. McCart
6. *"Bless the Lord, O My Soul": The New-York Liturgy of the Dutch Reformed Church, 1767,* by Daniel James Meeter
7. *The Eucharistic Service of the Catholic Apostolic Church and Its Influence on Reformed Liturgical Renewals of the Nineteenth Century,* by Gregg Alan Mast
8. *Moving toward Emancipatory Language: A Study of Recent Hymns,* by Robin Knowles Wallace
9. *Two Faces of Elizabethan Anglican Theology: Sacraments and Salvation in the Thought of William Perkins and Richard Hooker,* by Bryan D. Spinks
10. *The Language of Baptism: A Study of the Authorized Baptismal Liturgies of The United Church of Canada, 1925-1995,* by William S. Kervin

The Language of Baptism

A Study of the Authorized Baptismal Liturgies of The United Church of Canada, 1925-1995

William S. Kervin

Drew University Studies in Liturgy Series, No. 10

The Scarecrow Press, Inc.
Lanham, Maryland, and Oxford
2003

SCARECROW PRESS, INC.

Published in the United States of America
by Scarecrow Press, Inc.
A Member of the Rowman & Littlefield Publishing Group
4720 Boston Way, Lanham, Maryland 20706
www.scarecrowpress.com

PO Box 317
Oxford
OX2 9RU, UK

British Library Cataloguing in Publication Information Available

Library of Congress Cataloging-in-Publication Data
Kervin, William S., 1959–
The language of baptism : a study of the authorized baptismal liturgies of The United Church of Canada, 1925-1995 / William S. Kervin.
p. cm. — (Drew University studies in liturgy series ; no. 10)
Includes bibliographical references and index.
ISBN 0-8108-4653-5 (alk. paper)
1. United Church of Canada—Liturgy. 2. Baptism—United Church of Canada. I. Title. II. Series: Drew studies in liturgy ; no. 10.
BX9881 .K47 2003
264'.0792081—dc21

2002151532

∞™ The paper used in this publication meets the minimum requirements of American National Standard for Information Sciences—Permanence of Paper for Printed Library Materials, ANSI/NISO Z39.48-1992.
Manufactured in the United States of America.

In memory of

David R. Newman
Professor of Public Worship and Preaching
Emmanuel College, Toronto
1977-1990

Contents

Tables

Abbreviations

ASL (1984)	*A Sunday Liturgy for optional use in The United Church of Canada* (1984).
AV	Authorized Version.
BAS (draft)	A draft text of *The Book of Alternative Services of The Anglican Church of Canada.*
BAS	*The Book of Alternative Services of The Anglican Church of Canada* (1985).
BCO (1922)	*Book of Common Order for use in Church Services and Offices* (Presbyterian Church, Canada, 1922).
BCO (1932)	*The Book of Common Order of The United Church of Canada* (1932).
BCO (1940)	*The Book of Common Order of the Church of Scotland* (1940).
BCO (1964)	*The Book of Common Order of the Presbyterian Church in Canada* (1964).
BCP (1549)	*The Book of Common Prayer* (1549) in F. E. Brighton, *The English Rite*, Vol. II.
BCP (1552)	*The Book of Common Prayer* (1552) in F. E. Brighton, *The English Rite*, Vol. II.
BCP (1662)	*The Book of Common Prayer* (1662) in F. E. Brighton, *The English Rite*, Vol. II.
BCP (1892)	*The Book of Common Prayer* (Episcopal Church in the United States of America, 1892).
BCP (1918)	*The Book of Common Prayer* (The Church of England in the Dominion of Canada, 1918).
BCP (1928)	*The Book of Common Prayer with Additions and Deviations Proposed in 1928* (Church of England).
BCP (1959)	*The Book of Common Prayer* (The Anglican Church of Canada, 1959).

BCP (1962)	*The Book of Common Prayer* (The Anglican Church of Canada, 1962).
BCP (1979)	*The Book of Common Prayer* (The Episcopal Church, U.S.A., 1979).
BCR (1976)	*A Service of Baptism, Confirmation and Renewal* (The United Methodist Church, U.S.A., 1976).
BCW (1920)	*The Book of Congregational Worship* (Congregational Union of England and Wales, 1920).
BCW (1928)	*The Book of Common Worship* (Presbyterian, U.S.A., 1928).
BCW (1946)	*The Book of Common Worship* (Presbyterian, U.S.A., 1946).
BCW (1962)	*The Book of Common Worship* (The Church of South India, 1962).
BCW (1966)	*The Book of Common Worship: Provisional Services* (Presbyterian, U.S.A., 1966).
BPW (1949)	John Huxtable, et al., *A Book of Public Worship compiled for the use of Congregationalists* (1949).
BRBF (1986)	*Baptism and Renewal of Baptismal Faith for optional use in The United Church of Canada* (1986).
Bucer	Martin Bucer, *Censura* in E. C. Whitaker, *Martin Bucer and The Book of Common Prayer.*
BW (1986)	*Book of Worship: United Church of Christ* (U.S.A., 1986).
Calvin	John Calvin, *"The Form of Prayers, 1542,"* trans. J. D. C. Fisher in *Christian Initiation: The Reformation Period,* 112-177.
CGP	*Celebrate God's Presence: A Book of Services for The United Church of Canada* (The United Church of Canada, 2000).
CPB (1966)	*The Order for Confirmation with Provision for the Baptism of Persons Able to Answer for Themselves* (draft, The United Church of Canada, 1966).
DD (1874)	*The Doctrine and Discipline of the Methodist Church of Canada* (1874).
DD (1902)	*The Doctrine and Discipline of the Methodist Church* (Canada, 1902).
DD (1922)	*The Doctrine and Discipline of the Methodist Church* (Canada, 1922).
Dexter	Henry Martyn Dexter, *A Hand-Book of Congregationalism* (1880).
EUC	A draft order for baptism from Eden United Church, Mississauga, Ontario.
Forms	*Forms of Service for the Offices of the Church* (The United Church of Canada, 1926).
Hunter	John Hunter, *Devotional Services for Public Worship* (Congregational, 1880).

HWRP	Hymn-Worship Resource Project, The United Church of Canada.
Jackson	Samuel N. Jackson, *A Hand-Book of Congregationalism* (Canada, 1894).
Knox	John Knox, "The Order of Baptism," in *John Knox's Genevan Service Book,* William D. Maxwell, 105-111.
Luther (1523)	Martin Luther, "The Order of Baptism (1523)," in *Luther's Works,* Vol. 53, trans. Paul Zeller Strodach and Ulrich S. Leupold, 96-101.
Luther (1526)	Martin Luther, "The Order of Baptism Newly Revised (1526)," in *Luther's Works,* Vol. 53, trans. Paul Zeller Strodach and Ulrich S. Leupold, 107-109.
MSBC (1965)	*The Order for the Ministration of the Sacrament of Baptism to Children* (draft, The United Church of Canada, 1965).
NEB	The New English Bible.
ROP (year)	*Record of Proceedings of the General Council of The United Church of Canada.*
RSV	Revised Standard Version.
Sarum	"The Sarum Rite: The Order for the Making of a Catechumen, the Blessing of the Font, Baptism and Confirmation (1543)," in *Documents of the Baptismal Liturgy,* trans. J. D. C. Fisher, 231-253.
SB (1969)	*The Service Book for the use of ministers conducting public worship* (The United Church of Canada, 1969).
SS	*John Wesley's Sunday Service of the Methodists in North America.*
TEV	Today's English Version.
UCA	The United Church of Canada/Victoria University Archives, Toronto, Ontario.
UCC (adapted)	An order for baptism adapted from a draft of the United Church of Church of Christ *Book of Worship.*
VU	*Voices United: The Hymn and Worship Book of The United Church of Canada* (The United Church of Canada, 1996).
Year Book (year)	*Year Book & Directory,* The United Church of Canada.
Zwingli	Ulrich Zwingli, "Of Baptism (1525)," in *Christian Initiation: The Reformation Period,* trans. G. W. Bromiley, 126-131.

Acknowledgments

I would like to express my heartfelt thanks to all who have supported me in this work, from its dissertation form to the present. David Holeton graciously stepped in to direct the original research after the death of David Newman, providing wise guidance, and impressing upon me the importance of foundational historical research in liturgical theology. Friends and colleagues at Emmanuel College and the Toronto School of Theology continue to create an hospitable space for theological study and education. In particular, Peter Wyatt, Roger Hutchinson, Phyllis Airhart, and Fred Graham have given specific support to this project, and the staff of the United Church Archives at Victoria University remain a researcher's dream come true. Doug Fox, Lynda Katsuno, Ross Lockhart, and Kathryn Bonner provided skilled technical and research assistance. Thanks are also due to Kenneth Rowe, co-editor of this series, for his encouragement, and Nicole Averill and the staff at Scarecrow Press for their skill and patience.

Several institutions provided financial support for archival research, in particular, the Senate of Victoria University, Emmanuel College, the Social Sciences and Humanities Research Council of Canada, The Atlantic School of Theology, and The United Church of Canada.

On a more personal level, I remember also: the unfailing support of my parents, Dorothy and the late James Kervin; the friendship of the late Sylvia Dunstan, hymnwriter and liturgist; the inspiration of my first mentor in liturgical studies, the late David R. Newman; and, of course, Linda, of whom words fail and with whom even this was possible.

Finally, I am grateful to The United Church Publishing House for allowing me to reprint in full the liturgical texts relevant to this study. The following are reprinted with permission: *The Book of Common Order of The United Church of Canada* (Toronto: The United Church Publishing House, 1932), 97-112; *Service Book for the use of ministers conducting public worship* (Toronto: The United Church Publishing House, 1969), 39-74; *Baptism and Renewal of Baptismal Faith for optional use in The United Church of Canada.* The Division of Mission in Canada. (Toronto: The United Church of Canada, 1986), 8-15.

Introduction

Over the last three decades most of the major Christian denominations in North America and Europe have been involved in the examination and revision of their liturgical and pastoral practices surrounding Christian initiation. This activity has been precipitated by a convergence of several factors, among them, the reforms of the Second Vatican Council and the publication of the *Ordo Initiationis Christianae Adultorum*, The World Council of Churches' Faith and Order study *Baptism, Eucharist and Ministry*, contemporary scholarship on Christian initiation, and the context of the church in an increasingly post-Christian society.[1]

In 1977 the General Council of The United Church of Canada, responding to requests from congregations, began the task of examining available confirmation resources with a view to developing new ones. Within a year, however, the Task Force on Confirmation Resources had requested a larger mandate in order to examine the theology and practice of Christian initiation as a whole. Over the next six years the work of the Task Force on Christian Initiation resulted in two major reports, numerous congregational studies, countless submissions, and two churchwide precedent-setting remits requesting changes to the Basis of Union.[2] Eventually, in collaboration with the Working Unit on Worship and Liturgy, a new service of initiation, *Baptism and Renewal of Baptismal Faith*, was published "for optional use."[3] Related resources followed to support it which, in turn, functioned as a basis for revisions leading to the most recent services of initiation.

Each generation of liturgical resources has raised interesting questions about worship in the United Church, its history, theology, and practice—an area which has received surprisingly little scholarly attention.[4] With regard to Christian initiation in particular, it is noteworthy that in spite of the considerable amount of the church's energy and resources devoted to the subject over the years, the material remains largely unexamined. Such developments seem to have been overshadowed by other controversial issues which occupied the agenda of the United Church in the seventies and eighties, including inclusive language, human sexuality, sexual orientation, and the authority of scripture, to name but a few.

Upon closer examination, it can be shown that the United Church has studied the issue of Christian initiation several times during its relatively short history. Its liturgies have undergone at least four formal revisions to date. Within the last decade, a new generation of worship resources, *Voices United* and *Celebrate God's Presence,* has once again included the revision of services of initiation.[5]

Finally, on the pastoral level, many denominations have experienced in the renewal of initiation practices a renewal of their larger life and mission. A number of congregations in the United Church can testify to such results. It is becoming increasingly clear to many that, while Christian initiation is a complex issue, a multifaceted process in which historical, theological, pastoral, and liturgical dimensions converge, it is also one which possesses the potential for renewed understanding and commitment to the Christian faith in the context of contemporary life.

Purpose: Christian Initiation and United Church Worship

It is against this complex background of ecumenical development, liturgical scholarship, denominational history, and pastoral practice that this study will undertake an examination of the "authorized" (i.e., officially approved by the General Council) baptismal liturgies of The United Church of Canada from 1925 to 1995.

This research is an attempt to contribute to the discipline of liturgical study in at least two respects. First, as part of the larger issue of Christian initiation: as a major denomination, the history and development of Christian initiation in the United Church deserves to be studied as a contribution to the larger church and liturgical scholarship. Moreover, in the United Church context, it is a subject of continuing pastoral concern, but for which no developed critical liturgical study exists. This study hopes to take a step toward addressing this lacuna. An intended second contribution of this study relates to the issue of worship in The United Church of Canada generally. As a case study in one aspect of the liturgical history and theology of the United Church, such work can also contribute to the United Church's understanding of its own liturgical identity, an area which has only just begun to be examined in detail.

The thesis of this study is that, during the period in question, the authorized baptismal liturgies of The United Church of Canada show an evolution toward the classic (patristic) liturgical forms of Christian initiation gleaned from the liturgical scholarship of the day. An examination of each new generation of resources will show the introduction of several liturgical features reflective of the scholarship of the era, features which are very often experienced as "new" to the United Church at the time. Throughout the process of developing the material, the compilers consistently pressed for the use of more classic forms. This was tempered at each stage by a popular suspicion of those features which did not seem part of "Reformed" practice and theology or "United Church tradition."

The resulting compromise was that some forms were introduced, others were abandoned, and some were adapted for use within the United Church context of the time. The net result was, nevertheless, a gradual evolution in the direction of a greater catholicity of form and content.

To the extent that this study of authorized baptismal liturgies will serve as a case study in United Church worship, I believe these findings to be of significance. Often, for example, new liturgical resources born of the liturgical scholarship of the time raise popular concerns over a departure from United Church tradition. However, this study of baptismal liturgies will demonstrate that the United Church tradition has been surprisingly consistent in recovering "new" classic forms in each generation. Indeed, the accusation of betraying United Church tradition has been heard with the introduction of each generation of services, only to be forgotten in years to come. United Church tradition would appear to be, to use James White's description of Protestant worship, a "tradition in transition."[6]

In addition, certain lines of United Church liturgical evolution will be evident throughout this study, among them: unapologetic liturgical ecumenism (the liberal use and adaptation of material from other traditions); the tendency towards structural simplicity (that is, the integration of several previous orders into fewer and fewer orders); an increasing consciousness of lectionary and calendar in worship; an increasing appreciation of the classic "Word and table" shape of worship (and therein an increasing appreciation of sacramental celebration); more explicit participation of the gathered community in the words and actions of the liturgy; and the use of an increasing variety of biblical and liturgical metaphors, symbols, actions, and gestures.

This is not to suggest that the evolution of authorized baptismal liturgies (and United Church worship resources in general) is beyond criticism. Indeed, in the course of this study the discovery of a variety of provocative problems, surprising developments, and intriguing inconsistencies will lend more subtlety to our understanding. While the present work will stop short of an examination of the most recent generation of liturgical resources (*Voices United* and *Celebrate God's Presence*), it is hoped that insights from the first seventy years of the United Church will prove useful for liturgical scholarship yet to come.

Methodology: Expository Liturgical Theology

As already mentioned, and as the subtitle to this book suggests, this study will be limited in both content and scope—i.e., focused on the authorized baptismal liturgies from 1925 to 1995. Such a methodology is not meant to imply that these texts represent uniformity or normativity in the celebration of baptism as practiced in all congregations of the United Church.[7] Liturgical liberty is both a respected hallmark of and valued reality within United Church worship, and the celebration of baptism is no exception. However, it can be demonstrated that less liberty is usually taken in baptism than in most other orders of worship.

Similarly, where such creativity and experimentation are exercised in baptism it is most often in the form of a variation based upon the authorized text(s). Therefore, a consideration of the texts themselves is a productive method of liturgical study.

Regarding the seventy-year focus of this examination and the exclusion of the most recent generation of liturgical resources from consideration, the reasons are both practical and methodological. Practically speaking, the recently published resources, *Voices United* and *Celebrate God's Presence*, present a quantity of initiation-related material beyond the space available in this study. The baptismal texts alone in *Celebrate God's Presence*, for example, occupy over fifty pages. A detailed source commentary of these texts, in the style used in this study, warrants a separate piece of work. From a methodological perspective, the value of covering the ground preceding *Voices United* and *Celebrate God's Presence* lies in examining the foundational resources which continue to inform contemporary developments. As one who worked with the committees which produced these most recent resources, I have observed how future directions continue to depend upon assumptions about our liturgical past.

It is also worth noting that in spite of the United Church's popular concern about the content of worship, there is very little in the way of a developed tradition of the study of our liturgical texts, their origins and implications. It is hoped that this examination will contribute to the building of such a tradition. It is, to be sure, only a beginning to what must be carried on in further studies. Examinations of actual baptismal practice and popular liturgical style are also needed and would most certainly involve different methodological approaches, albeit those that could benefit from the findings of a study of the authorized texts.

This study is historical to the extent that archival information relating to the formation of the liturgies is an essential and important part, but it is not primarily a historical study. It is liturgical to the extent that authorized liturgical texts will form the basis of its analysis, but it will not attempt a thorough description of popular practice. It is theological to the extent that it raises theological issues in the analysis of the liturgies, but it does not attempt a systematic sacramental theology of baptism. It can best be described as an exercise in expository liturgical theology—that is to say, liturgical and theological reflection arising out of an examination and exposition of the texts in question. The texts will serve as a starting point for reflection and analysis. Throughout the study archival information on the formation and content of the texts will prove especially valuable and related information on the United Church context will be introduced where it illuminates the understanding of the texts and their function. I believe this to be a valid methodological approach insofar as it mirrors the way liturgical texts often function in the United Church—i.e., as a reference point for liturgical adaptation to a specific pastoral context.

Another practical reason for limiting the scope of this dissertation to the authorized baptismal liturgies is the quantity of information which could arguably be related to the broad area of Christian initiation. Historical, liturgical and theological works, church publications and curricula, congregational records, personal interviews, and surveys relating to popular practice could all be gathered within the scope of a study of Christian initiation. My focus on the baptismal liturgies themselves is intended to make a more manageable beginning. There is no pretense that this study exhausts the subject.

Thus, the primary sources forming the basis of this study are the period of the liturgical texts themselves and their respective sources. To support their examination, other primary sources are used: the archival materials which show the formation of the service books and their liturgies; the personal papers of some of the key figures responsible for the work of the worship committees of the United Church; and a number of articles bearing on the subject itself. Much of this material has not been documented or studied and therefore its use constitutes original research.

Material in the United Church *Year Books* and General Council *Record of Proceedings*, as well as *The New Outlook* and its successor *The United Church Observer*, will also shed light on the texts and their development at various points in the study. Some use of other church archival records, church documents and publications will also be made at various points. Secondary sources on Canadian church history, liturgy, and Christian initiation will contribute to the analysis.

Finally, two works relating to this study warrant particular mention and credit. Thomas and Bruce Harding's historical monographs, *Presbyterian, Methodist and Congregational Worship in Canada Prior to 1925* and *Patterns of Worship in The United Church of Canada, 1925-1987,*[8] provide an important overview of United Church worship in general and the formation of the service books and their major orders. This study of United Church baptismal liturgies builds upon the Hardings' foundational work by covering some of the same ground with respect to the formation and development of some of the liturgical texts. It differs from their work, however, insofar as it focuses specifically on the baptismal liturgies themselves and some of the issues raised. This allows for a more detailed treatment of some of the liturgical texts, an examination of other texts not covered in the Hardings's work, and a different interpretation of their overall development.

Structure: Four Eras of United Church Worship

This study is divided into four main parts. Part I, "The Founding Ethos and its Forms," will examine the contributions of the Congregationalist, Presbyterian, and Methodist churches to the baptismal liturgies which formed the United Church's first service book, *Forms of Service.*[9] This little-known and often overlooked service book will provide an interesting glimpse into the origins of United Church baptismal liturgies, the contributions of the founding traditions, and the birth of the United Church liturgical ethos.

Part II, "Coming of Age through Common Order," will examine the baptismal orders of *The Book of Common Order.*[10] It will include a brief overview of the formation of this United Church "classic," a detailed source commentary on the baptismal texts themselves, followed by an analysis of some of the liturgical and theological issues they raise. This part will demonstrate the degree to which the texts depend upon the liturgies of the reformers and the *Book of Common Prayer*. It will also show how the texts reveal the attempt to recover some of the classic liturgical forms available, and mark the beginning of a movement to replace the notion of profession of faith with a more "sacramental" notion of confirmation.

Parts III and IV, "Responding to the Contemporary" and "Ecumenical Convergence in Christian Initiation," will be organized along the same lines as part II, using the baptismal liturgies from the *Service Book*[11] and *Baptism and Renewal of Baptismal Faith*, respectively. The study of the *Service Book* texts will show, among other things, the rise of liberal United Church antisacramentalism with respect to baptism on the one hand and the emergence of confirmation as a "quasi-sacrament" on the other, and the introduction of several "new" classic liturgical forms. The study of *Baptism and Renewal of Baptismal Faith* will show the influence of the ecumenical liturgical movement on United Church worship.

All four parts will also seek to provide insight into the way in which liturgical texts are drafted and become officially authorized in the United Church. They will also illustrate the participation of the larger church in this process and some of the tensions which accompanied it. With respect to *The Book of Common Order*, the *Service Book*, and *Baptism and Renewal of Baptismal Faith*, the study will present commentaries documenting the sources of the texts to enable their use as a reference in further research. Finally, to the extent that the four main parts of this study also correspond to four past generations of United Church baptismal liturgies, they may be seen as indicative of four eras in United Church worship.

While this study seeks to demonstrate that the authorized baptismal liturgies of The United Church of Canada show an evolution toward classic liturgical forms, I do not consider the demonstration of this particular thesis as its most important contribution. Equally important, in my view, is the source work presented in the commentaries and the overall history of the development of the texts by the compilers. To be sure, a perspective on the development of baptismal liturgies in the United Church (and, by extrapolation, the development of United Church worship), is argued here. But it is also my hope that the value of the study extends beyond the particular thesis being put forward. As critical liturgical scholarship continues to develop in the United Church, I believe it important to do both foundational and interpretive work, while remaining open to alternative interpretations of the same data. To this end, this study concludes in part V, "The Language of Baptism and the Language of Worship," not only with a defense of the particular perspective presented here, but also with a brief consideration of some alternative interpretations worthy of further study, as well as brief comment in anticipation of future directions.

Notes

1. *Ordo Initiationis Christianae Adultorum* (Vatican City: Typis Polyglottis Vaticanis, 1972). The Canadian text is *Rite of Christian Initiation of Adults* (Ottawa: Canadian Conference of Catholic Bishops, 1987); *Baptism, Eucharist and Ministry*, World Council of Churches Faith and Order Paper, no. 111. (Geneva: World Council of Churches, 1982). First Canadian Edition (Toronto: The Anglican Book Centre, 1983).

2. *Christian Initiation: The Quest for Renewal*, Division of Mission in Canada, The Task Force on Christian Initiation (Toronto: The United Church of Canada, 1979); *The Report of the Project Group on Christian Initiation*, Division of Mission in Canada, The Project Group on Christian Initiation (Toronto: The United Church of Canada, 1983).

3. *Baptism and Renewal of Baptismal Faith for optional use in The United Church of Canada*, The Task Group on Christian Initiation, The Working Unit on Worship and Liturgy, Division of Mission in Canada (Toronto: The United Church of Canada, 1986) [*BRBF* (1986)].

4. Apart from a few short articles on different aspects of United Church worship, only a handful of significant studies in the area of its liturgy have been made: Alan Barthel, David R. Newman, and Paul Scott Wilson, *A Guide to Sunday Worship in The United Church of Canada* (Toronto: The United Church Publishing House, 1988); Charlotte Caron, *Eager for Worship: Theologies, Practices, and Perspectives on Worship in The United Church of Canada.* The McGeachy Papers, VII (Toronto: Division of Ministry Personnel and Education, 2000); William R. Plato, "Eucharistic Worship and The United Church of Canada" (Ph.D. diss., St. Michael's College, Toronto, 1974); Thomas R. Harding, *Presbyterian, Methodist and Congregational Worship in Canada Prior to 1925* (Toronto: Evensong, 1995); Thomas R. Harding and Bruce Harding, *Patterns of Worship in The United Church of Canada, 1925-1997* (Toronto: Evensong, 1996), monographs of Thomas Harding's graduate dissertations, "The Major Orders of *The Book of Common Order* of The United Church of Canada (1932): Sources and Development" (ThM. Thesis, Vancouver School of Theology, 1986) and "The Development of Liturgical Resources in The United Church of Canada: 1930-1986" (Th.D. diss., Trinity College, Toronto, 1990); William S. Kervin, "*Forms of Service (1926):* A Study in the Liturgical Ethos of The United Church of Canada," *Toronto Journal of Theology,* 17/2 (Fall 2001): 215-229; "The Language of Baptism: A Study of the Authorized Baptismal Liturgies of The United Church of Canada" (Th.D. diss., Emmanuel College, Toronto, 1994); "The Three Hymn Books of The United Church of Canada: The Dialectic of a New Song," *Touchstone*, 19/2 (May 2001): 6-21. Barthel, *et. al.* and Caron's works are general in scope. Plato's work has little bearing on this study in both subject and scope. My previous work, drawn from dissertation research, is incorporated into this study. Harding's work is also directly related. In the work which follows, I will cite the earlier and more thorough dissertation versions of Harding's monographs.

5. *Voices United: The Hymn and Worship Book of The United Church of Canada* (Toronto: The United Church Publishing House, 1996) [*VU*]; *Celebrate God's Presence: A Book of Services for The United Church of Canada* (Toronto: United Church Publishing House, 2000) [*CGP*].

6. James F. White, *Protestant Worship: Traditions in Transition* (Louisville: Westminster/John Knox Press, 1989).

7. For some methodological discussions on the implications of textual study, see, for example: Lawrence A. Hoffman, *Beyond the Text: A Holistic Approach to Liturgy* (Bloomington and Indianapolis: Indiana University Press, 1987); Frank Senn, "Protestant Worship: Does it Exist?" *Worship* 64, no. 4 (1990): 322-330; Keith Watkins, "Protestant

Worship: Many Traditions or One?" *Worship* 64, no. 4 (1990): 308-331; White, *Protestant Worship*, 13-24.

8. See n. 4 above.

9. *Forms of Service for the Offices of the Church* (Toronto: The United Church Publishing House, 1926) [*Forms*].

10. *The Book of Common Order of The United Church of Canada.* (Toronto: The United Church Publishing House, 1926) [*BCO* (1932)].

11. *Service Book for the use of ministers conducting public worship* (Toronto: The United Church Publishing House, 1969) [*SB* (1969)].

Part I
The Founding Ethos and Its Forms

Chapter 1
Baptism in the Founding Traditions and *Forms of Service*

A Starting Point for Study

Informed discussions of worship in The United Church of Canada tend to include some degree of respectful acknowledgment of the place of *The Book of Common Order* in the liturgical history of that denomination. This is as it should be, for as we shall see in its baptismal rites, it is a significant work of liturgical scholarship and important in the liturgical ethos of the United Church. Nevertheless, it is interesting to observe that such discussions seldom include any mention of the first service book in The United Church of Canada, *Forms of Service*. United Church historians seem to have little knowledge of it; liturgical scholars, little interest.[1]

This is both understandable and misleading. It is understandable to the extent that there is a sense in which *The Book of Common Order* can be thought of as the first service book of The United Church of Canada. But it is misleading to the extent that *Forms* was the first service book in the United Church and therein suggests a very different starting point for liturgical scholarship in that denomination. To be sure, *The Book of Common Order* was the first to provide the full range of liturgical resources, from orders of public worship and sacraments to occasional services and a "Treasury of Prayers." This was a new book with new liturgies for a new church and was meant to have a lasting effect. However, *Forms* is theologically and liturgically significant insofar as it is an expression of the intentional liturgical diversity which characterized early United Church worship. Indeed, the evidence suggests that until after the postwar period, when the United Church came of age and *The Book of Common Order* came into its own, it was *Forms* which best characterized United Church liturgical life. I will return to these considerations at the end of this chapter. For now, the implication is that if *Forms* is the proper starting point for the United Church service books, the founding traditions are the corresponding starting point for the study of United Church worship. Thus, in this study of authorized baptismal liturgies of The United Church of Canada, I will briefly examine the baptismal liturgies of the Congregational Churches of Canada, the Presbyterian Church in Canada, and the Methodist Church, Canada, endeavoring also to provide an overview of their relevant historical, theological, and liturgical context. An appreciation of the baptismal themes of the founding traditions will in turn lay some of the groundwork for an understanding of their United Church variations in *Forms* and later.

The Congregationalist Contribution

Congregationalists in Canada

The site of the first Congregationalist meeting place in Canada is now occupied by St. Matthew's United Church, Halifax, Nova Scotia. That plot of land can be seen as a symbol of the meandering journey of the Congregationalist tradition in Canada. It has been home to an Independent Dissenter's chapel, a Puritan meeting-house, a Presbyterian church, and now, a congregation of The United Church of Canada.[2]

In 1749 it was mostly Independents, with some Anglicans, who arrived in Halifax in response to the governor's invitation to found a new colony. The Dissenters' Chapel opened in March of 1751, but it soon became Mather's Meeting-house when they had to turn to the American Puritans for a minister. Waves of New England settlers brought rapid growth for a time, but this "boom" was to be short-lived.[3] The factors which precipitated the "bust" which followed illustrate the harsh realities of frontier life. Poverty-stricken pioneers could not support their churches and ministers. Henry Alline's "Newlight" evangelistic movement divided most of these churches, many of them becoming Baptist.[4] The politics of the American Revolution divided them further, prompting an exodus back to New England.[5] Finally, Congregationalism in Nova Scotia failed to organize itself sufficiently beyond the congregational level to secure its long-term future and withstand such pressures.[6] In short, poverty, piety, politics, and polity conspired against Congregationalist survival in Nova Scotia. Finally, after having gone over thirty years without a settled minister, Mather's Meeting-house turned to the Church of Scotland for leadership to become St. Matthew's Presbyterian Church.

Forced to start over, Congregationalism got its new lease on life in Upper and Lower Canada with Henry Wilkes as the catalyst. His work among the various missionary societies based in England, Scotland, and America helped establish the kind of infrastructure and systemic support needed to sustain church life on the frontier.[7] In this they had learned from the Maritime experience.

On the prairies and in western Canada, Congregationalism made an important but often overlooked contribution. While small in numbers, they were mighty in the spirit of the local "Union" churches which united members of many denominations and, in turn, made the ground in which the United Church took root more fertile. It has even been suggested that at the time of church union in 1925, while Presbyterian and Methodists were afraid of being swallowed by each other, "when they were not looking the Congregationalists swallowed them both."[8]

Congregationalism in Canada learned much from its journey from Halifax westward, from the gathering Dissenters to The United Church of Canada—much about independence and interdependence, separatism and survival, autonomy and unity. Such lessons deserve to be noted as a lasting, if subtle, contribution to The United Church of Canada. One could argue, for example, that the long-standing sympathies of the United Church toward frontier piety, practical ecumenism, and congregational independence are, at least in part, an expression of its Congregationalist genes. A consideration of Congregationalist baptismal orders bears this out.

Congregationalist Orders for Baptism

Congregationalists acquired their name from their passionate commitment to the autonomy and authority of the local congregation. As one early writer put it: "They [the English Puritans] hold and maintain that every Company, Congregation or Assembly of men, ordinarily joining together in the true worship of God, is a true visible church of Christ, and that the same title is improperly attributed to any other convocations, Synods, Societies, combinations, or assemblies whatsoever."[9] Accordingly, the gathered community of "covenant-members" ruled in matters of polity and worship. This has important ecclesiological implications, to which I will return below. It is raised here as an introductory caution, complicating the work of any study of worship and making it difficult to generalize about specific liturgical practices. The respect accorded the context of the local congregation meant that liturgical diversity was not only possible but encouraged.[10]

Keeping this in mind, the best place to begin is with an appreciation of the early Puritan critique of *The Book of Common Prayer*.[11] Early controversy centered around the doctrine of transubstantiation in the eucharist and the wearing of the surplice in the liturgy. Both were rejected as "Romish" beliefs and unbiblical customs which tempted the faithful to idolatry and superstition, compromising the integrity and faith of the Church.[12] These three principles—idolatry, superstition and scriptural warrant—were common themes which lay behind most of the Puritan objections. Among the other objections which followed were: the lack of simple, plain, and audible vernacular in the liturgy; the dependence on written and imposed texts; tiresome and long prayers, litanies, and psalms; brief and irrelevant collects; the confused and unintelligible reading of hymns; superstitious emphasis on prescribed gestures; the idolatry of images; the unscriptural observance of Lent and saints days; errors in the translation of lections; the use of lessons from the Apocrypha; the requirement to kneel to receive communion; and the private prayers of the priest at communion.[13] The use of the *BCP*, they argued, had created an experience of worship which was, all too often, simply a "confused murmur" and had rendered clerics "bare readers," and "blind guides," excluding the "gift of prayer"—that "one special qualification for the work of the ministry"—from worship.[14] For the Puritans, worship according to the *BCP* had been reduced to the mere ability to intone a stale text and follow prescribed forms, all of which flew in the face of a biblical and apostolic faith.

The application of such a critique to the baptismal liturgy resulted in several specific claims contrary to the present liturgical practice: only the children of believers who "made due profession of their repentance" should be baptized; proper notice and preparation should be given prior to baptism; questions should be addressed to the parents rather than the godparents; the font should be placed in a location fully visible to the congregation; the reference to biblical types of water in the "flood" prayer should be altered so as not to suggest that they were sanctified by Jesus' baptism; no implication should be given in the baptismal prayers that every child is "regenerated by God's Holy Spirit" in baptism; the practice of signing with the cross should be eliminated; private baptism and baptism by the laity should be discontinued; several changes should be made to the Catechism in keeping with actual practice and the scriptural witness; and confirmation should not be held up as more important than baptism (such as is implied when the bishop must preside) or a barrier to communion but should be discontinued and made into a requirement of instruction and examination.[15]

The Puritan distrust of liturgical texts caused them to prefer "forms," "orders of service," and "directories" over liturgies of common prayer. The following order, for example, was taught by a seventeenth century English Independent professor as representative of Congregationalist baptismal practice at the time.

> Short Introductory Prayer
> Discourse on a suitable text
> Prayer of Confession and Petition for Grace for the Parents
> Interrogation of Parents
> Pronouncement of the Triune Name and Baptism
> Charge to the Parents
> Prayer of Thanksgiving (for the family and its branches and for Christ's
> interest in the present generation)
> The Blessing[16]

One early American book does not even include an order of service for baptism, treating the subject generally in one paragraph.

> Baptism is usually administered by sprinkling, but as Congregationalists believe that the reverent application of water, in proper relations, *in any form* by a competent administrator, is baptism, candidates with whom it is a matter of conscience, are baptized by immersion. The form of words employed is simply that indicated by the Master [Matt. xxviii: 19] in his last command.[17]

Water and the trinitarian formula would seem to suffice.

In Canada, during the decades approaching the formation of the United Church, two Congregationalist service books were in popular use and can be viewed as indicative of the shape, content, and range of baptismal practice in this period: John Hunter's *Devotional Services for Public Worship* and Samuel N. Jackson's *A Hand-Book of Congregationalism*. While Hunter's work is more liturgically conservative than Jackson's, both presuppose the Congregationalist principle of liturgical freedom.[18]

Hunter's "An order for the Baptism and Dedication of Children" can be summarized as follows:

Scripture Sentences (many)
Address
Prayer (of Thanksgiving, for the Spirit, for the parents and the child)
Baptism
Declaration
Prayer (the Spirit's blessing on the child, parents, congregation, and Church)
Lord's Prayer
Benediction[19]

Several things about this service are noteworthy. The title may indicate either some degree of ambiguity about precise theological view of baptism, and/or an effort to provide for the option of dedication. The Address speaks of "the service in which we are now engaged" (it does not name it as a service of baptism *per se*) as one of "thanksgiving," "recognition," "testimony," "initiation," "dedication," and "consecration." The action of baptism itself provides the option of baptizing with the trinitarian formula or dedicating with an appropriate formula.[20] In short, all of the bases seem covered, from the Anglican to the Baptist! While this may appear ambiguous or radical to the liturgically conservative, from a Congregationalist perspective it could be viewed as more comprehensive and biblical, drawing upon a fuller range of baptismal meanings, resisting the temptation to settle on any one in particular, and providing for a range of pastoral and liturgical options relative to the congregational context. Thus, the liturgy suggests a wide range of Congregationalist baptismal practice and meaning at the turn of the century and implies a very liberal liturgical theology of initiation.

This is confirmed by several other features as well. A rubric introducing the service suggests that it was used during or after morning or evening worship, or on its own, and that by this time private baptisms were not unknown.[21] Note also that no questions are asked of the parents, nor is any baptismal symbol used in the form of an apostolic or other confession of faith. The address simply exhorts faith and counsels that participation in the rite is faithful testimony on the part of the parents and those gathered. There is, of course, no blessing of the water (this would have been viewed as superstitious or idolatrous) and the epiclesis is multiple and general, invoking the Spirit on all the action and the congregation in the numerous prayers. The dominant ethos of the order is simplicity and liberty.

Jackson's Canadian "Baptismal Service" represents a kind of middle ground between the American one-paragraph treatment and Hunter. (Once again, Canadians find themselves located somewhere between the Americans and the English.) The service can be outlined as follows:

Hymn (optional)
Scripture Sentences
Statement
Baptism
Prayer
Chant or Hymn (optional)
Benediction[22]

The rubrics make clear that the service is to be adapted as appropriate for children or adults. Again, no question is asked, the Statement serving as a combination of exhortation and address, to which the candidates or parents assent.

> Dearly beloved, believing that the promises of God extend to [you] [your offspring,] and that the ordinance of baptism is a seal of his grace, a sign of the work of the Holy Spirit in the heart; and considering it both a privilege and a duty thus to dedicate [yourself] [your children] to the service of God; you do now devote [yourself] [them] to the Lord to be his forever. [Relying upon divine grace for aid, you do solemnly engage to teach your children God's holy work and endeavour, with all your ability, to lead them in the way of life everlasting through our Lord Jesus Christ.].[23]

Baptism is "belief," "ordinance," "seal," "sign," "privilege," "duty," "dedication," "devotion." If the range of theological meaning seems broad, it is rooted in a theology of covenant, the promise being to "you and your children" (Acts 2:39). In spite of this foundation, however, the sense remains individualistic, leaving little explicit association between baptism and incorporation into the church.

Then follows baptism by sprinkling with the trinitarian formula. A closing rubric calls for extemporary Prayer and allows for an optional Chant or Hymn followed by a closing Benediction. It also betrays the occasional practice of private baptism.[24] The service leaves unclear the question of where in the regular service of worship baptism might have been celebrated.

On the level of liturgical action, Hunter's and Jackson's services share common elements. In both, questions or vows are not explicitly asked of the parents or candidates, assent to an address or exhortation being assumed. It could be that the questions dropped out with the Puritan omission of the use of godparents.[25] Congregationalists also here exhibit their Puritan discomfort with the historic creeds. Historically, baptismal questions and/or vows were most often structured along the lines of the Apostles' Creed, a statement which many early Puritans ceased to use in public worship because it was associated with "the corruptions of Rome" and was not scripture.[26] Many North American Congregationalists came to emphasize the experience of conversion over creedal assent.[27]

While the application of water "in the name of the Father and of the Son and of the Holy Ghost" is clearly the essential component of the rite, a curious variation on this is found in Jackson's order. The formula "I baptize thee

J__N__ [sic] into the name of the Father and of the Son and of the Holy Ghost"[28] tends more toward the practice of a naming ceremony. The water is most often applied by sprinkling, probably by a single application, since no specific mention is made of a three-fold application. Prominent baptismal fonts were not common in Congregationalist architecture. On the other hand, the Puritan desire for visible action was often met in those instances where a Presbyterian-style of baptism was followed. A metal ring attached to the pulpit held a basin and the child was passed up to the minister for baptism at the pulpit. Here even baptism is a proclamation of the Word. Most often a simple bowl placed on the communion table would suffice. The lack of emphasis on fonts permitted both easy adaptation for baptisms at home and the freedom for adult baptism by immersion. The use of the candidate's name was always called for.

This cursory examination of the baptismal liturgies of the Congregationalist tradition in Canada begs a deeper level of reflection. If, on the surface, the emphasis seems to have been on liturgical freedom, it is only because this is one expression of a more profound issue: the primacy of scripture. For early Puritans the Word of God was "the supreme liturgical criterion."[29] Theirs has been called a "rigorous biblicism" to the point of "hyper-Calvinism."[30] The notions of dominical institution and scriptural warrant are here taken to extremes.[31] Architecturally, to avoid any semblance of idolatry, they often went so far as to replace visual art and sculpture with biblical inscriptions. They rejected the high altar only to replace it with the elevated pulpit.[32] If the Reformers can be accused of making scripture a "paper pope," Congregationalists show us a particular example of the phenomenon of "the text as idol." One historian has called it "bibliolatry."[33]

Yet, even at such extremes, it should be kept in mind that for Congregationalists allegiance to the Word of God was intended as a witness to the freedom of the gospel. To put it another way, freedom in worship was not the absolute liberty to worship as one pleases (this would never have been tolerated), but rather freedom from the *Book of Common Prayer* and, more precisely, the freedom to worship according to God's Word. In this they shared common ground with the Reformers.[34]

In the baptismal orders examined above, such biblicism is manifested in the use of biblical texts functioning as scriptural warrants at or near the beginning of the services. In particular, Mark's story of Jesus' blessing the children (Mk. 10: 13, 14) and Matthew's "Great Commission" (Mt. 28:18-20) figure prominently, most often functioning together as a kind of dominical institution for baptism in general and infant baptism in particular. Acts 2:38, 39 is the primary text used to affirm the covenant promise "to you and to your children."[35]

Congregationalist liturgical freedom and the primacy of scripture also raises the issue of ecclesiology. Liturgical freedom is not only the freedom to worship according to the Word of God, but also the freedom to worship according to the ideal of the Apostolic Church, that goal of pristine simplicity which one Puritan called "the old glorious beautiful face of Christianity."[36] Congregationalist ecclesiology also rests upon a hermeneutics of biblicism to assert the catholicity of the congregation. To this end, many congregations formulated their own "confession of faith" or "covenant" articulating their contemporary appropriation of the apostolic faith—very often in terms which revealed a high degree of doctrinal debt to the Westminster Confession. "Covenant-membership" in the local congregation was granted to those who made public profession of Christ before the congregation.

This particular brand of covenant ecclesiology is evident at many points in the baptismal orders. The omission of godparents was related to the conviction that parents themselves should be answerable regarding spiritual responsibility for their children and the covenant which they enjoy. Originally, Congregationalists also objected to private baptisms on similar grounds. As a sacrament of the church, baptism should be administered in that context, the congregation thus living out its covenant responsibilities to God and one another through the corporate proclamation of the gospel and the mutual support and nurture of children and parents. Private baptism undermines these dimensions, inviting moralistic piety and individualistic faith.

Covenant ecclesiology is further evidenced as one looks beyond the baptismal liturgies themselves to the broader context of "Christian initiation." While space does not permit a detailed examination of Congregationalist life and piety, two features can be noted. First, the formal and informal catechesis nurtured by such customs as "expositions," "prophesyings," "readers services," and family worship.[37] Such practices affirm a vision of the covenant community that extends well beyond the Sunday liturgy.

Second, the importance of membership services. Hunter includes "A Dedication Service or, Order for the Admission of Baptised Persons to Full Communion with the Church."[38] It, rather than baptism, is the service which carries the connotation of initiation into the life of the church. Jackson's equivalent in the *Hand-book*, a service for the "Reception of Members,"[39] is more original. It seems to have fulfilled a variety of purposes, from the welcoming of new members from other traditions to profession or renewal of faith and the baptism of adults. This service contains more active congregational participation than the Baptismal Service.[40] It also speaks explicitly of the "Christian faith and covenant" in which all share. This suggests the important place given to congregational membership insofar as this service is more ecclesiologically well-rounded and liturgically sophisticated than the service of baptism. Furthermore, it is the first order of service in the book and is the only officially approved liturgical text. Such status is reminiscent of those Puritan beginnings where the admission to full "covenant membership" in a particular congregation by an individual was one of the pillars of the Congregationalist edifice. In New England and Canada it was often this profession of faith before the congregation, sometimes expressed as an experience of conversion or "holiness," which was understood as bringing the believer (and their children) into the covenant of the communion of saints. Again, there is a sense in which this was initiation; baptism was secondary—and an "open table" was waiting for all who could bear witness to this regenerating work of the Spirit in their lives.[41]

Finally, the evolving importance of this service, rather than that of baptism, reveals another aspect of Congregationalist piety at the turn of the century. Such considerations are best examined by reminding ourselves of Puritan origins in that period distinguished by the invention of the printing press and the subsequent popularization of the biblical text.

> [T]he Puritans were the educated middle class of the time. They were literate people who were on their way up socially and economically and had learned that politics could serve their personal advancement. In modern terms, they were pious yuppies. . . . Literacy had made these people much less dependent on visual images for information than their ancestors and at the same time made words, printed and spoken, far more important for the communication of truth. The linear mentality, of things happening one after another as in reading or preaching, had a stronger grip on their imagination than the all-at-once simultaneity of the visual.[42]

This worldview sets the stage for strong sympathies with the rationalism of the Enlightenment. By the eighteenth century, biblicism and empiricism had conspired to move the sacraments to the periphery of Congregationalist worship. By the nineteenth century, the normative liturgical experience was very much that of "Public Worship" rather than the Eucharist.[43]

Jackson's *Hand-Book* shows a similar shift from baptism to "Reception of Members." The didacticism of all the services also transposed Calvinist penitential piety into a nineteenth century moralistic key, emphasizing Divine immanentism, the historic Jesus, and the early Social Gospel.[44] While at the turn of the century Canadian Congregationalists may been more working class than their "pious yuppy" forebears, they still shared something of their antiestablishment zeal for authentic worship. They simply went about working out the implications of this in a new context.

In conclusion, what should one look for in the baptismal liturgies of the United Church as evidence of the Congregationalist contribution and influence? From among the several characteristic features and liturgical elements discussed, I would suggest the following list: 1. liturgical freedom embodied in simple directories; 2. biblicism, as evidenced by the prominence of particular scriptural warrants for liturgical action; 3. a congregational ecclesiology and covenant theology; 4. an antisacramental worldview marked by few symbols and an austerity of liturgical action; 5. more emphasis on "reception of members" or "admission to full communion" than on baptism.

The Presbyterian Contribution

Presbyterians in Canada

While the first Presbyterians in Nova Scotia were drawn largely from the New England colonies, immigration from the British Isles (mostly Scotland) dominated the picture after the American Revolution.[45] As always, frontier conditions presented serious challenges: it was impossible to communicate regularly with the Church of Scotland and thus benefit from its support and discipline; the presbytery system of organization and polity struggled to adapt to colonial geography; ministers of the Kirk were reluctant to leave the comfort of home and give themselves to voluntarily supported settlements; insistence upon the high standards of ministerial training in the face of few resources made the nurture of an indigenous ministry slow. In time, such obstacles were overcome. They asserted their own independence and adopted a more democratic style of decision making. They began to move beyond the inherited Old World divisions toward greater unity. They founded institutions for the education of their own clergy and the overall support of Christian education.[46]

This liberalizing trend continued in Upper and Lower Canada and westward. With the Anglicans as the state-supported church, Presbyterians were forced to contend with a radically different place in a new society, competing in a religious marketplace with other groups. This resulted in a combination of survivalist pragmatism and missionary concern, as evidenced by their organizational efficiency and stewardship, ecumenical cooperation and outreach. In this respect, the "provincialism of Scottish Presbyterianism" was less evident in the Canadian context. While some of this may be attributed to the influence of the U.S. churches, "the resulting blend" was "neither American nor British, but Canadian."[47]

The uniqueness of the Canadian ethos of Presbyterianism itself would seem to be tailor-made for the formation of The United Church of Canada. But one should not underestimate the degree to which Canadian Presbyterianism was also neither Kirk nor United, but Presbyterian. That is not to say that the idea of union was unknown to them. Nine regional unions, bringing together nearly twenty-four different groups, prepared the way for the formation of the Presbyterian Church in Canada in 1875. With this appearance of increasing ecumenical momentum fast on the heels of Confederation, one can be forgiven for surprise at the degree of Presbyterian resistance to church union which had gathered by 1925. One hundred and fifty thousand Presbyterians refused to join the United Church. Moreover, they continued to fight for the survival of Presbyterianism in Canada until 1939 when they won the legal battle for the use of the name "Presbyterian Church in Canada" through a parliamentary amendment of The United Church of Canada Act.[48]

The resilience of the Presbyterian tradition in this country is proven much by its continued existence outside the United Church as it is by the theology, worship, and polity of the United Church itself. A study of baptism in the Presbyterian tradition is at once a case study in Reformed worship, Presbyterian practice, and United Church identity.

Presbyterian Orders for Baptism

Presbyterians inherit their liturgical traditions more directly from Zwingli, Calvin, and Knox than do Congregationalists. Zwingli and Calvin, in spite of their significant differences, both set the Reformed liturgical experience in a cerebral and didactic, if eloquent, key. Both made the most of every available opportunity to instruct, teach, and exhort. It would almost seem to be as much a war on ignorance as sin, were it not for the dominance of Calvin's anthropology and resulting penitential piety.[49]

Knox was the main harbinger of these characteristics from Calvin's Geneva to the Scots.[50] While their first service book was the *Book of Common Prayer* (1552), they soon welcomed Knox's *Form of Prayers* (1556) as less conservative, formally adopting it in 1562. It became known as *The Book of Common Order*, seeing over seventy editions printed with only minor revisions, and continued to be the dominant liturgical form until it was replaced by *The Westminster Directory for the Public Worship of God* in 1645. It is, therefore, Knox's "The Order of Baptism" of the *Directory* which forms the liturgical and theological framework for Canadian Presbyterians. Knox's order can be summarized as follows:

Question ("Do you present this child," etc.)
Long exhortation (including exposition of scriptural warrants)
Apostle's Creed (said by father or godfather)
Prayer (for the Spirit, and the child)
Lord's Prayer
Baptism
Prayer (of Thanksgiving and for the Spirit)[51]

Like other Reformed rites, this is more than a minor revision of its medieval predecessors. It reflects an entirely new approach, attempting to take seriously the context of the baptism of children of Christian parents.[52] Because such children are heirs to the covenant of grace, no vicarious profession of faith on the part of the parents or godparents is necessary. The father or godfather confesses his own faith and that of church within which the parents promise to nurture the child. Exorcisms and renunciations are deemed inappropriate for children. Other "nonscriptural" elements such as the prayer for the sanctification of the water, chrism, and crossing are omitted. The lengthy exhortation dominates the rite. The intention is, first, to be true to biblical practice, or in the words of the subtitle to Calvin's *La Forme*, "*selon la coustume de L'Eglise ancienne*." This leads, second, to the simplification of liturgical action—nonessentials, save baptism in the triune name, having been stripped away.[53]

Baptism itself was most often performed by affusion.[54] Baptismal fonts were moved from their medieval location at the door to a place near the pulpit so as not to be, in Knox's words, "used in private corners, as charmes or sorceries, but left to the congregation, and necessarily annexed to the God's word."[55] For some, any font carried too many papist connotations and they opted for the simple basin placed on the communion table or in a bracket fixed to the pulpit.[56] The visual proximity to the pulpit was reinforced liturgically by placing the rite after the reading and preaching of the Word. For these reasons, the public Sunday-character of baptism was strictly defended, to the point of being law among the Scots.[57]

Knox's exhortation builds on Calvin's view of baptism, though it is less penitential and betrays some evidence of polemics against the Anabaptists.[58] Covenant theology dominates,[59] appealing to the Old Testament typology of circumcision and the New Testament metaphor of adoption. The first sentence presents the thesis clearly: "Then let us consider (dearly beloved) how almighty God hath not only made us his children by adoption and received us into the fellowship of his church: but also hath promised that he will be our God, and the God of our children unto the thousand [*sic*] generation."[60] This is, in turn, elaborated, explained, and defended with scriptural allusions woven throughout.

This covenant is both a retroactive and proactive promise—i.e., entailing "remission of sins in the blood of Christ Jesus" and "regeneration" in the power of the Holy Spirit. The congregation is exhorted to remember their baptism, its origins and meaning ("put in mind . . . the league and covenant made betwixt God and us"), and to examine and rededicate themselves. It ends with a charge to the godparents and the congregation to raise the child in the Christian faith.

It is also important to note that great care is taken at several points to caution that "this outward action" is not constitutive of salvation, that the work of the Holy Sprit is not dependent on "the visible water." It is one of God's "holy signs and badges" of the promise of grace, not the means by which it is obtained. God's work in Christ is the only means of salvation. To quote one commentator: "the washing in water is a demonstration and proof of the benefits which God will confer rather than the instrumental means by which he confers them."[61] This is entirely in keeping with what is without a doubt the most important Calvinist cornerstone of Presbyterian theology: the absolute sovereignty of God. (It is also that feature which often leads toward its penitential complement: the absolute depravity of humanity.) All Presbyterian sacramental theology must find its place in relation to this fundamental soteriological principle.[62]

In short, the Reformed theology of baptism which Canadian Presbyterians trace to Knox (and beyond to Calvin) emphasizes: God's sovereign action in covenant, adoption, remission of sins, regeneration; our remembrance of this by the outward washing of water and the inward working of the Holy Spirit in the life of the child in the context of the Christian family and congregation.

However, this theology is not inherited by Canadian Presbyterians directly through Knox's *Book of Common Order* but via *The Westminster Directory*. The *Directory* placed Knox's theology within a more Puritan liturgical framework. It was this combination which became normative for Presbyterians well into the early nineteenth century.[63]

The theological continuity is evident in the *Directory's* call for instruction "shewing" (in part):

> That this [baptism] is instituted by our Lord Jesus Christ: That it is a seal of the covenant of grace, of our ingrafting into Christ, and of our union with him, of remission of sins, regeneration, adoption, and life eternal: That the water, in baptism, representeth and signifieth both the blood of Christ, which taketh away all guilt of sin, original and actual; and the sanctifying virtue of the Spirit of Christ against the dominion of sin, and the corruption of our sinful nature: The baptizing, or sprinkling and washing with water, signifieth the cleansing from sin by the blood and for the merit of Christ, together with the mortification of sin, and rising from sin to newness of life, by virtue of the death and resurrection of Christ: That the promise is made to believers and their seed.[64]

This is to take place at the beginning of a simplified order structured as follows:

Exhortation
Prayer (for the Spirit, and the child)
Baptism
Prayer (of Thanksgiving, and for the Spirit)[65]

Gone is Knox's opening question of intent. The sponsor's profession of faith appears also to be missing, but was, in fact, later continued.[66] In contrast to Knox, the prebaptismal Prayer here calls for sanctification of the water.

Structurally, the *Directory's* service is Knox's order severely reduced to the form of a directory. This is not insignificant, for the liturgical liberty associated with a directory, as distinct from a "form of prayers" or "common order," invites a larger degree of liturgical variation and subsequent theological interpretation. The liturgical ethos invited by the *Directory* is particularly conducive to worship on the frontier. This may account in part for its popularity among Canadian Presbyterians. It also means that baptisms were approached with a high degree of liberalism, increasingly taking place at various points within the Sunday liturgy, at other times, and even privately. In this sense, the range of baptismal practices and associated meanings for Canadian Presbyterians in this period falls within a broad continuum embraced by the *Directory*, the liturgical result being not unlike that discussed above with respect to the Congregationalists.

The ambiguities of this state of affairs were beginning to be felt as early as the mid to later 1800s. Requests for more uniformity in worship came from synods, but the resulting committee of General Assembly eventually dissolved, unable to make any progress in the face of the particular loyalties of regional and congregational practices.[67] Another attempt met with more success, no doubt because the work was directed toward lay-led worship and those living in isolation from the regular services of an ordered ministry. The result, *Aids for Social Worship*,[68] was popular among pioneers, but it contained no services for sacraments. Nevertheless, it probably contributed significantly to the education of the laity with respect to the value of a form of prayers.

It was left to the homeland to be the catalyst for a new generation of service books. This was initiated with the publication of *Euchologion: A Book of Common Order*.[69] Its service for the baptism of infants is generally acknowledged as that from which "all modern Reformed rites are derived."[70] The outline of the order is:

Scripture Sentence (Ps. 124:8)
Scripture Readings, Exhortation & Exposition
  (on Mat. 28:18-20; Mk. 10:13-16; Acts 2:38-39)
Promises: Apostle's Creed & questions or question)
Prayer (for the child and the Spirit)
Baptism
Blessing: Apostolic or Aaronic
Declaration
Prayer (of Thanksgiving)

Lord's Prayer
Apostolic Blessing[71]

This order is, in most respects, a recovery of Knox, but not without significant influences from both the *Directory* and even the *Book of Common Prayer*. The vows restore the option of using the Apostle's Creed. The prebaptismal prayer relies on apostolic, *BCP*, and Catholic sources, with an epiclesis based on the *Directory*. The Aaronic blessing would have been familiar to Scots from Knox's Sunday Morning Service. The Declaration was taken from the "Savoy Liturgy" (1661) and the postbaptismal prayer combines phrases and ideas from both Knox and the Westminster Larger Catechism.[72]

Theologically, the order is most readily traced to Knox, as the exposition of the Matthean commission in the exhortation makes clear. Indeed, its opening lines also provide a good summary of a Reformed theology of baptism: "The sacrament thus instituted is a sign and seal of our ingrafting into Christ, of remission of sin by His blood, and regeneration by His Spirit, of adoption, and resurrection unto everlasting life; and by it we are solemnly admitted, by Christ's appointment, into His Church, and enter into an engagement to be the Lord's."[73] The operative metaphors are again "sign," "seal," "ingrafting," "remission," "regeneration," "adoption," "resurrection," "admission."

The second edition of *Euchologion* (1860) was the first Presbyterian book to provide an order for confirmation, influenced mostly by that of the Prayer Book. This is particularly significant in light of the fact that Knox's order and the *Westminster Directory* made no such provision. In this they followed Calvin, who had objected to the medieval practice of confirmation on the grounds that it was nonscriptural and that baptism was complete in itself. Thus Calvin emphasized education of the young in preparation for communion.[74] Canadian Presbyterians held to this "educational," as distinct from "sacramental," approach to the subject. They emphasized the family unit as the primary context for nurture in the faith.[75] In addition, both the Sunday School movement and nineteenth-century revivalism contributed to the growing desire for a formal confession of faith, the result being a marriage of educational and evangelical views of confirmation.[76] On the other hand, as educational and didactic models of baptism and confirmation grew in emphasis and popularity, the stage was also being set for the appropriation of confirmation as a kind of quasi-sacrament of educational maturity.

The third edition of *Euchologion* (1874) introduced a rite for the baptism of adults. It entailed only a minor change from that for infants, namely, with respect to the question after the opening scripture sentence and the "imposition of hands" (thus rendering the rite "baptism-confirmation").[77]

Even this cursory glance at the baptismal orders of *Euchologion* provides evidence that the compilers of the time were aware of some of the historical and liturgical material available. The result was a form impressive enough to leave its mark on Presbyterian baptismal liturgies well into the modern era.

What Presbyterian influences should one look for in United Church liturgies? From among the characteristics discussed, several liturgical features stand out: 1. Common order: with the influence of *Euchologion*, baptismal liturgies among Canadian Presbyterians began to shift back from the *Directory* toward Knox, from directories to "common order" and "forms"; 2. The theology of Knox (and Calvin): particularly by the use of theological vocabulary invoking God's sovereign action in covenant, adoption, ingrafting, remission of sins, and regeneration by the Spirit; 3. Scriptural warrants: particularly the continued use of the classic Reformed warrants (e.g., Mt. 28 and Acts 2), although perhaps not with the same intention as with the Congregationalists; 4. Promises and vows: the use of specific and intentional questions of intention and belief; 5. The use of a baptismal symbol: such as the Apostle's Creed; 6. Other common traditions rooted in Knox's orders: e.g., the use of the Aaronic Blessing and the Lord's Prayer.

In addition to these liturgical elements and features, one may also detect a certain characteristic loss, similar to the Congregationalist circumstances, of the corporate and ecclesiological character of the rite. The context of nineteenth-century liberalism and certain strains of individualistic evangelicalism would have supported this trend. Private baptisms can also be viewed as an expression of this context.

Finally, the overall tendency toward more structural uniformity along classic Reformed lines in baptismal rites can also be placed in the context of the new-found unity of the Presbyterian Church in Canada and the climate of nation-building following Confederation. This atmosphere contributed not only to the formation of The United Church of Canada, but before that, to the formation of the first service book for Canadian Presbyterians, *The Book of Common Order* (1922).[78] While this text was produced too close to union to have a discernible effect on those Presbyterians who became part of the United Church, it was, as we shall see, both in keeping with the characteristics of earlier texts and important to the United Church liturgical developments to follow.

The Methodist Contribution

Methodists in Canada

At the request of the Methodist Societies in America, John Wesley, the founder of Methodism, sent two missionaries to Philadelphia in 1769. Organization and extension, association and dissociation were swift in the coming decades.[79]

The Methodist Episcopal Church of North America was organized in 1784, embracing successful missions to both Nova Scotia and Upper Canada. However, with the political fall-out of the American Revolution, diverging allegiances became more pronounced. Upper Canadian Loyalists formed the Methodist Episcopal Church in Canada in 1828. Methodists in the eastern provinces tended to trace their lineage to the British Wesleyans and joined with the same in Upper Canada to become the Wesleyan Methodist Church in Canada in 1854. A union of the two in 1833 was short-lived, only to dissolve by 1840.[80] Subsequent years saw a variety of divisions and unions, including those involving such groups as the New Connexions (a British revivalist tradition), the Protestant Methodists, and the Bible Christians. This only added to the growing number of Methodist groups in British America. With the success of missions in the west, Wesleyans, Episcopals, Primitives, New Connexions, and Bible Christians colored the Canadian landscape, each claiming historical and theological superiority.[81]

In the face of such diversity and its associated tensions, the formation of a single Methodist body in 1884 seems almost miraculous. Yet, as with Congregationalists and Presbyterians, the Methodist Church (Canada, Newfoundland, Bermuda) was as much a product of the politics of nationalism as the piety of evangelism.[82] Indeed, it was perhaps the Methodist depth of national identity and breadth of political influence, more than that of the other founding partners, which fueled the formation of The United Church of Canada.

However, any historical outline of Methodism in Canada which portrays only a story of successive amicable unions belies the complexities of the "Methodist mind" and the important role of Methodism in Canadian religious and social history.[83] Without attempting to cover the ground which historians have done in far greater detail, it is important to appreciate the fact that the ethos of Methodism in Canada has the capacity to embrace both a John Wesley and a Salem Bland, pastors and politicians, revivalist piety and Social Gospel agenda. It is precisely the uniqueness of Methodism that it refuses to accept such easy categorizations as mutually exclusive, challenging one's conceptions of the categories themselves.[84] The United Church of Canada can learn much from its Methodist heritage which, at its best, brings vision to the tensions of faith and works toward the Reign of God on earth. It is against this backdrop and within this context that Methodists also struggled to work out their liturgical life together and make sense of the meaning of baptism.

Methodist Orders for Baptism

The foundational liturgical document for Methodists, Wesley's *Sunday Service of the Methodists in North America*[85] was accepted at the first Conference of the Methodist Episcopal Church in Baltimore in December of 1784. In the preface, Wesley made his views clear:

> I believe there is no liturgy in the World, either in ancient or modern language, which breathes more of a solid scriptural, rational Piety, than the Common Prayer of the Church of England. And though the main of it was compiled considerably more than two hundred years ago, yet is the language of it, not only pure, but strong and elegant in the highest degree. Little alteration is made in the following edition of it, (which I recommend to our Societies in America).[86]

Thus, it has been called "deeply conservative," "basically the work of one who loved the *BCP* and was determined to preserve it for others by adapting it to their changed circumstances."[87]

Because Wesley's service for "The Ministration of Baptism of Infants" is considered "the foundation for subsequent initiation rites in Methodism," it is an obvious starting point for this brief consideration of baptism in Methodism.[88] A structural comparison of Wesley's service with its counterpart in the *Book of Common Prayer* (1662), "The Ministration of Publick Baptism of Infants to be used in the Church" shows Wesley's dependence on the Prayer Book and his high regard for the Anglican form of this sacrament (see Table 1.1).

Table 1.1
A Structural Comparison of Baptism
in the *BCP* (1662) and Wesley's *Sunday Service*

"The Ministration of Publick Baptism of Infants to be used in the Church" *BCP* (1662)	"The Ministration of Baptism of Infants" John Wesley's *Sunday Service*
Rubrics (on polity and doctrine)	
Rubrics (at the font)	Rubrics (at the font)
Question ("Hath this child")	
Address ("Dearly beloved")	Address ("Dearly beloved")
"Flood" Prayer	"Flood" Prayer
Prayer ("Almighty . . . immortal")	Prayer ("Almighty . . . immortal")
Gospel (Mk. 10:13-16)	Gospel (Mk. 10:13-16)
Exhortation	
Prayer	Prayer
Address (to Godparents)	
Renunciation & Questions	
Prayers (four petitions)	Prayers (four petitions)
Prayer ("sanctify this Water")	Prayer ("sanctify this Water")
Naming (by Godparents)	Naming (by "Friends of the Child")
Baptism ("dip" or "pour")	Baptism ("dip" or "sprinkle")
Reception & Signation	Reception [no Signation][89]
Declaration	Declaration [altered]
Lord's Prayer	Lord's Prayer
Prayer ("We yield thee")	Prayer ("We yield thee") [altered]
Exhortation (to Godparents)	
Rubrics (doctrine and liturgy)	

Source: "The Ministration of Publick Baptism of Infants to be used in the Church" in F. E. Brightman, *The English Rite: Being a Synopsis of the Sources and Revisions of the Book of Common Prayer*, Vol. II, 2nd ed. rev. (London: Revinstons, 1921), 292-301; *SS*, 139-143.

A comparison of the services of adult baptism would show similar dependence and alterations at corresponding points.[90] Wesley did not include any rites for private baptism, confirmation, or the Catechism.

But it would be a grave error to draw simple conclusions on the level of content from such a comparison on the level of structure. In spite of his life-long convictions as a faithful priest of the Church of England, Wesley's Puritan sympathies are evident in the *Sunday Service* in general, in the baptismal liturgies in particular, and were to set important precedents for the future of Methodism.[91] If the chronological history of Methodism and the structure of its baptismal liturgies seem easy to outline, its theology and piety is much more complex. An appreciation of this context is essential to an understanding of the content of the liturgies of baptism.

The Methodist tradition has been variously characterized as "evangelical," "revivalist," and "missional."[92] At root is the Wesleyan commitment to the reality and necessity of the experience of personal conversion. Early Methodist organization, polity, and discipline can be viewed as a sophisticated infrastructure directed toward this end. The salvation of souls and the continued support and nurture of the converted was the aim of various social and liturgical innovations, including the use of societies, bands, classes, camp meetings, love feasts, and covenant renewal services. Wesley valued both the innovative "methods" of Methodism as well as the more traditional "means of grace" and frequent communion.[93] The result was a unique dialectic of Anglican discipline and Puritan dynamism, a full program of "conversion therapy," a tradition of Christian initiation.[94]

Doctrinally speaking, theological permission for the methods of Methodism derive from a basically Arminian position.[95] While there is a Calvinistic pessimism regarding human nature and original sin in Wesley, prevenient grace is also present, allowing all human beings to reach out toward God to receive justification and forgiveness and in response seek sanctification and Christian perfection through the various means of grace.[96]

The experience of conversion is the fulcrum point of this process. With respect to baptism, the theology of conversion becomes focused in the concept of "regeneration." A theological and liturgical analysis of Wesley's treatment of this subject provides the best window on his theology of baptism and its liturgical implications for subsequent generations of Methodists.

In the "Articles of Religion" of his *Sunday Service* Wesley omitted some references to the regenerative implications of baptism while including others. For example, in his Article "Of the Sacraments," Wesley omitted the reference to them as "certain sure witnesses and effectual signs of grace." The title of the Article "Of Sin after Baptism" was changed to "Of Sin after Justification" and each reference to "baptism" was changed to "justification," thus placing more emphasis on the experience of justification than the benefits of baptism. On the other hand, his Article "Of Baptism" continued to define baptism as "a sign of regeneration, or new birth," though the lengthy Prayer Book elaboration, which explained its results as "grafting," "forgiveness," and "adoption" "as by an instrument" was omitted.[97]

The same trend is evident in the content of Wesley's services of baptism as outlined above. In the service of infant baptism, while the references to "regeneration," "regenerate," "born anew," and "born again" in the opening address and prayers remain untouched, similar references in the postbaptismal declaration and prayer of thanksgiving are omitted. Later versions even omit some of the earlier references. Similar revisions are made to the order for adult baptism, including omissions from the exhortation after the gospel and in the including omissions from the exhortation after the gospel and in the postbaptismal prayers.[98]

It is not easy to interpret the precise intent and meaning of such changes. Wesley's choice to omit selectively certain, but not all, references to regeneration can seem somewhat confused. Nevertheless, one certain conclusion is that Wesley did not endorse a whole scale rejection of the regenerative implications of baptism. Too many references to it remain in the Articles and the liturgical texts. Some have suggested that because the 1784 texts are strong on regenerative implications and subsequent editions are less so, this indicates an evolution in Wesley's thinking on this subject which amounts to a gradual retreat from the concept of baptismal regeneration.[99] This perspective, it could be argued, would be in keeping with his efforts to deal with the increasingly nonsacramental and revivalist piety of the frontier context.

On the other hand, one could also argue that because all of the significant textual/liturgical changes with respect to regeneration *follow* the act of baptism itself, Wesley was affirming baptism as a *sign* of regeneration, but did not want to imply that it necessarily followed from it. "In short, Wesley does not eliminate the concept of baptismal regeneration but seems to remove any presumption of it."[100] This conclusion seems to best reflect Wesley's own thinking in this regard. Yet this is not without its problems. At issue is the relationship between conversion and baptismal regeneration.

It has been shown that after his Aldersgate Street conversion experience in 1738 Wesley added to his Anglican view of sacramental regeneration (as associated with baptism) a more experiential perspective (conversion as "adult regeneration"). Thus Wesley came to believe that regeneration was "given to infants in baptism as well as to adults at conversion."[101] But one may now ask: Where does this leave the efficacy of baptism? Does such a concept of regeneration drive a theological wedge between infant and adult baptism, leaving one with two baptisms?

Wesley defended the mutual compatibility of baptismal (or infant) regeneration and adult regeneration (or conversion) by appealing to the notion of conversion as "the new birth" and the classic catechetical definition of sacrament as "an outward and sensible sign" of an "inward and spiritual grace." This allowed him to argue that "baptism, the sign, is . . . distinct from regeneration, the thing signified," and conclude that "baptism is not the new birth," "they do not constantly go together."[102] But this argument is difficult to maintain, as the following passage reveals.

> A man may possibly be "born of water" and yet not be "born of Spirit." There may sometimes be the outward sign, where there is not the inward grace. I do not now speak with regard to infants: it is certain our church supposes, that all who are baptized in their infancy, are at the same time born again; and it is allowed that the whole office for the baptism of infants proceeds upon this supposition. Nor is it an objection of any weight against this, that we cannot comprehend how this work can be wrought in infants. For neither can we comprehend how it is wrought in a person of riper years. But whatever be the

case with infants, it is sure all of riper years, who are baptized, are not at the same time born again.[103]

Infants are regenerated at baptism and the guilt of original sin is washed away, but the benefits of this are lost with conscious sin. Thus, all adults, whether baptized as infants or not, require adult regeneration (the new birth of conversion) for salvation. This may or may not accompany adult baptism. For those adults baptized as infants, adult regeneration is, in effect, a *second* rebirth.[104]

But what are the implications of this? Is not infant baptism thus rendered "inconsequential for later adult life" and the "full worth" of adult baptism undermined?[105] Or is this a sophisticated reformed *and* evangelical theology of baptism?[106] Whatever may have been the result, it is clear that Wesley wanted to affirm both the "conscious instantaneous experience"[107] of conversion as the *locus theologicus* of the Christian life, and baptism as a traditional and ordinary means of grace in the church. If baptism was, *ex opere operato*, the sacrament of initiation, conversion was, *ex opere operato*, the experience of salvation.[108]

Such considerations constitute a revealing framework within which to locate the origin and development of Methodist baptismal liturgies. Wesley's liturgical revisions, including the omission of godparents, renunciation (in infant baptism only), signation, private baptism, and confirmation, can be understood as efforts to eliminate practices which detract from the importance of the personal experience of conversion and place undue emphasis on sacramental benefits. As Bernard Holland has put it: "Wesley did not exclude baptismal regeneration [from various points in the baptismal liturgies] because the converted had come to distrust it, but because the unconverted trusted it too greatly."[109] Holland's summary of Wesley's theology of baptism is in keeping with this analysis and can be summarized as in Table 1.2.

Later generations, however, seemed less concerned with Wesley's theological nuances, less concerned about trying to hold together the traditional doctrine of baptismal regeneration and the evangelical experience of conversion, than with meeting the immediate demands for the conversion of souls on the frontier. Despite Wesley's early preaching "On the Duty of Constant Communion" and "The Means of Grace," the content of his sophisticated dialectic did not survive the passage to North America.[110]

At the 1792 Conference of the Methodist Episcopal Church in Baltimore, only a year after Wesley's death, much of the *Sunday Service* was set aside for a chapter of "Sacramental Services &c" in the Methodist *Discipline*. Among the services which survived this transition were those for the baptism of infants and adults, the baptism of infants being the central baptismal rite.[111]

The changes to the 1792 service for infant baptism included the allowance for an extemporary address; the omission of several of the prayers (that before the gospel and those after the gospel and before baptism); the omission of the declaration and the prayers of thanksgiving after baptism. The structural result was a greatly simplified liturgy and the loss of the essential characteristics of the Prayer Book form.

On the level of content, such changes meant that noteworthy phrases were omitted. Several references to "forgiveness of sin," "regeneration," being "born again," and the "mystical washing" of baptism either fell out of the rite with the omission of their associated prayers or were edited out of the remaining texts. In the order for adult baptism, the same approach was taken, with the significant exception of allowing a reference to remission of sin and regeneration in the prayer before the gospel.[112]

In summary, the rite leaves behind Wesley's attempts to nuance the rite with respect to the dialectical theology of baptismal regeneration discussed above. The method of liturgical revision is more reactionary than proactive, more revision by omission than reconstruction. Wesley himself had set this methodological precedent in his own work. Ironically, it was now being used to undermine his own vision of baptism.

Table 1.2
Wesley's Theology of Infant and Adult Baptism Compared

Infant baptism is:	Adult baptism is:
1. a sign of regeneration (meaning: forgiveness of original sin; adoption as a child of God; reception of the Holy Spirit; made heir to the kingdom of heaven);	1. a sign of regeneration (meaning: forgiveness of original and former sins; reception of the Holy Spirit; made heir to the kingdom of heaven);
2. a means of "unconditional" (though not "necessary") grace;	2. a means of "conditional" (though not "necessary") grace;
3. full admission and reception into membership of the church (no confirmation is necessary);	3. full admission and reception into membership of the church (no confirmation is necessary);
4. dedication of the child to God by the parents (and "Friends of the Child");	4. an act of public confession of faith (private baptism is not encouraged);
5. an occasion of prayer for the future nurture and faithfulness of the child.	5. an occasion of prayer for the future nurture and faithfulness of the candidate.

Source: Bernard G. Holland, *Baptism in Early Methodism* (London: Epworth Press, 1970), 138-139, 182, 186.

By 1874, a decade before the formation of the Methodist Church, Canada, the authorized services for infant and adult baptism in the Methodist Church of Canada remained essentially the same, with the exception of the addition of several more scripture passages.[113] By this time, however, a service for the "Reception of Members" (subtitled "form of receiving persons into the church after probation") had been added, involving a long exhortation on the blessings and responsibilities of membership in the "household of God" followed by a profession of faith and reception to communion.[114] Its content presupposed a probationary and catechetical period. One suspects, therefore, that the introduction of this order was an attempt to fill the vacuum left by Wesley's omission of confirmation. Holland argues that Wesley's "irresolution" surrounding confirmation and reception of members, the fact that "Wesley had not spelled out his intentions plainly enough, . . . paved the way for later Methodist indecisiveness."[115]

By 1902, the service of adult baptism showed interesting evidence of both simplification and recovery. There were fewer prayers before baptism, thus omitting more regenerative implications. Even the opening address was altered to emphasize profession of faith and admission to the church rather than remission of sins. However, the postbaptismal exhortation to the godparents from the Prayer Book had been moved so as to become a general prebaptismal exhortation, and the postbaptismal words of reception had found their way back in. The service for the "Reception of Members" remained essentially the same as that of 1874. As the theology of regeneration continued to recede from view, the overall theological impression created by the services was that of an emerging emphasis on Wesley's other themes of profession of faith and reception into the church.[116] These developments signify the beginning of a two-fold trend which will reemerge in *The Book of Common Order*: the continued theological simplification (if not erosion) through the omissions of classic doctrinal themes and the selective recovery of Prayer Book liturgical forms.

This is also evident in the 1922 order. By then, three years before the formation of the United Church, the services of infant and adult baptism presented "reception" as the dominant metaphor. A service for "advancement from Catechumen Membership to Adult Membership" had joined that for "reception into Full Membership," referring to baptism as "dedication" and "reception." But again, another Prayer Book/Wesley prayer had been included in the rite. The result was, at least on the level of structure, surprisingly Wesleyan.[117]

Thus, one can detect two parallel trends in Canadian Methodist baptismal liturgies. One has to do with sacramental theology, the other with liturgical forms. On the one hand, if the sacramental theology of Wesley was present at all by now, it was only a distant memory. None of the sophistication of the *Sunday Service* remained. Canadian Methodist piety was formed more by the frontier, the camp meeting, and the love feast than by Wesley's conception of the means of grace.[118] The Word preached and sung was more prominent than that enacted at table or font. A study of Methodist liturgical space confirms this. The development of Methodist architecture tended to emphasize the evangelical centrality of the Word while the Word in water (and sacrament) receded from prominence.[119] Similar observations apply to Methodist hymnody, one of its best sources for liturgical theology. In spite of the significant number of hymns devoted to baptism by the Wesleys, few of them actually got into Canadian hymn books.[120]

On the other hand, British Wesleyan sympathies for the *Sunday Service* were not entirely lost.[121] Prayer Book liturgical forms tended to be recovered (albeit, often significantly revised by the method of omission). After some alterations with a view to greater simplification, successive versions of the baptismal texts gravitated back toward the original Wesleyan forms. Ironically, by 1922, the liturgy of baptism in the Methodist Church, Canada, seemed, structurally speaking, more Wesleyan than it had been when the denomination was founded nearly a century earlier. Significant liturgical developments are also evident with the addition of services for the reception and admission of members. These can be viewed as an attempt at recovering confirmation-like rites to fill the gap left by Wesley in this regard. Some historians have suggested that, as Methodists became less outcast and more mainstream, their establishment tastes allowed some of the liturgical practices of the established church to appear more attractive than ever before on this continent.[122] By the nineteenth century, Methodism's evangelical roots tended to become either increasingly absent in an increasingly established church, or expressed in various efforts to "Christianize the social order."[123] In such a climate the sacramental piety of its founder is long gone but the residual traces of his much-loved Prayer Book are found in a service of baptism now recast as one of the many sociocultural rites of passage of a "Christian" nation.

Methodism is a highly complex tradition, and its baptismal liturgies are an interesting window on such complexities. It has been demonstrated that the dimensions of this window are framed by Wesley's liturgical roots in the Prayer Book, his own liturgical theology of baptism, the revivalist piety of the frontier, and the coming of age of establishment Methodism in Canada. Like Wesley himself, Methodist baptismal liturgies are complex and defy easy generalization.

For the purposes of this study, however, I pose the same question as I have asked at the close of the previous sections: What will be the signs of Methodist influence in subsequent United Church baptismal liturgies? The dominant features can be summarized as: 1. an ambiguity or tension around the meaning of baptismal regeneration and conversion; 2. similar ambiguities around notions of "confirmation," "reception," and "profession of faith"; 3. the tendency to maintain or recover certain aspects of the language, forms, and structures of the Prayer Book; 4. the tendency to engage in liturgical revision by the process of omission; 5. and, perhaps, in keeping both with the general outlook of Wesley and his North American descendants, the willingness to engage in liturgical adaptation according to the changing context of the church.

Forms of Service

The First Service Book in The United Church of Canada

It has been suggested that the spirit of union in which the United Church was born was more pragmatic than radical.

> The dominant note sounded by those who conceived a united church in Canada was neither the novelty of establishing a new tradition nor the authority commanded by a common tradition but the richness to be achieved by bringing diverse traditions together. Implicit in the enterprise, no doubt, was the thought

> that the denominational dowries represented parts of an original treasure that had been parceled out and needed only to be brought together. The emphasis was on the diversity, however, and on the sharing that union would bring.[124]

This observation holds true on the level of liturgy. While the inaugural service of June 10, 1925 was not without liturgical innovation, the emphasis was more on "blending traditions" than founding new ones or recovering old ones.[125] This was most clearly articulated in the constitutionally enshrined principles of *The Manual* concerning worship and polity. Section 121 in the first edition outlines the authority of the General Council, including its power "to legislate on matters respecting the doctrine, worship, membership, and government of the Church,"[126] subject to the following three conditions:

> First, that before any rule or law relative to these matters can become a permanent law of the church, it must receive the approval of a majority of the presbyteries, and if advisable, pastoral charges also. Second, that no terms of admission to full membership shall be prescribed other than those laid down in the New Testament. Third, that the freedom of worship at present enjoyed in the negotiating churches shall not be interfered with in The United Church of Canada.[127]

These powers have remained unchanged to this day.[128] The first condition relates to the practice of plebiscites or "remits," subjecting official liturgical developments to democratic approval. This will become particularly significant in the seventies and eighties with respect to the United Church studies of Christian initiation. The second condition is an affirmation of a Reformed identity on these matters (though here it is not without Puritan overtones). The third protects the liturgical freedom of the founding traditions.

The thesis that liturgical uniformity was not the goal of organic unity is further supported by the fact that United Church polity has, from the beginning, placed authority over liturgical matters with the session of the congregation.[129] As the relevant sections of *The Manual* state:

> It shall be the duty of the session to have the oversight of
> i. the admission of persons into full membership and the granting of certificates of removal. . .
> iii. the administration of the sacraments. . .
> v. the order of public worship, including the service of praise, and the use made of the church edifice. . .
> vii. to keep [sic] a register of baptism, marriages, and burials.[130]

It is in the context of this polity that the formation and use of *Forms of Service* is best understood.

The first General Council of The United Church of Canada, meeting in Toronto one week after the inaugural service, appointed a Committee on Church Worship and Ritual and instructed it to print

> in a pamphlet form . . . certain Forms of the uniting Churches, more particularly those relating to Baptism, Marriage, Burial of the Dead, Reception of Members, the Ordination and Induction of Elders, the Ordination and Induction of a Minister, and the form of administration of the Lord's Supper which was used at the Inaugural Service of the United Church, for optional use by congregations.[131]

The committee presented its work, *Forms of Service*, to the second General Council in 1926, having interpreted its mandate with care. It did not draw on forms from outside the uniting churches, but selected only "certain Forms" which seemed "best fitted to meet the needs of The United Church."[132] Furthermore, only minor rubrical adaptations were made in keeping with newly established polity and procedures, and "without touching the structure and substance of the Forms."[133] Thus, the spirit of liturgical freedom enshrined in the polity of the United Church was translated into its first service book. Phrases like "authorized for voluntary use" and "for optional use" became established as important rubrical qualifiers which have characterized official United Church liturgical texts ever since.

The sources for *Forms* reflected the historical and liturgical developments already outlined, and anticipated future directions by drawing upon the most recent texts available. The service books to which the committee turned were the Presbyterian *Book of Common Order* (1922), the Methodist *Doctrine and Discipline* (1922), and the Congregationalist *Book of Congregational Worship* (1920).[134] As the dates imply, all of the books were relatively new to their respective traditions.

As shown in the previous sections of this study, *The Book of Common Order* (1922) was the first Canadian service book for Canadian Presbyterians, *Euchologion* and the *Westminster Directory* having dominated until then.[135] The Methodists enjoyed a more steady stream of successive revisions to the *Doctrine and Discipline*. Congregationalists had no officially authorized service book, tending to worship somewhere between Hunter's *Devotional Services for Public Worship* and Jackson's *A Hand-Book of Congregationalism*. The *Book of Congregational Worship* (1920) was just beginning to become known at the time of union, having come with the approval of the Congregational Union of England and Wales.[136]

While all the sources were contemporary by the standards of the time, the resulting selections were weighted in a decidedly Presbyterian direction. In total, *Forms* presents twelve Presbyterian orders, four Methodist orders, and four Congregationalist orders. This ratio is further reduced in the case of the sacraments, of which four are Presbyterian and one is Congregationalist. Methodist orders show up most notably in reception into full communion, marriage, ordination, and the "setting apart of deaconesses."[137]

The significance of *Forms* in the United Church is often overlooked. As shall be demonstrated later, all indications are that it was the United Church's preferred service book until after World War II. The initial reception of *The Book of Common Order* (1932) was, at best, lukewarm; at worst, negative. Clergy and congregations had grown attached to *Forms* and continued to use it, seeing no need for anything new. It was not until the changed circumstances of the postwar era that *Forms* faded from dominance.[138]

With this in mind, one can place *Forms* next to the Basis of Union and *The Manual* in importance. These were among the first articulations of identity for the new United Church. The church which *Forms* embodied was characterized by a vision of polity which valued the richness of the founding traditions and attempted to protect their respective liturgical freedom. Nevertheless, I would argue that it is a mistake to conclude from early United Church polity and *Forms* that the liturgical life of the new United Church was simply an exercise in business as usual. Clergy now had in their hands a service book in which they saw not only the familiar, but also the less so. The act of placing such a text in the hands of worship leaders could not help but expose them to broader liturgical horizons, however subtle such exposure might have been. Such a situation held within it the opportunity to educate each tradition in some of the liturgical practices of the others. Indeed, it permitted and invited each to experience something of the worship life of their newly adopted siblings. One should not underestimate the potential impact of nearly two decades of this kind of exposure, formation, and transition. This gradual and subtle blending of traditions, this mingling of liturgical experiences, was the substrate in which the liturgical identity of the United Church was formed—one characterized both by the Reformed tradition and nineteenth century liturgical liberalism. In the end, it was *Forms* which set the stage and established the precedent for the eclectic mining of traditions which would come to characterize all United Church liturgical revisions, from *The Book of Common Order* to the present.

Forms of Service and Baptism

From among the denominational baptismal liturgies and practices already outlined, *Forms* included two orders for the baptism of infants, one order for the baptism of adults, and three orders for the reception of baptized persons into full communion. These selections may be taken as indicative of the general liturgical trends with respect to baptism in this first period of United Church life. In this section, I will briefly point to the essential features of these orders, noting those aspects which stand out as significant developments in, or departures from, the denominational characteristics already outlined.

The "First Order for the Sacrament of Baptism: Infants" in *Forms* was taken from the Presbyterian *Book of Common Order* (1922). The structure of the order was as follows:

Hymn
Scripture
  Matthew 28:18-20
  Deuteronomy 6:5-7 (optional)
  Mark 10:13-16
Instruction
Prayer (for the Spirit)
Questions

Baptism
Aaronic Blessing
Declaration
Prayers (of Thanksgiving)
The Lord's Prayer
Hymn
Benediction[139]

Several aspects of this order were noteworthy. First, it is structurally very similar to the standard *Euchologion* order.[140] However, this is the second of the two orders for infant baptism in *BCO* (1922). While both are descendants of *Euchologion*, the second is the more contemporary and simple of the two. Thus, the Committee chose not to emphasize the first and more traditional order, the content of which is based more explicitly on the classic language of the Prayer Book, Knox, and *Euchologion*.

Second, some interesting editorial changes were being made on the level of content, including: the omission of the prefatory rubric regarding the celebration of baptism within the context of public worship (though perhaps the presence of a hymn presupposes it); the omission of the covenant text (Gen. 17:7) from the selection of scriptural warrants (though reference to covenant theology remains in the Instruction); and the omission of the doctrinal rubrics from the *Westminster Directory* following the order.[141] Where the service did retain some of the familiar turns of phrase from the Prayer Book, Knox, and *Euchologion*, it simplified them.[142] Perhaps the most significant feature of this order, as compared to the first order in *BCO* (1922), is that it omitted all classic Reformed (i.e., Knox's) references to "ingrafting" and "adoption," as well as Prayer Book references to "regeneration."[143] The only remaining regenerative implication left in the Instruction was the reference to the "renewal of our nature by the Holy Spirit."

> Dearly Beloved,
>
> We have heard with what kindly words and gesture our Lord Jesus Christ received little children who were brought to Him, thereby assuring us that He will embrace our children within the arms of His love and protection. St. Paul has taught us that the children of believing parents are to be numbered among the people of God, and St. Peter that the promise is to us and to our children.
>
> This Sacrament of Baptism signifies the cleansing of our hearts by the grace of Jesus Christ and the renewal of our nature by the Holy Spirit. It is the recognition of our children's birthright in the household of faith, and the rite of admission into the visible Church. It seals the sacred bond in which God assures to them His fatherly love and care, and in which they are engaged to confess Christ and be His faithful people.
>
> In this act parents dedicate their children to the Father who gave them, and receive them again from His hands as a sacred trust, to be brought up for His Kingdom and service.[144]

Following, as it does, after the opening scriptural warrants, the result was a service in which Jesus's reception of children is the dominant scriptural metaphor and the theology of covenant was the operative doctrine. Any of the potential controversies inherited from the Reformed or Prayer Book liturgies were avoided by omission.

This was the case to an even greater extent in the "Second Order for the Sacrament of Baptism: Infants" in *Forms*. Its simple structure was:

Scripture (Mark 10:13-16)
Questions
Baptism
Aaronic Blessing
Declaration
Rubric (on Prayer, The Lord's Prayer, Hymn and Benediction)[145]

This Congregationalist order occupied less than two pages in *Forms*. It was much more simple than even Hunter's and Jackson's earlier texts. Elements in common with the other order in *Forms* included the biblical text, the Aaronic Blessing, the Declaration (though the order of the last two were reversed and the wording was slightly altered), and use of the trinitarian formula in the baptism itself. However, there was no Address or Instruction, the Markan text having been left to establish the biblical and theological framework of the rite. Given the long-standing Congregationalist suspicion of creedal confession, the use of the Questions is noteworthy. On the other hand, its content could hardly have been mistaken as confessional or creedal: "We give you welcome in the Name of the Lord. Do you present this child for Christian Baptism; and do you solemnly promise that *he* be brought up as a Christian child in the nurture and admonition of the Lord?"[146] The order was indeed a striking example of Puritan simplicity.

Taken together, these services for infant baptism show that while covenant theology was present, it was not communicated through the classic Reformed vocabulary of ingrafting and adoption. The language of baptism had shifted. It was now less traditional and conservative, more contemporary and liberal, and marked by simplicity. God's love and acceptance of children was the primary emphasis, their admission and welcome into the church and their dedication to God's service dominated. Adoption into the covenant had become reception into the congregation.

While at first glance this shift may seem insignificant, upon closer examination it proves to be quite substantial. In particular, it involves a reinterpretation of God's action in baptism from the active to the more passive. God no longer adopts in baptism, but simply receives. Later developments would continue the variations on these emerging themes.

Forms contains only one order for adult baptism, "An Order of the Sacrament of the Baptism of Adults," which was also taken from *BCO* (1922).[147] In the tradition of *Euchologion*, this Presbyterian order was essentially an adaptation of the first order for infant baptism in *BCO* (1922) and involved, among other things, some minor revisions to a few of Knox's classic prayers. The consistency in liturgical structure and content in the two services in *BCO* (1922) was somewhat compromised given that the first order for infant baptism was omitted from *Forms*. On the other hand, more of the language of Knox was carried forward and liturgical variety was heightened.

Only one rather curious change was made to the order in the transition from *BCO* (1922) to *Forms*. The line "after His resurrection and before His ascension to the right hand of God" was omitted from the opening introduction to the Matthean warrant.[148] Perhaps Congregationalist objections to creedal language lie behind the deletion.

Two additional features of this Presbyterian order are noteworthy, the first having to do with the explicit mention of adoption. The exhortation reads, in part, "This Sacrament is a sign and seal of the cleansing of our hearts by the grace of Jesus Christ; of the renewal of our nature by the Holy Spirit; of adoption into the household of faith, and admission, by Christ's appointment, in His Church."[149] Adoption (and perhaps an allusion to baptismal regeneration in the phrase "renewal of our nature") here seems to be more appropriate to the baptism of adults than infants. While Knox might puzzle over this limitation of adoption to adults only, Wesley would have been pleased with such a view of baptismal regeneration.

The second feature relates to the use of a question involving renunciation—presumably deemed more appropriate for adult baptism. The question, "Do you confess your sins and turn from them with godly sorrow?" was a contemporary Presbyterian adaptation of *Euchologion*'s "Do you, with heartfelt sorrow for your sins, renounce the devil, the world, and the flesh?"[150]

Together, the services for the baptism of infants and adults illustrate a contemporary Reformed perspective, mostly that of Canadian Presbyterians. From one vantage point, they communicated some of the traditional theological concepts of baptism with ambiguity. From another, they did so with greater simplicity, liberalism, and modernity. On some concerns they were merely silent. Overall, one is struck by their simplicity, their straightforward emphasis on the reception of the individual into the church, and a liturgical focus on scripture, prayer, and the sprinkling of water with the (western) trinitarian baptismal formula. Thus, little else seems important.

Forms also contained three orders for "The Reception of Baptized Persons into Full Communion," one from each of the three founding traditions.[151] These orders and their selection for *Forms* graphically illustrate both diversity and ambiguity in the meaning and practice of reception, profession of faith, and confirmation. Their titles alone testify to this fact. While they were each given the same title in *Forms*, their original titles are the first clue that they were not simply three versions of the same service. The Methodist order appeared as "Advancement from Catechumen Membership to Adult Membership" in the *Discipline*. The Presbyterian order was "An Order for the Admission of Baptized Persons to Full Communion" in *BCO* (1922). The Congregationalist order was "The Reception of Church Members at Holy Communion" in the *Book of Congregational Worship* (1920). A brief comment on each will draw out some of their differences.

The first (Methodist) order in *Forms* addressed "young people" as its candidates.[152] While this might suggest images of a confirmation liturgy, there was no

BCP-like prayer for the Spirit (though extempore prayer is invited) and no kneeling or laying on of hands. The service consisted of an exhortation to fulfill the obligations of one's baptism, questions regarding profession of faith and acceptance of the discipline of the church, and a congregational affirmation of the advancement of the candidate(s) to adult membership. While mention was made of the "privileges and duties" of adult membership and "diligent use of the means of grace" (in the United Church version only), no specific mention was made of participation in the Lord's Supper.[153]

The opening rubric to the second (Presbyterian) order in *Forms* articulated the intended function of the service: "Those who profess their faith in Christ, and desire publicly to confirm their Baptismal vow and to be received into full Communion, shall be admitted by the Minister and Elders in the presence of the Congregation."[154] Thus, the service covered a range of meanings, including profession of faith, confirmation of vows, reception into full communion, and admission to full membership. This service also contained an explicit renunciation (as in the service of adult baptism) and reference to admission to the Lord's Supper. In addition, it included an optional section to be used for the reception of communicants "from other Churches or Congregations of the same Church."[155]

As a whole, the ecclesiology of this rite was enhanced by the participation of elders, mention of the session and its implied authority, and declarations of welcome. In particular, the giving of "the right hand of fellowship" was significant, functioning in place of a laying on of hands as the climactic liturgical gesture, and therein reinforcing the overall sense of the service as one of reception rather than confirmation.[156]

The third (Congregationalist) order in *Forms* was more explicit about its function in its original title, "The Reception of Church Members at Holy Communion."[157] Indeed, the closing rubric advised that in the communion service the minister could distribute the elements directly to the new communicants.[158] In its original Congregationalist form, it was the first of the initiation orders, placed before the orders for baptism. One wonders about the extent to which this reflected its perceived importance relative to baptism.

The Puritan simplicity of this brief order again stands out. Scriptural warrants pointed to the church as the body of Christ and the sheep of his fold. However, the questions, as with the other orders in *Forms*, also contained reference to "essential agreement with the faith and order of The United Church of Canada." This formulation was a uniquely United Church invention, resulting from the union negotiations in which the Congregationalist delegation expressed hesitancy about any statement which would tie faithfulness to doctrinal or creedal assent.[159] Even this formulation is surprising, however, given that no questions of any kind appeared in the original order. In addition, references to kneeling have been omitted in the United Church version. Finally, in spite of the clear focus on reception to communion in the service, the prayer preceding the giving of the right hand of fellowship was the Prayer Book confirmation prayer. In short, the Congregationalist order in *Forms* struggled to remain faithful to its Puritan roots in the new context of the United Church.

As one can see, the services of reception in *Forms* covered a range of meanings including welcome, reception, admission, and profession of faith. Prayer Book confirmation elements mingled with Reformed profession of faith turns of phrase. This spectrum reflected both the liturgical diversity and theological ambiguity of the times, one which would continue to haunt future developments.

When the services of reception are placed alongside the baptismal liturgies, the emerging picture is one of Reformed practices dominated by Presbyterian forms gravitating toward Congregationalist simplicity. The theological liberalism of the times and the evangelical sensibilities of Methodism and Congregationalism converge in such a way as to push the rites in the direction of simpler and more populist forms.

The rites proclaimed baptism as reception into the "congregation of Christ's flock."[160] Children were received by the grace of their birthright upon profession of their parents' or sponsors' faith, and dedicated to God's service. Adults were received upon their profession of faith and confession of sin and "engaged as Christ's faithful soldier and servant."[161] Beyond these theological common denominators, the nuances of the rites diverged into the variety of meanings outlined above.

Finally, it is helpful to place the orders for baptism and reception in *Forms* in the context of the formal doctrinal affirmations of the United Church. How does the liturgical vision of the rites compare with the theological vision articulated in the Articles of Faith of the Basis of Union of The United Church of Canada?

A detailed study of the Articles of Faith is beyond the scope of this study. For our purposes, those of primary relevance include Articles IX, X, XI, XII, XV and XVI.[162] Article IX, "Of Regeneration," illustrates the spirit of Articles IX through XII.

> We believe in the necessity of regeneration, whereby we are made new creatures in Christ Jesus by the Spirit of God, who imparts spiritual life by the gracious and mysterious operation of His power, using as the ordinary means the truths of His word and the ordinances of divine appointment in ways agreeable to the nature of man.[163]

The "necessity of regeneration" to become "new creatures" is here affirmed. The other articles of this group elaborate that the "saving grace" of faith is "always accompanied by repentance" and the "conscious assurance" of our "justification" and "adoption." Thus, regenerated and justified, we grow through the power of the Holy Spirit. The "evidence" of this "saving faith" is a "holy life" and the "perfection" of God's love in us.[164]

The evangelical spirit of these articles stands in accordance with much of the Methodist piety already examined. To the extent that this lacked clarity in relation to baptism, it should come as no surprise to find that the role and place of baptism in the process of regeneration, justification, and sanctification is not clearly defined. Where it is alluded to, as in the quotation above, it is only by implication in the reference to "ordinances of divine appointment *in ways agreeable*" to human nature [italics added]. This is further qualified insofar as it is rooted in the "mysterious operation" of God's power. The result is a theology which stops short of any explicit affirmation of baptismal regeneration.

Explicit mention of baptism is contained in the more traditional Articles XV and XVI, "Of the Church" and "Of the Sacraments," respectively. The former states that the church consists "of those who profess faith in Jesus Christ and obedience to Him, together with their children, and other baptized children." The latter places both baptism and the Lord's Supper in the context of covenant theology. As "signs and seals" of the covenant, they are "means of grace," sources of "strength and comfort," and ordinances for confession of faith in the world. The "proper subjects" of baptism are believers and "infants presented by their parents or guardians."[165] While no specific mention is made of confirmation, profession of faith, or reception to full membership, the obligation of nurture is impressed upon both parents (or guardians) and the church in the expectation that "their children will, by the operation of the Holy Spirit, receive the benefits which the sacrament is designed and fitted to convey." The roots of the United Church's "open table" tradition are seen in the fact that admission to the Lord's Supper is extended to all who make "a credible profession of faith in the Lord Jesus Christ and of obedience to his law."[166]

The doctrinal room and theological flexibility of such statements reflects what has been observed in the liturgical texts themselves. It also sheds light on the spirit of union which produced both the Articles of Faith of the Basis of Union and *Forms*. Chalmers has characterized the Basis of Union as a document which combined "Calvin's logic" with "Wesley's emotions."[167] Grant has argued that it was a conservative consensus document aimed more at smoothing the way for union than blazing a trail marked by contemporary theological precision.[168] Of the Articles of Faith, it has been demonstrated that "the main desire of the men who gave us these Articles was not to prepare a new creed but to restate the ancient faith in such a way that the distinctive emphases of Presbyterianism and Methodism, Calvinism and Arminianism, would both be recognized."[169]

The liturgical ethos of *Forms* was an expression of this same theological climate. The orders for baptism embraced the spectrum of practice from Presbyterian to Congregationalist. The orders for reception represented each of the founding traditions. The insertion of such revealing phrases as "essential agreement" in the questions of some of the orders respected Congregationalist sensibilities. On the question of who should receive baptism, Methodist liberal sensibilities were respected by the omission of the traditional reference to the *Directory* in the rubrics of the Presbyterian order. In general, all potentially problematic allusions and references in the texts were simply omitted.

To be sure, such an approach did not represent a systematic resolution of theological difficulties. It was, like the formation of the United Church itself, a style of blending traditions, in which *Forms* was to liturgy what the Articles of Faith and the Basis of Union were to doctrine and polity. This process of liturgical blending contained both risk and potential. Among the risks: the setting in motion of a jumbled package of meanings and traditions containing mutually exclusive contradictions and the creation of a liturgical climate so liberal as to be devoid of identity and substance. Among the potential benefits: a renewed catholicity resulting from the sharing of diverse liturgical traditions and a new climate of ecumenical tolerance modeled on the experience of rich liturgical diversity. The compilers of *The Book of Common Order* would have to reveal their preference in their efforts to take the United Church into its next stage of liturgical development.

Conclusions

In the first part of this study, I have shown that *Forms of Service* is the logical starting point both for the study of United Church worship in general and its authorized baptismal liturgies in particular. Because *Forms* was a compilation of orders from the founding traditions, it was necessary to examine the contributions of each of those traditions. A brief overview of the Congregationalist, Presbyterian, and Methodist traditions, followed by an examination of their primary baptismal orders, suggested a variety of dominant features to look for in the continued development of United Church baptismal liturgies. For the sake of convenience, they are summarized in Table 1.3.

Table 1.3
Features of Baptismal Orders in the Founding Traditions

Congregationalist	Presbyterian	Methodist
• liturgical freedom and simple directories	• common order via Knox	• ambiguity surrounding regeneration
• biblicism, heavy use of scriptural warrants	• language of Knox and Calvin (e.g., God's sovereignty, covenant, adoption, ingrafting, remission of sins, regeneration)	• ambiguity surrounding confirmation, reception, and profession of faith
• congregational ecclesiology and covenant theology	• reformed scriptural warrants (Mt. 28 and Acts 2)	• selective use of Prayer Book
• antisacramental, few symbols, austere liturgical action	• intentional promises and vows	• liturgical revision by omission
• emphasis on "reception" and "admission"	• other features: Apostles' Creed; Aaronic Blessing; Lord's Prayer	• liberal liturgical adaptation

An examination of *Forms* has demonstrated its significance both to the birth of the United Church liturgical ethos and to the development of its baptismal liturgies. While *Forms* borrowed more heavily from the Presbyterian tradition than either the Congregationalist or Methodist, it was also an expression of the commitment to liturgical diversity affirmed in the formation of the United Church. The baptismal orders introduced into the United Church context were of contemporary Presbyterian and Congregationalist origin, while those for reception reflected the practices of each of the founding traditions. The baptismal rites showed evidence of a tendency toward increased simplicity and liberal modernization at the expense of some traditional theological language. Those for reception tended to reflect both the liturgical diversity and theological ambiguity that characterized the understanding of the rite at the time.

Finally, it has been further demonstrated that all the orders were now being used within a new theological and liturgical context—one characterized primarily by that blending of traditions which was the spirit of United Church union. This was the liturgical ethos within which the compilers of *The Book of Common Order* would craft their new baptismal liturgies.

Notes

1. I have yet to encounter any specific comment on *Forms* by Canadian church historians, in spite of their clear appreciation for the significance of the *BCO* (1932). E.g., John Webster Grant, *The Canadian Experience of Church Union* (London: Lutterworth Press, 1967), 60-61; "Blending Traditions: The United Church of Canada," in *The Churches and the Canadian Experience*, ed. John Webster Grant (Toronto: Ryerson, 1963), 142-143. Liturgical scholars tend to speak of *BCO* (1932) as the United Church's "first service book." E.g., Alan Barthel, et. al., *A Guide to Sunday Worship*, 1; Charlotte Caron, *Eager for Worship*, 23. Evidence of an appreciation of the significance of *Forms* is only beginning in United Church liturgical study. E.g., Thomas Harding, "The Marriage Services of the United Church of Canada: Stages on a Liturgical Journey," *Toronto Journal of Theology* 7, no. 2 (1991): 169-195. For a detailed assessment of the significance of *Forms*, see William S. Kervin, "*Forms of Service (1926):* A Study in the Liturgical Ethos of The United Church of Canada," *Toronto Journal of Theology* 17, no. 2 (Fall 2001): 215-229. This research led to the first reference to *Forms* in United Church worship resources. *CGP*, 2.

2. Helpful sources include: Horton Davies, *The Worship of the English Puritans* (Westminster: Dacre Press, 1948); Earl B. Eddy, "The Congregational Tradition in Canada," in *The Churches and the Canadian Experience*, 25-37; J. Clark Saunders, "Congregationalism in Manitoba, 1879-1937," in *Prairie Spirit: Perspectives on the Heritage on The United Church of Canada in the West*, ed. Dennis L. Butcher, et al. (Winnipeg: University of Manitoba Press, 1985), 122-146; Bryan D. Spinks, *Freedom or Order? The Eucharistic Liturgy in English Congregationalism, 1645-1980* (Allison Park: Pickwick, 1984); White, *Protestant Worship*, 117-134. Congregationalist terminology can be confusing, complicated both by Old World divisions and New World permutations. Separatists saw separation as the only faithful response to the corruption of the Church of England. Some are also classified as Independent because they rejected Presbyterian proposals for organizational reform. The more moderate Puritans renounced separation, seeking instead to faithfully reform and "purify" the established church from within. In

the Canadian context, Eddy speaks of Independent and Congregational streams within the larger Congregationalist tradition. In the American context, White speaks of Separatists and Puritans under the umbrella of Congregationalism. The term *Congregationalist* does not dominate until we reach North American soil. In a sense, the terms *Separatist* and *Puritan* become somewhat anachronistic after the 1662 Act of Uniformity. In North America all are now Dissenters by choice, Congregationalists in theology, and Independent or Presbyterian in polity. Spinks, 1-29.

3. By 1776 over 90 percent of Nova Scotia's 20,000 residents were Protestant, and over half of these were New England Congregationalists. Nancy Christie, "In These Times of Democratic Rage and Delusion: Popular Religion and The Challenge the Established Order," in *The Canadian Protestant Experience*, ed. George A. Rawlyk (Burlington: Welch, 1990), 9-47; cf. Eddy, 30.

4. "[T]he religious landscape of Nova Scotia was completely reshaped by the New Light stir." Christie, 21. For more on the New Light movement, see George A. Rawlyk, *Ravished by the Spirit: Religious Revivals, Baptists and Henry Alline* (Montreal & Kingston: McGill-Queen's University Press, 1984).

5. Christie, 41-43.

6. Eddy, 31-33; Christie, 9-10.

7. Eddy, 33-35; Samuel N. Jackson, *A Hand-Book of Congregationalism* (Toronto: Congregational Publishing Company, 1894), 136. [Jackson].

8. Saunders, 146.

9. William Bradshaw, 1605, cited in Jackson, i [spelling modernized].

10. One cannot help but notice the same feature within United Church worship, where the session (or its equivalent) has oversight in matters of worship. In this sense, the United Church continues to be very congregationalist. Thus, the study of liturgy in the United Church can learn much from the way in which historians have dealt with the liturgical ethos of the Congregationalists. E.g., Davies; Harding, "The Major Orders," 43-55; Bard Thompson, *Liturgies of the Western Church* (Philadelphia: Fortress Press, 1961), 311-321; White, 117-134.

11. The primary sources are collected and examined in Edward Cardwell, *A History of Conferences and Other Proceedings Connected with the Revision of the Book of Common Prayer: From the Year 1558 to the Year 1690.* 3rd edition. (London: Oxford University Press, 1849).

12. Cardwell, 3-7. As other controversies unfolded, the beliefs and practices which fell under their critical eye were viewed not only as "badges and tokens of Romanism," but "the outward signs of an episcopal church in subjection to state authority." As such, they were a fundamental breach of the first commandment. Cardwell, 121.

13. "The Exceptions Against the Book of Common Prayer" (1661), in Cardwell, 303-335. See also 32-41; "Millenary Petition," 130-133; "Hampton Court Conference," 167-212; "Letter from Patrick Galloway," 212-217; "The First Address and Proposals of the Ministers," 277-286; and other primary documents, 48-62.

14. "Exceptions," 304-309; Thompson, 312-313, 318-319; White, 123-125, 128-129.

15. "Exceptions," 323-330; see also 39, 40, 50, 141. Of the sign of the cross in baptism, a continuing symbol of the Puritan critique of the *BCP* liturgy, it was said that "the duties whereunto we are really obliged by baptism [are] more expressly fixed to that airy sign than to this holy sacrament" (310). For a response to such critiques, see "The Answer of the Bishops to the Exceptions of the Ministers," 335-363.

16. Davies, 220.

17. Henry Martyn Dexter, *A Hand-Book of Congregationalism* (Boston: Congregational, 1880), 85. [Dexter].

18. John Hunter, *Devotional Services for Public Worship*. 8th edition. (London: Dent & Sons, 1903). Hunter's *Devotional Services* has been called "by far the most outstanding and influential liturgical compilation of nineteenth century Congregationalism." (Spinks, 109.) It did not go out of print until 1949. The 1903 edition was still in use in 1975. What began as an Independent directory for a particular congregation and included only a few prayers and responses, eventually grew to over three hundred pages, gradually gravitating back toward the *BCP* and resulting in the style of a Reformed *Forms of Service* or Presbyterian *Book of Common Order*. My copy of the eighth edition (it was in its final form by the seventh edition of 1901) contains many *BCP*-like elements including orders for morning and evening prayer, litanies and prayers of intercession, collects and prayers for the Christian year, and a lectionary.

Jackson's *Hand-Book* was "prepared at the request of the Congregational Union of Ontario and Quebec" and was intended to be "as complete a compendium of Congregationalism, as [the author's] ability and limited space . . . would warrant." (Jackson, iv). To this end, it also includes chapters on history and polity. The chapter "Congregational Church Services" claims to draw on "practices which are common in our churches" (47) as well as those which had received official approval. Included are orders for the reception of members, baptism, communion, marriage, and burial. Scriptural warrants comprise the major portion of the orders. Simple directories are also provided for the "Church Service," "Ordination or Installation," "Laying of Corner-Stone," and "Church Dedication." The directories are simple in the extreme. While it owes much to Dexter in its structure, it is more comprehensive in its content. For a commentary on the book and its eucharistic orders in particular, see Spinks, 109-121.

19. Hunter, 157-162.

20. The formula for dedication is: "In the faith and fellowship of the Church of Christ, I dedicate thee to God, our Father in Heaven. Amen." Hunter, 161.

21. The rubric reads: "The Service may be used after Morning or Evening Prayer, or at any convenient point in either, or by itself, at the home." Hunter, 157.

22. Jackson, 146-147.

23. Jackson, 147.

24. "If it is desired to lengthen the service, as at the home, other scripture selections may be read, as 1 Samuel 1: 21-23." Jackson, 147.

25. Horton Davies, "Baptism: Congregationalist," in *A New Dictionary of Liturgy and Worship*, ed. J. G. Davies (London: SCM Press, 1986), 64.

26. Davies notes that sometimes the Creed was replaced in worship with the congregation's own "covenant." Davies, *English Puritans*, 273-277.

27. Randolph Charleton Chalmers, *See The Christ Stand! A Study in Doctrine in The United Church of Canada* (Toronto: The Ryerson Press, 1945), 76-78.

28. Jackson, 147. The origin of this particular formulation is unclear.

29. Davies, *English Puritans*, 49.

30. White, 118. The term *hyper-Calvinism* is Peter Toon's, from *Hyper-Calvinism* (London: Orange Tree, 1967), and is used especially in Spinks's work. Calvin would allow considerable flexibility in his application of the criterion of a scriptural basis for worship, depending on the pastoral and historical circumstances. In other words, biblical practices could be discarded if they had become freighted through misuse, and nonbiblical practices could be tolerated if edifying and done "decently and in order." Congregationalists were much less patient. For them, the Word of God alone was the sole and supreme norm. "[T]he Puritans had no intention of canonizing Reformed practice. Their criterion was the Word of God, by which all Geneva and Zurich were also to be judged." Thompson, 319.

31. For an almost comical list of liturgical proof-texting, see Davies, *English Puritans*, 49-56.

32. Eddy, 28.

33. Davies, *English Puritans*, 178.

34. Thompson, 319-321.

35. While the liturgies always make provision for freedom to include other texts, one cannot help but wonder about the polemical context of the use of the most popular passages and the extent to which they are offered as a defense for the baptism of children.

36. John Owen, in Thompson, 317.

37. White, 124-125; Thompson, 313, 322; William D. Maxwell, *John Knox's Genevan Service Book* (Edinburgh: Oliver and Boyd, 1931), 177. A variety of such customs were modeled on the practices of Zwingli and Knox. See also Davies, *English Puritans*, 278-285.

38. Hunter, 163-166. It is modeled on the *BCP* confirmation rite in structure, action, and function, though Congregationalists preferred the notion of profession of faith, rejecting confirmation as an unbiblical "invented" sacrament. It is interesting to note, nevertheless, that the service comes complete with kneeling (which would never have been tolerated by the early Puritans), laying on of hands, and a final prayer that God will "confirm us all in Thy truth and Spirit." The service makes clear that baptized persons do not participate in the Lord's Supper until such an admission takes place.

39. Jackson, 144-146.

40. Provision is made for the corporate confession of the Apostles' Creed. The congregation stands to welcome the new member into the fellowship and acknowledge their corporate promise of Christian love and support.

41. Chalmers, 65-66, 77.

42. White, 124. North American Congregationalists also became known for their liberal socio-cultural sensibilities, including the founding of Yale and Harvard, Chalmers, 78.

43. Spinks, 111.

44. Spinks, 110.

45. Helpful sources include: N. Keith Clifford, *The Resistance to Church Union in Canada: 1904-1939* (Vancouver: University of British Columbia Press, 1985); John Webster Grant, *The Canadian Experience of Church Union*; *The Church in the Canadian Era*, 1st edition. 1972 (Burlington: Welch, 1988); William D. Maxwell, *A History of Worship in the Church of Scotland* (London: Oxford University Press, 1955); John Thomas McNeill, *The Presbyterian Church in Canada: 1875-1925* (Toronto: Presbyterian Church in Canada, 1925); John S. Moir, *Enduring Witness: A History of the Presbyterian Church in Canada* (Toronto: Bryant Press, 1974); N. G. Smith, "The Presbyterian Tradition in Canada," in *The Churches and the Canadian Experience*, 38-52; Neil G. Smith, Allan L. Farris and H. Keith Markell, *A Short History of the Presbyterian Church in Canada* (Toronto: Presbyterian Publictions, 1967).

46. Moir, 36-44, 50-73; Smith, 36-43; Smith, et al., 23-25, 38-40, 43, 51. Originally, three strands of Presbyterians seemed to live on in North America: Secessionists were Voluntarists, rejecting state support or interference of any kind; Free Church Presbyterians rejected government interference, but would accept their support; the Auld Kirk desired a legal relationship with the state and would thus tolerate some state control. Such divisions were challenged when Kirk congregations could attract only Secessionist ministers. In time, with the absence of state support, the previous divisions began to appear increasingly anachronistic and union was entertained.

47. Moir, 146-169, 181-191; Smith, 43-47; Smith, et al., 51-55. On American influence, Smith notes: "Proximity to the United States involved all the churches, more or

less, in a process of Americanization. While maintaining strong Scottish ties, the Canadian [Presbyterian] church was influenced by the propaganda for the temperance movement in the United States, by the American Sunday School movement, and to some extent by American revivalism." Smith, 45.

48. Clifford, 9; Moir, 128-145; Smith, 45-50; Smith, et al., 52-55. Clifford's presentation of the events leading up to and following union is interesting in that they are viewed not from the vantage point of a 1925 failure, but a 1939 success—a provocative case study in the relationship between denominationalism and ecumenism. An overview of the crisis is found in Moir, 195-223. See also Smith, et al., 70-91.

49. White describes the chief difference between Zwingli and Calvin as "essentially a matter of piety." Zwingli held to a belief in the "disjuncture between the physical and the spiritual," denying that the former could lead to an understanding of the latter and was thus critical "of the use of physical objects and actions in worship." Calvin held to a more biblical view of the role of material things in pointing to spiritual realties. "There is a world of difference between Calvin's concept of the importance of signs for humans to experience God's self-giving, and Zwingli's dualism between nature and spirit." Nevertheless, Calvin, for all his reform of medieval worship, was entirely medieval in his view of humanity and his subsequent piety. His eucharist, for example, seems to combine two sacraments, penance and eucharist, in one. White, 60-66.

50. Maxwell has demonstrated the extent to which Knox's liturgy is indebted to Calvin's *La Forme des Prières*—which is, in turn, dependent on the earlier work and revisions by Bucer, Schwarz, and Luther. Maxwell, *A History of Worship in the Church of Scotland* (London: Oxford University Press, 1955), 42-49; *John Knox's Genevan Service Book*. For the purposes of this study, I will use the latter, a critical edition of Knox's "The Order for Baptism" [Knox], when citing the original source.

51. Knox, 105-120. Maxwell shows that this particular order, much like the work as a whole, is "derived almost in its entirety from Calvin; here and there, there are slight deviations, but none of these are important liturgically or doctrinally." Maxwell, *Genevan Service Book*, 48.

52. The medieval rites were "designed in the first place for the baptism of adult believers" and adapted for infants by simply directing the questions to sponsoring adults. John M. Barkley, *The Worship of the Reformed Church* (London: Lutterworth Press, 1966), 93.

53. "[T]he Reformers saw in the simple sign of washing such rich biblical meaning that they wanted to make this basic sign a prominent part of their worship." Hughes Oliphant Old, *Worship That Is Reformed According to Scripture* (Atlanta: John Knox Press, 1984), 16.

54. Whether it was a single or triple affusion is unclear. John M. Barkley, "Baptism: Reformed," in *A New Dictionary*, 73.

55. Knox, 105.

56. This was the origin of the Congregationalist practice. J. G. Davies, "Baptistery," in *A New Dictionary*, 81.

57. Maxwell, *Genevan Service Book*, 111-113. Old notes the extent to which Bucer, Zwingli, Calvin, and Knox were united on this question. Old, 17-18.

58. Maxwell, *Genevan Service Book*, 116.

59. Old contends that from Zwingli and Bullinger onward "covenant theology became the Reformed sacramental theology." Old, 19.

60. Knox, 105 [language modernized].

61. J. D. C. Fisher, "Lutheran, Anglican, and Reformed Rites," in *The Study of Liturgy*, eds. Cheslyn Jones, Geoffrey Wainwright, and Edward Yarnold, SJ (London: SPCK, 1978), 123.

62. Chalmers, 46-47. According to Chalmers, the Calvinist vision of the sovereignty of God in Presbyterianism carries with it a variety of implications. Salvation is only by grace through faith; there is no room for penance or priestly ritual, there is only Christ and salvation in him by grace through faith. Thus, Presbyterian sacramental theology attempts to avoid the extremes of "magic" and "memorialism," Lutheranism and Zwinglianism, by regarding the "elements as signs of grace, visible expressions of the Word, conveying Christ to the believer by faith in a real spiritual manner." (Chalmers 47.) Following from this, the church is the priesthood of all believers, the Body of Christ, and a church polity of ecclesiastical democratic representative government is the logical result.

63. White, 71; Maxwell, *A History of Worship*, 102.

64. "The Directory for the Public Worship of God," in *Confession of Faith. Larger Catechism. Shorter Catechism. Directory of Public Worship* (Toronto: Presbyterian Publications, 1900), 108. The exhortation is essentially the doctrine as presented in Chapter XXVIII of the Confession of Faith. Both go on to affirm that: infants of "one or both believing parents" are suitable candidates for baptism; water in the triune name by sprinkling or pouring is the method; baptism is unrepeatable; and grace is "not so inseparably annexed unto it, as that no person can be regenerated or saved without, or that all that are baptized are undoubtedly regenerated." *Confession of Faith*, 30.

65. "Directory," 108-110.

66. Barkley, *Worship*, 94.

67. Moir, 170-171.

68. *Aids for Social Worship: Being Short Services of Prayer and Praise for the use of Christians*. Prepared by a special committee under the Authority of the General Assembly of the Presbyterian Church in Canada (Toronto: Westminster Press, 1900).

69. *Euchologion. A Book of Common Order. Being Forms of Prayer, and Administration of the Sacraments, and Other Ordinances of the Church.* Church Service Society. 7th ed. (Edinburgh: William Blackwood and Sons, 1896).

70. Barkley, *Worship*, 94; Barkley, "Baptism," *A New Dictionary*, 73.

71. *Euchologion*, 304-312.

72. Barkley, "Baptism," *A New Dictionary*, 73; Knox, 92.

73. *Euchologion*, 305.

74. The title in the second edition of *Euchologion* (1869) was "An Order for the Confirmation of Baptismal Vows and Admission to the Lord's Table." The title in the seventh edition (1896) was "The Order for the Admission of Catechumens to the Confirmation of the Baptismal Vow, and to the Participation of the Lord's Supper." Barkley suggests that these orders are at the root of a growing confusion around confirmation. Similar developments will be discussed in reference to the development of the United Church. Barkley, 117; *Euchologion*, 313. There was some discussion at the Westminster Assembly favoring a service of admission to the Lord's Supper, but those seeking it were unsuccessful. Barkley, *Worship*, 116.

75. Grant notes that "the true high priest of Presbyterian worship was the head of the family," and the catechesis leading to communion was "especially intense." John Webster Grant, *George Pidgeon* (Toronto: Ryerson, 1962), 6-7.

76. Smith, 45.

77. The question is: "Do you present yourself for holy Baptism, desiring to be ingrafted into the body of Christ?" *Euchologion*, 320. See also Barkley, "Baptism," *A New Dictionary*, 76.

78. *Book of Common Order for use in Church Services and Offices* (Toronto: Oxford University Press, 1922). [*BCO* (1922)].

79. Helpful sources include: Phyllis D. Airhart, *Serving the Present Age: Revivalism, Progressivism, and the Methodist Tradition in Canada* (Kingston: McGill-Queen's University Press, 1992); Frank Baker, "The Trans-Atlantic Triangle: Relations between British, Canadian, and American Methodism during Wesley's Lifetime," *Bulletin of The United Church Archives*, no. 28 (1979); Dennis L. Butcher, et al., eds., *Prairie Sprit*; Goldwin French, *Parsons & Politics: The Role of The Wesleyan Methodists in Upper Canada and the Maritimes from 1780-1855* (Toronto: Ryerson, 1962); "The People Called Methodists in Canada," in *The Churches and the Canadian Experience*, 60-81; Grant, *The Canadian Experience of Church Union; The Church in The Canadian Era; A Profusion of Spires; Religion in Nineteenth-Century Ontario* (Toronto: University of Toronto Press, 1988); Francis Dean Mercer, "The Liturgical and Sacramental Development of the Free Methodist Church in Canada, with Special Attention to the Rituals of Baptism and the Lord's Supper" (Th.D. diss., Trinity College, Toronto School of Theology, 1991); John S. Moir, ed., *The Cross in Canada* (Toronto: Ryerson, 1966); George A. Rawlyk, ed., *The Canadian Protestant Experience*; Alexander Sutherland, *Methodism in Canada: Its Work and Its Story* (Toronto: Methodist Mission Rooms, 1904); David Lowes Watson, "Methodist Spirituality," in *Protestant Spiritual Traditions*, ed. Frank C. Senn (New York: Paulist Press, 1986), 217-273.

80. French's summary of the early differences between the two groups is instructive. Both professed "devotion to the Wesleyan tradition" and to the "search for lost souls," but those in the east were more conservative in their evangelical approach while the Upper Canadians "were still a band of enthusiasts." The former were still dependent on the homeland. The latter identified more with the Canadian context, prompting them to become more socio-politically involved. French, *Parsons and Politics*, 78-79. Cf. Mercer, 120-121.

81. French, "The People Called Methodists in Canada," 76-77. For essays on the spread of Methodism to the west, with comments on work among aboriginal peoples, see Gerald Hutchinson, "British Methodists and the Hudson's Bay Company, 1840-1854," in *Prairie Spirit*, 28-43; John Badertscher, "As Others Saw Us," in *Prairie Spirit*, 44-64.

82. For discussions on the relationship between nationalism and piety, see: Airhart, "Ordering a New Nation and Reordering Protestantism, 1867-1914," in *The Canadian Protestant Experience*, 98-138; *Serving the Present Age;* French, "The People Called Methodists in Canada," 77-81.

83. The "Methodist mind" is French's phrase in "The People Called Methodists in Canada," 69. French explores the complexities of Methodism's role in Canadian history in *Parsons & Politics*, 278-290. See also Sutherland, 6-7.

84. Consider the contrasts that are held together in Methodism. Wesley's theology and piety was both evangelical and social, reformed and catholic, revivalist and sacramental. French, *Parsons & Politics*, 1-16; Watson, "Methodist Spirituality," 217-230; White, *Protestant Worship*, 150-158. In the Canadian context, Bland was equally paradoxical, "realistic and mystical," political and devotional. Richard Allen, "Salem Bland and the Spirituality of the Social Gospel: Winnipeg and the West, 1903-1913," in *Prairie Spirit*, 132-217. Airhart's *Serving the Present Age* challenges narrow conceptions of revivalist piety through her analysis of revivalism as a tradition with a dynamic capacity for contextual adaptation. Christie notes the countercultural character of evangelical piety. Christie, "In These Times of Democratic Rage and Delusion," 9-47. Both place the rise of progressivism and the Social Gospel in the context of evangelical revivalism. On the Social Gospel, see Richard Allen's definitive study *The Social Passion: Religion and Social Reform in Canada 1914-1928* (Toronto: University of Toronto Press: 1973). Similarly, Grant challenges the equation of evangelism with conservative fundamentalism, placing evangelism at the heart of the United Church identity. Grant, "The United Church

and Its Heritage in Evangelism," *Touchstone* 1, no. 3 (October 1983): 6-13. For further comments on the term *evangelical*, see Grant, *A Profusion of Spires*, ix.

85. White, speaking in an American context, calls it "the foundation stone for subsequent Methodist worship in this country." White, "Introduction," in *John Wesley's Sunday Service of the Methodists in North America* (Nashville: The United Methodist Publishing House, 1984), 7 [*SS*] when quoting from Wesley's liturgical text.

86. *SS*, A1.

87. White, "Introduction," 10-11.

88. White, "Baptism: Methodist," in *A New Dictionary*, 68; "Introduction," 13.

89. A few versions of the 1784 texts retain signation but most omit it. All subsequent editions dropped it. Bernard G. Holland, *Baptism in Early Methodism* (London: Epworth Press, 1970), 180; White, "Introduction," 30.

90. In adult baptism the exhortation and the postbaptismal signation are again omitted and an altered form of the closing prayer of thanksgiving from the order for infant baptism replaces the final prayer. The alterations to most of the prayers are along the same lines as those for infant baptism. Cf. *BCP* (1662), 761-777; *SS*, 143-149. Cf. Holland, 182-188; Mercer, 168-169; White "Introduction," 30.

91. For a summary of the Puritan influence on Wesley's *Sunday Service*, see Mercer, 26-37. This included changes to the Psalter and lessons, omission of the Apocryphal readings, provision for more extemporaneous prayer, omission of confirmation, and the suppression of both Lent and the sanctoral cycle.

92. Grant, "The United Church and Its Heritage in Evangelism," 6; White, *Protestant Worship*, 151.

93. Note that "Methodist" was at first a derogatory nickname given to the members of the Oxford Holy Club in which Wesley was a member. They were derided for their commitment to the disciplines of fasting, charitable works, and frequent communion. For a summary of Wesley's views of the means of grace, see Mercer, 8-25. For a discussion summarizing Methodist revivalist methods see Mercer, 56-67.

94. Watson's synthesis is that Anglicanism provides the "forms" and Puritanism the "dynamic." Watson, 217-222. See also Grant, *A Profusion of Spires*, 29. "Conversion therapy" is borrowed from Kavanagh. E.g., Aidan Kavanagh, *On Liturgical Theology* (New York: Pueblo, 1984), 167.

95. Watson, 254; Chalmers, 96-114.

96. French, *Parsons & Politics*, 5-7.

97. *SS*, 306-312.

98. *SS*, 139-143. See also comments by Holland, 178-181; Mercer, 168-173; White, "Baptism: Methodist," 68.

99. Holland, 181, 182, 186.

100. White, "Introduction," 20.

101. Holland, 13, 35. For an overview of Wesley's encounter with the Moravians, see Mercer, 13-15.

102. John Wesley, "The New Birth," in *Wesley's Doctrinal Standards: Part I. The Sermons*, ed. N. Burwash (Toronto: William Briggs, 1881), 446-455.

103. Wesley, "The New Birth," 453.

104. Holland, 66-72; Mercer, 141-159.

105. Holland, 66-72. Ole Borgen defends Wesley against this accusation, arguing that such a conclusion is a result of a misunderstanding of his vocabulary of *regeneration*, *new birth*, and *conversion*. They are, he argues, not synonymous throughout Wesley's writings, but are used in a variety of ways with different connotations in different contexts. Ole E. Borgen, *John Wesley on the Sacraments* (Grand Rapids: Francis Asbury Press, 1972), 148-160. Cf. Mercer, 162-168.

106. Holland notes that "evangelicals of the eighteenth century, for all their stress upon the universal necessity of adult conversion, believed that regeneration is also given in infant baptism." Holland, 129.

107. This is Holland's definition of what Wesley means by conversion. Holland, 35.

108. Cf. Mercer, 151-153.

109. Holland, 135.

110. For perspectives on the reasons behind this phenomenon see: Bedell, 13-18; Mercer 47-47; Watson, 225-233, 235-240, 253-256; White, *Protestant Worship*, 154-156, 162.

111. The others included were the services for weddings, burials, and some parts of the ordination rites and the Lord's Supper. White, "Introduction," 12; *Protestant Worship*, 158; Kenneth B. Bedell, *Worship in the Methodist Tradition* (Nashville: Discipleship Resources-Tidings, 1976), 55.

112. Mercer, 174-180.

113. *The Doctrines and Discipline of the Methodist Church of Canada. 1874* (Toronto: Samuel Rose, 1874), 131. [*DD* (1874)]. The additional scriptural texts in the service of infant baptism show evidence of a Puritan-like concern with warrants (perhaps with polemical overtones) focusing particularly on texts which reflect covenant theology (e.g., Gen. 17:7, Acts 2:39; 3:13, 14, 29) and the mode of sprinkling (e.g., Ez. 36:25).

114. *DD* (1874), 129-140.

115. Holland, 142.

116. *The Doctrine and Discipline of the Methodist Church 1902* (Toronto: William Briggs, 1902), 277-289. [*DD* (1902)].

117. *The Doctrine and Discipline of the Methodist Church Canada 1922* (Toronto: Methodist Book and Publishing House, 1923), 335-350. [*DD* (1922)].

118. Harding, "The Major Orders," 32-36; Mercer, 26-37

119. See White, *Protestant Worship*, 163, for his comments on Methodism's "Akron Plan" of liturgical space. Its central pulpit, organ, and choirloft, together with its excellent acoustics and sightlines, emphasized preaching and music. Little attention was given to the font or its placement. The Oxford Movement also influenced nineteenth century Canadian Methodist architecture, leading to chancels and high altars, especially in the larger urban churches. This often reflected the displacement of an evangelical approach by a more establishment ethos.

120. Holland, 163-169; Watson, 240-243; White, *Protestant Worship* 153, 157-158, 164-165; Harding, "The Major Orders," 31.

121. Bacon has suggested that Canadian Methodists, especially on the east coast, used the *Sunday Service* more than their counterparts in the rest of Canada. Douglas A. Bacon, "The Impact of a Study of Christian Worship on a Congregation of The United Church of Canada," D.Min. project report (Drew University, 1982), 33. See also: Harding, "The Major Orders," 28; Mercer, 122-123, 138.

122. French, *Parsons & Politics*, vii, 278; White, *Protestant Worship*, 111-112, 162-166. White's comments on the influence of aestheticism, restorationism, and the Oxford Movement on Methodist worship can be placed in this context.

123. *Christianizing the Social Order*, The Board of Evangelism and Social Service (Toronto: The United Church of Canada, 1934). The Social Gospel and Methodist involvement in education and politics can be placed in the context of this tradition—i.e., not so much a turning away from evangelical roots as an affirmation of them in a new context.

124. John Webster Grant, "Blending Traditions: The United Church of Canada," in *The Churches and the Canadian Experience*, 136-137.

125. The service in the Mutual Street Arena, Toronto, is noteworthy for introducing into United Church liturgical usage the practice of simultaneous communion in which all communicants, upon receiving the elements in their pews, wait to partake with the presider as one body. The official act of union included a brief address by the leaders of the founding denominations. Each spoke of the heritage brought to the union by their tradition, concluding with the words: "Receive ye our inheritance among them that are sanctified." Grant, "Blending Traditions," 135, 138; *The Manual* (Toronto: The United Church Publishing House, 1928), 7-12. [*Manual* (1928)].

126. *Manual* (1928), 85.

127. *Manual* (1928), 85.

128. *The Manual 2001* (Toronto: United Church Publishing House, 2001), 27. [*Manual* (2001)].

129. The sole exception to this is the questions to candidates in the service of ordination. This is the only liturgical matter which is ruled on directly by General Council. Cf. *Manual* (1928), 47; *Manual* (2001), 30, 56-57; *SB* (1969), unnumbered 3; David R. Newman, "Ordination in The United Church of Canada: An Essay in Liturgical Theology," *Toronto Journal of Theology* 2, no. 1 (1986): 94-104.

130. Cf. *Manual* (1928), 58-59; *Manual* (2001), 21.

131. *The Year Book and Record of Proceedings* (Toronto: United Church Publishing House, 1952), 215. The committee of four was made up of G. Hanson (Presbyterian), D. L. Ritchie (Congregationalist), S. P. Rose (Methodist), and R. E. Welsh (Presbyterian). Hanson did not, in the end, serve with the committee, leaving it a committee of three—one Presbyterian, one Methodist, one Congregationalist. Ritchie was Principle of Congregational College, Montreal. Welsh, the secretary of the committee, was the chair of the Presbyterian committee which produced *BCO* (1922).

132. *The Year Book and Record of Proceedings* (Toronto: United Church Publishing House, 1926), 387; *Forms*, v.

133. *The Year Book and Record of Proceedings* (Toronto: United Church Publishing House, 1926), 387; *Forms*, vi.

134. *Forms*, vi-ix.

135. Cf. *Forms*, ix and *BCO* (1922), 4.

136. *Book of Congregational Worship*, Congregation Union of England and Wales (London: Trumbull & Spears, 1920). [*BCW* (1920)].

137. *Forms*, i-iii.

138. The evidence for this becomes clear in the context of the reception of *BCO* (1932). This will be discussed further in chapter 2.

139. Cf. *Forms*, 19-25; *BCO* (1922), 117-126.

140. Cf. *Euchologion*, 304-312.

141. These traditional *Directory* notes included statements about baptism as a public act of the church ("in the presence of the Congregation"), its proper administration by "a Minister of Christ," the proper candidates for baptism ("infants of one or both believing parents"), and as noted in the discussion with respect to the Presbyterian orders, the statement from the Confession of Faith that "grace and salvation are not so inseparably annexed unto this ordinance as that none can be regenerated or saved without it." *BCO (1922)*, 121.

142. E.g., the "kindly words and gesture" exhortation, the "God and Father of our children" prayer for the Spirit, the Aaronic blessing, and the declaration of reception were all simplified and modernized.

143. Cf. *BCO* (1922), 117 and 123.

144. *Forms*, 20-21.

145. The service was reproduced unchanged from *BCW* (1920). Cf. *Forms*, 26-27; *BCW* (1920), 47-48

146. *Forms*, 26.

147. Cf. *Forms*, 28-32; *BCO* (1922), 127-129.

148. Cf. *BCO* (1922), 127; *Forms*, 28.

149. *Forms*, 28.

150. *BCO* (1922), 128; *Forms*, 29; *Euchologion*, 322.

151. *Forms*, 33-43. The order in which they were presented was Methodist, Presbyterian, and Congregationalist. Cf. *DD* (1922), 348-350; *BCO* (1922), 130-133; *BCW* (1920), 45-46. The only other services which provided a similar balance of representation in *Forms* were those for ordination.

152. *DD* (1922) contains another order for Reception into Full Membership for baptized adults taking up the responsibilities of "full" membership in the Methodist Church. *DD* (1922), 345-348.

153. The United Church version of all three services in *Forms* was also adapted to include appropriate references in the questions, including the phrase "essential agreement with the faith and order of The United Church of Canada as set forth in the Basis of Union." The significance of the phrase "essential agreement" here and in ordination services in the United Church relates to the noncreedal convictions of the Congregationalists. This will be noted again in the context of the discussion on the *BCO* (1932) orders.

154. *Forms*, 36.

155. *Forms*, 38.

156. Note, however, that the words *confirm* and *strengthen* are used in the closing prayers. *Forms*, 40.

157. *BCW*, 45-46.

158. *Forms*, 43.

159. Chalmers, 120-121.

160. The *BCP*-like words are common to all the orders in the postbaptismal declarations. *Forms*, 23, 27, 31. Cf. *BCP* (1662), 741.

161. *Forms*, 31.

162. *Manual* (1926), 16-18.

163. *Manual* (1926), 16. It is interesting to note that the term *Holy Spirit* was used in the Articles of Faith, while *Holy Ghost* was used in the liturgies.

164. *Manual* (1926), 16-18.

165. Chalmers notes that this was a compromise between the Methodist liberalism (which would turn no child away) and Presbyterian conservatism (which held to the *Directory* principle of baptizing only believers or children of believing parents.)

166. *Manual* (1926), 18.

167. Chalmers, 118.

168. Grant argues that the Articles of Faith of the Basis of Union were the least of the unionists' worries, having been completed by 1908 with very little difficulty. Others have also noted their conservative, nonpolemical, and noncontroversial nature, even suggesting that this may have been due to the advanced age of the men of the Union Committee. In addition, the pragmatism of the time favored social involvement over theological restatement. Chalmers, 122; Grant, *The Canadian Experience of Church Union*, 31-36; *The Church in the Canadian Era*, 106-110; C. E. Silcox, *Church Union in Canada* (New York: Institute of Social and Religious Research, 1933), 127; Robert A. Wright, "The Canadian Protestant Tradition," *The Canadian Protestant Experience*, 151-152; John H. Young, "Sacred Cow or White Elephant? The Doctrine Section of the Basis of Union," *Touchstone* 16, no. 2 (May 1998): 29-46.

169. Chalmers, 120.

Part II
Coming of Age through Common Order

Chapter 2
Baptism in *The Book of Common Order*

The Book of Common Order

In presenting *Forms of Service* to the 1926 General Council, the Committee on Church Worship and Ritual recommended that further steps be taken toward the production of a more comprehensive book. The words of the Committee provide a glimpse of its intentionally catholic vision.

> The recommendation of your Committee is that the General Council should appoint . . . a select representative Committee . . . to sift and unify the material in use within the uniting Churches, and with a catholic interest in all other helpful material, to compose a comprehensive Book of Worship and Ritual, subject to the judgement of the General Council.[1]

In fact, the work had already begun. A report to the same General Council from the Presbyterian committee which produced *The Book of Common Order* (1922), the Committee on Public Worship and Aids to Devotion, pointed out that several members in the Toronto area had surveyed a number of liturgical resources in preparation for further work. The materials gathered were then placed "at the service of any Committee which the General Council . . . [saw] fit to appoint for the objects in view."[2] In response to these developments the Committee on Church Worship and Ritual was immediately expanded and interpreted its mandate as twofold: the production of a new hymn book and a Book of Common Order.[3]

The work on a new hymn book proceeded quickly and resulted in the production of the booklet *Songs of the Psalter* and later *The Hymnary of The United Church.*[4] In spite of some lively initial criticism, *The Hymnary* was to become a Canadian classic, due mostly to the vigorous scholarship of Alexander MacMillan.[5] The same "catholicity of taste"[6] he brought to the production of the Presbyterian *Book of Praise* years earlier is evident throughout this work. Indeed, the catholic concern for "a collection . . . widely representative of the Hymnody of the Church Universal" was defined as the "larger aim of the compilers," while the "second purpose" was that of honoring the hymnody of the founding communions of the United Church.[7] Thus, *The Hymnary* stands as the first example of the Committee's liturgical vision, one which interpreted the mandate of a "united and uniting church" as a call to mine the entire wealth of the Christian liturgical heritage, not simply the immediate resources of the founding traditions.[8]

The Book of Common Order was part of this same vision and is appropriately placed within the same context. What Alexander MacMillan was to *The Hymnary*, Richard Davidson was to *The Book of Common Order.*[9] Within months of beginning work on *The Hymnary* a subcommittee led by Davidson began work on *The Book of Common Order*. As Professor of Old Testament Literature, History, and Exegesis and a lecturer in worship at Union College, he brought an impressive degree of both passion and scholarship to the task.[10] By the 1928 meeting of General Council, draft orders for Ordination, Induction, Lord's Supper, Baptism, and Confirmation were ready to be distributed to presbyteries for consideration and response.

Presbytery responses to the draft orders were numerous and varied, ranging from "commendation" to "minor adjustments." One respondent bluntly labeled it "impracticable for common use." Davidson summarized the responses for the Committee by reporting that one half were explicit in "appreciation," most of the others approved "implicitly" with some notations, and most of the criticisms generally entailed a call for greater simplicity and likeness to *Forms*. A survey of the actual submissions, however, suggests that he put the best possible face on the situation.[11] Work on the draft orders continued until the 1932 General Council, where motions for the acceptance of the work were passed with a surprising lack of controversy or discussion.[12]

Unlike the colorful correspondence surrounding *The Hymnary*, the pages of the church's official weekly, *The New Outlook*, were largely silent on *The Book of Common Order*.[13] No doubt one writer had it in mind, however, when, only weeks after the 1932 General Council, he wrote of "the dangers of ritualism," and the need to prize "virtue in variety, divineness in diversity."[14] Over a year after the book was published, another writer puzzled over the continuing silence about the book, especially in light of the fact that controversy had been predicted by some and the book was "heralded abroad" by others. He further suggested that a companion to the book, along the lines of that being produced by MacMillan for *The Hymnary*, was needed to encourage and explain its intended usage.[15]

In fact, such a companion was a goal of Davidson and the Committee, as the introduction as the 1928 drafts made clear:

> The Committee has in preparation a Handbook to accompany the Book of Orders. The Handbook will contain in regard to each Order:
>
> (a) A statement of its meaning and intention.
> (b) A sketch of history showing how it has come to be what it is today.
> (c) An explanation of its structure (rationale).

> (d) Practical hints for carrying it through. This would be an amplification in freer form, of the compressed rubrical directions contained in the Order.[16]

It is not clear why it never materialized.

On the other hand, the silence was not so puzzling to one anonymous correspondent. The reason was, put simply, its "formalism." "I have never heard a minister mention [*The Book of Common Order*]. They know that those who follow John Wesley in his fight for freedom from formality in worship would revolt. . . . [The church is] drifting slowly into formalism and it does not matter to . . . [some] whether a prayer comes from a minister's left breast or from his right pocket." Noteworthy in the context of this study, he also went on to illustrate his point with reference to baptism.

> [A] baby is taken to church, forcibly baptized, its name placed on the cradle roll of the Sunday School, then it is advanced from class to class, until it is finally told to join the church. Obediently it takes the step, without, in too many cases, knowing anything about being "born again." For this class ready-made prayers do as well as any. . . . It is like a child asking a lawyer to request a gift of parents. Let our ministers preach repentance, conversion, and personal communion with God, and if the people accept this they will not need a book of prayers. For the United Church to adopt formalism in worship means its spiritual death.[17]

A vaguely supportive note was sounded in one article, but again no mention was made of the book in particular: "The United Church of Canada is now in the process of making new traditions. It has discarded some old ones and is questioning the values in others. Replacements will be necessary."[18] This writer was in a minority of two out of a total of five.

The popular reaction to *The Book of Common Order* stands in contrast to its more scholarly reception. One religion columnist called it a "venerable cathedral," "the most comprehensive expression of corporate worship thus far at the disposal of the universal church."[19] William Maxwell spoke of it as "a monumental piece of work."[20] In particular, "An Order for the Celebration of The Lord's Supper and Holy Communion" came to be regarded by some as "a model for the climax of Free Church worship."[21]

But such recognition was a long time coming. The minutes of the Committee on Church Worship and Ritual reveal that, on at least one occasion, there was serious concern about the book's reception. The Committee even recommended to General Council that it urge all ministers to use the book and, moreover, that its use in the courts and colleges of the church be legislated. There is, however, no evidence to suggest that the General Council acted upon this recommendation. To have done so would have been surprising in view of the polity of the United Church in matters of worship.[22]

In addition, as already noted, many of the presbytery responses to the draft orders expressed satisfaction with the status quo as set forth in *Forms of Service*.[23] Such evidence demonstrates that denominational liturgical allegiances were strong and *Forms* was the favored text for the first generation of United Church clergy.

This time lag between the publication and appropriation of *The Book of Common Order* is important to consider. Beyond such reasons as simple disapproval or the liturgical sensibilities characteristic of the founding traditions, additional factors shed some light on the development of worship in The United Church of Canada.

As discussed with respect to *Forms* in part I above, one must again take seriously the spirit of union itself. The liturgical freedom symbolized by *Forms* and constitutionally entrenched in the Basis of Union was itself a "union spirit" much needed during the first period of United Church history, one which helped to cement and solidify the new relationships of union. A liturgical debate, at either the national or congregational level (or both), pitting the hallowed traditions of one communion against another, was something few would have wanted and seems to have been instinctively avoided as counterproductive by most.

On another level, the realities of the Depression seemed to bring more urgent issues before the church. Soon war began to loom on the horizon and the church became increasingly immersed in heated debates about pacifism, followed by the anxious and stressful years of the war itself. In this context, the significance of a new service book seemed to drop in priority.

On the pedagogical front, one must also recognize that it takes time for any liturgical resource to be taught to clergy and appropriated by congregations. Davidson, well aware of the liturgical literacy that such a work demanded, issued "A Warning" in one version of his introduction of the draft orders: "The Book is no substitute for study and hard-won understanding. The use of set forms to the edification of the people is always a difficult task. To use any book well involves great labour and much patience and long practice."[24] In his presentation to the 1932 General Council he cautioned: "For the Lord's sake, don't use this book unless you know how."[25]

However, in the absence of both a "companion" or "handbook" and an intentional plan for liturgical education or renewal, it was left to the gradual emergence of a new generation of clergy who, having been schooled in the meaning and use of the new resource, could usher it into popular use. The slow transfusion of such new blood can easily take a decade or two before it accumulates in enough measure to significantly change the liturgical life of the church.

In short, whether because of the realities of union, Depression, or war, or for reasons of apathy, antipathy, or ignorance, *The Book of Common Order* did not come of age until after the Second World War. One historian's summary of this general context sheds some helpful light on the dynamics of a period within which we can locate this particular liturgical phenomenon:

> It is said that the generation of 1914-1945 presided over Canada's emergence as a full-fledged nation. . . . In virtually every walk of life, the Canadian nation that emerged from the Second World War barely resembled that which had entered the first. Various institutions, social patterns, cultural and intellectual precepts, and political ideas were fractured and then recast during this tumultuous period.[26]

A new country and a new church emerged together after the war, each ready to embrace symbols of a national identity.[27] *The Book of Common Order*, together with a generation of clergy, by now more accustomed to its use, were ready and available to assist in the task.

Finally, on the liturgical level, it may have been the very strength of the work which contributed to its initial weakness. Paradoxically, its sophisticated catholicity had as much to do with its short-term failure as its long-term success. Unionists committed to exploring the diversity of *Forms of Service* interpreted the catholicity of *The Book of Common Order* with suspicion. Its efforts to recover many of the classic turns of phrase of the Reformed and Anglican liturgies and restore a more balanced experience of Word and sacrament appeared too "ritualistic" and "Anglican" to many. Its acknowledged "indebtedness to the service books of the ancient and mediaeval Church, . . . the Anglican and Lutheran Communions, and those of Scottish and American Churches"[28] was seen by some more as a weakness than a strength. It took several decades before the United Church had sufficient distance from the founding traditions to appreciate *The Book of Common Order* on its own terms. When talk of a new service book began again in the fifties and sixties, commentators would routinely speak of it with fondness and loyalty.[29]

The quintessential expression of this United Church version of catholicity is summed up in the phrase, "ordered liberty," a careful attempt to balance the activity of the Spirit and the wisdom of the ages. The classic exposition of this principle is contained in the preface to *The Book of Common Order*. It warrants quotation in full:

> In the Churches which united to form The United Church of Canada there was an ordered liberty in common worship. They followed lines marked out by the Apostolic practice and hallowed by the general usage of Christendom, but they shrank from a uniformity that might quench the Spirit of God in the soul of man. In our worship we are rightly concerned for two things: first, that a worshipping congregation of the Lord's people shall be free to follow the leading of the Spirit of Christ in their midst; and secondly, that the experience of many ages of devotion shall not be lost, but preserved, experience that has caused certain forms of prayers to glow with light and power.
>
> This book has been prepared by the Committee on Church Worship and Ritual of The United Church of Canada. The aim of the Committee has been to set forth orders that are loyal to the spirit of Christ and loyal to the experience of the Church of all ages and of all lands; orders that carry on the devotional usage of the three united Communions in their living integrity. It is hoped that they may prove fit to be regarded as normative, and also be found flexible enough for the many-sided life of a growing Church.
>
> The Committee prays that those who use this book may be enabled by it to enter more fully into the rich heritage of Christian worship, and find that the good Shepherd has there provided for his flock "green pastures" and "waters of comfort."[30]

This is the standard which the Committee set for itself, which the United Church officially approved as its liturgical vision, which its people came to own in the fifties and sixties, and according to which this study must evaluate the baptismal liturgies of *The Book of Common Order*.

In the sections which follow, I will begin with a detailed commentary on the sources of the texts themselves, followed by a discussion of some of the theological and liturgical issues they raise. The commentaries in this and the remaining parts of this study will be presented in a format conducive to easy reference and documentation. The analysis which follows the commentaries will be organized under a series of relevant headings.

A Commentary on the Texts

AN ORDER FOR THE BAPTISM OF CHILDREN[31]

Of the immediate sources, only the Congregationalist speaks of "children" rather than "infants" in the title.[32]

The Minister may, before the administration of the Sacrament, give instruction touching its nature and meaning, using, if he will, the Exhortation placed at the end of this Order.

The opening rubric points to the practice of the time: preparation or catechesis was an option left to the discretion of the minister.

THE INTRODUCTION

The Minister, standing at the Font, shall say to the Parents or Sponsors) of the child,

This rubric allows for the possibility of baptismal sponsors other than parents.

Do you here present this child, earnestly desiring that *he* be received by Holy Baptism into the fellowship of the Church of Christ?

Answer. I do.

The question is a recovery of the practice of Calvin and Knox. Calvin's simple "Do you present this child to be baptized?"[33] was expanded by Knox to "Do you present this child to be baptized, earnestly desiring that he may be ingrafted in the mystical body of Jesus Christ?"[34] In keeping with the tendency shown in the orders of the founding traditions and *Forms*, the United Church version shies away from the mystical and typological language of "ingrafting," favoring the language of "reception."

Then shall the Minister say one or other of the Prayers following.

Almighty God and merciful Father,

The opening address and relative

who of thine infinite goodness has called us into thy Church, and promised to be our God and the God and Father of our children; Graciously look upon this child, whom we now offer and dedicate unto thee; and vouchsafe to receive *him* into the fellowship of thy Son Jesus Christ, that as a living member of his Body *he* may be sanctified by the Spirit, and made partaker of the fullness of thy heavenly grace through Jesus Christ our Lord. *Amen.*

clause of the first prayer are classic phrases from the baptismal liturgies of the Reformed tradition, traceable to Calvin and Knox.[35] This particular version is a skillful combination of two prayers which appear in the 1922 Presbyterian *Book of Common Order.*[36] What distinguishes this one from its forerunners is its location and function. The sources show that it was traditionally offered immediately following the exhortation and just before baptism, thus serving to reinforce the message of the former and invoke the Spirit's blessing on the latter. Its use here in the Introduction causes it to function more as a general opening prayer of invocation.

Almighty and immortal God, the aid of all that need, the helper of all that flee to thee for succour, the life of them that believe, and the resurrection of the dead: We call upon thee for this child, whom we bring to thee in this holy Sacrament. Receive *him,* O Lord, as thou has promised by the well-beloved Son, saying, Ask, and ye shall have; seek, and ye shall find; knock, and it shall be opened unto you; So give now unto us that ask; let us that seek find; open the gate unto us that knock; that his child may become and ever remain Christ's true disciple, and may attain to the eternal kingdom which thou hast promised by Christ our Lord. *Amen.*

This is also a well-known prayer, as evident in the Sarum usage of the Roman rite, Martin Luther's orders for baptism, the Prayer Book, and Wesley.

In most Roman usage it was a prayer of "catechising a catechumen" associated with exorcisms. Luther's first order of baptism (1523), a conservative translation of a Roman rite, retained it in full.[37] His second (1526) was more radical, eliminating much of the ceremonial, especially that associated with exorcisms. A version of this prayer remained, however, as an opening prayer of invocation associated with the signing with the cross.[38]

Cranmer knew it from the Sarum rite, where it was said over male candidates in the exorcisms of "Order for Making of a Catechumen."[39] In his Prayer Book of 1549 most of the Sarum text was combined with some of Luther's.[40] His 1552 revision, informed by Bucer, disassociated it from the exorcisms and used it more simply as one of the opening prayers.[41] Wesley followed this use (as found in the 1662 Prayer Book), however, it was not included in the service of infant baptism in the Canadian Methodist *Doctrine and Discipline*.[42] Thus, it is the 1552/1662 Prayer Book usage which is the source of its presence and function here.

As observed in the liturgies of the founding traditions and *Forms*, the United Church version omits the Prayer Book and Wesley phrases regarding "remission of their sins by spiritual regeneration" and "heavenly washing," thus avoiding possible theological controversy by referring only to the "the holy sacrament" and "Christ's true disciple." As a result, the petition to "receive" the child dominates.

Then shall the Minister say,

Hear the words of the Gospel according to Saint Mark, in the tenth chapter, at the thirteenth verse.

Luther and Zwingli used the Gospel of Mark in their liturgy, while Sarum and Calvin tended to use Matthew 19.[43]

They brought young children to Christ, that he should touch them; and his disciples rebuked those that brought them. But when Jesus saw it, he was much displeased, and said unto them, Suffer the little children to come unto me, and forbid then not; for of such is the kingdom of God. Verily I say unto you, Whosoever shall not receive the kingdom of God as a little child, he shall not enter therein. And he took them up in his arms, put his hands upon them, and blessed them.

This particular version of Mark 10 is the Prayer Book's[44] and was common to Methodists, Presbyterians, and Congregationalists. However, Presbyterians also took care to include the text of dominical institution, the so-called Great Commission of Matthew 28.[45] The use of Mark draws attention to practice of baptizing infants rather than the institution of baptism in general.

Then may the Minister make this brief Exhortation upon the words of the Gospel.

Beloved, you hear in this Gospel the words of our Saviour Christ, that he

The origins of the exhortation can be traced at least to 1543 to a conference commanded the children to be brought unto him; how he blamed those that would have kept them from him; how he exhorteth all men to follow their innocency. You perceive how by outward gesture and deed he declared his good will toward them; for he took them in his arms he laid his hands upon them, and blessed them. He is the same yesterday and today and forever. Doubt not therefore, but earnestly believe, that he loveth this child; that he is ready to receive *him*, to embrace *him* with the arms of his mercy, and give *him* the blessing of eternal life.

in Bonn in which Melanchthon and Bucer presented their reformed Church Order. Cranmer possessed a Latin copy of the document and it influenced his much-abridged version on the level of both content and function and settled into the Prayer Book tradition from the beginning.[46] While variations on it appear in Canadian Presbyterian orders,[47] the United Church version is very much a return to the Prayer Book tradition. However, it is interesting to note that it comes not simply from the expected Canadian Anglican source. In fact, the last sentences of the prayer (beginning "Doubt not") owe much to the particular text of the "Alternative Order" composed for the proposed 1928 Prayer Book.[48]

THE PROMISES

Then shall the Minister say unto Parents (or Sponsors),

For as much as you desire and claim these blessing for your child, you will now engage, on your part, to perform those things which God requireth of you, that the good will and pleasure of your heavenly Father may not be hidden from your child.

Anglicans, Methodists, and Congregationalists would have been familiar with the exhortation-like style of this statement which functions both to recapitulate what has gone before and introduce what is to come. For Methodists, such an exhortation often replaced questions.[49]

I ask therefore,

Do you confess Jesus Christ as Saviour and Lord?

Answer. I do so confess.

Do you promise, as God shall give you Grace, to bring up this child in the knowledge and love of God, to the end that in all things *he* may grow up into union with Christ?

The form of the first question is noteworthy in that it is neither trinitarian nor explicitly creedal, but simply a confession of Jesus Christ as Savior and Lord. This style is quite Congregationalist, while the second question is more Presbyterian. The absence of a renunciation in the questions is in keeping with the practice of the founding traditions at the time of union.[50] An optional form based on the Apostles' Creed is provided in the "Appendix" but the presence of these questions in the main body of the text seems to indicate a preference on the part of the compilers.

Then shall follow this Prayer.

Grant, O Lord, to these thy servants grace to perform the things which they have promised before thee, and sanctify with thy Spirit this child now to be baptized according to thy Word; through Jesus Christ our Lord. *Amen.*

The choice of this prayer, from a contemporary American source,[51] is worth comparing with the optional prayers provided in the liturgy in the "Appendix" below. In contrast to any suggestion of a blessing of the water or any references to the symbol of water itself, the emphasis in this prayer is on grace for the parents/sponsors to perform their duties and the Spirit's blessing upon the child. However, an additional problem is introduced. The prayer contains the curious petition to "sanctify . . . this child" who is about to be sanctified in the act of baptism itself, as if to imply some distinction between the prayer and the act, a separation of the action of the Spirit from the action of baptism.

THE BAPTISM

Then the Minister (taking the child in his arms, or leaving it in the arms of one of the Parents or Sponsors) shall say,

The rubrics, probably influenced by the same American source as the preceding prayer, allow for the variety of practices at the time.[52]

What is the name of this child?

The explicit naming of the child was common to the practice of all three uniting denominations, as, of course, was the traditional (Western) form of the trinitarian formula.[53]

And then, naming it after them, he shall pour or sprinkle water upon the head of the child, or dip the child in the water, saying,

N. I Baptize thee In the name of the

Regarding the method of the baptism itself: while sprinkling no doubt dominated, Presbyterians spoke of both sprinkling and pouring;[54] Methodists may have known of three-fold dipping via Anglicanism and Wesley, though

Father, and of the Son, and of the Holy Ghost. *Amen.*

few probably practiced it (the *Discipline* spoke simply of "baptism");[55] similarly, Congregationalist books simply directed the minister to "baptize."[56]

Then the Minister shall say,

We receive this child into the congregation of Christ's flock, that as a member of the family and household of God *he* may be nurtured and grow strong, and continue Christ's faithful servant unto *his* life's end. *Amen.*

The wording of this simple declaration is an intriguing journey of liturgical redaction. In the medieval Latin rites the service of baptism was preceded by prayer and consignation at the church door. Both Luther's and Cranmer's first revisions kept this practice, while their later versions abolished it. Cranmer's second revision (1552) took some of the words of the prayer into the postbaptismal signation where it lodged firmly in the Prayer Book tradition.[57]

Canadian Methodists came to use a version which omitted the reference to (and action of) the sign of the cross and included a reference to instruction and training "in the doctrines, privileges and duties of the Christian religion."[58] One Congregationalist version is closer to the spirit of the Prayer Book than that of the Methodists.[59] The Presbyterians modified it to perhaps its simplest form.[60] The United Church version is perhaps closest to that of the Methodists, pared down to the declaration of reception with the imagery of family and Christian nurturing dominating.

And the Minister may bless the child, saying,

While this rubric does not intend that laying on of hands occur here, one cannot help but wonder if it happened on occasion.

The Lord bless thee, and keep thee: the Lord make his face to shine upon thee, and be gracious unto thee: the

The use of the Aaronic blessing can be found in Luther and Calvin, but was popularized especially by Knox's

Lord lift up his countenance upon thee, and give thee peace. *Amen.*

Sunday Morning Service.[61] Congregationalists and most Presbyterians came to use it also in baptism, however both tended to place it immediately after the baptism itself, before the declaration.[62] In the proposed 1928 Prayer Book it is also found at the close of the "Alternative Order."[63]

THE PRAYERS

Then shall the Minister say,

Let us pray.
Most holy and merciful Father, we give thee hearty thanks that thou hast numbered us amongst thy people, and dost also call our children unto thee, marking them with this Sacrament as a singular token and badge of thy love. Wherefore we beseech thee to confirm thy favour more and more toward us, and to take into thy tuition and defence this child, who we offer and present unto thee with common supplications. Grant that *he* may know thee *his* merciful Father, through thy Holy Spirit working in *his* heart, that *he* may not be ashamed to confess the faith of Christ crucified; but may continue his faithful servant, and so prevail against evil that in the end *he* may obtain the victory, and be exalted into the liberty of thy kingdom; through Jesus Christ our Lord. *Amen.*

One or other of the next two prayers is to be used.

The giving of "hearty thanks" is an opening line well known in the postbaptismal prayers of the Prayer Book tradition (beginning in 1552).[64] The petition near the end of the first prayer, that the child "may not be ashamed to confess the faith of Christ crucified" is in both the medieval language of confirmation and the Prayer Book's prayer at the postbaptismal signation discussed above.[65] The substance of the prayer is essentially the same as the option to follow. The wording is exactly that found in the American Presbyterian order.[66]

Or else,

Most holy and merciful Father, who does not only beautify and bless us with common benefits, but dost also heap upon us most abundantly rare and wonderful gifts: We lift up our eyes and minds unto thee, and give thee most humble thanks, who does call our children unto thee, marking

This prayer is a revision of Knox's postbaptismal prayer, though some of the phrases can be detected in Calvin's rite.[67] The wording is found in the first Canadian Presbyterian order; the second order contained a further revision.[68]

Both this and the previous prayer are

them with this Sacrament as a singular token and badge of thy love. Confirm this thy favour more and more towards us, we beseech thee, and take this infant into thy tuition and defence, that *he* may perceive thee continually to be *his* merciful father, through thy Spirit working in *his* heart, by whose divine power *he* may so prevail against evil, that in the end, obtaining the victory, *he* may be exalted into the liberty of thy kingdom; through Jesus Christ our Lord. *Amen.*

so similar as to cause one to question why both were needed. Could it be that, in view of the dash of memorable Prayer Book phrases in the first prayer, it was a way in which to appeal to Anglican liturgical sensibilities in a time of increasing union discussions?

In addition, it is worth noting that these two prayers provide the only occasion in the service in which evil is in any way named.[69] This is as close as the rite gets to a renunciation.

Then may follow this Prayer for the Home.

Almighty God, our heavenly Father, whose blessed Son did share at Nazareth the life of an earthly home: Bless, we beseech thee, the home of this child, and grant wisdom and understanding to all who have the care of *him*; that *he* may grow up in thy constant fear and love; through the same thy Son Jesus Christ our Lord. *Amen.*

This optional prayer is a contemporary composition from the proposed 1928 Prayer Book.[70]

Then shall be said by all,

Our Father, who art in heaven, Hallowed be thy name; Thy kingdom come; Thy will be done; In earth as it is in heaven. Give us this day our daily bread. And forgive us our trespasses, As we forgive them that trespass against us. And lead us not into temptation; But deliver us from evil: For thine is the kingdom, The power, and the glory, For ever and ever. *Amen.*

The location of the Lord's Prayer in baptismal rites varies historically. In 1549 Cranmer placed it before the baptism itself (following the opening exhortation and before the corporate confession of the Creed).[71] In 1552 it was moved to its present Prayer Book position after the baptism itself (following the declaration and before the postbaptismal prayer).[72] Calvin and Knox preferred the former location,[73] Methodists the latter.[74] Later Presbyterians would provide both options.[75] In one Congregationalist book it is in the latter location for infant baptism and in the former for adult baptism.[76] This United Church location seems to fit the movement of the liturgy nicely, acting as a communal bridge between the pastorally-focused "Prayer for the Home" and "The Duties of the People" to follow.

THE DUTIES OF THE PEOPLE

And the Minister shall say to the People this, or the like, Exhortation.

Brethren, this child has now been received into the bosom of the Church of God. You who have participated in this holy act are called, together with the parents (or sponsors), to take care that *he* may grow up in the nurture and admonition of the Lord, to lead a godly and Christian life. Consider this your part and duty, and support this child with constant love, and wholesome example, and faithful prayer. May the Lord grant you grace for this work. *Amen.*

The first line of the "Duties of the People" is as much another declaration as it is an exhortation and could be experienced as repetitive. Regardless, the practice of a postbaptismal exhortation on the duties of the godparents has long been part of the Prayer Book tradition.[77] The phrase, "received into the bosom of the Church of God," is reminiscent of Knox's "received into the bosom of Christ's congregation," as is the general spirit of the rest of the exhortation. The significant difference, however, is that Knox used it as a prebaptismal exhortation directed toward the parents, the form most familiar to the Presbyterian tradition.[78]

Thus, it would appear that this particular text is a new variation on historic themes, a case of Presbyterian content being adapted to fit within the Prayer Book structure and set apart with its own heading in the contemporary style of the proposed 1928 "Alternative Order."[79] It now functions within a United Church context in which the "people"/congregation are the godparents.

Then the Minister shall say to the Parents (or Sponsors),

Go in the peace of the Lord. *Amen.*

If Baptism be administered otherwise

The dismissal "Peace be with thee" is not found in any of the orders of the founding traditions or the immediate *than at Public Worship, the Minister shall dismiss them that are gathered with this Blessing.*

The grace of the Lord Jesus Christ, and the love of God, and the communion of the Holy Spirit, be with you. *Amen.*

sources and thus appears to be an "innovation introduced by the compilers."[80]

In light of the rubric and blessing which follows it, this usage makes clear that it is intended to function in the context of public worship, giving closure to the baptismal rite and assuming the use of a later blessing at the close of the service as a whole. The rubric, similar to that in the 1928 Prayer Book order,[81] suggests that private baptisms were not unknown. "The Grace" blessing appears specifically in the Presbyterian and Methodist orders for baptism in the context of public worship.[82]

It belongs to the Church, as well as to the Parents (or Sponsors) to see that children who have been baptized are taught the substance of Christian faith and duty. And when they come to years of discretion they are to own for themselves the covenant of their baptism; they are to confess Jesus Christ as their Saviour and Lord, and engage themselves to be his disciples.

In case of extreme urgency it shall suffice if the child be named, and water poured or sprinkled upon its head, with the words,

N. I baptize thee in the name of the Father, and of the Son, and of the Holy Ghost. *Amen.*

These two final rubrics deal with the Church's obligation to see that baptized children are instructed and nurtured in faith, the expectation of a later (adult) profession of faith, and the provision for emergency or clinical baptism. The latter reinforces the view of the compilers that "the core of the rite is the use of water with the words: "N. I baptize thee, etc.,"[83]

The use of such rubrics is somewhat reminiscent of those often included in Presbyterian liturgies.[84] This United Church approach is somewhat "softer," avoiding the Presbyterian practice of quoting from the *Westminster Directory*. Moreover, attention to the subject of emergency baptism may also be viewed as a curious concession to popular ideas about the link between salvation and baptism. This is in direct contrast to the Presbyterian rubrics which took care to avoid any such equation.[85]

APPENDIX

AN EXHORTATION

Which may be used before the Sacrament of Baptism is administered.

Dearly beloved, the Father in heaven, who has received us into the fellowship of his Church, has promised to be our God and the God and Father of our Children; which covenant he renews in this Sacrament of Baptism given to us as a sign and seal of the washing away of our sins, and our ingrafting into Christ.

You that are fathers and mothers may take hence most singular comfort in seeing your children thus received into the bosom of Christ's Church, and by this you are admonished that you bring them up in piety and virtue, remembering that their Father in heaven careth for them.

The first element in the "Appendix" is an optional exhortation which consists, for the most part, of two paragraphs taken from Knox's much longer pre-baptismal exhortation. Most of his classic turns of phrase, well known to Presbyterians, are retained, the notable exception being the definition of baptism as "adoption."

On the other hand, Knox's metaphor of "ingrafting" is inserted at this point, having been left out of the introductory question at the beginning of this order. This definition of the sacrament as a "sign and seal" and "our ingrafting into Christ" was also prominent in the Canadian Presbyterian exhortation.[86] Similarly, the metaphor of "washing," reminiscent of the Prayer Book, is inserted here, having been left out of the second opening prayer in this order.

Such editorial practices again illustrate and confirm the hesitancy and ambiguity around such metaphors of baptism as "sign and seal," "ingrafting," "washing," and "adoption." And yet the compilers of *The Book of Common Order* did not want to lose them entirely. Having systematically omitted them from the order they have given them "optional" status by placing them in the Appendix.

A CONFESSION OF FAITH

Which may be used in place of the first question (as equivalent thereto), asked of Parents of Sponsors.

Do you believe In God the Father Almighty, Maker of heaven and earth;

This alternate question appears, at first, glance to be the historic creed of and in Jesus Christ, his only Son our Lord, who was born into the world, and who suffered for us; and in the Holy Ghost, the Holy Catholic Church, the Communion of Saints, the Forgiveness of sins, and the Life everlasting?

Answer. I do.

baptism, the Apostle's Creed, in interrogative form, but a close look finds it to be a baptismal symbol of the Committee's own creation.[87]

The phrase "who was born into the world, and who suffered for us" replaces all the Christological details of the Apostles' Creed from "who was conceived by the Holy Ghost, born of thc Virgin Mary" to "from then he shall come to judge the quick and the dead." Furthermore, "the resurrection of the body" has been deleted from between "the forgiveness of sins" and "the Life everlasting."[88]

PRAYERS

One or other of which may be used in place of that beginning, Grant, O Lord.

Either of the two prayers provided, if used, would find their place immediately before the baptism itself, thus functioning in close association with the baptismal action/water, one of the main references of both prayers. Both provide the sole possibility for any reference to Matthew 28 in the service.

I

Almighty, everlasting God, whose most dearly beloved Son Jesus Christ, for the forgiveness of our sins, did shed out of his most precious side both water and blood; and gave commandment to his disciples, that they should go teach all nations, and baptize them In the name of the Father, and of the Son, and of the Holy Ghost: Regard, we beseech thee, our supplications; and grant that this child, now to be baptized, may receive the fullness of thy grace, and be found at last in the number of thy faithful and elect children; through Jesus Christ our Lord. *Amen.*

The first prayer is found in the 1549 Prayer Book as the last prayer in the rite for the blessing of the font.[89] In 1552 this rite was intcgratcd into the baptismal liturgy, this prayer being its remaining vestige.[90] In this, together with his editing of the prayer, Cranmer followed Bucer's recommendation that "all suggestion that the water is consecrated . . . [be] removed."[91] Its contemporary source for the United Church could be either Anglican or Methodist.[92]

II

Almighty, everlasting God, *whose beloved Son became man for us men and for our salvation*, and gave commandment to his disciples that they should go teach all nations, and baptize them In the name of the Father, and of the Son, and of the Holy Ghost: *hear, we beseech thee, the prayer of thy people: set apart this water to the holy use unto which thou has appointed it*; and grant that this child, now to be baptized therein, may receive the fullness of thy grace, *and ever remain* in the number of thy faithful and elect children: through Jesus Christ our Lord. *Amen.*

The second prayer is a United Church revision of the first, edited as indicated. [Compare italicized portions; italics mine.]

It is interesting, if not curious, to note that, on the one hand, the first prayer's references to the "water and blood" flowing from Jesus' side (a biblical allusion to John 19:34) have been omitted from the second prayer, while, on the other hand, a petition to "set apart" the water for "holy use" has been inserted. In a United Church context, those with Puritan suspicion of any metaphors remotely resembling consecration would find little solace in such options.

Because the "Grant, O Lord" prayer of earlier in the order (which either of these two prayers would replace) asks the Spirit's blessing upon only the child (with no mention of water), these prayers provide the only opportunity for any mention of the symbol of water in baptism and the Spirit's work through it. The compilers chose not to avail themselves of the Anglican and Methodist versions of Luther's classic "Flood Prayer" near the beginning of the service.[93]

AN ORDER FOR
THE RECEPTION TO
FULL COMMUNION

AND THE CONFIRMATION OF
THOSE WHO HAVE BEEN
BAPTIZED[94]

When children who have been baptized are come to years of discretion, and have been taught the substance of Christian faith and duty, they are to be

The upper title dominates the original text appearing in larger type and at the head of each subsequent page. The lower title is a subtitle in smaller print on the first page only. Their use appears to be a combination of the Congregationalist, Presbyterian, and Anglican titles of the time. If this is true, it is convenient for a "uniting" church. However, the explicit use of the term "confirmation" is puzzling, given that it was not used in any of the contem-

brought before the church, that they may openly confess for themselves Jesus Christ as their Saviour and Lord. And they are to be assured that the Lord who now comes to them with his grace and strength will never fail them; and in particular that he will meet them at his own Table to their lives' end.

Upon the day appointed an Address, touching the meaning of the action, may be given by the Minister. Then all that are to be received shall stand before the Minister, and he shall speak to them in this wise.

porary orders of the founding traditions, nor in the Basis of Union of the United Church.[95] This is the first glimpse of a tendency to begin using the vocabulary of confirmation. One again wonders about the desire of the compilers to show some sympathy for the Anglican liturgical tradition.

From another perspective, it could be viewed as an intentional reversal and revision of that of the title of the American Presbyterian rite, "The Order for the Confirmation of Baptismal Vows and Reception to the Lord's Supper."[96] Such a reversal results in an emphasis on "reception" over "confirmation" and a theological clarification of the action of confirmation (i.e., candidates are confirmed, not vows). However, the opening exhortation which follows the rubrics speaks of both "ratifying" one's vows as well as the confirmation of the person.

Beloved in the Lord, in your baptism you were received into the fellowship of Christ, sealed as members of the family and household of God, and engaged to be the Lord's. Now you come, of your own choice, to ratify the solemn covenant and vow then made in your behalf, to profess your faith in the Lord Jesus, and to consecrate yourselves to him. Doubt ye not, but earnestly believe that he waiteth to receive you, and that he will confirm and strengthen you anew by his Holy Spirit, that ye may grow more and more in the knowledge of God, and be enabled to keep his covenant steadfastly to the end.

The Address begins with lines reminiscent of the American Presbyterian order, with some significant changes.

The reference to baptism as "engrafting into Christ" has been omitted and one's "covenant and vow" is here "ratified" (Prayer Book language), not "confirmed."[97]

The "Doubt ye not" closing line is a composition based on the closing lines of the Prayer Book's exhortation for baptism of adults, the necessary changes having been made for the context of confirmation.[98]

I ask you therefore before God and this congregation.

The Reformed emphasis on public profession of faith is alluded to in the introduction to the questions. While the specific use of the phrase "before

God and this congregation" is not found in any of the immediate Presbyterian, Methodist, or Congregationalist sources, it is present in the questions of the American Presbyterian rite and as the Anglican "Alternative Order."[99]

Do you believe in God the Father Almighty, Maker of heaven and earth; and in Jesus Christ, his only Son our Lord, who was born into the world, and who suffered for us; and in the Holy Ghost, the Holy Catholic Church, the Communion of Saints, the Forgiveness of sins, and the Life everlasting?

Answer. I do.

While the so-called short form of the Apostles' Creed[100] was not the preferred option in the baptism of children, it is for those who can answer for themselves.

Reformed practice can vary widely with the questions of confirmation, especially the first. The practice of the time ranged from more simple questions regarding faith in Jesus Christ, to belief in the Trinity.[101] In spite of its problems, the recovery here of a more creedal-like first question can be viewed as an attempt on the part of the compilers to return to a more catholic or historic confession of faith.

Will you then endeavour to keep God's holy will and commandments, and to walk in the same all the days of your life?

Answer. I will.

The second question can be found in this form in the Canadian Anglican rite.[102]

Do you promise to make diligent use of the means of grace, and in all things to seek earnestly the peace and welfare of the Church of God?

Answer. I do so promise, God being my helper.

The third question is reminiscent of *Euchologion*,[103] the source for the Presbyterian question inserted into the Congregationalist and Methodist orders in *Forms*.[104] In this United Church version the traditional promise to "submit yourselves to all the ordinances of Christ" is omitted, perhaps because its meaning is covered in the promise to "make diligent use of the means of grace." Also, "work and worship of the Church" is replaced with the more general "peace and welfare of the Church."[105]

Then shall the Minister say,

Let us pray.
Almighty and everliving God, strengthen, we beseech thee, these thy servants with the Holy Spirit the Comforter, and daily increase in them thy manifold gifts of grace; the spirit of wisdom and understanding; the spirit of counsel and might; the spirit of knowledge and true godliness; fill them, O God, with the spirit of they holy fear; and keep them in thy mercy unto life eternal; through Jesus Christ our Lord. *Amen.*

This classic confirmation prayer comes into United Church usage via the Prayer Book tradition, the contemporary source being the Canadian order of 1918.[106] This version omits the Prayer Book's relative clause, a remembrance of the regenerative powers of baptism.[107] The prayer also points to the compilers' practice of using "Holy Spirit" in prayers and blessings, but "Holy Ghost" in creedal and trinitarian constructions.[108] Note also that the editors have restored the order of the scriptural allusions to that of the biblical text (Isaiah 11:2).[109]

Then the Minister (laying his hand if such be his discretion, upon the head of every one in order kneeling before him) shall say,

This rubric is significant when placed alongside the contemporary rites of the founding churches. They did not speak explicitly of laying on of hands but tended to emphasize "the right hand of fellowship."[110] This version, while giving room for "discretion," attempts to restore the historic action. It is found, verbatim, in the American Presbyterian source.[111]

The God of all grace, who hath called you unto his eternal glory by Jesus Christ, confirm you to the end, that ye may be blameless in the day of our Lord Jesus Christ. *Amen.*

The first option for the prayer of confirmation/blessing is a creative linking of two biblical verses which deal with confirmation in the sense of strengthening.[112]

Or else,

Defend, O Lord, this thy child (or servant) with thy heavenly grace that *he* may continue thine for ever; and daily increase in thy Holy Spirit more and more, until *he* come unto thy everlasting kingdom. *Amen.*

The second option is the traditional Prayer Book "Defend, O Lord" prayer, found also in some Congregationalist and Presbyterian sources.[113]

Then shall the Minister say,

Let us pray.
Almighty God, our heavenly Father, we give thee hearty thanks and praise that thou has not withheld thy loving kindness from these thy children (or servants), but hast given them shelter within the covenant of thy peace, and makest them to sit down at thy Table. We entreat thee of thy great mercy to perfect in them the good work thou has begun, that they, being defended by thy fatherly hand, and strengthened with might by the Spirit, may be enabled to keep this covenant without spot, unrebukable, until the day our Lord Jesus Christ. *Amen.*

The immediate source for this prayer is the American Presbyterian rite.[114] It serves to reinforce the notion of "reception to communion" (which many of the contemporary confirmation rites did not emphasize) by alluding to the Table and therein supporting the movement of the liturgy toward that end. However, such implications are not followed through in the rest of the order, there being no specific mention, rubrical or otherwise, of a preference to continue with the celebration of Holy Communion.

Our Father who art in heaven, hallowed by thy name; Thy kingdom come; Thy will be done; In earth as it is in heaven. Give us this day our daily bread. And forgive us our trespasses, As we forgive them that trespass against us. And lead us not into temptation; But deliver us from evil: For thine is the kingdom, The power, and the glory, For ever and ever. *Amen.*

The use of the Lord's Prayer after the laying on of hands with prayer is a Prayer Book custom[115] which would no doubt find little objection in the founding churches of the United Church. The location here is similar to Presbyterian usage, following and/or concluding the prayers.[116]

After which may follow this Ascription of Praise.

Now unto him that is able to keep you from falling and to present you faultless before the presence of his glory with exceeding joy; to the only wise God our Saviour, be glory and majesty, dominion and power, both now and ever. *Amen.*

The Ascription is from Jude 24 and was used in this manner in the American Presbyterian order.[117] By using a benediction which would not be repeated later, it serves the liturgical function of bringing the rite to a close without implying an end to the service in which it takes place.

A public service for the Reception to Full Communion and the Confirmation of Baptized Persons is not to be regarded as an invariable condition of full membership; the occasions when it may be necessary or proper to follow

This disclaimer is also taken from the American service.[118]

another manner being left to the prudence and judgement of the office-bearers of the Church.

Reviewing the preceding unit of action from the laying on of hands and its rubric to the Ascription and the concluding doctrinal rubric, it seems clear that the structure and content of the "confirmation" portion of the rite relies very much on the American *Book of Common Worship.*

APPENDIX

A PROFESSION OF FAITH

Again, as in the Order for the Baptism of Children, an "Appendix" provides for other options.

Instead of the short form of the Apostles' Creed this question, as equivalent thereto, may be used.

Note that the rubric is the first reference to the compilers' own invention, a "short form of the Apostles' Creed."

Do you now for yourselves profess the Christian faith in which you were baptized?

This alternative question is reminiscent of the first questions in both *Euchologion* and the American order and provides an explicit link with the candidates' baptism.[119]

CONCLUSIONS

Which may be used after the Lord's Prayer and in place of the Ascription of Praise.

The two concluding options provide an interesting study in liturgical accommodation, honoring the practices of the founding traditions.

I

The Minister may say to all that have been received,

In the name of the Lord Jesus Christ, I receive and welcome you to the fellowship of his Table, and to all the privileges of full communion with the Church of Christ.

And the blessing of God Almighty, Father, Son and Holy Spirit, be upon

The first option recalls in words the concluding gesture of "the right hand of fellowship" common to the founders.[120] It was Methodist practice to "heartily congratulate" candidates at this point in the service, while Presbyterians would "admit and welcome" them "to the fellowship of the Lord's you, and remain with you always. *Amen.*

Table" at a point earlier in the service. Methodists also spoke of "the privileges of full communion."[121]

Thus, this first option combines several familiar features, with an emphasis on admission to the Table and its implications.

II

Where it is the custom, all may covenant together as followeth. The Minister shall first say to them that have been received,

Beloved of the Lord, baptized in the name of the Father, and of the Son, and of the Holy Ghost, you have already confessed the faith of Christ before his people, and given yourselves to God in the everlasting covenant of grace. And now that you cordially join yourselves with this Church of Christ, you promise to wait diligently upon its ordinances, to study its peace and prosperity, to pray and labour for its edification and fruitfulness, and to live with this people of God in Christian fellowship. Do you so promise?

The second option is reminiscent of the place of covenanting in the early Congregationalist tradition as discussed in part I above. Unlike the first option, it explicitly invites the hospitable hand shake (see the closing rubric below). It also bears a significant resemblance to the American and Canadian Presbyterian rites for the reception of communicants from other churches/congregations.[122]

Answer. I do.

The members of the Church shall then stand, and the Minister shall say,

We the members of this Church, do affectionately welcome you into this household of faith. We pledge to you our sympathy, our help, and our prayers, that you may evermore increase in the knowledge and love of God. We trust that by his grace we may all walk worthy of the calling where with we are called, with all lowliness and meekness, forbearing one another in love; giving diligence to

The pledge, made by the Minister on behalf of the congregation, performs much the same function as "The Duties of the People" in the baptism of children.

keep the unity of the spirit in the bond of peace, and remembering all Christ's sheep that wander and go astray, that they may be gathered and brought home to his fold. God grant that, serving and being served, we may together be prepared for the perfect fellowship of the saints above.

Here may the Minister give to each of the newly-received the right hand of welcome. Then may follow a Benediction.

AN ORDER FOR
THE BAPTISM OF SUCH AS ARE
OF RIPER YEARS

AND ARE ABLE TO ANSWER FOR
THEMSELVES[123]

The title is closest to those of the Prayer Book and Methodist traditions. Congregationalists and Presbyterians tended to use the phrase "baptism of adults."[124]

The Minister may, before the administration of the Sacrament, give instruction touching its nature and meaning, using, if he will, the following Exhortation.

The rubric renders the exhortation optional, a departure from the immediate sources.

Hear the words of the Gospel of our Lord and Saviour according to St. Matthew.

All power is given unto me in heaven and in earth. Go ye therefore, and teach all nations, baptizing them in name of the Father, and of the Son, and of the Holy Spirit: teaching them to observe all things whatsoever I have commanded you: and lo, I am with you always, even unto the end of the world.

Reformed practice tended to begin with the Matthew text (28:18-20). Presbyterians often called them the "words of institution."[125] Methodists used this text as well (but not Wesley), preceded by a longer exhortation-like preface.[126]

St. Peter also, on the day of Pentecost, called upon the people, saying, Repent, and be baptized, every one of you, in the name of Jesus Christ, for

The use of the Acts text (2:38-39) is common to all the immediate sources, save some Congregationalist orders.[127] The emphasis on repentance and rethe remission of sins, and ye shall receive the gift of the Holy Spirit. For the promise is unto you, and to your children, and to all that are afar off, even as many as the Lord our God shall call.

mission of sins is in contrast to the avoidance of such implications in the Baptism of Children and Reception to Full Communion.

Doubt ye not, therefore, but earnestly believe that he will number among his people these persons (or this person), coming unto him by faith, that he will grant *them* remission of *their* sins, and bestow upon *them* the blessing of eternal life, and make *them* partakers of his everlasting kingdom.

The "Doubt ye not" exhortation has its roots in the Prayer Book. This version opens with lines from the Canadian and American Presbyterian orders and closes with a return to the original Prayer Book wording. Noteworthy is the omission of the phrase "truly repenting and" immediately before "coming unto him by faith."[128]

As a whole, it contains Prayer Book content in a Presbyterian mode. The theological content of the former is transposed into a form and location more familiar to the latter. As with the Address in the order for Reception to Full Communion, the American Presbyterian order provides the closest model.[129]

If the Presbyterian exhortation is a first cousin to the Prayer Book, this United Church version is a second cousin aware of its genealogy.

THE BAPTISM

The Minister, standing at the Font, shall say to the persons to be baptized.

Well-beloved, who are come hither desiring to profess your faith in Christ and to receive Holy Baptism, you have heard that our Lord Jesus Christ hath promised in his Word to grant forgiveness of sins and his Holy Spirit unto all that repent and turn unto him; which promise, he, for his part, will most surely keep and perform.

Wherefore, after this promise made by

The introduction to the promises is essentially that of the Prayer Book with minor revisions consistent with earlier changes.

In keeping with the compilers' avoidance of explicit renunciation, the Prayer Book's closing call to "renounce the devil and all his works, and constantly believe God's holy Word, and obediently keep his commandments" has been changed to "follow

Christ, you must also faithfully, for your part, promise in the presence of God and this congregation to follow Christ as your Lord and Master, turning away from what he forbiddeth and doing whatsoever he commandeth.

Christ as your Lord and Master, turning away from what he forbiddeth and doing whatsoever he commandeth."[130]

And he shall ask each of them, severally, these questions following.

Do you believe in God the Father Almighty, Maker of heaven and earth; and in Jesus Christ, his only Son our Lord, who was born into the world, and who suffered for us; and in the Holy Ghost, the Holy Catholic Church, the Communion of Saints, the Forgiveness of sins, and the Life everlasting?

This particular use of the baptismal symbol (creed) has already been noted. In this context it is worth adding that the use of the full Apostles' Creed in the interrogative form was common to adult baptismal orders of the Anglicans, Wesley, the Methodists, and some Presbyterians.[131]

Answer. I do.

Will you then endeavour to keep God's holy will and commandments, and to walk in the same all the days of your life?

Answer. I will.

The Prayer Book and Methodist question in the rite for adults is: "Wilt thou then *obediently* keep God's holy will," [italics mine]. The use of "endeavour to keep" is found in the Canadian Anglican rite for confirmation and was used in the United Church's order for Reception to Full Communion above.[132]

Do you promise to make diligent use of the means of grace, and in all things to seek earnestly the peace and welfare of the Church of God?

Answer. I do so promise, God being my helper.

This question, as discussed earlier with respect to its use in the order for Reception to Full Communion, is rooted in the confirmation service of *Euchologion.* Contemporary influences can be found in both the American Presbyterian order and the Canadian Presbyterian order for the reception of communicants from other churches or congregations.[133]

The symmetry of the order to Reception to Full Communion above is clearly evident; the questions are the same for both of the orders.

Then shall follow this Prayer.

We beseech thee, O Lord, that it may please thee to receive, and to sanctify with thy Spirit, these persons (*or* this thy servant) now to be baptized according to thy Word; that *they* may obtain the fullness of thy grace, and ever remain in the number of thy faithful children; through Jesus Christ Our Lord. *Amen.*

This prayer for the Spirit's blessing upon the candidate(s) is found in the American Presbyterian order.[134]

Then shall the persons presenting themselves for Baptism kneel, and the Minister shall pour or sprinkle water upon their heads severally, calling each by name, and saying,

In both Reception to Full Communion and adult baptism the rubrics call for kneeling.

N. I baptize thee In the name of the Father, and of the Son, and of the Holy Ghost. *Amen.*

Then shall the Minister say,

We receive these persons into the congregation of Christ's flock, that as living members (*or* a living member) of the same, *they* may be made *partakers* of the fullness of divine grace, and grow up into union with Christ who is our Saviour and Lord.

Some of the background to the declaration following the baptism has been discussed in the context of the Order for the Baptism of Children. It is interesting to note that the reference to "the family and household of God" has been omitted (replaced by "the same") —i.e., "the congregation of Christ's flock." Was it too infantile for adult baptism? The use of a similar declaration in adult baptism was common to Anglicans (though with signation) and Presbyterians.[135] The prayer "that they be made partakers" suggests that the closing lines may have been inspired by those of the opening Exhortation.

THE CONFIRMATION

The Confirmation rite contained within this service of baptism follows very closely the corresponding section of the order for Reception to Full Communion.

The closest immediate source among rites of adult baptism appears to be the American Presbyterian order, though this United Church version is still more elaborate.[136]

Then shall the Minister say,

Let us pray.
Almighty and everlasting God, strengthen, we beseech thee, *these* thy *servants* with the Holy Spirit the Comforter, and daily increase in *them* thy manifold gifts of grace; the spirit of wisdom and understanding; the spirit of counsel and strength; the spirit of knowledge and true godliness; fill *them*, O Lord, with thy spirit of thy holy fear; and keep *them* in thy mercy unto life eternal; through Jesus Christ our Lord. *Amen.*

Only minor editorial changes have been made—or did the editors miss them? For example, this first prayer is identical to that in the previous order, save that the changeable words are italicized in this version and "might" has been altered to more closely resemble the original Prayer Book's "strength" (though not quite "ghostly strength").

Then the Minister (laying his hand, if such be his discretion, upon the head of every one in order kneeling before him) shall say,

The rubrics are repeated again, while in the prayer to follow, "you," and "your" has reverted to "thee" and "thou."

The God of grace, who hath called thee unto eternal glory by Jesus Christ, confirm thee to the end, that thou mayest be blameless in the day of our Lord Jesus Christ. *Amen.*

Or else,

Defend, O Lord, this thy servant with thy heavenly grace, that *he* may continue thine for ever; and daily increase in thy Holy Spirit more and more, until *he* come unto thy everlasting kingdom. *Amen.*

"Servant" replaces child (*or* servant), but the use of "may" remains (note "mayest" in the previous prayer).

Then the Minister shall say,

Let us pray.
Almighty God, our heavenly Father, we give thee hearty thanks and praise

This prayer from the American Presbyterian rite has been used again, as that thou has not withheld thy loving kindness from these thy children (*or* servants), but has given them shelter within the covenant of thy peace, and makest them to sit down at thy Table. We entreat thee of thy great mercy to perfect in them the good work thou hast begun, that they, being defended by thy fatherly hand, and strengthened with might by thy Spirit, may be enabled to keep this covenant without spot, unrebukable, until the day of our Lord Jesus Christ. *Amen.*

with the practice of following it with the Lord's Prayer. It is also found in that source's rite for adult baptism.[137]

And all shall say together the Lord's Prayer.

After which may follow this Blessing.

The Lord bless you, and keep you: the Lord make his face to shine upon you, and be gracious unto you: the Lord lift up his countenance upon you, and give you peace. *Amen.*

The order for Reception to Full Communion closed with an Ascription of Praise from Jude 24. Here the compilers have returned to the use of the Aaronic blessing, as in the baptism of infants, but "thee" has been modernized to "you."

Where is it desireable a candidate may be dipped in the water.

In keeping with the liturgical freedom affirmed in the Basis of Union, allowance is made for the possibility of baptisms by immersion (though this rubric could be clearer).

Forasmuch as by this rite there is admission to full membership in the Church, the essential parts of the two foregoing Orders are included in this Order.

Here the compilers seem to wish to emphasize that, due of the form and content of this order, nothing else is needed to complete the rite of adult baptism; i.e., adult baptism grants full membership. And yet by including "The Confirmation" in this order the implication is that indeed something is needed to make adult baptism complete. This is a precursor to what will become an increased emphasis on "confirmation."

A PROFESSION OF FAITH

Instead of the short form of the Apostle's Creed, this question, as equivalent thereto, may be used.

Do you believe in God, Father, Son, and Holy Spirit; and do you confess the Lord Jesus Christ as your Saviour and Lord?

Yet another variation on the question combines a trinitarian and Christological confession into one, reminiscent of some aspects of Congregationalist practice.[138] The rubric implies that such baptismal symbols are interchangeable.

Notes

1. *Year Book* (1926), 388. Cf. *Forms*, ix.

2. *Year Book* (1926), 357.

3. *Year Book* (1926), 76, 90; United Church of Canada/Victoria University Archives [UCA], The Committee on Church Worship and Ritual, Records (Old Files), Minutes, Vol. 1, p. 1 [cited in Part II of this study as "Minutes"]; W. Morrison Kelly, "Fifty Years of Worship in the United Church," *Gathering: A Packet for Worship Planners*, Advent/Christmas/Epiphany (1985), Study Papers, 2. Twenty-seven members were appointed at the 1926 General Council, including P. M. Macdonald as convener and A. MacMillan as secretary. Among them, Richard Davidson, G. D. Kilpatrick, A. MacMillan, H. Matheson, and R. E. Welsh had served on the Committee on Public Worship and Aids to Devotion in the Presbyterian Church in the production of the *Book of Praise* and *BCO* (1922). Welsh was also the Presbyterian behind *Forms*. S. P. Rose (also behind *Forms*) and H. E. Thomas had worked on revisions to the Methodist *Discipline*. Matheson, librarian at Union (later Emmanuel) College, was also an acknowledged liturgical expert.

4. *Songs of the Psalter* (Toronto: The United Church Publishing House, 1927); *The Hymnary of The United Church of Canada* (Toronto: The United Church Publishing House, 1932).

5. For a sense of the popular reaction to *The Hymnary* see the "Readers Forums" in the 16 January to 20 February 1929 issues of the church's weekly, *The New Outlook*. The editors, overwhelmed by the flood of letters, brought the discussion to an "abrupt close" on 20 February (p. 29), arguing that the spectrum of opinion had been fully represented and it was now the Committee's task to take this into account. Articles on the hymns of the church and the new book were also published in the same publication before and after the publication of the work, including: Alexander MacMillan, "A New Musical Triad: (24 June 1925): 14; "Church Praise in The United Church of Canada" (24 June 1925): 14; W. Harold Young, "The New Hymnary" (30 July 1930): 731, 743; W. S. Dingham "The Making of the Hymnary" (3 June 1931): 517, 518. For responses from the presbyteries to the outlines see, UCA, The Committee on Church Worship and Ritual, Records (Old Files), Correspondence, Files 18-24. See also N. Keith Clifford, "No Easy Process: Alexander Macmillan and the Birth of *The Hymnary*," *Touchstone* 8:1 (January 1990): 30-43.

6. This is Grant's phrase in "Blending Traditions," 143.

7. *Hymnary*, v-vi. Grant has observed that "the proportion of selections from the Wesley's, the Scottish Psalter and Isaac Watts comes out very close to the formula of two, two and one by which seats on the joint union committee were assigned" (Grant, *The Canadian Experience of Church Union*, 60). But an overall catholicity still dominates to the extent that the Committee saw its range of resources to include "canticles of the ancient Church, translations and transfusion of early and mediaeval Greek and Latin hymns, songs of the time of the Reformation and period following and . . . the treasures of modern hymnody" (*Hymnary*, v.).

8. Grant, "Blending Traditions," 142-143; *The Canadian Experience of Church Union*, 60-61. For a study of *The Hymnary* in relation to other United Church hymn books, see, Kervin, "The Three Hymn Books of The United Church of Canada: The Dialectic of a New Song," *Touchstone* 19/2 (May 2001): 6-21

9. Grant, "Blending Traditions," 143. In Dow's words, "*The Book of Common* is above all else [Davidson's] monument." John Dow, "Richard Davidson: Churchman," in *The Living Church*, ed. Harold W. Vaughan (Toronto: The United Church Publishing House, 1949), 18.

10. Davidson held the same position at Knox College. Union was soon to become Emmanuel College, of which Davidson became principal in 1932. The contribution of Hugh Matheson, librarian at Knox College and later Emmanuel, to the formation of *BCO* (1932) was also significant. The personal papers of both show copious correspondence on liturgical matters and their work on *BCO* (1932). See UCA, Richard Davidson, Personal Papers and UCA, Hugh Matheson, Personal Papers.

11. Davidson, Personal Papers, Box 12, Files 213-238.

12. The Committee's progress is recorded in successive volumes of the *Year Book* (Toronto: The United Church Publishing House, 1928-1993). [*Year Book* (year)]. E.g., *Year Book* (1928), 87, 93-94, 143, 415, 452; *Year Book* (1930), 217; *Year Book* (1932), 24, 34, 36.

13. Harding has recounted the various reactions and responses, including some of those discussed below, in "The Major Orders," 120-125, and "The Development of Liturgical Resources," 14-22. Harding also argues that an editorial bias of *The New Outlook* against *The Book of Common Order* explains some of the silence on the subject.

14. Fred Smith, "Spiritual Calisthenics," *The New Outlook* (26 October 1932): 1001.

15. G. Campbell Wadsworth, "'The Book of Common Order' in Our Readers' Forum," *The New Outlook* (14 February 1934): 109. MacMillan's companion was *Hymns of the Church: A Companion to The Hymnary of The United Church of Canada* (Toronto: The United Church Publishing House, 1935).

16. Davidson, "Introductory Notes for the Executive Committee," *Draft of Orders*, 6 in Personal Papers, Box 6.

17. Anonymous, "'The Book of Common Order' in Our Readers' Forum," *New Outlook* (6 June 1934): 430.

18. Aubrey Fullerton, "The Oughtness of Traditions," *New Outlook* (10 January 1934): 23.

19. J. K. Unsworth, "Many Communions Contribute to New Volume of Liturgy," *The Daily Colonist*, Victoria, B.C. (27 November 1932): 12; and "Liturgical Forms of New Book Show Social Sympathy," *The Daily Colonist* (4 December 1932): 10; cited in Harding, "The Major Orders," 120-121.

20. William D. Maxwell, cited by G. Campbell Wadsworth, "The United Church Communion Rite of 1932," *Canadian Journal of Theology* 12 (1966): 110. Maxwell was a student of Davidson's and served for a time on the Committee before moving abroad to study the Scottish liturgy. His work, *John Knox's Genevan Service Book*, was dedicated to Davidson. *Genevan Service Book*, v.

21. Raymond Abba, *Principles of Christian Worship* (London: Oxford University Press, 1957), 171; Cf. Newman's assessment of the rite in David R. Newman, "Worship in The United Church of Canada," *Worship* 53 (1979): 538-548.

22. "Minutes," Vol. 2: 79.

23. See "Returns from Presbyteries," Davidson, Personal Papers, (Files 236-238). Montreal Presbytery, for example, objected simply on the grounds that *The Book of Common Order* was "not needed," and that *Forms* was "enough." Medicine Hat Presbytery expressed their strong allegiance to *Forms*. Halifax Presbytery requested that the "orders" be called "forms."

24. Davidson, "Introduction to Draft Orders," *Draft Orders*, 1, in Personal Papers, Box 12.

25. Davidson recalling his 1932 remarks, in "The Book of Common Order and The Book of Common Prayer," *Cap and Gown Magazine* (April 1937): 16.

26. Robert A. Wright, "The Canadian Protestant Tradition," *The Canadian Protestant Experience*, 139.

27. John G. Stackhouse, "The Protestant Experience in Canada Since 1945" in *The Canadian Protestant Experience*, 199. Stackhouse relates the conservatism of the postwar years to the desire for stability after upheaval; the church and its worship served as an important expression of this need for normalcy.

28. "Acknowledgements," in *BCO*, back of title page.

29. E.g., W. Morrison Kelly, "Liturgical Trends in The United Church of Canada," *Anglican Dialogue* (Autumn 1967): 18; G. Campbell Wadsworth, "The United Church Communion Rite of 1932," *Canadian Journal of Theology* 12 (1966): 116.

30. *BCO* (1932), iii. The text of the preface is Davidson's revision of the report to the 1928 General Council and the "Introduction" to the *Draft of Orders*. Cf. *Year Book* (1928), 415, 452; Davidson, "Introduction to Draft Orders," *Draft Orders*, 1, in Personal Papers, Box 12.

31. *BCO* (1932), 97-103. Cf. Harding's overview of the sources for this order in "The Major Orders," 104-112.

32. *BCW* (1920), 47.

33. For the original see John Calvin, *La Forme des prières et chants ècclesiastiques, Genève 1542; facsimilé de l'édition originale* (Kassel: Barenreiter, 1959). There is no evidence in the archival records that the compilers of the United Church orders worked from original texts, nor evidence to indicate which translations they had in hand as working copies. For the purposes of this study and its commentaries I cite the critical text and thereafter refer to an established English translation. In the case of Calvin's *La Forme des prières* it is J. D. C. Fisher's translation, "The Form of Prayers and Ecclesiastical Chants with the Manner of Administering the Sacraments and Solemnizing Marriage According to the Custom of the Ancient Church, 1542," in *Christian Initiation: The Reformation Periods. Some Early Reformed Rites of Baptism and Confirmation and Other Contemporary Documents*, ed. J. D. C. Fisher (London: S.P.C.K., 1970), 112-117. [Calvin]. Calvin, 113.

34. Knox, 105.

35. Calvin, 115-116; Knox, 110.

36. *BCO* (1922), 119, 124.

37. "Das tauff buclin verdeutscht" in *D. Martin Luthers Werke*, Vol. 12 (Weimer: H. Bohlau, 1883-1914), 42-46. "The Order of Baptism," in *Luther's Works*, Vol. 53, trans. Paul Zeller Strodach and Ulrich S. Leupold, ed. Helmut T. Lehman (Philadelphia: Fortress Press, 1965), 96-103. [Luther (1523)]. Luther (1523), 96-97.

38. "Das tauffbuchlin auffs new zu gericht" in *D. Martin Luthers Werke*, Vol. 19, 539-541. The English translation cited here is "The Order of Baptism Newly Revised," in

Luther's Works, Vol. 53, trans. Paul Zeller Strodach and Ulrich S. Leupold, ed. Helmut T. Lehman, 107-109. [Luther (1526)]. Luther (1526), 107.

39. "The Sarum Rite: The Order for the Making of a Catechumen, the Blessing of the Font, Baptism and Confirmation (1543)," in *Documents of the Baptismal Liturgy*, trans. J. D. C. Fisher, ed. E. C. Whitaker (London: S.P.C.K., 1960), 231-253. [Sarum]. Sarum, 234.

40. *BCP* (1549), 728, 730. See also Fisher's comments in *Christian Initiation: The Reformation Period*, 90-91.

41. *BCP* (1552), 729, 731. Cf. Martin Bucer, *Censura* in E. C. Whitaker, *Martin Bucer and The Book of Common Prayer* (Essex: Mayhew-McCrimmon, 1974), 92. [Bucer].

42. Cf. *SS*, 140; *DD* (1874), 129-132; *DD* (1922), 335-339. It is interesting to note that while the prayer was omitted from the service in both *DD* (1874) and *DD* (1922), in the former it was simply moved from the "Ministration of Baptism to Infants" to the "Ministration of Baptism to Adults." See *DD* (1874), 133.

43. Ulrich Zwingli, "Works" in *Corpus Reformatorum* Vol. 91, 93 ed. C. G. Bretschneider (Lasis Sax: Schwetschke, 1834-1860), 334-346, 710-713. Ulrich Zwingli, "Of Baptism," in *Christian Initiation: The Reformation Period*, 126-131. [Zwingli]. Cf. Luther (1523), 98-99; Luther (1526), 108; Zwingli, 127 with Calvin, 115 and Sarum, 237.

44. *BCP* (1549), 730; *BCP* (1552), 731; *BCP* (1662), 731.

45. Cf. *DD* (1874), 131-132; *DD* (1922); *BCO* (1922), 117, 123; *BCW* (1920), 47; *Forms*, 20, 26.

46. Cf. *BCP* (1549), 732; *BCP* (1552), 733; and Fisher's comments in *Christian Initiation: The Reformation Period*, 54, n. 3.

47. *BCO* (1922), 117-118, 123-124.

48. Cf. *The Book of Common Prayer with Additions and Deviations Proposed in 1928* (London: Cambridge University Press, 1928), 275, with *The Book of Common Prayer and Administration of the Sacraments and other rites and ceremonies of the Church according to the use of The Church of England in the Dominion of Canada* (Toronto: Oxford University Press, 1918), 294-295. [*BCP* (1928); *BCP* (1918)].

49. E.g., *BCP* (1918), 295-296; *DD* (1922), 338, Jackson, 147.

50. See *BCW* (1920), 27, *Forms*, 26, and *BCO* (1922), 119.

51. *The Book of Common Worship* (Philadelphia: Presbyterian Board of Publication and Sabbath School Work, 1928), 41. [*BCW* (1928)].

52. *BCW* (1928), 41. Maxwell notes in the 1920s, for example, "the present common Scottish custom of baptizing the child while in the father's arms." He goes on to comment that "all the rubrics in Calvin's Service Books are silent, as are all the English books" on such details. Similarly, it is difficult to be precise about the specifics of Canadian practices. Maxwell, *Genevan Service Book*, 119, n. 23.

53. See, for example, *DD* (1922), 339; *BCO* (1922), 120; *BCW* (1920), 47.

54. *BCO* (1922), 125, 128.

55. Three-fold dipping is directed in the rubric of *BCP* (1540), 740. Simply "dip" is the direction in *BCP* (1552), 741 and *BCP* (1918), 298. Both ask that it be done "discreetly and warily." "Baptize" is the simple directive in *DD* (1874), 132, and *DD* (1922), 339.

56. *BCW* (1920), 47. Baptism by immersion was not unknown among Congregationalists.

57. See Fisher's comparison of Luther's (1523) order and its counterpart in a contemporary usage of the Roman rite, Fisher, *Christian Initiation: The Reformation Period*, 9. Cf. Also, Luther (1523), 96-97; Luther (1526), 107; *BCP* (1549) 728, with *BCP* (1552) 741, 743.

58. Though it is not present in the *DD* (1874), it has been recovered by *DD* (1922), 339: "We receive *this child* into the congregation of Christ's flock, that *he* may be instructed and trained in the doctrines, privileges, and duties of the Christian religion, and trust that *he* will be Christ's faithful servant unto *his* life's end."

59. The Canadian Prayer Book reads: "We receive this Child into the Congregation of Christ's flock, and do sign *him* with the sign of the Cross, in token that hereafter *he* shall not be ashamed to confess the faith of Christ crucified, and manfully to fight under his banner against sin, the world, and the devil, and to continue Christ's faithful soldier and servant unto *his* life's end. Amen." *BCP* (1918), 298. A Congregationalist version reads: "We receive this child into the congregation of Christ's flock, in the trust that hereafter he shall not be ashamed to confess the faith of Christ, valiantly to fight under His banner against all evil, and to continue Christ's faithful soldier and servant unto his life's end. Amen." *BCW* (1920), 48.

60. The Canadian Presbyterian version reads: "This child is now publicly received into the congregation of Christ's flock, and is engaged to confess Christ and to be his faithful servant. Wherefore receive ye *him* in the Lord as Christ also received us to the glory of God." *BCO* (1922), 125. Another version is found in the first order at 126k identical to that of *BCO* (1896), 310.

61. Knox, 92, and Maxwell's comments, *Genevan Service Book*, 102, n. 12.

62. *BCW* (1920), 47, 48; *BCO* (1922), 120, 125.

63. *BCP* (1928), 277.

64. *BCP* (1552), 745; *BCP* (1662), 745. Cf. *BCP* (1918), 299.

65. *BCP* (1549), 728; *BCP* (1552), 741; *BCP* (1662), 741; *BCP* (1918), 298.

66. *BCW* (1928), 41.

67. Knox, 110-111. Cf. Calvin, 155-156.

68. *BCO* (1922), 120, 125.

69. Knox's version spoke of prevailing "against Satan." Knox, 111.

70. *BCP* (1928), 277.

71. *BCP* (1549), 732.

72. Cf. *BCP* (1552), 743; *BCP* (1918), 299.

73. Calvin, 116, Knox, 110. Maxwell notes that "the Lord's Prayer was repeated at this point in all the Reformed Liturgies" (Maxwell, *Genevan Service Book*, 119, n. 21).

74. To be more precise, *SS*, 142 and *DD* (1874), 132, place it after the baptism, while *DD* (1922), 339, omits it (but the familiar option for "extempore prayer" remains).

75. Cf. *BCO* (1922), 119, 126.

76. Cf. *BCW* (1920), 48, 49.

77. *BCP* (1549), 744; *BCP* (1552), 745; *BCP* (1662), 745; *BCP* (1928), 300.

78. Cf. Knox, 109, and *BCO* (1922), 118-119, n. 1.

79. *BCP* (1928), 277.

80. Harding, "The Major Orders," 111. Zwingli used a similar form of dismissal in baptism in his second revision of the Zurich Order: "The Lord be with you. Go in peace." Zwingli, 131.

81. *BCP* (1928), 277.

82. *BCO* (1922), 121, 126; *DD* (1922), 339.

83. "Notes on Some of the Orders," in *BCO* (1932), vi.

84. E.g., *BCW* (1928), 42; *BCO*, (1922), 121.

85. Cf. *BCO* (1922), 121.

86. Knox, 105-110; *BCO* (1922), 117-118.

87. For the technical use of the term *baptismal symbol*, see J. N. D. Kelly, *Early Christian Creeds*, 3rd ed. (New York: Longman, 1991).

88. While there is historic precedent in Protestantism for use of an emended form of the Creed, it is found in the form of a three-fold questioning and "the resurrection of the flesh [body]" is certainly not omitted. E.g., Luther (1523), 99; Luther (1526), 109. The *BCP* (1549) followed a three-fold form using the full (unabbreviated) Creed. *BCP* (1549), 736. The *BCP* (1552) Prayer Book used the entire Creed as a single question. [*BCP* (1552)], 737.

89. *BCP* (1549), 740.

90. *BCP* (1552), 741.

91. Fisher, *Christian Initiation: The Reformation Period*, 109, n. 2. For Bucer's objections see, Bucer, 8-90.

92. *BCP* (1918), 296-297; *DD* (1922), 338-339.

93. Cf. Luther (1523), 97; Luther (1526), 107-108; *BCP* (1918), 293; *DD* (1922), 336.

94. *BCO* (1932), 104-108.

95. The other titles are "The Reception of Church Members at Holy Communion" (Congregationalist) in *BCW* (1920), 45; "An Order for the Admission of Baptized Persons to Full Communion" (Presbyterian) in *BCO* (1922), 130; "Advancement from Catechumen Membership to Adult Membership" (Methodist) in *DD* (1922), 348; in *Forms* all these titles become "The Reception of Baptized Persons into Full Communion" (*Forms*, 33, 36, 41); the Anglican order is "The Order of Confirmation or Laying on of Hands Upon Those That Are Baptized and Come to Years of Discretion," *BCP* (1918), 330.

96. *BCW* (1928), 47. The more minor changes of "The" to "An" and "Lord's Supper" to "Full Communion" is in keeping with the language of the founding traditions.

97. While "Beloved in the Lord" is used in *BCO* (1922), 130, most of the opening words are closer to *BCW* (1928), 47. The latter reads, in part: "Dearly beloved, in your Baptism you received the sign and seal of your engrafting into Christ, and were solemnly engaged to be the Lord's. And forasmuch as you now desire to confirm the covenant then made in your behalf, and to obey His commandment."

98. *BCP* (1918), 313-314.

99. See *BCW* (1928), 47, and *BCP* (1928), 296.

100. This is the compilers' name for this baptismal symbol. *BCO* (1932), 112.

101. The Methodist question was "Do you love and trust the Lord Jesus Christ as your Saviour, Friend and Guide?" *DD* (1922), 349. The Presbyterian question was "Do you receive and confess the Christian faith, believing in God the Father as your heavenly Father, in Jesus Christ as your Lord and Saviour, and in the Holy Spirit as your Sanctifier?" *BCO* (1922), 130-131.

102. *BCP* (1918), 334; and also the "Alternative Order" of *BCP* (1928), 296.

103. The question there is "Do you promise to submit yourselves to all the ordinances of Christ, to use faithfully the means of grace, and to give to the relief of the poor, and the furtherance of the gospel, as the Lord may prosper you?" *BCO* (1896), 315.

104. The Presbyterian question is "Do you promise to submit yourselves to all the ordinances of Christ, to make diligent use of the means of grace, and faithfully to support the work and worship of the Church?" *BCO* (1922), 131. Cf. *Forms* 35, 37, 42.

105. This wording is also very close to that of the Canadian Presbyterian order used for the reception of communicants from other churches or congregations and the American Presbyterian order for the baptism of adults. Cf. *BCO* (1922), 131; *BCW* (1928), 44,

106. *BCP* (1549), 794; *BCP* (1552), 795; *BCP* (1662), 795; *BCP* (1918), 334. Yet another version was also known to Presbyterian rites, where it was abbreviated and incorporated into a longer prayer. E.g., *Euchologion*, 317 and *BCO* (1922), 132. Fisher notes that the roots of this classic prayer for confirmation can be traced via Sarum usage to the sixth century *Gelasian Sacramentary*. In both uses it immediately precedes the

episcopal confirmation/anointing. Fisher, *Christian Initiation: The Reformation Period,* 241, n. 3. See also Sarum 252.

107. *BCP* (1918), 334.

108. This is evident throughout all of *BCO* (1932).

109. In this they followed the Presbyterian use of Isaiah's lines in the prayer. See *BCO* (1896), 317, and *BCO* (1922), 132.

110. See "the right hand of fellowship" in: *BCO* (1922), 133; *DD* (1874), 140; *DD* (1902), 288; *BCW* (1920), 46. While not explicitly mentioned in *DD* (1922), 350, former practice and the phrase "we heartily congratulate you" may imply that practice. (See also the comments on the "Conclusions" below.)

111. *BCW* (1928), 48.

112. 1 Peter 5:10 (AV): "But the God of all grace, who hath called us unto his eternal glory by Christ Jesus, after that ye have suffered a while, make your perfect, stablish strengthen settle you." 1 Corinthians 1:8 (AV): "Who ["our Lord Jesus Christ" (v.7)] shall also confirm you unto the end, that ye may be blameless in the day of our Lord Jesus Christ."

113. E.g., *BCO* (1896), 317; *BCW* (1920), 46; *BCW* (1928), 48; *Forms* 43. The Anglican use of the prayer begins with the 1552 Prayer Book, perhaps inspired by some of the phrases of the Strassburg rite of baptism, but more likely phrases from Bucer. See *BCP* (1552), 795, and Fisher's comments, *Christian Initiation: The Reformation Period,* 251, n. 3, 252-253, n. 2. It is found in the 1918 Canadian rite and in the "Alternative Order" of 1928. *BCP* (1918), 335; *BCP* (1928), 296.

114. *BCW* (1928), 48.

115. Though not in *BCP* (1549) or (1552), it is found in *BCP* (1662), 797; *BCP* (1928), 294, 297; *BCP* (1918), 335. While it is placed after the laying on of hands, it is before the postconfirmation prayer, unlike *BCO* (1932).

116. *BCO* (1922), 133. The Presbyterians placed it at the structural climax of their order, that is, after the prayers and just before the giving of the "right hand of fellowship."

117. *BCW* (1928), 48. It is also commonly found in the "Treasury of Prayers" sections of many service books, including that of The United Church. See *BCO* (1932), 46; *BCO* (1896), 283; *BCW* (1928), 151.

118. *BCW* (1928), 49. Both the American and Canadian Presbyterian orders for the baptism of infants took care to make a similar theological clarification following those orders, based on the Westminster "Confession of Faith." *BCW* (1928), 42. While no such rubric was included after the United Church's Order for the Baptism of Children, it was thought necessary here.

119. The use of the Apostles' Creed is introduced in *Euchologion* with similar wording: "Do you receive the doctrine of the Christian Faith into which you were baptized, whereof we make confession, saying, I believe in God?" *BCW* (1896), 314. The first question in the American order is: "Do you here, in the presence of God and this congregation, confess Christ as your Lord, and adhere to that Christian faith wherein you were baptized?" Both, no doubt, have their roots in the Prayer Book question. See *BCP* (1918), 333.

120. E.g., *BCW* (1920), 46; *BCO* (1922), 133. This practice probably continued, even in the absence of rubrical direction.

121. E.g., *DD* (1922), 350. The Canadian Presbyterian order used a declaration earlier in the service (probably based on *Euchologion,* 315-316), the substance of which read: "In the Name of Jesus Christ, the great King and Head of the Church, and by the authority of the Session of this congregation, I do now admit and welcome you to the fellowship of the Lord's Table and to all the privileges of full communion with the

Church of Christ." *BCO* (1922), 131. The United Church version combines the *Euchologion* form with a portion of the blessing used at the conclusion of the Canadian Presbyterian order. See *BCO* (1922), 133.

122. Cf. *BCO* (1922), 131; *BCW* (1928), 50. The latter includes an address, which reads in part: "Dearly beloved, having before made public confession of your faith in Christ . . . you now promise to wait diligently upon its ordinances, to study its peace and prosperity, and to yield becoming submission to its government and discipline?" A pledge said by the minister on behalf of the (standing) congregation follows.

Together, the two concluding options appended in the *BCO* (1932) rite serve to provide the substance for The United Church's "An Order for the Reception of Communicants from Other Churches," *BCO* (1932), 113-124. I have chosen not to detail or examine this rite in this study, as it adds nothing new to the previous rites. However, two observations are in order: First, the separation of such a membership rite from baptism clearly follows the American Presbyterian source (demonstrating once again a reliance on that text), which is to be distinguished from that of the Canadian Presbyterian source (which integrates it into the confirmation service, thereby placing it in closer proximity to baptism itself). See *BCO* (1922), 131. Second, its continued presence as a separate rite can be seen to honor the Congregationalist practice of reception into covenant membership within the United Church.

123. *BCO* (1932), 109-112.

124. *BCP* (1918), 310, called it, "The Ministration of Baptism to such as are of Riper Years and Able to Answer for Themselves." *SS*, 143: "The Ministration of Baptism to such as are of Riper Years." *DD* (1922), 340: "The Ministration of the Sacrament of Baptism to such as are of Riper Years." *BCW* (1920), 49: "Baptism of Adults." *Euchologion* (1896), 320: "The Order for the Baptism of Adults." *BCW* (1928), 43: "The Order for the Administration of Baptism to Adults and their Reception to the Lord's Supper." *BCO* (1922), 127: "An Order for the Administration of Holy Baptism to Adults."

125. Cf. *Euchologion* (1896), 320-321; *BCW* (1928), 43; *BCO* (1922), 127.

126. Cf. *DD*, (1922), 340; *SS*, 143; *BCP* (1918), 310. With the introduction of the comparable Prayer Book service in 1662, the dominant Anglican text was John 3:1-8 (Jesus with Nicodemus on being born of the "water and the Spirit"), read after the opening prayers. However, an allusion to Mark 16:15-16, the synoptic parallel to the Matthean text, is found in the Prayer Book's scriptural exhortation following the lesson. *BCP* (1962), 765, 767; *BCP* (1918), 313-314.

127. In the Prayer Book tradition it is again found in the scriptural exhortation (n. 4 above).

128. *BCO* (1922), 127: "Doubt ye not, therefore, but earnestly believe, that He will number among His people this person, *truly repenting and* coming unto Him by faith." Is it too much to suggest that the compilers were embarrassed by the call to repentance? And yet it is present in the Acts text. Compare the closing lines with the traditional *BCP* ending: "that he will grant *them* remission of *their* sins, and bestow upon *them* the Holy Ghost; that he will give *them* the blessing of eternal life, and make *them partakers* of his everlasting kingdom." *BCP* (1662), 767; *BCP* (1918), 313-314.

129. *BCW* (1928), 43.

130. *BCP* (1662), 769; *BCP* (1918), 314-315.

131. E.g., *BCP* (1662), 771; *BCP* (1918), 315; *DD* (1922), 519; *SS*, 146-147; *Euchologion*, 322.

132. Cf. *BCP*, (1662), 771; *BCP* (1918), 316, 334; *DD* (1922), 342; *BCP* (1928), 296.

133. Cf. *Euchologion* (1896), 315. *BCW* (1928), 44, reads, in part: "do you promise to make diligent use of the means of grace"; *BCO* (1922), 131 reads, in part: "Do you

promise to persevere in the diligent use of the means of grace, and earnestly in all things to seek the peace and welfare of the Church?"

134. *BCW* (1928), 44.

135. Cf. *BCP* (1662), 773; *BCP* (1918), 317; *Euchologion*, (1896), 324-325; *BCO* (1922), 129; *BCW* (1928), 45. Methodists alluded to many of the same ideas in a prayer clearly based on the same Prayer Book source (though without signation). E.g., *DD* (1922), 343.

136. *BCW* (1928), 45-46.

137. *BCW* (1928), 45.

138. *BCW* (1920), 50.

Chapter 3
Liturgical Reform, United Church-Style

The commentary in chapter 2, in addition to providing a detailed description of the sources of the baptismal texts in *The Book of Common Order*, has raised a variety of theological and liturgical issues for further consideration and analysis. In this and the other similar chapters of this study, the commentaries will serve as a means by which to introduce and raise such issues. Four common areas will be addressed with respect to each generation of texts: structure, scripture, pneumatology, and ecclesiology. A variety of other issues will also be discussed under a selection of headings appropriate to the particular texts and their context.

While this approach cannot claim to produce results that are exhaustive, it will prove instructive with respect to the development of the rites. In this chapter, several features of the baptismal liturgies of *The Book of Common Order* will be studied, among them: the extent to which they depend on the liturgies of the Reformers and the Prayer Book; the extent to which they reflect the liturgical forms of the founding traditions; the efforts made by the Committee to recover more catholic liturgical forms; and, the beginning of a trend away from the notion of profession of faith toward "confirmation." As a whole, it provides a picture of liturgical reform, United Church-style.

Structure

It has been suggested that the most primitive level on which any liturgical rite operates is the level of structure.[1] According to this method of liturgical analysis, structure is the key to liturgical function and theological meaning. In the case of the baptismal liturgies of *The Book of Common Order*, structural considerations prove particularly revealing.

Davidson himself once commented that the orders for baptism and "confirmation" were essentially those of *The Book of Common Prayer*.[2] To investigate this claim, Table 3.1 below compares the structure of the 1932 service with the major sources already identified in the foregoing commentary.

Table 3.1
A Structural Comparison of Orders for the Baptism of Children

BCO (1932)	*BCP* (1662)	*BCP* (1928)	*BCO* (1922)	*BCW* (1928)	*DD* (1922)	*BCW* (1920)
INTRO.						
question	question	question				
	exhort.	exhort.		exhort.	exhort.	
prayer	prayers	prayers			prayers	
Mk.	Mk.	Mk.	Acts		Gen.	Mk.
			Mk.		Acts	
			(John)		Gal. Ez.	
					Mk.	
exhort.	exhort.	exhort.	exhort.		exhort.	
	prayer	prayer	prayer		prayers	
						welcome
PROMISES		PROMISES				
exhort.	exhort.	exhort.				
	renunc.	renunc.				
questions	questions	questions	questions	questions		questions
prayer	prayers	prayer		prayer		
		BLESSING				
		WATER				
BAPTISM		BAPTISM				
baptism	baptism	baptism	baptism	baptism	baptism	baptism
			blessing			
declar.	declar. &	declar. &	declar.		declar.	
	signation	signation				
blessing					blessing	blessing
						& declar.
PRAYERS		THANKSG.				
	Lord's P.	Lord's P.				
thanksg.	thanksg.	thanksg.	thanksg.	thanksg.		
Lord's P.			Lord's P.	Lord's P.		Lord's P.
DUTIES		DUTIES				
exhort. to	exhort. to	exhort. to				
parents	godpar.	godpar.				
		question				
dismissal		dismissal				
or		*or*				
blessing		blessing	blessing	blessing		
rubrics			rubrics	rubrics		
APPENDIX						

As can be seen, the almost total structural convergence of the United Church order (first column) with the 1662 *Book of Common Prayer* order (second column) generally supports Davidson's claim. But the table also shows, as the commentary has implied, another significant influence. There is an even greater structural convergence of the United Church order with that of the "proposed" 1928 version of *The Book of Common Prayer*. In particular, the use of headings to demarcate the structure of the rite, and therein the purpose of its respective sections, is clearly inspired by this source. Archival records show that such headings were introduced into the United Church texts late in the drafting process. While Davidson and Matheson began the work on the texts as early as May of 1928, the headings were not inserted until perhaps as late as January of 1932 in the next to last revision. Up to this point the 1662 text was the predominant structural influence in the drafts.[3] Such last-minute additions were possible only because the 1928 Prayer Book was a revision based on the 1662 text.

In the United Church version the heading "The Introduction" was added to the first section, while "The Blessing of the Water" and its related material was omitted. "The Thanksgiving" became "The Prayers" and, in keeping with Reformed ecclesiology, "The Duties of the Godfathers and Godmothers" became "The Duties of the People." One result of these developments was that the organization of liturgical texts through the use of subject headings has become standard practice in the United Church ever since.

While specific structural influence of the 1928 Prayer Book on the Order for the Baptism of Children is significant, Table 3.1 also demonstrates the degree to which the structure of the rite would also be generally familiar to the founding traditions of the United Church. In fact, an overall parallel in the structure and movement of the rite exists among all the orders. From one perspective, there is a sense in which the 1932 text can be viewed as a kind of blending and convergence of the Presbyterian, Methodist and Congregationalist orders, the net result being an elaboration and expansion of all three—an interesting metaphor for union. From another perspective, this is achieved by an appeal to the Church of England's rite and can therefore be viewed as a move in a decidedly Anglican direction. Both perspectives have some merit. The scale is tipped, however, on the level of content. As the commentary has shown, while all three traditions are represented in various portions of the order, Presbyterian and Prayer Book elements dominate, the language of the latter being strongest.

With respect to the order for Reception to Full Communion, the compilers chose not to avail themselves of a similar use of headings, save in the "Appendix." Table 3.2 below shows that the reliance on general Prayer Book structures was shared by all of the sources. But the commentary has also demonstrated that the action beginning with the laying on of hands reveals that the most direct influence on the United Church order is the American Presbyterian rite.

In the case of adult baptism, the compilers returned to the use of 1928 *BCP*-like headings to clarify the structure of the rite, adapting them in this case for an order which combined, in the words of the closing rubric, the "essential parts" of both previous orders to produce one full rite of baptism and reception/"confirmation." Table 3.2 shows the almost equal partnership of Prayer Book, Methodist, and Presbyterian influences.

Table 3.2
A Structural Comparison of Orders for
Reception to Full Communion or "Confirmation"

BCO (1932)	*BCP* (1662)	*BCP* (1928)	*BCO* (1922)	*BCW* (1928)	*DD* (1922)	*BCW* (1920)
						readings
			names	names	names	
exhort.	exhort.	exhort.	exhort.	exhort.	exhort.	exhort.
		RENEWAL				
		renunc.				
questions	questions	questions		questions	questions	
			declar.		declar.	
			(reception)			
		CONFIR.				
		(hymn)				
prayer	prayer	prayer				
hands &	hands &	hands &		hands &		
prayer	prayer	prayer		prayer		prayer
	Lord's pr.	Lord's pr.				
prayer	prayer	prayer	prayers	prayer	prayer	
Lord's pr.			Lord's pr.			
		CONCLU.				
	prayer	prayer				
		commis.				
			right hand			right hand
			(hymn)			
ascription				ascription		readings
	blessing	blessing	benedict.		names	
Appendix						

As Table 3.3 below shows, the orders for adult baptism in the *BCP* and the founding traditions did not view the laying on of hands as necessary.[4] It was the American Presbyterian rite which provided for baptism and *BCP* "confirmation"-like hand laying in one order. This seems to have caught the imagination of the compilers. The American order also contained confusing rubrical directions in an effort to integrate the liturgies of adult baptism, "confirmation," and reception of members from other churches.[5] The United Church texts eliminated some of the rubrical confusion only to introduce others.

Clearly the compilers did not intend that some combination of the three orders be celebrated together on one occasion. Any celebration of, for example, both the baptism of children and adults, or adult baptism and Reception to Full

Communion (of those previously baptized), would have resulted in the repetition of several of the prayers.

Table 3.3
A Structural Comparison of Orders for Adult Baptism

BCO (1932)	*BCP* (1662)	*BCP* (1928)	*BCO* (1922)	*BCW* (1928)	*DD* (1922)	*BCW* (1920)
						Ps.
						prayers
	exhort.	exhort.				
	prayers	prayers				
Mt.; Acts	Jn.	Jn.	Mt.	Mt.; Acts		Ep.
exhort.	exhort.	exhort.	exhort.	exhort.	exhort	
			Acts.		Mt.; Acts	
			exhort			
	prayers	prayers				
						welcome
		PROMISES				
BAPTISM						
exhort.	exhort.	exhort.			exhort.	
	Renunc.	Renunc.			Renunc.	
questions	questions	questions	questions	questions	questions	questions
prayer	prayer	prayer	prayer	prayer		
	prayer	BLESSING				
		WATER				
baptism	baptism	BAPTISM	baptism	baptism	baptism	baptism
			blessing		prayer	
declar.	declar.	declar.	declar.	declar.	declar.	
	signation	signation				signation
						charge
CONFIR						
hands &				hands &		
prayer				prayer		
		THANKSG.				
	Lord's P.	Lord's P.				
prayer	prayers	prayers	prayer	prayer	prayers	
Lord's P.			Lord's P.		Lord's P.	
blessing			benedict.			blessing
		DUTIES				
	exhort.	exhort.			exhort.	
						prayer
				ascription		ascription
	the grace	(blessing)			the grace	the grace
APPENDIX						

More significantly, the structure (and content) of the order for adult baptism shows a significant departure from the practice of the founding traditions in its integration of a *BCP*-like order for "confirmation" into the rite. The implication is that it is necessary for, in the words of the closing rubric, "admission to full membership."

As a whole, all three United Church orders emphasize mostly Prayer Book and Presbyterian content, with Methodist and Congregationalist contributions present, but to a much lesser degree. The compilers sought to integrate some of the practices of the latter traditions through the use of appended options. In fact, however, the use of such options in the case of the baptism of children would only result in the rite seeming even more Anglican and/or Presbyterian than it already was. The "Conclusions" appended to the order for Reception to Full Communion achieve a more representative result and allowed for the liturgy to seem significantly more Methodist or Congregationalist, depending upon the choices. Similarly, the alternate question provided in adult baptism would make for a more Congregationalist approach to the action of baptism.

It is interesting to note that the drafts of the orders show that the appendixes developed as much for reasons of simplicity as liturgical flexibility and variety. Early drafts attempted to integrate most of this material into the main body of the orders themselves. Had this approach been successful, the results may have proved preferable in terms of giving better and more explicit representation of the founding traditions. However, the resulting length of the orders (especially with the exhortations and conclusions included) and the tendency toward repetition prompted the Committee to append such components to the end of the order.[6]

This structural analysis has shown that while a certain degree of structural unity, clarity, simplicity, and sophistication is present in the orders, the introduction of "confirmation"-like structures was a significant (if not surprising) development. The compilers may have underestimated the liturgical contributions and overestimated the liturgical literacy of some of their constituents. Methodists and Congregationalists, for example, could be forgiven for frustration at seeing some favored practices appended to the orders. More to the point, it is unlikely that many "free" Methodists and Congregationalists would have been interested in seeking out the liturgical liberties and options they were being offered in the work. To them the book probably appeared as simply another example of either Prayer Book ritualism or Presbyterian formalism. On the other hand, could any "text" hope to convert such parties to the merits of such a liturgical approach? While the structure of these rites reveals some attempts at uncovering common liturgical ground among the founding traditions, it is mostly within the context of a move in a decidedly Prayer Book and Presbyterian direction.

Scripture

One of the weakest aspects of the orders is the use of scripture. The emphasis on Mark's account of Jesus' acceptance of children in the order for infant baptism shows a readiness to accept both the Prayer Book form and the practice of infant baptism as normative. Here the Committee could have benefited, at the very least, from a closer consideration of the merits of some of the Presbyterian and Methodist sources in which other texts were used. While the prayers in the "Appendix" provide for the possibility of a somewhat wider range of biblical allusions in the liturgy, they do not make up for the reading of scripture as such.

The sole reliance on Mark 10 in the baptism of children persisted in the drafting process in spite of the complaints of at least one presbytery and one Committee member. Camrose Presbytery objected to it in their response to the draft orders.[7] A draft by William Maxwell for infant baptism titled "An Order for the Administration of Holy Baptism" took the classic Reformed approach on this issue, giving priority to the Matthean commission/resurrection appearance.[8] Especially interesting is the fact that the minutes of the Committee show a concession in this direction was considered at one point, incorporating the opening lines of the Methodist *Discipline's* exhortation into the "Introduction."[9] The lines in question include an explicit reference to the Matthean text: "Dearly Beloved: Forasmuch as our Lord Jesus Christ gave commandment to His Church to make disciples of all nations, baptizing them into the name of the Father, and of the Son, and of the Holy Spirit, and whereas these person here present do bring *this* child. . . ."[10] However, these lines do not appear in any subsequent draft and there is no record of the process behind their disappearance.

In the Order for the Baptism of Adults the compilers did take the lead of their founding partners by using both the Matthean commission and Acts 2. Presumably these texts were deemed more suitable for adults.

For Reception to Full Communion no scripture readings were included. The compilers chose not to be influenced by the Congregationalist order featured in *Forms* which included several passages on the church, the Body of Christ, and the "Good Shepherd."[11] In addition, it may be significant that they did not use the Acts 8 or 19 texts of the Canadian *BCP* (1918).[12] In this they may have been refusing to suggest that "confirmation" was a pneumatic event. Instead Davidson crafted an optional "confirmation" prayer based on the "strengthening" texts from the Epistles.

Thus, with respect to the reading of scripture, the orders followed Prayer Book practice in the case of the baptism of children, that of the founding traditions in the case of the baptism of adults, and Methodists and Presbyterians in Reception to Full Communion.

Pneumatology

The role of the Holy Spirit in these orders is, of course, more complex than that implied by simply the absence of particular scriptural texts in the order for Reception to Full Communion. The commentaries have also raised particular developments surrounding "regeneration" and "confirmation" which relate to the Spirit. Before turning to these concerns, I wish to comment on a related issue, namely that of renunciation and the blessing of water. While these are not necessarily related pneumatological issues, the Committee saw them as connected and dealt with them as such.

The commentary and structural analysis shows the absence of any explicit renunciation and blessing of the water in the orders for baptism, in spite of otherwise strong Prayer Book influences. On these matters, the Committee followed, for the most part, Presbyterian and Congregationalist practice.[13] These traditions shared, to varying degrees, many of the Puritan-based sensibilities discussed in chapter 1. Among these can be included the objection to vows taken on behalf of others and any liturgical acts which could tempt superstition or imply idolatry. The former counsels against the use of an explicit renunciation in the context of infant baptism; the latter against the blessing of water.

William Maxwell, for one, was not swayed by such traditional objections. His drafts for adult and infant baptism included both: a renunciation worded "Do you, (in the name of this child) renounce the vanity of the world, the lusts of the flesh, all evil works and ways?" and a blessing of the water (complete with Sursum Corda) based on that of the 1928 Prayer Book.[14] The minutes record that May 27, 1927, was Maxwell's last meeting with the Committee before leaving for England "for two or three years."[15]

A later draft of the order for infant baptism from Davidson's typewriter also included a renunciation worded "Do you, in the name of this child, renounce the vain pomp and glory of the world, the sinful desires of the flesh, and all evil works and ways?" and a simplified version of Maxwell's prayer for the blessing of the water (without the Sursum Corda).[16] Even drafts of the order for "confirmation" contained a creative attempt at a contemporary renunciation: "Do you here, in the presence of God and of his congregation, renounce all selfishness and cruelty, falsehood and pride, and the vices which degrade our human nature, so that you will not be led by them?"[17] Gradually, however, all such renunciations and explicit blessings of the water were dropped.[18]

Writing as minister of Emperor's Gate Presbyterian Church in London, Maxwell argued the catholic case first to Hugh Matheson: "The Hymnary delights me, and the Orders, I think, are very good, with the exception of Baptism, where, I am astonished to note, you have no prayer of Consecration of the water. . . . I do not see that there is much to be gained from departing from the old form of renunciation in the questions."[19]

On the subject of the consecration of the water he argued that while Calvinist practice had none, this was a departure from the Reformed tradition of the *Westminster Directory* and in need of correction. While ignored by Presbyterians in England, Canada, and the United States, he noted, the Church of Scotland had recently seen fit to restore it, thereby recovering a more catholic and Presbyterian practice. He closed his letter "pleading" for a reopening of this discussion. A day later he wrote to Davidson and the Committee, again expressing his concern over these "grave faults."[20]

Though Maxwell's drafts and related pleas seemed to have affected Davidson's drafts, the Committee's wishes prevailed. The minutes record the decision that the renunciation "be not so included, although a truth contained within it may be fittingly included if otherwise expressed."[21] To this end the postbaptismal prayers in the order for the baptism of children pray, in Presbyterian fashion, that the power of the Spirit may enable the child to "prevail against evil." Furthermore, as pointed out in the commentary, the exhortation before the promises in adult baptism calls the candidate "to follow Christ as your Lord and Master, turning away from what he forbiddeth and doing whatsoever he commandeth," a revision of the Prayer Book's reference to "renounce the devil and all his works, and constantly believe God's holy Word, and obediently keep his commandments." In the order for Reception to Full Communion the references are more oblique, exhorting the candidate to keep the commandments of God and praying that he or she may "be blameless." Thus the language of renunciation in the orders as a whole is, at most, oblique or implied.

The issue of baptismal epiclesis was treated in much the same fashion. In the orders for both infant and adult baptism the Spirit is invoked upon the candidate, though in the case of infants the second prayer of the "Appendix" allows for the possibility of prayer that the water be "set apart" for "holy use."[22]

What semblance of renunciation and baptismal epiclesis remained in the orders seemed due to Maxwell's persistence *in absentia*. What is interesting about the discussion around these issues is the fact that they will be resurrected in the eighties with *Baptism and Renewal of Baptismal Faith*.

Though the practice of renunciation and the blessing of water have not been a significant part of the United Church tradition *per se*, efforts to recover them have been with United Church worship committees from the beginning. The puzzlement of some at their "sudden" appearance may be fruitfully placed in this larger historical context.

Other areas of pneumatological concern relate to the subjects of "confirmation" and "regeneration." It has already been noted that the most explicit invocations of the Spirit in the orders for baptism are directed upon the candidates themselves. In addition, postbaptismal prayers include petitions for the future work of the Spirit in the life of the individual. It is, however, in the prayers associated with the laying on of hands that the liturgical picture begins to get more complicated. On the one hand, the words of the opening exhortation to Reception to Full Communion or "Confirmation" define the purpose of the rite as a "strengthening" by God's Holy Spirit that one may "grow more and more in the knowledge of God" and "keep [God's] covenant steadfastly to the end." On the other hand, the prayer before the laying on of hands is the prayer for the Spirit's "manifold gifts of grace" and gravitates precariously toward the implication of a specific gifting of the Spirit. In one of Davidson's drafts he even included an opening rubric suggesting the singing of *The Hymnary's* "Veni Creator Spiritus," a hymn traditionally associated with ordination.[23] His words in the "Introductory Notes for the Executive Committee" of the draft orders clearly reveal his own belief that "confirmation" was a "catholic" and "Reformed" practice worthy of recovery.

> The Committee has not hesitated to use the word "Confirmation." It belongs to our Reformed tradition. John Calvin in the sixteenth century vindicated the word and the rite. So did Richard Baxter in the next century and so did Charles Hodge more recently. Both the word and the idea appear generally in Presbyte-

> rian Orders. The Committee in the Order has been jealous of its evangelical contents; on the one hand the young person "confirms" (i.e. ratifies) the vows made on his behalf at his baptism; on the other hand, the Lord comes to meet the young person at this critical period of his life with "confirming" (i.e. strengthening) grace. The word puts emphasis on the Christian, as compared with the merely human significance of the rite, the subject of the verb "confirm" is God more than man.[24]

Hence the subtitle to the rite is "the Confirmation of Those Who Have Been Baptized." This in spite of several calls from some Presbyteries to "delete" the term from the title and, in some instances, the entire order from the book.[25]

In its final form various senses of "confirmation" are simultaneously operative in the rite, among them: a specific pneumatic event (if it can be suggested that the *Veni Creator* be sung, there would appear to be operative a particular gifting of the Spirit); a general invocation of the Spirit (in the sense of "strengthening"); a "profession of faith" (in the Reformed sense of a "confirmation" of baptismal vows following upon instruction); Reception to Full Communion (this Congregationalist-like sense is made even stronger when the alternate "Conclusions" are used and/or Holy Communion follows).

One can only conclude that, in spite of the efforts of the compilers to recover and/or clarify the meaning of this rite, the result was that the seeds of future confusion had been sown (or perhaps the ambiguities of the Methodist heritage discussed in chapter 1 continued to be unwittingly harvested). With this order "confirmation" had begun to become part of the United Church's approved liturgical vocabulary.

In what sense does the action of the Spirit include the work of regeneration? In the order for baptism some of the vocabulary which often accompanies the language of regeneration is present (i.e., "repentance," "remission," "forgiveness"). Similarly, in all three orders the invocation for the present and future work of the Spirit is present. However, the fact that the specific omission of the Prayer Book references to regeneration and forgiveness of sins were deleted from the prayer before the laying on of hands is testimony to the avoidance of regenerative implications in adult baptism and "confirmation."

More noteworthy is the order for infant baptism, which operates as a foundational rite for the other two. As the commentary has shown, this order is consistent in its deletion of specific Prayer Book phrases such as "remission of sins," "spiritual regeneration," "heavenly washing," "adoption," and "ingrafting." This language of regeneration, so present in the classic Reformed texts, the Prayer Book and Wesley, is conspicuous by its absence in this United Church rite. With the loss of much of this classic language the substance of baptismal regeneration is eviscerated. The desire by Wesley, for example, to define and distinguish the character of regeneration in infant and adult baptism is not a concern here.

What baptismal paradigm has taken its place? From an analysis of key words it is clear that the dominant language of the order for infant baptism is that of "reception." It dominates the order from the opening question and prayers, through the gospel reading and its exposition, to the postbaptismal declaration, the duties of the people, and the appended alternate exhortation (though this does contain the only Reformed reference to "ingrafting into Christ" in the order). The opening prayers also carry the sense of offering and dedication. As has been shown, in Reception to Full Communion the metaphor of reception operates in conjunction with "confirmation," "strengthening," and profession of faith. Only the Order for the Baptism of Adults carries any latent classic regenerative connotations.

Thus, the texts continue in the spirit of *Forms* and the founding traditions. Avoidance of potential controversy is achieved by omission. The result is a tendency in a Congregationalist direction, toward reception rather than regeneration.

In summary, one can see how the operative pneumatology of the orders is both complex and fraught with ambiguities indicative of the period (as seen in *Forms*) and reminiscent of the Methodist orders (as discussed in chapter 1). This is further complicated by the introduction of a particularly unique style of "confirmation," the necessity of which is implied in order to complete one's baptism by being received into "full membership." While the compilers seem to have wanted the Spirit to be evident and active in the rites, they erred on the side of pushing the operative liturgical theology in a surprisingly "sacramental" direction through the use of their appropriation of "confirmation."

Ecclesiology

Pneumatological considerations such as the loss of the classic vocabulary of regeneration also have implications for the theology of covenant in these orders and therein their resulting ecclesiology.

Metaphors of "adoption" and "ingrafting" no longer play the essential role they had in the classic Reformed texts. The remaining vestige of this tradition—Calvin and Knox's thankful acknowledgment that God has "promised to be our God and the God and Father of our children"—takes on an even more important role in this reoriented context and is called upon to bear most of the weight of a theology of covenant. It is this covenant into which candidates are "received." This is the root metaphor for infant baptism. "Confirmation" involves both a Divine and human ratification of this covenant, a strengthening in and for it, as well as a reception into its fuller privileges. Adult baptism involves its profession.

Covenant theology is also reinforced in the orders through the language of congregation, community, hospitality, "household," home (i.e., the specific use of the 1928 *BCP* "Prayer for the Home" in the baptism of infants), nurture, parenthood ("Father"), and childhood. It becomes ecclesiologically explicit in "The Duties of the People" where the congregation replaces the godparents of the Prayer Book tradition and all are charged to offer support, love, example, and prayer for the candidates.

The alternate "Conclusions" in Reception to Full Communion draw cleverly on some of the practices of the founding traditions, providing for the possibility of enactment in liturgical gesture with the "right hand of welcome" and Holy Communion. Given that the latter is the symbol of the new covenant *par excellence*, it is noteworthy that its celebration is not more strongly encouraged. Equally noteworthy is the fact that these ecclesiological and liturgical dimensions are omitted from the "confirmation" section of the order for adult baptism, leaving it with a largely individualistic character. With this, the concluding rubrical claim that all the "essential parts" are contained in the combined order is even more suspect.

In spite of such shortcomings, the ecclesiology of covenant remains the most important theological concept operative in the orders. It is the most explicit example of the United Church's appropriation of its Reformed theological roots. One final observation on this subject has as its focus these very roots. The orders do not value the role of elders in the rite through the presentation of candidates by the Clerk of Session or some other such action. Presbyterian practice was strong in this regard. It was an important way of communicating the leadership of the laity and the priesthood of all believers. To the extent that the practices of the founding traditions would have continued in many congregations, one is probably safe in assuming that this custom often continued in spite of its omission in the orders.

Other Issues

Placement

The above discussion of the ecclesiology of covenant has already led to a consideration of some issues on the level of liturgical action. In addition to these, one notes the ambiguity in the orders in terms of their placement in the context of worship.

First, while the context of public worship was the preferred Reformed practice, no rubrics specifically reflect or direct this. Most of the Reformed liturgies of the time at least called for the singing of a hymn and therein implied such a context. Indeed, the closing blessing in the order for infant baptism and its related rubric shows that private baptisms were not unknown and provision for them had been conceded. Yet no rubrics are provided to suggest what one should do with "The Duties of the People" in such circumstances. In such cases this section becomes superfluous and the ecclesiology of the rite is compromised. The same could be said of the effect of the closing rubrics in the order for Reception to Full Communion and its relegation of the communal liturgical action to the appended "Conclusions." The individualistic tendencies of the order for adult baptism could also be taken to suggest that a private celebration of baptism was acceptable.

Second, the orders do not locate the rites specifically within orders for public worship or Holy Communion. Are they to take place at the beginning of worship or following the sermon? On any occasion of public worship or preferably (only?) in conjunction with Holy Communion? Such questions have important implications for the function of the orders and their meaning.

Calendar, Lectionary, and Hymnody

Similar questions could be raised with respect to their placement in the Christian year. The "Table of Lessons" with associated collects in *The Book of Common Order* was a bold addition, but it did not identify particular seasons, Sundays, or texts appropriate for baptism.[26] Its concern was primarily homiletical rather than liturgical. Of course, the "free church" tradition of preaching tended either to ignore this lectionary system or, at most, engage it very liberally. As articles on worship in the *New Outlook* demonstrate, a liturgical consciousness of the Christian calendar was either totally absent or nascent in the United Church at the time.[27]

Similarly, *The Hymnary* was organized not seasonally but theologically and thematically.[28] With respect to baptismal hymns, while a search in the thematic index could result in some finds related to baptismal themes, only three are presented in the section organized specifically for that purpose. All of them focus on the baptism of children.[29]

Liturgical Space

Because liturgical action always implies spatial arrangements, a consideration of baptismal space in United Church architecture can be instructive. To my knowledge, no thorough or systematic study of United Church liturgical architecture has been undertaken. I would classify United Church liturgical space under three general headings: the Reformed plan; the Akron plan; the "neo-Gothic" plan. Various combinations of the three can exist together.

In the Reformed plan the atmosphere is plain and simple, the lines are straight and the dominant shape is rectangular or square. The pulpit is central and dominant, often on an elevated platform. The communion table is small, plain, and on floor level, often flanked by elders' chairs. There may or may not be a baptismal font; sometimes a portable basin is attached to the pulpit or placed on the table for baptism. In either case the arrangement speaks of the centrality of the Word. As mentioned in chapter 1, this plan was favored mostly by Presbyterian and Congregationalist congregations.

In the Akron plan, named after is first home in Akron, Ohio,[30] organ pipes, choir loft, pulpit, table and Communion rail exist in descending order at the front of the church. Often curved pews face them on a "raked" or sloping floor. A covered font is nearly always present, though it is often placed aside on floor level and can be even out of sight when not in use. This space speaks again of the centrality of the Word, but with its own brand of considerable eucharistic piety evident in the kneeling rail. Fine acoustical and performance properties conducive to vibrant music and hymnody are also present. This plan was favored by Methodists of the nineteenth century.

The neo-Gothic plan is a nineteenth century revival of the two-room medieval cruciform plan. Congregational seating is in the nave, choir seating in the chancel. The choir (or "split chancel" as it is often popularly called in the United Church) separates the lectern from the pulpit and places the "altar" in the center of the chancel space, often near or against the east wall. This churchly style was revived by Pugin and the Cambridge Camden ecclesiologists, adopted by the Oxford movement in Anglicanism, and taken up by others. Large cathedral-like stone churches were built in this style in urban centers at the turn of the century. In the boom of the fifties and sixties yet another offshoot, one generation removed from this, was taken up in a simplified form in "A-frame" suburban churches. Prefabricated construction methods and a combination of wood and steel materials contributed to their ubiquitous arrival on the scene. In both cases a font is present, usually on the lectern side on the floor (the right, facing the chancel)—but again little is made of it when baptism is not taking place. This space speaks of the centrality of the sacrament of Holy Communion. The plan was adopted by a wide variety of nineteenth century established urban churches and promoted by many architectural and liturgical "experts" for the new United Church. Metropolitan United Church in Toronto, for example, formerly referred to as the "Cathedral of Methodism," was rebuilt in this style in the late twenties and heralded as a model church at the time.[31]

Such United Church liturgical plans betray a lack of intentional baptismal piety and consciousness. A survey of articles by many of the architectural and liturgical experts of the United Church of this period confirms this.[32] In the expositions and explanations of the architectural trends of the time, the font—its placement, meaning, and significance—seldom warrant mention at all.[33] One only has to reflect on the portability (and often invisibility) of the fonts of United churches to appreciate the fact that the spirituality of baptism has been, at best, of only passing interest to those designing liturgical space. When seen in conjunction with the lack of any intentional focus on the water itself in the orders, we are presented with a strong liturgical and symbolic manifestation of a theological and practical reality. The claim of *The Book of Common Order* that "the core of the rite is the use of water with words: N. I baptize thee, etc."[34] has little to do with the symbol of water or an appreciation of the significance of baptismal space and more to do with a form of sacramental minimalism, the liturgical results of which undermined the best liturgical intentions of *The Book of Common Order*.

United Church Publications

This consideration of some of the "other issues" related to the baptismal liturgies of *The Book of Common Order* would not be complete without reference to some of the United Church documents and official publications which followed *The Book of Common Order*. Many of these provided guidance for clergy and educators in the area of Christian education and baptismal catechesis and preparation. Thus they provide an important systematic reference point with which to compare the liturgical theology of the orders themselves.

Even before *The Book of Common Order* was published, the General Council had already begun receiving requests to clarify the meaning of church membership, particularly in relation to children. Often this revealed discomfort regarding the practice of infant baptism.[35] In the face of such requests, the United Church was supportive of early efforts to articulate the theology of the new church, to expound on the Articles of Faith of the Basis of Union, and to provide a defense of its catholic and Reformed heritage. Kilpatrick's *Our Common Faith* was one such popular early effort.[36] However, his Reformed defense of the orthodoxy of infant baptism and United Church practice[37] did not quell the questions for long. With the publication of *The Book of Common Order* the issue began to ferment again and the General Council soon formed a Commission on Christian Faith as part of the Board of Evangelism and Social Service to give guidance on these and other theological questions.

The General Council enlisted the leadership of none other than Richard Davidson to lead the Commission. As the "guiding mind of the Commission,"[38] he had a large influence in the drafting of its two major publications, *A Statement of Faith* and *A Catechism*, the latter being based on the former.[39] John Dow, also a member of the Commission and professor of New Testament at Emmanuel College, was also asked by the Commission to write *This is Our Faith* as an "exposition of the Statement of Faith."[40] This became a Canadian best-seller with over six printings and 10,000 copies, including printings in Great Britain. To this list one can add Davidson's own booklet *The Meaning of Baptism*, also published by the Board of Evangelism and Social Service.[41] It is interesting to note that what one United Church theologian has called "a rising theological interest in religious education"[42] coincided with the end of the war, and the coming of age of the United Church, and was precipitated in part by issues related to baptism and membership.

The relevant section of *A Statement of Faith* reads, in part:

> Section X—THE SACRAMENTS—We believe in the Sacraments of Baptism and the Lord's Supper are effectual means through which, by common things and simple acts, the saving love of God is exhibited and communicated to His people, who receive them in faith.
>
> We believe that in Baptism men are made members of the Christian society. Washing with water in the name of the Father, the Son, and the Holy Spirit signifies God's cleansing from sin and an initial participation in the gifts and graces of new life. The children of believing parents are baptized and nurtured in the family of God so that they may in due time take upon themselves the yoke of Christ.
>
> . . . So we acknowledge Baptism as God's appointed means of grace at initiation into the Christian fellowship.[43]

This statement is not in conflict with the orders themselves, though it is unclear whether "men" in the second paragraph refers to all persons (adults and children) or only adults. If it is the latter, the implications are interesting to consider. With the baptism of adults being treated first in this section, the construction seems to imply that the baptism of children follows from it. Both Dow's exposition of this section and Davidson's writing on the subject support this view of the historical development of baptism, infant baptism being seen as a later result of the convergence of the sociology of the household and the theology of covenant.[44] While this has some historical merit, the United Church texts are clearly constructed in the reverse order, the baptism of children being the normative rite, the baptism of adults being derivative.

The comparable sections in *A Catechism* read:

> 32. WHAT IS SACRAMENT?—A Sacrament is an act of worship instituted by Christ in which He joins material things with the inward working of the Holy Spirit to set forth and communicate to believers the saving love of God.
>
> 33. WHAT ARE THE SACRAMENTS OF THE NEW TESTAMENT?—The Sacraments of the New Testament are Baptism, by which we are admitted into the Church, and the Lord's Supper, by which we grow in the fellowship of Christ.
>
> 34. WHAT IS BAPTISM?—Baptism is a Sacrament in which, by the cleansing with water in the name of the Father, the Son, and the Holy Spirit, we are received into the Church of Christ, and are engaged to be wholly and always His.
>
> 35. WHY ARE THE CHILDREN OF BELIEVING PARENTS BAPTIZED IN INFANCY?—The children of believing parents are baptized in infancy because they are born within the fellowship of the Church and Christ claims them for His own.
>
> 36. WHAT IS REQUIRED AFTER CHILDREN ARE BAPTIZED?—When children are baptized, Christ entrusts them to their parents and the Church to be so cared for and instructed that when they grow up they will make public profession of their faith in Him as the Saviour and Lord.
>
> 37. WHAT FOLLOWS WHEN THOSE BAPTIZED IN INFANCY PROFESS THEIR FAITH IN CHRIST?—When those baptized in infancy profess their faith in Christ, God confirms and equips them as soldiers of the Cross, and the Church receives them into full communion with all its rights and duties.
>
> 38. WHAT IS REQUIRED OF THOSE WHO COME IN ADULT YEARS TO BE BAPTIZED?—Before those who come in adult years are baptized, they must turn away from what Christ forbids, commit themselves wholly to Him, and promise to do what He commands; at their baptism God confirms then as soldiers of the Cross, and the Church receives them into full communion with all its rights and duties.[45]

These passages highlight baptism as admission and reception (numbers 33, 34). The verb "cleansing," like "washing" in the *Statement*, seems to be a favored image, though the liturgies themselves pay little attention to liberal use of water. A sense of adoption is captured in the phrase "engaged to be wholly and always His" and "claims them for His own" (numbers 34, 35), though the word is not used. The theology of covenant is clearly the basis for the defense of infant baptism (number 35). The ecclesiological dimensions of family and the household of faith are implied in number 36.

It is interesting to note that what the orders call Reception to Full Communion or Confirmation, the *Catechism* calls profession of faith (numbers 36, 37).

This is defined as God's action of confirming and equipping in number 37. The use of the phrase "soldiers of the Cross" (numbers 37, 38) is noteworthy given that it is not used in any of the orders. Moreover, "soldier" is specifically deleted from the Prayer Book-based postbaptismal declaration so that "Christ's faithful soldier and servant" becomes simply "Christ's faithful servant." Finally, the reminder that one must "turn away from what Christ forbids" and "promise to do what He commands" (number 38) recalls the subtle remnants of renunciation in the order for adult baptism.

Davidson's *The Meaning of Baptism* puts forward an even more catholic view than both the orders and the Commission's statements. He is much more explicit and intentional about the need for "the renunciation of the world" in both baptism and profession of faith.[46] He is more evangelical regarding the regeneration of both infants and adults and their "new allegiance" resulting from God's action of "ingrafting" into the Body of Christ.[47] He seems more conscious of the responsibilities of the parents and the church in Christian nurture and instruction than in the orders.[48]

On the subject of "confirmation," he takes care to make the point that God is "the subject of the verb 'confirm.'" "God is the dominating figure and chief actor in the action."[49] Finally, throughout the essay his wide-ranging use of scripture makes the orders seem biblically barren by comparison.

In spite of the publication of these documents, the 1952 General Council again instructed the Commission to provide "guidance on the doctrine and practice of Infant Baptism."[50] In 1954, the document *The Doctrine and Practice of Infant Baptism* was presented, given "general approval" and "commended . . . to congregations, . . . ministers and sessions in particular for their guidance and study."[51]

This document refers to the widespread "considerable debate regarding the significance and efficacy of Infant Baptism."[52] This is not difficult to imagine during these years of greatest church growth. It is reflected not only in the United Church context by the request for the General Council study itself, but also by the famous Barth and Cullman debate of this period.[53] Building on the previous work of the Commission, the United Church statement argues from a classic catholic and Reformed understanding of infant baptism (indebted more to Cullman than Barth). To this end, it contains a concise summary of the history of infant baptism, noting: 1) the practice of the early church is consistent with New Testament doctrine; 2) the emphasis on family life in the early church favors the practice of infant baptism; 3) the theology of covenant supports the practice; 4) more than mere dedication, infant baptism has to do with God's initiative in Jesus Christ, human witness in the world, and the church's responsibility to children; 5) the contemporary importance of the home in supporting the practice.[54] The document addresses the critiques of those supporting believers' baptism, no doubt because they were exerting significant influence from within and outside the church.

Finally, it is concrete and practical regarding the obligations and responsibilities of parents, church, session, and members. These involve guidance on such topics as pastoral oversight, emergency baptisms, counsel against indiscriminate baptism, the proper subjects for baptism, the context of public worship, the responsibilities of the Session and parents, and the role of sponsors. This application of liturgical practice and theological understanding to the specifics of United Church policy and practice was the specific mandate given by General Council to the Commission for this task. The results make it among the most valuable documents on the subject at the time.

The Doctrine and Practice of Infant Baptism can be viewed as a completion of the work begun with *The Book of Common Order* baptismal liturgies. The Commission located its work firmly within this context by excerpting the relevant sections from the Basis of Union, *A Statement of Faith*, *The Catechism*, and *The Book of Common Order* in an appendix titled "Pronouncements of The United Church of Canada on the Sacrament of Baptism."[55] With its publication the orders now had a body of theological exposition and polity guidelines reflective of United Church liturgical practice. In conclusion, in addition to any of the theological subtleties, ambiguities, or contradictions contained in these documents, one particular development should be noted. With the publication of *The Doctrine and Practice of Infant Baptism* one sees the use of the term *confirmation* for the first time in an official policy statement of the General Council of the United Church.[56] It would appear that, twenty-two years after its rather confused introduction into United Church liturgical life through *The Book of Common Order*, it has finally made its way into popular liturgical vocabulary and consciousness.

Conclusions

The Book of Common Order liturgies for baptism and "confirmation" serve to illustrate the liturgical gains and losses of union and the politics of liturgical revision in the newly formed United Church. As such, they provide us with a case study in the first systematic attempt at liturgical reform in The United Church of Canada.

We have seen that the Congregationalist emphasis on liturgical freedom embodied in simple directories and the heavy use of extended scriptural warrants is absent in the new orders. On the other hand, if former Congregationalists could countenance the "formalism" of the orders (which was probably unlikely), they would find traces of their covenant ecclesiology as well as an emphasis on "reception" and "admission" in rites, notwithstanding a certain sacramental minimalism.

Similarly, former "free" Methodists for whom the influence of *The Book of Common Prayer* had been long forgotten would no doubt be put off by the Prayer Book style of the orders, though there was little in their content to offend *per se*. Indeed, a Methodist-like "revision by omission" of potentially controversial concepts such as regeneration continued, as did the language of reception and "confirmation" (with all of its ambiguities). Former urban Methodists or British Wesleyans who were interested in liturgical renewal would have found the orders exciting in the recovery of the liturgical cadences of the Prayer Book within a liberal theological context.

Of all the founding traditions, former Presbyterians would have felt the most at home in these orders. The tradition of "common order," the familiar language of some of the scriptural warrants and the vows, several typical phrases form the vocabulary of the Reformers (including the specific recovery of some of Calvin's and Knox's prayers), and the particular manner in which the Aronic Blessing and the Lord's Prayer were used would all have been familiar and significant touchstones.

The ratio of Presbyterian, Methodist, and Congregationalist seats assigned to the Union Committee which formed the United Church was 2:2:1, respectively.[57] If this balance was any indication of the relative numbers of the founding constituencies, it would have been reasonable to expect more of an equal balance between the Presbyterian and Methodists liturgical traditions in the orders than was the result. If "ordered liberty" was intended as the operative ethos of the orders, as the preface to *The Book of Common Order* stated, the final emphasis seemed to be more on order than liberty. In fact, it was *The Book of Common Prayer* which figured most significantly in the new orders. This fact no doubt contributed to the book's initial cool reception.

In 1920, the Lambeth Conference called upon all Anglicans to actively support initiatives for union. While this did not directly effect the formation of the United Church, it is clear that the compilers of *The Book of Common Order* were not unconscious of the potential impact that a collection of liturgies sympathetic to the Anglican tradition might have in future union discussions. It was not unreasonable, therefore, for them to anticipate future directions in ecumenical union and liturgical convergence. It is interesting that Davidson spoke little of it. His characterization of the orders as Presbyterian forms with Methodist content was clearly only partially true.

The evidence for Anglican influence in the context of this study is compelling: the dominance of Prayer Book language in the prayers of the orders; the strong influence of the 1928 "proposed" Prayer Book on the structure and content of the forms;[58] the willingness to embrace the concept and form of "confirmation"; even the poorly executed attempt at catholicity with the "short form of the Apostles' Creed"—all overwhelmingly demonstrate Anglican influence in the production of *The Book of Common Order* baptismal rites.[59]

At least one presbytery, in responding to the draft of the orders, was bold enough to address the matter: "We regret that we have the suspicion that in compiling these Orders, the Committee is catering to a communion that has rebuffed our advances toward Union, and hopes to conciliate this Church by pointing out how much of her Orders has been incorporated in The United Church of Canada."[60] This was not the first time the United Church was accused of courting the Anglicans, nor would it be the last. One writer crudely referred to this liturgical trend as "aping the Anglicans."[61]

While Anglican influence on the *BCO* orders cannot be denied and was often cited as a reason for their rejection, the fact remains that there were also many who spoke of their "simplicity and orderly form of procedure,"[62] even praised them for being "most beautiful."[63] Davidson himself had concluded of the work: "It ought to be much better; I am mighty thankful it is not worse."[64] The same "catholic interest"[65] of the compilers which got them into difficulty on a variety of liturgical, theological, and pastoral fronts was also the same characteristic which allowed them to look beyond the immediate traditions of the founding denominations in crafting something of lasting value. By the forties and fifties members of the United Church were ready to embrace the dignified cadences of these orders. They came to be loved by a generation of United Church persons and characterized the language of prayer for its clergy.

As *Forms* had been the first service book *in* the United Church, *The Book of Common Order* had truly become the first service book *of* The United Church—the first attempt at comprehensive liturgical reform, United Church-style. One of the implications of this was that what was at first regarded either as an innovation or a departure came to be viewed as normative for later United Church practice.

Notes

1. E.g., Aidan Kavanagh, "Confirmation: A Suggestion from Structure," *Worship* 58 (1984): 386-395; *Confirmation: Origins and Reform* (New York: Pueblo, 1988); Robert F. Taft, *Beyond East and West: Problems in Liturgical Understanding* (Washington, D.C.: The Pastoral Press, 1984); "The Structural Analysis of Liturgical Units: An Essay in Methodology," *Worship* 52 (1978): 314-329.

2. Davidson, "The Book of Common Order and The Book of Common Prayer," 15.

3. UCA, Davidson, Personal Papers, Box, 14; "Minutes" of 1 May 1928, Vol. 1: 61; 26 January 1932, Vol. 2: 59-64. Davidson's library contains a copy of the *BCP* (1928) text; a signed draft for "Confirmation" by Maxwell in Box 14 cites it.

4. However, the Congregationalist order followed Anglican practice in its inclusion of a postbaptismal signation!

5. *BCO* (1922), 131, is not as confusing as *BCW* (1928), 44-45, 48.

6. Davidson, Personal Papers, "Drafts" in Box 12, Box 14. Unfortunately, many of the drafts are neither numbered nor dated, but earlier ones are conspicuous by their length and marginal notes. One draft, dated February 1932, is the first example of the Order for Reception to Full Communion with the Appendix complete except for sub-headings. Doctrinal and liturgical rubrics also gravitated to the end of liturgies in successive drafts, rather than preceding the orders as in the Prayer Book and many Presbyterian texts. Drafts dated May 20, 1932, show that such editing of the rubrics continued up until the last minute.

7. Davidson, Personal Papers, Box 12, "Returns from Presbyteries."

8. Davidson, Personal Papers, "Draft" signed by Maxwell, Box 14.

9. "Minutes" of 16 April 1931, Vol. 2: 33.

10. *DD* (1922), 335.

11. *Forms* (1926), 41.

12. *BCP* (1918), 331-332.

13. As the commentary has shown, while the preunion Congregationalist and Presbyterian orders often included reference to the Spirit's help in "prevailing against evil," the only invocation of the Spirit was upon the candidate, not the water. E.g., *BCO* (1922), 119-120; *BCW* (1920), 50-51. On the other hand, the Methodist order for infant baptism

included a baptismal epiclesis and the order for adult baptism retained the Prayer Book renunciation. Cf. *BCP* (1662), 769; *DD* (1922), 518, 341. However, none of the baptismal services included in *Forms* contained either a renunciation or blessing of water. *Forms*, 19-32.

14. Davidson, Personal Papers, "Draft" signed by Maxwell, Box 14.

15. "Minutes" of 27 May 1927, Vol. 1: 60.

16. Davidson, Personal Papers, "Draft" dated March 1928, Box 14.

17. Davidson, Personal Papers, "Draft" dated March 1928, Box 14.

18. Davidson, Personal Papers, "Draft" dated 27 April 1928, Box 14. This one contains no renunciation but continues to include the full blessing of the water prayer. Other drafts show that attempts at crafting a renunciation for the orders for adult baptism and confirmation were given up by 1931 and 1932, respectively.

19. UCA, Hugh Matheson, Personal Papers, Correspondence, letter dated 26 September 1928.

20. Davidson, Personal Papers, Correspondence, Box 1, letter dated 27 September 1928.

21. "Minutes" of 16 April, 1931, Vol. 2: 34.

22. Notations in a "Draft" dated 26 January 1932 suggest moving the "Water Prayer" to the Appendix. Richard Davidson, Personal Papers, Box 14.

23. Davidson, Personal Papers, "Draft" dated February 1932, Box 14.

24. Davidson, Personal Papers, Box 12. "Draft of Orders," 5.

25. Davidson, Personal Papers, Box 12, "Returns from Presbyteries."

26. *BCO* (1932), 49-74.

27. The one exception found to this is one by Maxwell, "On Observing the Christian Year," *New Outlook* (28 March 1928): 4, which speaks of the calendar primarily as a help in preaching. Seasons in which themes of dedication and instruction are dominant are noted, but no specific mention is made of any seasonal relation to baptism.

28. "Contents," *The Hymnary*, xii-xiii; "Times and Seasons" refer to the natural year.

29. *The Hymnary*, numbers 217-219 and notes. Hymns for adult baptism and confirmation dealing with themes of decision and discipleship are suggested in the notes.

30. White, *Protestant Worship*, 163-164.

31. "Metropolitan Church: Symbol of Reunion," *New Outlook* (26 February 1930): 198-199.

32. A representative selection of articles from the special "Architecture Number" issues of *The New Outlook* can be found in the bibliography to this study. The UCA collection of the Committee on Church Architecture also provides an interesting study on the subject, though without any consciousness of baptismal space.

33. One exception is notable: Hugh Matheson, "The Interior Arrangement of a Church: Some Applications of the Principles of Public Worship to the Art of Church Building," *New Outlook* (8 February 1928): 7-8. Matheson goes so far as to speak of the font as the place where there are "rich meanings of life given, of incorporation into the beloved community of the Spirit, and with is obligations and commitments, both on behalf of the baptized and the community." Further, it is to be "set in an area of its own" where the "whole body should be able to join in the action." And yet in the floor plans no font is present!

34. "Notes on Some of the Orders," in *BCO* (1932), v.

35. See, for example, *Year Book* (1930), 29.

36. Thomas Buchanan Kilpatrick, *Our Common Faith* (Toronto: The Ryerson Press, 1928).

37. Kilpatrick, *Our Common Faith*, 187, 193-197.

38. John Dow, "Preface," in *This Our Faith*, n.p. An editor called Davidson "one of the most influential thinkers in the Church." "The Purposes of the New United Church Catechism," *Saturday Night* (15 April 1944): 22-23.

39. *Statement of Faith*, Commission on Christian Faith, Board of Evangelism and Social Service (Toronto: The United Church of Canada, 1940); *Catechism*, Commission on Christian Faith, Board of Evangelism and Social Service (Toronto: The United Church of Canada, 1942). See also, "The Purposes of the New United Church Catechism." The article notes that, at the time of writing, over 32,000 copies of *Statement* had been printed and circulated and comments that the *Catechism* contains the "same faith as that of *The Hymnary*, and *The Book of Common Order*."

40. John Dow, *This Is Our Faith: An Exposition of the Statement of Faith of The United Church of Canada* (Toronto: The United Church of Canada, 1943).

41. Davidson, *The Meaning of Baptism*, Board of Evangelism and Social Service (Toronto: The United Church of Canada, 1943).

42. Randolph Carelton Chalmers, *See the Christ Stand! A Study in Doctrine in The United Church of Canada* (Toronto: The Ryerson Press, 1945), 229.

43. *Statement of Faith*, 7.

44. Dow, *This is Our Faith*, 191-192; Davidson, *The Meaning of Baptism*, 16.

45. *Catechism*, 6.

46. Davidson, *The Meaning of Baptism*, 7, 10. 18, 23, 25.

47. Davidson, *The Meaning of Baptism*, 12, 14-18, 26.

48. Davidson, *The Meaning of Baptism*, 24.

49. Davidson, *The Meaning of Baptism*, 26.

50. By this time the Commission was now led by John Line, Davidson having died in 1944.

51. "Foreword," *The Doctrine and Practice of Infant Baptism*, The Commission on the Christian Faith, Board of Evangelism and Social Service (Toronto: The United Church of Canada, 1954), back of cover.

52. *Doctrine and Practice*, 1.

53. Karl Barth, *The Teaching of the Church Regarding Baptism*, trans. E. Payne (London: SCM Press, 1948); Oscar Cullman, *Baptism in the New Testament*, trans. J. K. S. Reid (London: SCM Press, 1950).

54. *Doctrine and Practice*, 6-7.

55. *Doctrine and Practice*, 10-12.

56. While the word is defined simply as "profession of faith" in the document, there is no hesitation in the use of the term. *Doctrine and Practice*, 6, 8-9.

57. Grant, *The Canadian Experience of Church Union*, 60.

58. Note however that there was one unique feature of the 1928 Prayer Book which the compilers did not embrace: The Blessing of the Water. *BP* (1928), 276, 287.

59. Harding has also noted that "the service in *The Book of Common Order* which most closely parallels the *Book of Common Prayer* is The Order for the Ordination of Ministers." "Major Orders," 128.

60. Davidson, Personal Papers, Box 12, "Returns from Presbyteries."

61. Chalmers, *See The Christ Stand!*, 236. However, Chalmers goes on to praise the high quality of *BCO* (1932).

62. Davidson, Personal Papers, Box 12, "Returns from Presbyteries."

63. Davidson, Personal Papers, Box 1, Correspondence, an unidentified letter dated 12 January 1929.

64. Davidson, Personal Papers, Box 14, an undated letter to "Hugh" (Matheson?).

65. *Year Book* (1926), 388.

Part III
Responding to the Contemporary

Chapter 4
Baptism in the *Service Book*

The *Service Book*

If there was ever a "bad time" to produce a new generation of liturgies in the history of the United Church, it was probably the "seething sixties."[1] No one could have predicted the "boom" of the fifties followed by the "ferment" of the sixties—the dynamic of church growth and consolidation followed by the beginning of erosion and fragmentation. With the ground shifting so rapidly under the feet of the Committee on Worship and Ritual, the challenges were considerable. This is the complex context of the production of the successor to *The Book of Common Order*, the *Service Book*. The complexities of the time are reflected in the work itself.

Grant describes the beginning of the postwar period as follows:

> The first sign of an upswing appeared in the Sunday schools, where enrollment doubled and quadrupled as war veterans sought to ensure that their children would inherit the Christian values they had fought to preserve. Then, when ministers suggested that children were likely to take Christianity seriously only if they saw evidence of the parents' interest, young couples took the hint and began to attend church with unaccustomed regularity. They sometimes found sermons difficult to understand, and the next step was enrollment in study groups. Indeed, the range of possible activities seemed to be almost limitless. Women's organizations flourished, men's clubs came alive, and service projects abounded. Many church buildings were rarely out of use during waking hours.[2]

As has been noted already, this large scale turn toward the church permitted the coming of age of the United Church and of *The Book of Common Order*. It was the time of the largest growth of the churches in the twentieth century.[3] Membership in the United and Anglican churches rose by 25 percent. In 1951, the number of "persons under pastoral care" in the United Church broke through the two million mark. By 1960, the official "membership" advanced beyond one million.[4] Over fifteen hundred churches or halls and 600 new manses were built between 1945 and 1965. "Boom still Booms!" proclaimed the *United Church Observer* in April of 1961: "The United Church continued to open a new church, church hall, or manse every other day, including Sundays."[5]

But what such appearances of growth and stability failed to communicate was an erosion taking place beneath the surface. In 1946, 60 percent of Canadian Protestants reported that they had attended church in the last 7 days. By 1956, that number was 43 percent; by 1965, 33 percent. As a percentage of the total population, the mainline Canadian churches were, in fact, declining in numbers.[6]

Consciousness of this erosion became explicit in the sixties. The number of baptisms in the United Church (both children and adults), which had been increasing steadily since 1925, began to drop steadily beginning in 1958. This downward trend was evident in Sunday schools beginning in 1961 and membership by 1965.[7]

The effect of this "decade of ferment,"[8] the sixties, was evident in the worship life of the United Church. Harding has called it "the time of unrest" in United Church worship.[9] Several issues of the *Observer* featured a colorful procession of different kinds of "experimental" worship.[10] An iconoclastic use of poetry, drama, dance, gesture, popular music, and secular symbols characterized the ethos of these events. "Immediacy," "relevance," "creativity," and "celebration" were their bywords. Weeknight meetings and special "happenings" were particular opportunities for their expression. In many congregations the Gestetner machine was embraced as the technological key to liberating worship from the anachronistic constraints of the past. "Chats," "dialogues," "reflections," and "multi-media presentations" replaced many Sunday sermons. "Folk music was invading the choir, psychiatry the pulpit, journalism the text."[11] The medium was meant to be the message in this McLuhanesque foray into "contemporary worship."

When the Committee on Worship and Ritual received its mandate to "restudy and revise" *The Book of Common Order* from the 1958 General Council, its members had no idea that they were in for a decade-long journey through such turbulent times.[12] In 1964, after six years of at least monthly meetings (at least a full day each month) and one year away from the originally expected publication date, the Committee suggested 1968 as a more likely possibility.[13] By 1966, with the sixties "seething" around them, Richard Davidson, Chair of the Committee and son of the guiding force behind *The Book of Common Order*, was expressing "embarrassment" to the General Council about the Committee's "continuing change in its own thinking." "Work, which it thought complete and acceptable several years ago," he acknowledged, "now must be updated."[14] Presbyteries were calling for more "contemporary" services than the drafts they had seen and the Committee was forced to begin considering revisions of their revisions.[15] In 1968, when the "final" version of the *Service Book* was presented to the General Council, a formal request was made for the addition of contemporary alternative versions for the major orders.[16] This work was hastily completed in two months. The arrival of the first bound copy of the finished *Service Book for the use of ministers conducting public worship* was celebrated with enthusiasm and great relief at the April meeting of the Committee in 1969.[17]

By the time the book was published, Davidson must have felt like he was trying to navigate in the eye of a storm. On the one hand, he had led the Committee through to the production of a hard-bound book of orders. On the other hand, he was trying to address the church's desire for experimental worship, "throw-away material for a throw-away age," as he once described it.[18] As the work on the *Service Book* came to an end, they began to address this need by providing experimental liturgies for certain occasions and publishing them in the Committee's *News-Letter.*[19] While the *Service Book* itself was prompting little reaction at all, this work brought "the largest [response] the Committee [had] ever received by mail."[20] It was impossible for the Committee to keep up with the demand. Mimeographed packages were crisscrossing the country and regional committees were being assigned the task of producing original seasonal material.[21] In May of 1969, the "Celebration" project was born to support this demand in experimental worship. Its offices were located in a Toronto church with Davidson as a member of the Advisory Committee and Ron Atkinson its Director.[22] Atkinson traveled the country conducting workshops, seminars, and liturgical "happenings" that often provoked controversy.[23] The work also entailed the publication of related multimedia resources in the "Celebration Catalogue."[24]

After two frenetic years, Atkinson left. The Celebration Project became the Celebration Committee and was placed within the newly formed Division of Mission in Canada and encouraged to work more closely with the Committee on Church Worship.[25] The work of the latter began to diminish in intensity while the Celebration Committee continued to become firmly established within the church structures, especially through the success of its catalogue of worship resources. This was eventually supported with the appointment of John Ambrose as "Special Assistant—Worship" in July of 1973.[26] By 1974, the Celebration Catalogue had become the popular quarterly *Getting It All Together: A Packet for Worship Planners.*[27]

As the seventies drew to a close, the Committee on Church Worship finally completed the last stage of its 1958 mandate to revise *The Book of Common Order* with the publication of the *Service Book for use in Church Courts.*[28] By this time the intensity of "experimental worship" was waning and budgetary pressures were intensifying. The rise of the profile of the ecumenical movement in liturgical renewal provided some of the theoretical foundations on which the Celebration Committee and the Committee on Church Worship could be reconciled and integrated within the Division of Mission in Canada. The new Committee on Liturgy was now poised to take the United Church into the next era of liturgical renewal.[29]

In his report to the 1962 General Council, Davidson outlined the process of their work in compiling the *Service Book*: 1. the possible structure and content of the order in question was studied by the Committee as a whole; 2. work on a first draft was assigned to a subcommittee; 3. drafts were presented to the larger Committee for discussion and critique; 4. further revisions were made by the subcommittee and subsequent presentations and discussion followed as necessary; 5. three copies were mailed to the presbyteries for consideration and response; 6. presbytery responses were considered by a different subcommittee than the one which produced the draft; 7. presbytery responses were discussed by the larger Committee and the final revisions were made. A long list of local and internationally recognized consultants also received drafts of the orders for comment.[30] In addition, it became clear that the passion of the discussion among the presbyteries required that the drafts also be circulated more widely. To this end, copies of the draft orders were published in booklet form and sent to each pastoral charge for trial use and response.[31]

Early efforts were also made to communicate with the church about the work via the *Observer*. However, as with *The Book of Common Order*, either the editors of the magazine, or church members, or both, were not very enthused about the project. Articles on experimental worship seemed to attract much more attention.[32]

The liturgical vision of the Committee is outlined in the introduction to the *Service Book*.[33] Its first lines are more apologetic in tone than the articulation of the concept of "ordered liberty" in *The Book of Common Order*. They no doubt arose out of the context of continuing objections to the use of liturgical forms in the process of drafting and trial use.

> The services in this book are for the guidance and assistance of those leading or sharing in public worship. They are not provided to enforce compliance or uniformity.
>
> In the United Church of Canada there are no prescribed forms of worship, except part of the ordination service. Worship in the United Church of Canada is guided by directories. This means that liberty is given to each minister to use his own words in any prayer. In a directory rubrics refer to structure and content, not language. It is in this context that the use of "shall" and "may" in the rubrics is to be understood. "Shall" indicates not prescription but preference, a recommendation that an act should be done or a type of prayer said. "May" suggests some particular act or prayer but without the preference involved in "shall."
>
> The prayers and scripture readings in the various services and in Section II, Material for Services of Worship, are samples of what may be appropriately used in public worship. Freedom is given to any minister to adapt them to local circumstances or to provide his own.[34]

The introduction goes on to speak of "three general concerns" which "underlie the services in [the] book and have helped to shape them." Moreover, it suggests, "these concerns are not peculiar to The United Church of Canada but are characteristic of liturgical revision in other churches."[35]

The first concern is "the unity of word and sacrament."[36] This is perhaps the most important contribution of the *Service Book* orders. It is evident in the structure of all the major orders insofar as the structure of the Lord's Supper is the preferred model. As will be demonstrated in the commentary and analysis to follow, this finds particular expression (and runs into interesting difficulties) in the orders for baptism. In the case of the orders for public worship, this principle meant that with the *Service Book, Westminster Directory* and Morning Prayer structures were replaced by more eucharistic forms.

The second and third underlying concerns had to do with "worship as action."[37] The intent here was to express the active character of worship, that "worship is something which is done." This was spoken of first with respect to God's action in word and sacrament; second, with respect to the active response of the people; and third, with respect to the kinds of communal participation in the liturgy as a whole. These principles are evident in such features as the "Approach-Word-Response" structure of all the major orders; the unison prayers, litany forms, responses, psalmody; the use of vernacular and contemporary biblical translations (e.g., RSV, NEB); the variety of forms of address to God ("thou" in the "first" version of the major orders, "you" in its "contemporary" counterparts); the dimensions of "social action" implied in the use of commissionings, and the content of the thanksgivings and intercessions. It was for the purposes of this increased level and variety of congregational participation that the *Service Book for the use of the people* was published the same year.[38] It contained "the basic services, a collection of prayers (as in the *Service Book for the use of ministers*) and an arrangement of the prose psalms."[39]

The *Service Book* represents a very significant development in the ethos of United Church worship. No doubt a good deal of this evolution was influenced by the participatory richness of much of the experimental worship being explored at the time. It was theologically supported by the breakdown of the dichotomy between the sacred and the profane, and psychologically reinforced by similar attention to the unity of the mind and the body.[40] While the expression of such emerging concepts in the *Service Book* was conservative, the results did enhance the ecclesiological dimensions of United Church worship. More of the people were actively involved in more of the worship than ever before. Such developments can also be seen as providing the foundation on which continued evolution in the direction of a greater consciousness of symbol and sacrament, gesture and movement were to build. The *Service Book* manifestations were, to be sure, far from holistic and, as will be demonstrated in the case of the baptismal orders, reflected the Reformation proclivity for sacramental minimalism.

A Commentary on the Texts

AN ORDER FOR
THE BAPTISM OF CHILDREN[41]
based on the foregoing outline

The title of the 1965 draft was "The Order for the Ministration of the Sacrament of Baptism to Children." The objections of presbyteries and ministers prompted a return to that of the 1932 *Book of Common Order*.[42]

The order provides a full order of worship based on the First Order for Holy Communion and the Second Directory in *BCO* (1932).[43]

The Approach

The people having assembled, the minister shall call them to worship with sentences appropriate to the season of the Christian Year, or one or both of the following,

The opening rubrics, like those which follow for the prayer of approach, the prayer for grace, and the scripture lessons, are noteworthy in that they reveal a consciousness of the Christian Year.

Thus says the Lord: "Fear not, for I have redeemed you; I have called you by name, you are mine."

Isa. 43.1

If any one is in Christ, he is a new creation; the old has passed away, behold the new has come.

II Corinthians 5.17

The scripture passages reflect the Committee's desire to emphasize "God's initiative" in baptism and the "newness of life" which results.[44] Of course, as the rubric points out, they are optional.

A prayer of approach appropriate to the season of the Christian Year shall be said, or the following,

O Lord, our God, who has commanded the light to shine out of darkness and has called us to praise the and to seek thy grace; accept this our sacrifice of worship; make us to be children of light and of day and heirs of thine eternal inheritance; bestow thy mercy upon us, and grant that we may ever glorify thy holy name; through Jesus Christ our Lord. **Amen.**

This optional prayer is a revision of that found in the "Materials for Services of Worship" section of the *Service Book,*[45] which is, in turn, a revision of a prayer of invocation found in the "Additional Material for Public Worship" section of a Congregationalist source.[46] It is also found in the Canadian *BCP* order for family morning prayer.[47] Its allusions to "light," "children of light," and "heirs of thine eternal inheritance" seemed to make it attractive to the compilers for the purposes of the baptism of children.

A hymn of praise shall be sung.

There is no suggestion that the hymn should be of any particular theme other than praise.

A prayer of confession shall be said by minister and people.

Almighty God,

This prayer would be familiar to many

Father of our Lord Jesus Christ,
Maker of all things,
Judge of all men:
we acknowledge and confess
our manifold sins
which we, from time to time,
have committed
by thought word and deed,
against thy divine majesty.
We do earnestly repent,
and are heartily sorry for these our misdoings.
Have mercy upon us,
have mercy upon us,
most merciful Father.
For thy Son our Lord Jesus Christ's sake forgive us all that is past,
and grant that we may
hereafter serve and please thee
in newness of life
to the honour and glory of thy name;
through Jesus Christ our Lord. Amen.

United Church persons because of its use as one of the two prayers of confession included in *The Hymnary* (No. 771) and in both of the 1932 orders for The Celebration of the Lord's Supper.[48] Interestingly enough, the 1932 structure was not modified to correspond with the other 1969 forms of confession in Lord's Supper and Public Worship (which provide for "private confession" and an Agnus Dei or Kyrie).[49]

Its more distant origins can be traced through the 1662 *BCP* and Cranmer's communion order for 1548 to Bucer and Melanchthon's Latin text for Archbishop Hermann's Consultation.[50] For United Church purposes, it comes to *The Book of Common Order* via the Prayer Book and Wesley.[51] Its use here in baptism is original.

The minister shall give an assurance of pardon.

Hear words of scripture which declare forgiveness of sins.
If we confess our sins, he is faithful and just and will forgive our sins and cleanse us from all unrighteousness.
Therefore I assure you who turn to him in repentance and faith that God forgives you your sins.

Then may be sung a doxology, or a suitable hymn of praise.

The 1965 draft contained the familiar assurance of pardon based on John 3:16, probably inspired by the same 1932 source as the prayer of confession, and perhaps influenced by the Congregationalist rite.[52]

This text, on the other hand, is based on 1 John 1:9, a simplified version of that in the *Service Book* orders for the Lord's Supper. While the introduction makes its scriptural base more explicit than the others, the concluding assurance is more conditional ("I assure you who turn"). The other versions conclude more unconditionally: "I assure you that."[53]

The Word

A prayer for grace appropriate to the season of the Christian Year shall be

There was no "prayer for grace" in the 1965 draft, however the following *said, or the following,*

O God our Father, whose blessed Son of Jesus Christ is the way, the truth and the life; enlighten us by they word, empower us with thy Spirit and strengthen us in the faith into which we have been baptized; through the same Jesus Christ our Lord. **Amen.**

"prayer of supplication" was placed after the assurance of pardon and before the "Word" section:

> O God our Father, whose blessed Son Jesus Christ has been given all authority in heaven and on earth, and who hath commanded us to go forth and make disciples of all nations: Strengthen us in the faith into which we are baptized; fill us with the power of the Spirit; and keep us ever in thy glorious presence; through Jesus Christ our Lord. Amen.[54]

It would appear that the final form is a simplified and less explicitly baptismal version of the draft text.

A lesson from the Old Testament, or from a book of the New Testament other than a gospel, or both, appropriate to the season of Christian Year, shall be read.

A psalm or canticle shall be said or sung, with this conclusion wherever appropriate.

Glory be to the Father,
and to the Son,
and to the Holy Spirit;
as it was in the beginning,
is now, and ever shall be:
world without end. Amen.

A lesson from the gospels, appropriate to the season of the Christian Year, shall be read.

A hymn or anthem shall be sung.

This rubric is consistent with those for Lord's Supper and Public Worship, all of which are based on the tradition of the first order for the Lord's Supper in the *Service Book* and the second directory for Public Worship in *The Book of Common Order*.[55]

The result can be placed in the context of two-fold new emphasis evident in the *Service Book* with respect to scripture: lessons are to be chosen "appropriate to the Christian Year" and a lesson from a gospel is to be heard each week. This is in contrast to the *BCO* which advised any number of readings from one to three, including the possibility of "one Lesson only . . . taken out of the New Testament."[56]

The Gloria Patri is associated with the use of psalms in the First Directory for Public Worship of the *BCO*.[57] The fact that it has become part of the "Word" section of the major *Service Book* orders, surviving the shift to structures based upon the *BCO*'s Second Directory, is testimony to the place it had won in popular piety. In the *Service Book for the use of the people* it is called that "ancient hymn," "with which the Church has traditionally set the Christian seal upon Hebrew spirituality."[58]

A prayer for illumination may be said.

Gracious God, who dost teach and guide thy people by thy holy word: show us thy truth, and reveal anew unto us the greatness of thy love; through Jesus Christ our Lord. **Amen.**

A sermon shall be preached.

The use of this particular prayer for illumination is something of a curiosity, as is their function in the *Service Book* generally. Three observations are in order.

First, no other prayers for illumination appear in any other orders, in spite of several being included in the "Material for Services of Worship."[59]

Second, in their work on the first order for the Lord's Supper, the Committee decided to move such a prayer to the beginning of the "Word" section to become a prayer for grace.[60] This structure was consistently followed in all other orders, with the exception of this Order for the Baptism of Children.

Third, it would seem that the Committee did not notice the fact that, according to their own principles, the change of the prayer of supplication in the 1965 draft to a prayer for grace (as discussed earlier) renders this prayer redundant.

In general, the location and role of this prayer illustrates the functional ambiguities among collects, prayers for grace, and prayers for illumination in the *Service Book* as a whole.

Prayer or an ascription shall follow.

Now unto the God of all grace, who hath called us unto his eternal glory by Christ Jesus, be glory and dominion for ever and ever. **Amen.**

This ascription of glory, based on Peter 5:10, can be found in the "Treasury of Prayers" of *The Book of Common Order* and in many other similar collections.[61]

The banns of marriage may be published and any necessary announce-

ments shall be made.

The Action

The offerings of the people shall be collected and presented, and an offertory prayer said.

The headings of the order and their significance with respect to liturgical structure will be discussed in more detail in the next chapter.

O Lord our God, send down upon us thy Holy Spirit, we pray thee, to cleanse our hearts, to hallow our gifts, and to perfect the offering of ourselves to thee; through Jesus Christ our Lord. **Amen.**

The offertory prayer is a slight revision of that found in the third order for Public Worship of *The Book of Common Order of the Church of Scotland.* The compilers have simply replace "beseech" with "pray," and added "through Jesus Christ our Lord" and a unison "Amen."[62]

A hymn shall be sung, during which the children to be baptized shall be brought forward by their parents (or sponsors) and presented by an elder.

There is no mention of the desire for a baptismal hymn, though it was probably a popular custom.[63] This rubric does, however, constitute the first explicit mention of the role of the elders in a United Church baptismal rite. In this we are probably witnessing a case of liturgical reform catching up with the popular practice.[64]

The minister shall say,

Hear the command of the risen Christ: All authority in heaven and on earth has been given me. Go therefore and make disciples of all nations, baptizing them in the name of the Father and of the Son and of the Holy Spirit, teaching them to observe all that I have commanded you; and lo, I am with you always to the close of the age.
Matthew 28.18-20

Hear also the record of our Lord's concern for children.

They were bringing children to Jesus, that he might touch them; and the disciples rebuked them. But when Jesus

The inclusion of the Matthean text follows the favored sources of the Committee and signals a slight broadening of the scriptural base of the rite beyond the 1932 order's sole reliance on Mark 10.[65]

There was much discussion and revision of the scriptural content of this order, the details and significance of which will be discussed more fully in the chapter to follow. At this point, it is worth noting simply that the 1965 draft contained Mark 1:9-11 (Jesus' baptism by John), Matthew 28:18-20, and Acts 2:28-39 (Peter's call to repentance and baptism at Pentecost). In the end the use of Mark 10 was reinstisaw it he was indignant, and said to them, "Let the children com to me, do not hinder them; for to such belongs the kingdom of God. Truly I say to you, whoever does not receive the kingdom of God like a child shall not enter it." And he took them in his arms and blessed them, laying his hands upon them.

Mark 10.13-16.

tuted and the John the Baptist and Pentecost texts were dropped.[66]

The minister shall say to the parents (or sponsors),

In baptism we celebrate God's love,
a love revealed in the life, death
and resurrection
of our Lord Jesus Christ,
a love which has surrounded
this child from *his* beginning.
In baptism we proclaim that God
has acted to save *him*.
He washes *him* in his cleansing waters
and adopts *him* as a member
of his family,
incorporating *him* into the living
body of Christ.
In baptism we dedicate *him*
to God's purposes,
knowing that even though we may
falter, God will not,
that he will continue,
through his Spirit,
the work begun this day,
a work in which life triumphs
over death.

This "Teaching," as it is called in the "Outline,"[67] also went through a wide range of forms and revisions.

The 1965 draft contained simply the following statement:

> Jesus Christ is the same yesterday, and today, and forever. He loves and seeks this child. He is ready to receive *him* into the family and household of God, and to make *him* an heir of the Kingdom of heaven.[68]

It is clearly drawn from the closing lines of the 1932 Exhortation, functioning along the lines common to Canadian Presbyterian sources.[69]

Later drafts also attempted various versions of the more lengthy and traditional "Beloved in the Lord" statements.[70]

The Committee abandoned both styles when Ron Atkinson offered to attempt something more contemporary, a "poetic statement" using "rhythmic parallelism." His original went as follows:

> We celebrate the love of God in Holy Baptism.
> He invites us to offer and dedicate these children.
> He makes them his own and cherishes them.
> He washes them in his cleansing waters and immerses them in his

New Creation.
He brings them into the communion of His Son for the life together of the Body of Christ.
He pours upon them the gifts of His Holy Spirit and assures them of newness of life.
By his great love, He gives them victory of life over death and liberates them from darkness to light.
We celebrate with thanksgiving the love of God and renew our fellowship in the household of faith
where love is at work, from beginning to end.[71]

The theological and liturgical significance of these developments will be discussed in more detail below.

I ask therefore, do you present this child, earnestly desiring that by holy baptism he be made a member of the church of Christ?

Answer.
I do.

This is a revision of the opening question of the 1932 order: "Do you present this child, earnestly desiring that *he* be received by Holy Baptism into the fellowship of the Church of Christ?"[72]

With this, some of the language of Knox is carried forward, though the traditional location has been shifted from its place in the introduction to association with the promises and profession of faith.

The people shall rise and the minister shall say,

Beloved in the Lord, do you receive this child in Christ's name as we have been received, promising to support him with constant love, wholesome example, Christian teaching and faithful prayer? Are you willing to accept so great a responsibility?

Answer.
We are willing, God being our helper.

In the 1965 draft this was in the form of an exhortation directed toward the people, modeled on the "Duties of the People" of the 1932 order.[73] The interrogative form makes the congregation's role more explicit, as does the action of standing. The phrases "support . . . with constant love, wholesome example . . . and faithful prayer" are from the 1932 Exhortation.[74] While its relocation to this position before baptism recovers something of its origins in Knox, its form as a congregational vow is reminiscent of the Baptism of the Infants in the Church of South India.[75]

Then may the Apostles' Creed be said by all.

The rubric in the 1965 draft read "The Apostles' Creed shall be said by all" and was introduced with the words: "Let us profess the faith of the Church as it is declared in the Apostles' Creed."[76] Its preferred or optional status, its location before or after the vows, and the role of creeds in general was a subject of much discussion within the Committee.[77]

It is worth recalling that a so-called short form of the Apostles' Creed was placed in the appendix of the 1932 order.[78] In the end, the Committee's desire to recover some of the historic and liturgical significance of this baptismal symbol is undermined by the final form of the rubric and the absence of the text itself.

The minister shall say to the parents (or sponsors).

I ask you before God and his congregation, do you profess your faith in God your heavenly Father, in Jesus Christ your Saviour and Lord, and in the Holy Spirit your Teacher and Guide?

Answer.
I do.

The congregation's profession of faith leads to that of the parents, followed by promises. This is a synthesis of Scottish, Canadian, and South Indian questions.[79] The parental profession of faith replaces "confess" with "profess" and "Holy Spirit as your Sanctifier" with "Holy Spirit your Teacher and Guide." The answer in the 1965 draft was "I do so confess."[80]

Will you bring up your child in the knowledge and love of God, teaching him the truths and duties of the Christian faith?

Answer.
I will, God being my helper.

Though the first promise of the draft order shows some influence from the South Indian rite,[81] the final version turns more directly toward the Canadian Presbyterian source:

Do you promise in dependence on

> divine grace, to teach him the truths and duties of the Christian Faith; and by prayer, precept and example, to bring him up in the knowledge and love of Christ and of His Church?[82]

Will you make a Christian home for him, so fashioning your lives that he may come to know Christ as his Lord and Saviour?

Answer.
I will, God being my helper.

The second is a combination of the first two South Indian promises, which read:

> Will you, by God's help, provide a Christian home for this child and bring *him* up in the worship and teaching of the Church, that *he* may come to know Christ *his* saviour?
> Will you do so order your own lives that you do not cause this little one to stumble?[83]

Will you encourage him to seek confirmation, so that being strengthened in faith by the Holy Spirit and nurtured at the Table of the Lord, he may go forth to serve God faithfully in the world?

Answer.
I will, God being my helper.

The third promise is also a revision of the corresponding South Indian text:

> Will you encourage *him* later to be received into the full fellowship of the Church by Confirmation; so that, established in faith by the Holy Spirit, he may partake of the Lord's Supper and go forth into the world to serve God faithfully in his Church?[84]

With this (third) question we encounter the first use of the term "confirmation" in the body of an authorized United Church liturgy.[85]

Note also that the *Service Book* answers to the promises are influenced by those of the South Indian rite, which uses "We will, God being our helper," in contrast to the Presbyterian "I do."[86]

The people shall be seated and the minister shall say,

Almighty and eternal God, whose beloved Son our Lord Jesus Christ has bidden us made disciples of all nations baptizing them in thy name: sanctify

This prayer of invocation was created with phrases drawn from its parallel prayers in *The Book of Common Order*. The opening lines are inspired by with thy Spirit, we pray thee, this child now to be baptized according to thy word; through Jesus Christ our Lord. **Amen.**

the "Appendix" prayers, with the closing lines taken from their counterparts (the "Grant, O Lord" prayer before baptism).[87]

It is interesting to note that the 1965 draft presented a very different prayer in this location, a revision of the traditional Scottish Presbyterian epiclesis, with a reference to Jesus' blessing of the children added (since the Mark 10 text was not used elsewhere).[88] However, popular objections to the petitions "Bless this water for use in thy Holy Sacrament" were strong. The compilers were finally forced to resort to the 1932-style prayer of invocation of the Spirit upon the child only. In so doing they continued the problematic implication of a separation between the action of the Spirit from the action of baptism itself. Such developments raise interesting issues of baptismal epiclesis and regeneration to which I will return below.

The minister (taking the child in his arms, or leaving him in the arms of one of the parents or sponsors), shall say,

The procedure here is the same as that of *The Book of Common Order.*[89]

What is the name of this child?

Having named him, he shall sprinkle water on the head of the child, saying,

N. *Christian names*, I baptize you in the name of the Father, and of the Son, and of the Holy Spirit. **Amen.**

"Pour" and "dip" have been dropped from both the 1932 and 1965 draft rubric. "Sprinkle" reflects the dominant United Church practice.[90]

After those presented for baptism have been baptized the minister shall say,

In the name of the Lord Jesus Christ, the King and head of the Church, I declare that *N. Christian names and surname* has now been received into

This departure from the well-known *Book of Common Order* declaration, "We receive this child into the congregation of Christ's flock,"[91] is inspired the holy catholic church.

by the both Congregationalist and Presbyterian sources. A Congregationalist source reads, in part: "M.N., in the name of the Lord Jesus Christ, I declare that you have been received into membership of the Church by baptism."[92] The Church of Scotland text begins: "According to Christ's commandment this child is now received into the membership of the holy Catholic Church."[93] The strength of this declaration causes one to suspect apologetic motives, perhaps in relation to the context of Anglican-United dialogue.

And the following shall be said or sung.

The Lord bless you and keep you: the Lord makes his face to shine upon you, and be gracious unto you: the Lord lift up his countenance upon you, and give you peace. **Amen.**

Again, as in the 1932 order, the Aaronic blessing closes the action of baptism.[94] The option to sing is supported by the popular "Hebrew Benediction" found at No. 762 in *The Hymnary.*

The Response

In the 1965 draft the remainder of the service was contained under the third and final heading "The Action."[95] The use of "The Response" here is yet another sign of the Committee's struggles with the liturgical structure of the rite. As we shall see, the rubrics appended to the close of this order draw even more attention to such problems.

Prayers of thanksgiving and intercession shall follow.

All glory be unto thee, O Lord our heavenly Father, for the creation of the world, for the gift of life, for making man in thine own image and for thy love for all thy children.

All blessing be unto thee for sending

The development of the prayers of thanksgiving and intercession is an interesting study in the Committee's attempts to appropriate historic liturgical forms.

Originally the thanksgivings were distinct from the intercessions, the latter being located after the sermon and before the baptism.[96]

The first drafts of the thanksgivings

thy Son Jesus Christ to redeem us from sin and death and to open to us the gate of life eternal.

All praise be unto thee for giving the Holy Spirit and for his work in thy Church and the world to revive, uphold and guide us.

All thanksgiving be unto thee, O God, Father, Son and Holy Spirit, for this sacrament by which thou has received *this child* into the family and household of faith, making *him* thine own. **Amen.**

experimented with the form of a litany. Soon the Committee turned to the berakah form, complete with Sursum Corda and the familiar Prayer Book and *BCO* preface: "It is very meet, right, and our bounden duty, that we should at all times, and in all places, give thanks unto thee."[97]

Presbytery comments on this prayer were reported as "evenly divided," however a survey of the actual responses from both ministers and presbyteries shows this to be rather optimistic characterization.[98] At the very least, they were almost unanimous in their opinion that the order as a whole was "too long and formal" and this prayer in particular was "ornate" and "pretentious," appropriate perhaps to the context of the Lord's Supper, but not the "simplicity" of baptism.[99]

For some time after this critique the Committee experimented with a return to a litany form.[100] Eventually, the congregational responses were dropped and the four sections were combined for a single voice. Nevertheless, the berakah origins of this prayer linger on in the final version: "All glory be unto thee. . . ." "All blessing be unto thee. . . ." "All praise be unto thee. . . ." "All glory be unto thee. . . ."

In retrospect, one is reminded of the draft attempts in the 1932 texts to use the berakah form for the blessing of the water. These too met with a similar fate. This classic liturgical form will wait until the eighties before it will be reappropriated in baptism.

Remember, O God, *this child*, that as he grows in knowledge of thy truth *he* may be led to acknowledge Jesus Christ as Lord and Saviour.

Remember, O God, the parents of *this*

The prayers of intercession began not only in a different location but also in a different form.

Early drafts attempted various forms of litanies. The Committee soon settled on a form based on a version of the *child* that they may be strengthened to keep the promises they have made and so to live that *their child* shall see in them what it means to follow Christ.

Remember, O God, all those who have not yet given themselves to Christ, that they may come to confess their faith and know the joy of salvation.

Other prayers of intercession may be said.

litany of St. John Chrysostom taken from *The Book of Common Order.*[101] In the 1965 draft the text called for "silence" after each petition, followed by "Lord, hear our prayer," with the people responding "And in thy mercy answer." The response to the final petition even included the Chrysostom-like response "Help, save, pity and defend us, O God, by thy grace."[102]

The same criticisms of the berakah form of the thanksgiving were leveled at the litany form. In particular, as late as March of 1968, the Executive of General Council charged that the service as a whole was much too long and this prayer was singled out as playing a part in the problem.[103] With little time left before going to press, the litany form, its traditional content, and its location in the liturgy were all abandoned. The responses were dropped, the intercessions were joined to the thanksgivings, and this new prayer was written.[104]

Then the minister and people shall say,

Our Father, grant that we who have been baptized may be true to thee to our life's end. In thy great mercy unite us at the last with all thy children in the joy and glory of thine eternal kingdom. And to thee, Father, Son and Holy Spirit, be all blessing, praise and thanksgiving for ever and ever. Amen.

This unison prayer appears to be an original composition inspired by the spirit of similar prayers in other orders. Several phrases are reminiscent of the Presbyterian and Congregationalist versions which pray for the life-long faithfulness of all the baptized and their unity in God's kingdom.[105]

The Lord's Prayer shall be said by minister and people

Our Father, who art in heaven,
hallowed be thy name,
thy kingdom come,

The Lord's Prayer concludes the prayers, as in the 1932 order and the contemporary Presbyterian orders.[106]

thy will be done,
on earth as it is in heaven.
Give us this day our daily bread,
and forgive us our trespasses
as we forgive those who
trespass against us,
and lead us not into temptation
but deliver us from evil.
For thine is the kingdom,
the power and the glory,
for ever and ever. Amen.

The United Church propensity to lay-out unison prayers in boldface sense lines is evident throughout the *Service Book* and is applied even to the familiar text of the Lord's Prayer (though, curiously, not the preceding prayer!). Indeed, it was the *Service Book* which began and effectively institutionalized this practice in the United Church.

A hymn shall be sung.

The minister shall dismiss the people with a blessing.

The grace of the Lord Jesus Christ, and the love of God, and the fellowship of the Holy Spirit, be with you all. **Amen.**

Following the hymn, the Grace closes the service, the Aaronic blessing having been used following the baptism itself.

The sacrament of baptism will normally be administered in the presence of the congregation, following the order set out above. If special circumstances require a shorter order, it is recommended that the order begin with a suitable approach, followed by the segment of the above order beginning,

> *"A hymn shall be sung, during which the children to be baptized shall be brought forward by their parents (or sponsors) and presented by an elder."*

and ending with the blessing of the child.

> "The Lord bless you and keep you: the Lord make his face to shine upon you, and be gracious unto you: the Lord lift up his countenance upon you, and give you peace. **Amen.**"

These rubrics emphasize the expectation that the full order will be used in the context of congregational worship. They do not elaborate on the conditions which constitute "special circumstances." One suspects that it is a concession to criticisms regarding the service's length.

One must assume that "extreme urgency" (such as "clinical baptism") is not intended by "special circumstances" since it is spoken of separately. In any case, the rubric effectively undermines the very goals that the provision of a full order sought to achieve.

The service shall conclude with prayers of thanksgiving and intercession, the Lord's Prayer and a blessing.

In the case of extreme urgency, it will be sufficient to name the child, sprinkling or pouring water on his head and saying,

N. *Christian names,* I baptism you in the name of the Father, and of the Son and of the Holy Spirit. **Amen.**

If the sacrament of the Lord's Supper is to be celebrated the dedication of the offering should be transferred from the place given in the above service, the following order being observed:

> *after the blessing of the child a hymn shall be sung, the bread and wine prepared, an offertory prayer said and the minister shall proceed in the order for the celebration of the Lord's supper. The prayers of intercession shall be said after all have communicated.*

It is desirable that a short order for the celebration of the Lord's supper be used.

The barriers to achieving a truly full sacramental rite with this particular order become more pronounced when an attempt is made to celebrate the Lord's Supper. Here the structural complications militate against a liturgical celebration of both sacraments. The implications of this will be discussed in more detail in the analysis which follows a similar examination of the other baptismal orders in the *Service Book.*

ANOTHER ORDER FOR
THE BAPTISM OF CHILDREN[107]
based on the foregoing outline

Upon presentation of the "final" draft of major orders of the *Service Book* to the 1968 General Council, an amendment to the motion of acceptance was passed requesting that "contemporary" versions of the orders for Baptism, Confirmation, Marriage, and Burial also be included.[108] With so little time left before publication, the Committee chose not to attempt a comprehensive drafting process, settling for a revision based on the previous order. Thus, unlike the previous order which took over eight years to produce, this order was developed in six months. Its first draft was left largely intact.[109]

The Scripture Sentences, Prayer of Approach, Prayer for Grace, and Lessons, should be appropriate to the season of the Christian Year.

The rubrics call again (this time in summary form) for a consciousness of the Christian Year.

The Approach

Scripture Sentences

God's promise was made to you and your children, and to all who are far away—all whom the Lord our God calls to himself.

Acts 2.39

When anyone is joined to Christ he is a new being: the old is gone, the new has come.

2 Cor. 5.17

Isaiah 43:1 in the first order is replaced by Acts 2:39, making covenant theology as it applies to children more explicit. The Corinthians passage is retained. The translation for both is "Today's English Version" rather than the Revised Standard Version.[110]

Prayer of Approach

As on a first day you began the work
of creating us;
as on a first day you raised your
Son from the dead;
so on this first day, good Lord,
freshen and remake us:
and as the week is new, let our
lives begin again
because of Jesus who shows us
your loving power.
Amen.

The Prayer of Approach is one of the "Opening Prayers" for "general use" in the Congregationalist collection, *Contemporary Prayers.*[111] Following the Corinthians passage, the metaphor of "newness" dominates the opening.

Hymn of Praise

Prayer of Confession

Father, we have sinned
in many ways.
We have not loved you with
all our hearts.

This prayer is also strongly influenced by the language of the confessions included in the Congregationalist collection. In particular, note the opening

We have not loved one another as we should.
Sometimes we have let pride rule us,
sometimes anger;
sometimes our sin
has been carelessness;
sometimes resentment, or
impatience, or greed.
Forgive us.
We need your love.

lines of one prayer:

> God our Father,
> We have sinned against you
> In thought, word and deed:
> We have not loved you with all our heart;
> We have not loved our neighbour as ourselves.[112]

The modern "sometimes" language together with the naming of "pride," "anger," and "resentment" are found in other prayers of the same collection.[113]

Assurance of Pardon

Here is good news:
Christ Jesus came that we might
have life, life in all its fullness:
to forgive us in our failures,
to accept us as we are,
to set us free from evil's power,
to make us what we were meant to be.

Doxology or Hymn of Praise

Again, the source is the Congregationalist collection. Compare this Assurance of Pardon with:

> Listen—
> Here is good news:
> "Christ Jesus came into the world to save sinners"
> —to forgive you in your failure
> —to accept you as you are
> —to set you free from evil's power
> and make you what you were meant to be.[114]

The New English Bible quotation from 1 Timothy 1:15 has been replaced with a Today's English Version quotation from John 10:10 and the pronoun "you" has been changed to "we." The latter is evidence of the discussions in the Committee about the "priestly" role in worship in reference to contemporary worship.[115]

The Word

Prayer for Grace

Father, in the gospel of Jesus Christ you have assured us that we and our children are yours. Give us the will to

The "Prayer for Grace" appears to be an original composition, but is influenced by the style of some of the

accept this heritage and the courage to grasp it; through Jesus Christ our Lord.
Amen.

"Supplications" in *Contemporary Prayers.*[116]

Lessons (from the Old Testament, or an Epistle, or both)
Psalm (with "Glory be to the Father")
Gospel
Hymn or Anthem
Sermon
Banns and Announcements

As evident throughout the order, the rubrics have been simplified and abbreviated to the point of titles. In addition, some of the features of the pervious order have been omitted: the provision "or Canticle" with the Psalm; the anomalous "Prayer for Illumination" before the sermon; the "prayer or ascription" following the sermon.

The Action

Offertory

God, you have given us life and its many resources. You have entrusted them to us to use wisely and unselfishly. Accept our gifts, and accept us; in Jesus' name we ask. Amen.

Hymn (during which the child to be baptized is brought forward by his parents (or sponsor) and presented by an elder.) The elder says:

I present to you Mr. and Mrs. N. M. (or these parents) whose *child is* to be baptized.

The Offertory prayer also appears to be an original composition of the Committee, again clearly influenced by the style of some of those found in *Contemporary Prayers.*[117]

Unlike in the previous order, or in the contemporary sources, words of presentation are here provided for the elder. More significant is the fact that in this order the presentation follows immediately after the Offertory and Hymn, while in the previous order it occurs after the exhortation and before the questions. No reason for the change is recorded in the minutes.[118]

Statement (optional)

After his resurrection Jesus said to his disciples: I have been given all authority in heaven and on earth. Go, then, to all peoples everywhere and make them my disciples; baptize them in the name of the Father and of the Son and of the Holy Spirit, and teach them to obey everything I have commanded you.

Note that in this order the Statement has become "optional."

In spite of an early attempt at a revision based on the statement in the previous order,[119] this text follows closely that provided in the "Order for Baptism" in *Contemporary Prayers.*[120] Among the changes worth noting are: the sole scriptural warrant has been rendered in Today's English version;

And remember! I will be with you always, to the end of the age.

Matthew 28.18-20

When people became Christian in the early church, they were baptized as Jesus had been; that is they went down under the water and came up again. This meant that they were dying to their old way of life and being born into a new life. Jesus made this possible by his own death and resurrection.

Although, in our tradition, people are seldom baptized by going down under the water, the meaning is the same. Baptism stands for the new life God gives us through Jesus. It proclaims that God has made us members of his family.

Since a child cannot understand what is being done, his parents and the church act on his behalf. The parents promise to bring him up in the Christian faith. We, the church, promise to help them. It is our hope and prayer that when he is old enough to understand, he will speak for himself and choose to be confirmed as one of Christ's people.

the historically dubious phrase "as Jesus had been" has been inserted; "and rising again to a new way of life" has been changed to "and being born into a new life;" "It declares that God gives us the Holy Spirit as the guarantee of eternal life" has been deleted from after "It proclaims that God has made us members of his family."

Note also that an earlier draft had rendered the last line in the above paragraph: "It proclaims that God has adopted us as his children." Some Committee members argued that "adoption" was not "our theology of baptism" and that it undermined the notion of prevenient grace. A vote on leaving the reference to adoption in passed by only two votes. Further discussion produced "made us members of his family" as a compromise.[121]

In particular, a comparison of the final paragraph with the original text proves interesting:

> But since a little child cannot understand this at the time, *his* parents and the Church must promise to bring him up in the Christian faith, so that he has every opportunity to confirm and complete his baptism by choosing for himself to follow Christ to serve him as a member of his Church.[122]

Again, as in the first order, the specific reference to confirmation in the exhortation is a United Church first.

While some improvements have been made in the United Church version of this exhortation, the text remains thoroughly didactic, in keeping with the first lines of the original: "We are now going to administer the sacrament of baptism to. . . . What does this mean?"[123] In this sense, the concerns noted at the time by John Webster Grant are justified:

> It is a pity that we can only produce a mirror or shadow of someone else's work. Even though devised by a small committee of English Congregationalists, this is too much individual Micklem [*Contemporary Prayers*] for me. However, I have consistently preferred no statement, believing that the service should explain itself.[124]

Questions and Promises

(to the parents) Mr. And Mrs. N.M., you have brought your *son* here for baptism. Do you believe in God and his love?

Yes, we do.

The simplification of the questions is evident, though the first sentence repeats the sentiments of the presentation which was moved to before the exhortation. The result is a combination of the question of intent ("do you present . . ., earnestly desiring") and the question on profession of faith. Intent is assumed with "you have brought." The profession of faith in the previous order dealt explicitly with all three persons of the Trinity.[125] Here it is expanded into three separate questions.

Do you believe that God has made himself known to men in Jesus of Nazareth, who lived and died and lives again?

Yes, we do.

Do you believe that God by his Spirit is active in the world to direct and strengthen you?

Yes, we do.

For the second question, the Committee rejected "Are you trying to be followers of Jesus?" One member called it "pretty thin," arguing further that "Baptism is always a place for strong doctrinal statements. There should be a question regarding belief here."[126]

The result, however, is that while the second and third questions may be more substantial, the first remains "pretty thin" by comparison. The final editing of all the questions was done in conjunction with those for the second (contemporary) Order for Adult Baptism and Confirmation.[127]

Will you do your best to provide a Christian home for your *child*, and will

This question was produced by combining the opening phrases of the third you encourage *him* to seek confirmation?

and fourth questions in the previous order. Again references to "confirmation" are introduced. The answers to all these questions omit the phrase "God being our helper."

(the congregation stands)

Do you, the members of this church, receive *this child* and promise to help in the Christian training of all children under your care?

Yes, we do.

The question to the congregation in this order follows, rather than precedes, those to the parents of sponsors, In addition, nowhere is the use of the Apostles' Creed suggested.

The particular wording of this question is influenced somewhat by *Contemporary Prayers*: "Do you, the members of this church, promise to play your part in the Christian upbringing of this child?" However, the changes both broaden and narrow the scope of its counterpart in the previous *Service Book* order. It broadens it to include "all children" under the congregation's care; it narrows it to "Christian training."[128]

Let us pray in silence for the gifts of God's Spirit.

The prayer for the Spirit has been simplified to the point of silent prayer. There is a precedent for a specific invitation to silent prayer in the South Indian rite.[129]

Baptism (minister takes the child in his arms).

(to the parents)
What is the name of this child?
N. *Christian names*

N. *Christian names*, I baptize you in the name of the Father, and of the Son, and of the Holy Spirit.
Amen.

Some simplification is also evident in the act of baptism itself: there is no mention of the provision for leaving the child in the arms of the parents, nor is any particular mode of baptism mentioned.[130]

Declaration and Blessing

N. *Christian names and surname* has been received into the Christian church. May God bless you and keep you and give you peace.

The declaration and blessing is a combined simplification of those of the previous order. "In the name of the Lord Jesus Christ" and reference to the "holy Catholic church" have been omitted. The blessing is loosely based on the Aaronic blessing.[131]

The Response

Prayer of Thanksgiving

God of our fathers
and of our children,
with joy we praise you,
we thank you,
we honour you.
For your love which has made us
and supports us,
we praise you.
For your gift of life embodied in
these children,
we thank you.
For this sacrament
by which they are received
into your family,
we honour you.
God of our fathers
and of our children,
with joy we praise you,
we thank you,
we honour you for ever.

While the minutes suggest that the prayer of thanksgiving is influenced by some of the ideas in the prayer after baptism in *Contemporary Prayers*, it also seems stylistically inspired by one of the Opening Prayers for use "when children are present" in the same source. In particular, the use of "we praise you, we worship you, we thank you" is noteworthy.[132]

The opening and closing phrase "God of our fathers and of our children" is somewhat reminiscent of the 1932 orders' use of Calvin and Knox.[133]

Prayer of Intercession

Father, keep *this child* in your truth as he grows in mind and body. Keep these parents in your love as they guide *their child* in the truth. Keep us also that we may be faithful to you.

In keeping with the final structural revisions of the first order, the Prayers of Thanksgiving and Intercession are combined. The text is simple and original.[134]

Other Intercessions

Lord's Prayer

Our Father in heaven,

The Committee was inspired by an

holy be your name,
your kingdom come,
your will be done,
on earth as in heaven.
Give us today our daily bread.
Forgive us our sins
as we forgive those who
sin against us.
Save us in the time of trial,
and deliver us from evil.
For yours is the kingdom,
and the power,
and the glory forever. Amen.

"Appendix" of translations and paraphrases of the Lord's Prayer in *Contemporary Prayers* to include a version from the Consultation on Church Union in this order.[135]

Hymn

Blessing

The grace of the Lord Jesus Christ, and the love of God, and fellowship in the Holy Spirit, be with you all. **Amen.**

The order closes, as in the first order, with a hymn and a blessing, though the extended rubrics have been omitted.[136]

AN ORDER FOR
ADULT BAPTISM
AND CONFIRMATION[137]
based on the foregoing outline

Until after the 1966 draft, the title was "The Order for Confirmation with Provision for the Baptism of Persons Able to Answer for Themselves."[138] The Committee again heeded the advice of others that the indefinite article "An" was more appropriate "because we have no mandatory orders in the United Church."[139]

The reversal of the title, placing "adult baptism" before "confirmation," is ironic given that it would be used more for the latter than the former. The implications of this will be discussed in the next chapter.

Again, as with the orders for the baptism of children, the structural innovation is that of providing a full order of worship. Furthermore, this order also provides one service for both adult baptism with confirmation and/or the confirmation of those baptized in infancy. While other contemporary orders either separated these rites altogether or brought them together in different combinations, one can detect a trend in some Presbyterian rites toward integration.[140] The United Church order builds on this trend, effectively combining the two 1932 orders for adult baptism and Confirmation.[141]

The Approach

The candidates for confirmation being in the front pews, the minister shall call the people to worship with sentences appropriate to the season of the Christian Year or one or more of the following.

The rubrics provide guidance for the logistics of presentation to follow later. Otherwise, they duplicate those in the Order for the Baptism of Children.

They who wait for the Lord shall renew their strength, they shall mount up with wings like eagles, they shall run and not be weary, they shall walk and not faint.

Isaiah 40.31

The scripture sentences are different from those for the Baptism of Children. The minutes of the Committee do not record any particular reasons for the choice.

Wait for the Lord; be strong, and let your heart take courage; yea, wait for the Lord.

Psalm 27.14

The hour is coming, and now is, when the true worshippers will worship the Father in spirit and truth, for such the Father seeks to worship him.

John 4.23

A prayer of approach appropriate to the season of the Christian Year, or the following shall be said,

Almighty and most gracious God, from whom comes every good and perfect gift: help us so to ask that we may receive, so to seek that we may

The optional prayer of approach opens with an address and relative clause from a Prayer Book collect.[142] To this is added the familiar petition based on

find, so to knock that the door of thy mercy may be opened to us; through Jesus Christ our Lord.
Amen.

Matthew 7:7-8. This petition is common to the opening prayer in the 1932 Order for the Baptism of Children and the Prayer Book's rites.

> And, as thou has promised in thy Holy Word, saying, Ask, and ye shall have; seek, and ye shall find; knock, and it shall be opened unto you: So give now unto us that ask, let us that seek find; open the gate unto us that knock.; . . . through Jesus Christ our Lord. Amen.[143]

A hymn of praise shall be sung.

A prayer of general confession shall then be said by minister and people.

O God,
Father, Son, and Holy Spirit,
we confess to thee and to all the
company of heaven
and to one another
that we have sinned in thought,
word and deed, and by omission,
through our fault,
our own grievous fault.

Then the minister shall call the people to make their private confession of sin, saying,

Let each of us in silence humbly confess his sins to almighty God.

After a period of silence the following may be sung or said,

O Lamb of God, who takest away
the sin of the world;
have mercy upon us;
O Lamb of God, who takest away
the sin of the world;
have mercy upon us;
O Lamb of god, who takest away
the sin of the world;

The structure and content of confession follows that established for the first Order for the Celebration of the Lord's Supper.[144] Initially, the structure in the drafts of both the Lord's Supper and adult baptism and confirmation was reversed, with the call to private confession at the beginning, followed by the Kyrie eleison, the unison prayer of general confession, the Agnus Dei, and the assurance of pardon.[145] The decision was made because of the perception that general confession could more effectively prepare the congregation for the silence of private confession. In addition, the Kyrie eleison was omitted, no doubt influenced by the criticism from some presbyteries objecting to the use of too many traditional liturgical forms.[146]

The unison prayer is based on the alternative Confession in the second 1932 order for the Lord's Supper (which is based, in turn, on the *Confiteor* of the Roman Mass).[147] A musical setting for the Agnus Dei is included at No. 757 in *The Hymnary.*

grant us thy peace.

The minister shall give an assurance of pardon.

Hear the good news and rejoice: God so loved the world that he gave his only Son, that whoever believes in him should not perish, but have eternal life. Therefore I assure you who turn to him in repentance and faith that God forgives you your sins.

The assurance of pardon, based on John 3:16, is a combination of scripture taken from the 1965 draft order for the Baptism of Children and the last sentence from the final version.[148]

In the 1966 draft of this order the assurance was introduced with the words "Our Saviour Christ said."[149]

A doxology or suitable hymn of praise may be sung.

The Word

A prayer for grace appropriate to the season of the Christian Year, or the following, shall be said,

Almighty and ever blessed God, who has given thy word to be a lamp unto our feet and a light unto our path: pour out upon us thy Holy Spirit that with humble and receptive hearts we may learn what thou wouldst have us do, and fashion our lives in obedience to thy holy will; through Jesus Christ our Lord. **Amen.**

While the relative clause of this prayer ("who hast given") is closest to a Scottish Presbyterian source,[150] the remainder of the prayer owes more to the following Congregationalist source:

> O Lord God, who has left unto us thy holy Word to be a lamp unto our feet and a light unto our path; give unto us all thy Holy Spirit, we humbly pray thee, that out of the same Word we may learn what is thy blessed will, and frame our lives in all holy obedience to be the same, to thine honour and glory and the increase of our faith: through Jesus Christ our Lord. Amen.[151]

A lesson from the Old Testament, or from a book of the New Testament other than a gospel, or from both, appropriate to the season of the Christian Year, shall be read.

And one of the following psalms shall be sung or said,
Psalm 27; Psalm 63; Psalm 119.33-40.

It is interesting to note that particular psalms are suggested only in this order, though no reason for this depar-

After the psalm shall be sung or said,

Glory be to the Father,
and to the Son,
and to the Holy Spirit;
as it was in the beginning
is now, and ever shall be:
world without end. Amen.

A lesson from one of the gospels appropriate to the season of the Christian Year shall be read.

A hymn shall be sung.

A sermon shall be preached.

A prayer or an ascription shall follow.

Now to him who by the power at work within us is able to do far more abundantly than all we ask or think, to him be glory in the Church and in Christ Jesus to all generations, for ever and ever.
Amen.

Banns of marriage may be published and such announcements as are needful and fitting shall be made.

The Action

*If there are no candidates for baptism the paragraphs marked * shall be omitted.*

A hymn shall be sung.

The minister shall say,

*Hear the record of the baptism of our Lord Jesus Christ and of the descent of

ture is recorded in the minutes of the Committee.

The absence of a prayer for illumination before the sermon (as in the Order for the Baptism of Children) is a return to the structure of the other orders.[152]

The optional ascription is the RSV text of Ephesians 3:20. It is included in the "materials for Services of Worship" section of the *Service Book*, the AV of it having been included in the 1932 "Treasury of Prayers."[153]

Like the Order for the Baptism of Children, the headings of the various structural components of the liturgy have undergone various changes, the details and significance of which shall be discussed in the following chapter.

All of the scripture passages are from the RSV.

the Holy Spirit upon him.

In those days Jesus came from Nazareth of Galilee and was baptized by John in the Jordan. And when he came up out of the water, immediately he saw the heavens opened and the Spirit descending upon him like a dove; and a voice came from heaven, "Thou art my beloved Son; with thee I am well pleased."

Mark 1.9-11.

The use of the passage on Jesus' baptism for adult baptism is an innovation for United Church orders, one especially noteworthy given that it is not included in any sources used by the Committee.[154] The introduction to the reading suggests the Committee's desire to unify baptism and confirmation in the case of adults and emphasize the gift of the Spirit in this baptism.

*Hear the command of the risen Christ.

Jesus came and said to them, "All authority in heaven and on earth has been given to me. Go therefore and make disciples of all nations, baptizing them in the name of the Father and of the Son and of the Holy Spirit, teaching them to observe all that I have commanded you; and lo, I am with you always, to the close of the age."

Matthew 28.18-20

The use of the Matthean text follows both the Order for the Baptism of Children and some of the sources.[155]

Hear the record of our risen Lord's give of the Holy Spirit to his disciples.

Jesus said them again, "Peace be with you. As the Father has sent me, even so I send you." And when he had said this, he breathed on them, and said to them "Receive the Holy Spirit."

John 20.21,22

The passages to be read for confirmation (i.e., those not marked *) clearly set the stage for a pneumatological interpretation. The use of the passage from John is novel when compared with the Committee's sources.[156]

Hear the record of the gift of the Holy Spirit to the church at Samaria.

Now when the apostles at Jerusalem heard that Samaria had received the word of God, they sent to them Peter and John, who came down and prayed for them that they might receive the Holy Spirit; for it had not yet fallen on

Acts 8 is used in the Canadian Prayer Book.[157]

any of them but they had only been baptized in the name of the Lord Jesus. Then they laid their hands of them and they received the Holy Spirit.

Acts 8.14-17

The minister shall say to the people.

By baptism we are made members of the church of Jesus Christ and are adopted into the family and household of God.

When those who have been baptized as children have grown up and have been taught the essentials of Christian faith and duty they come before the church to own for themselves the covenant of their baptism. In this act they confess Jesus Christ openly as Saviour and Lord, that they may be confirmed by the Holy Spirit and welcomed to the Lord's Table.

*These same blessing of confirmation are also conferred upon those who not having been baptized as children do now confess Jesus Christ as Saviour and Lord and are through baptism received into his church.

The statement is a revision of the 1932 "Beloved in the Lord" statement for Reception to Full Communion.[158]

The use of the term "adoption" in the opening line is inconsistent with the explicit decision to delete it from the contemporary Order for the Baptism of Children.[159]

The closing line of the second paragraph goes so far as to identify the Holy Spirit as the agent of confirmation. Moreover, the third paragraph, in speaking of the "blessings of confirmation" effectively relinquishes the classic Reformation position on confirmation vis-à-vis baptism. The Reformers would contend that all these blessings are proper to baptism. Thus, the United Church version of confirmation has taken on a distinctive pneumatic character.

The people may stand and say the Apostles' Creed.

The candidates shall remain seated.

In this order there is no promise on the part of the people to support the candidates, even though it was given greater attention in the order for children.[160]

The option for the use of the Creed applies to the people only, reminiscent of the Canadian Presbyterian order.[161] Furthermore, the Creed has been placed before the presentation and questions in this order rather than as a climax to the questions (as in the first Order for the Baptism of Children).

Then, the people standing, the clerk of session shall call the candidates by

The role of clerk of session is again brought out in the presentation of the *name (Christian name and surname). They shall rise and the minister shall say to them,*

candidates.

I ask you before God and this congregation,

Do you profess your faith in God your heavenly Father, in Jesus Christ your Saviour and Lord, and in the Holy Spirit your Teacher and Guide?

Again, as in the Order for the Baptism of Children, the first question is based on that of Scottish and Canadian Presbyterian rites.[162]

Answer.
I do.

Will you be faithful in joining with the Lord's people in the worship of God, in studying the Bible and in prayer?

Answer.
I will, God being my helper.

This question is based on two from the South Indian rite: "Do you promise to join with your fellow Christians in worship on the Lord's Day, and especially in the Lord's supper?" and "Do you promise to be faithful in reading or hearing the Bible, and in prayer?"[163] The omission of any reference to the Lord's Supper undermines the initiatory significance of the rite.

Will you enter into the life and work of the church, supporting it with your gifts and sharing in it mission to all men?

Answer.
I will, God being my helper.

The next two questions are original compositions of the Committee inspired by some of the nearby sources. For example, the 1966 draft of this question on the "life and work of the church" shows the influence of the 1932 question on the "peace and welfare" of the church.[164]

Will you endeavour daily to respond to God's love, to do his will, and to fulfill your Christian calling and ministry in the world?

Answer.
I will, God being my helper.

Similarly, the draft of the following question shows the influence of both the 1932 order and some Presbyterian sources.[165]

Then the hymn Come, Holy Ghost, our souls inspire *or* O Holy Spirit, by whose breath *may be sung.*

The operative pneumatic presuppositions of rite are further reinforced by the suggestion of these particular hymns, as if to suggest confirmation was the ordination of the laity.

The people shall be seated but the candidates shall remain standing. The minister shall say,

Let us pray in silence that God in his loving kindness may pour out his Holy Spirit upon these his servants.

Here silence shall be kept for a space, after which the minister shall say,

For the same reasons already discussed elsewhere, early drafts of a prayer blessing the water were eventually dropped.[166] The use of silence and the associated rubrics show the influence of the South Indian rites.[167]

Almighty and everlasting God, who of thine infinite mercy and goodness didst give Jesus Christ thy Son to be our Saviour; we pray thee to sanctify with thy Spirit thy servants who are to be (*baptized and) confirmed according to they word; through the same Jesus Christ our Lord. **Amen.**

This prayer is a revision of the prayer after the vows in the 1932 order for adult baptism, which read, in part: "We beseech thee, O Lord, . . . sanctify with thy Spirit, these persons (*or* this thy servant) now to be baptized according to they Word."[168]

*The clerk of session shall summon by name each candidate for (*baptism and) confirmation.*

**A candidate to be baptized shall kneel at the font, and the minister shall sprinkle or pour water on his head, saying,*

*N. *Christian names*, I baptize you in the name of the Father, and of the Son, and of the Holy Spirit. **Amen.**

In the first Order for the Baptism of Children, the rubric mentioned only "sprinkle" as the mode of baptism, while here "sprinkle or pour" is suggested.[169]

**After baptism the minister shall say,*

*In the name of the Lord Jesus Christ, the King and Head of the Church, I declare that N. Christian names and surname is now received into the holy catholic church.

The declaration is the same Congregationalist and Presbyterian-inspired text as found in the first Order for the Baptism of Children.[170]

The candidate kneeling, the minister shall lay hands upon his head and say,

In the 1932 order the rubric was less directive, suggesting that the minister only lay on hands "if such be his discretion."[171] It seems that sensitivity to the Congregationalist objections to confirmation were no longer an issue.

The minutes record a particularly revealing discussion regarding the question of whether the laity should be involved in the laying on of hands. One member of the Committee suggested that, even though the United Church does not hold to a strict "mechanical" view of apostolic succession, there was a value in laity being involved here in order to express the "continuity of the Church" through the priesthood of all believers. Another countered that "ordination of the laity does not mean ordination *by* the laity." At least some members thought confirmation was indeed "ordination of the laity."

In the end, it was concern over ecumenical relations that settled the argument about who should lay on hands. As one member put it, "We are at the point where we do not want to make conversation with the Anglicans more difficult." The resolution was "to leave the laying on of hands by the minister only, but to attempt greater lay participation in the service."[172] Again, as in *The Book of Common Order* rites, the possibility of union with the Anglicans was influencing the work of the Committee.

Confirm, O Lord, this thy servant by the Holy Spirit that he may continue thine forever.

The people and the candidate shall say,

Amen.

The candidate shall rise and remain standing.

The actual prayer of confirmation used in this order is a departure from classic Prayer Book text, as found in the 1932 order.[173] The explicit use of the word "confirm" is noteworthy. As will be seen below, it is translated as "strengthen" in the second Order for Adult Baptism.

After each candidate has been confirmed the minister shall say to him,

Go into the world in the power of the Holy Spirit to fulfill your high calling as a servant and soldier of Jesus Christ.

And the clerk of session shall extend the right hand of fellowship.

Considerable discussion took place in the Committee regarding the use of the word "soldier." In light of the comments of presbyteries in 1965, the word was dropped. A month later it was back in. Three months later, the sole woman on the Committee objected to it on the grounds that it was a "very masculine term" and suggested that the word "ambassador" replace it. The response of the Committee is tersely noted: "The Committee felt that it was a bit late to reopen this issue which had been pretty well discussed."[174] It is interesting to recall that "soldier" was deleted from the declaration in the 1932 Order for the Baptism of Children.[175] Here we have an interesting precursor to the many discussions to come on inclusive and militaristic language.

After all the candidates have been confirmed they shall say together with the minister,

Teach us, good Lord, to serve thee as thou deservest; to give and not to count the cost; to fight and not to heed the wounds; to toil and not to seek for rest; to labour and not to ask for any reward, save that of knowing that we do thy will; through the same Jesus Christ our Lord. **Amen.**

The use of this prayer, based on the Prayer of St. Ignatius of Loyola, is an innovation not found in any of the sources.

The candidates shall return to their places in the congregation.

The Response

The offerings of the people shall be collected.

The offering has been moved from its position at the beginning of "The Action" in the baptism of children.[176]

The offerings shall be presented and an offertory prayer shall be said.

O Lord God, Ruler of all things and Father of all men, accept, we pray, the offerings of thy people. Consecrate them by thy Spirit for the spread of thy gospel, and grant us willing hearts and ready hands to use all thy gifts to thy glory; through Jesus Christ our Lord. **Amen.**

The offertory prayer is not found in any of the immediate sources, though some turns of phrase are reminiscent of prayers found in the Congregationalist *Book of Public Worship.*[177]

Prayers of thanksgiving and intercession shall follow.

O Lord our God, all glory be unto thee for making us in thine own image and calling us to be stewards of thy good gifts.

The prayers of thanksgiving are essentially those written for the first Order for the Baptism of Children.[178]

All blessing be unto thee for sending thy Son Jesus Christ to redeem us from sin and death, and to open to us the gate of life eternal.

All thanksgiving be unto thee for giving the Holy Spirit and for his work in thy church and world to revive, uphold and guide us.

All praise and honour be unto thee, O god, Father Son and Holy Spirit, for ever and ever.
Amen.

Let us pray for the peace of the whole world, for the extension of God's kingdom and for the salvation of all men. *Silence.* Lord, hear our prayer:

The intercessions use the Chrysostom-based prayer originally composed for use in the first Order for the Baptism of Children.[179] Neither criticisms regarding the length of the prayer or objections to the use of historic forms made any difference in this case.

People.
And in thy love answer.

Minister.
Let us pray for the well-being of the churches of God and for the unity of

them all, that they may fulfill their mission in the world. *Silence.* Lord, hear our prayer:

People.
And in thy love answer.

Minister.
Let us pray for ministers of word and sacrament, for missionaries, for elders and teachers, and for all who bear office in the church, that they may be faithful to the work committed to them. *Silence.* Lord, hear our prayer:

People.
And in thy love answer.

Minister.
Let us pray for all who profess the name of Christ, and especially for those who this day have confessed him as Saviour and Lord, that they may be kept in the way of salvation. *Silence.* Lord, hear our prayer:

People.
And in thy love answer.

Minister.
Let us pray for the lonely and the troubled, for the sick and the sorrowful, and for those to whom death draws near, that they may be comforted. *Silence.* Lord, hear our prayer:

People.
And in thy love answer.

Minister.
Remembering what thy love has accomplished in thy saints, and thy faithfulness to those who have gone before us into thy presence, we commend ourselves and one another, and all our life, to Christ our Lord.

People.
Help, save and strengthen us,
O God, by thy grace.
Amen.

The Lord's Prayer shall be said by minister and people.

The use of the Lord's Prayer at this point follows the pattern of the first Order for the Baptism of Children.[180]

Our Father, who art in heaven,
hallowed be thy name,
thy kingdom come,
thy will be done,
on earth as it is in heaven.
Give us this day our daily bread,
and forgive us our trespasses
as we forgive those who trespass against us,
and lead us not into temptation,
but deliver us from evil.
For thine is the kingdom, the power and the glory,
for ever and ever. Amen.

A hymn shall be sung.

The minister shall dismiss the people with a blessing.

The Lord bless and keep you: the Lord make his face to shine upon you, and be gracious to you: the Lord lift up his countenance upon you, and give you peace. And the grace of the Lord Jesus Christ and love of God and the fellowship of the Holy Spirit be with you all.
Amen.

The Aaronic blessing has been moved from its more traditional location following the declaration and combined with the Grace for a double (?) benediction.[181]

If the sacrament of the Lord's supper is to be celebrated, in place of THE RESPONSE shall be inserted THE WORD OF GOD ENACTED from an order for the celebration of the Lord's supper. Prayers of intercession shall be included in the post-communion prayers.

The closing rubrics again raise structural questions which warrant a fuller discussion below. At this point, it is worth noting that the rubric concerning those "received by transfer or certificate" places this action with the announcements at the close of "The Word" and thus before and separated

If there are any to be received by transfer or certificate this may be done after the announcements have been made.

from "The Action" of baptism and/or confirmation. In any case, it is a little late in the order to discover what could have happened long before.

ANOTHER ORDER FOR
ADULT BAPTISM
AND CONFIRMATION[182]
based on the foregoing outline

The production of this "contemporary" order was mandated in conjunction with that for the baptism of children, and produced by the same hasty process. Thus, it is both a revision of the previous Order for Adult Baptism and Confirmation and follows closely the same sources and style as the second (contemporary) Order for the Baptism of Children.

The Scripture Sentences, Prayer of Approach, Prayer for Grace, and Lessons, should be appropriate to the season of the Christian Year.

The rubrics throughout the order are simplified and abbreviated along the same lines as the second Order for the Baptism of Children.[183]

The Approach

Scripture Sentence

Since Jesus was delivered to you as Christ and Lord, live your lives in union with him. Be rooted in him; be built in him; be consolidated in the faith you were taught; let your hearts overflow with thankfulness.
Colossians 2.6,7

This New English Version of the Colossians text replaces the three texts from the Revised Standard Version in the first order for Adult Baptism and Confirmation.[184]

Prayer of Approach

How generous you are, God.
You give good gifts to men.
Give us freedom to ask;
give us openness to receive;
may our search for fullness of life
be satisfied,
through Jesus Christ our Lord. **Amen.**

The Prayer of Approach is a contemporary revision of the prayer in the first order.[185]

Hymn of Praise

Confession

We confess we have not
been honest with you, God
we have not been honest with each other.
We think, speak and act in ways that deny love:
we put self first;
we speak to hurt;
we turn our back on need.
Forgive us.

The Confession is a further revision of that of the contemporary Order for the Baptism of Children.[186] The result is more a confession of dishonesty than sin.

The Agnus Dei (which followed the silence itself in the first order) has been dropped, while the silence itself has been retained. There was no silent confession in either of the orders for the baptism of children (perhaps out of fear of noisy children?).[187]

(Silent Confession)

Assurance of Pardon

God loved the world so much that he gave his only Son, that everyone who has faith in him may not die but have eternal life. Trust him, and you shall have new life.
Thanks be to God.

The Assurance of Pardon renders John 3:16 in the New English Version and has replaced "Therefore I assure you who turn" with "Trust him."[188]

The Word

Prayer for Grace

O living Word,
in a world of many voices you
define what is important,
Give us insight to know what to do;
give us strength to do it. **Amen.**

This Prayer for Grace is an original composition of the Committee. It is unusual for a liturgical prayer in that it is addressed to the second person of the Trinity.[189]

Lessons from the Old Testament,
(or an Epistle, or both)
Psalm (the "Glory be to the Father")
Gospel
Hymn or Anthem
Sermon
Banns and Announcements

The abbreviated rubrics follow the practice established for the second Order for the Baptism of Children. Again, the provision "or Canticle" with the Psalm and the "prayer or an ascription" following the sermon have been omitted.[190] In addition, the specific psalms suggested in the first Order for Adult Baptism and Confirmation have been deleted.[191]

Action

"The Action" follows the structure and

*(If there are no candidates for baptism omit the paragraphs marked *.)*

Hymn

Scripture Record and Teaching

content of the first order. The only changes involve those to the introductory sentences and the use of Today's English Version of the texts.[192]

*This is what the Gospel says of Jesus' own baptism:

Jesus came from Nazareth, in the region of Galilee, and John baptized him in the Jordan. As soon as Jesus came up out of the water he saw heaven opening and the Spirit came down on him like a dove. And a voice came from heaven; "you are my own dear Son, I am well pleased with you."

Mark 1.9-11

Compare the following corresponding introductions from the first order: Hear the record of the baptism of our Lord Jesus Christ and of the descent of the Holy Spirit upon him;

*After his resurrection Jesus said to his disciples:

I have been given all authority in heaven on earth. Go, then, to all peoples everywhere and make them my disciples; baptize them in the name of the Father and of the Son and of the Holy Spirit, and teach them to obey everything I have commanded you. And remember! I will be with you always, to the end of the age.

Matthew 28.18-20

Hear the command of the risen Christ;

When Jesus gave the Holy Spirit to his disciples, after the resurrection, he said to them:
Peace be with you. As the Father sent me, so I send you. He said this, and then he breathed on them and said, Receive the Holy Spirit.

John 20.22

Hear the record of our risen Lord's gift of the Holy Spirit to his disciples;[193]

In Acts we have an account of the gift of the Holy Spirit to the church at Samaria:

Hear the record of the gift of the Holy Spirit to the church at Samaria.

The apostles in Jerusalem heard that the people of Samaria had received the word of God; so they sent Peter and John to them. When they arrived, they prayed for the believers that they might receive the Holy Spirit. For the Holy Spirit had not yet come down on any of them; they had only been baptized in the name of the Lord Jesus. Then Peter and John placed their hands on them, and they received the Holy Spirit.

Acts 8.14-17

(The minister may say to the people)

In baptism we celebrate a new beginning. We are received into the Church. In Christ God says 'Yes' to use.

In confirmation we respond with 'Yes' to God, and we proclaim that God alone makes the difference to human life.

In confirmation we are strengthened by the Holy Spirit; we are welcomed to Christ's table; and we are commissioned to serve in the world.

The content of the "Teaching," as it is called in the outline,[194] is very loosely based on the statement in the previous order. Compare, for example, the first paragraph with: "By baptism we are made members of the church of Jesus Christ and are adopted into the family and household of God."[195]

The more direct influence, however, is on a stylistic level. The structure and style is modeled on the Teaching in the first Order for the Baptism of Children. Compare, for example, the opening phrases of each paragraph with: "In baptism we celebrate," "In baptism we proclaim," and "In baptism we dedicate."[196]

A Creed (optional)

This reference to "A" Creed is noteworthy, given that all other references in the baptismal liturgies have been to the Apostles' Creed. It is also interesting in light of the fact that the use of any creed was omitted from the second Order for the Baptism of Children. This is the first intentional permission for the use of other baptismal symbols. This is a direct result of the Committee's discussions with the Committee on Christian Faith regarding the use of creeds in general, the Apostles' Creed in particular and the so-called A New Creed.[197]

An elder presents the candidates. He says

I present to you N. *Christian names and surnames* for *baptism and confirmation.

As in the second Order for the Baptism of Children, specific words of presentation are provided.[198] Curiously, however, in this case the presentation is given to any "elder," whereas in the first Order for Adult Baptism and Confirmation it was the "clerk of session."[199] No reason is given for the change.

Questions and Promises (to the candidates)

Do you believe in God and in his love?

Yes, I do.

The first three questions, each dealing with one person of the Trinity, are the same as those in the second Order for the Baptism of Children.[200]

Do you believe that God has made himself known to men in Jesus of Nazareth, who lived and died and lives again?

Yes, I do.

Do you believe that God by his Spirit is active in the world to direct and strengthen you?

Yes, I do.

Do you commit yourself to God, Father, Son, and Spirit to be his for ever?

Yes, I do.

This question on commitment is somewhat redundant given those which precede and follow it.

Will you meet regularly to celebrate his presence and discern his truth?

The fifth question is a contemporary (and weaker) wording of the second question in the previous order: "Will

Yes, I will.

you be faithful in joining with the Lord's people in the worship of God, in studying the Bible and in prayer?"[201]

Will you act responsibly in your private and public life?
Yes, I will.

Similarly, this rewording is based on a corresponding question in the previous order: "Will you endeavour daily to respond to God's love, to do his will, and to fulfill your Christian calling and ministry in the world?"[202]

Will you take an active part in Christ's service to all men?

Yes, I will.

The final one is based on the question: "Will you enter into the life and work of the church, supporting it with your gifts and sharing in its mission to all men?"[203]

Three observations on the questions as a whole are noteworthy: first, the function of the fourth question is, as already mentioned, unclear; second, it is also unclear why the order of the final two questions has been reversed from that of the previous order; third, subsequently, the number of questions seems unnecessary (there are seven questions in this order rather than four as in the other orders.[204])

Let us pray in silence for the gifts of God's Spirit.

No hymn for the Spirit is suggested in this order, and the use of silent prayer follows the pattern in the second Order for the Baptism of Children.[205]

**Baptism (candidate kneeling)*

N. *Christian names* I baptize you in the name of the Father, and of the Son, and of the Holy Spirit. **Amen.**

The rubric in the first order, in which the clerk of the session "summons by name each candidate" and the minister baptizes by sprinkling or pouring, has been omitted.[206]

**Declaration*

N. *Christian names and surname* has been received into the Christian Church.

The Declaration is a simplification of that in the previous order, along the lines of the second Order for the Baptism of Children.[207]

Laying on of Hands

By the gift of your Spirit, God, strengthen N. ***Christian names*** that he may be true to you all his life.

The rubrics around the act of Confirmation have been omitted (i.e., "The candidate kneeling," the "Amen," "The candidate shall rise," etc.).

"Strengthen" has replaced "confirm" in the confirmation prayer. Compare with: "Confirm, O Lord, this thy servant *N.*__ by the Holy Spirit that *he* may continue thine forever."[208]

Commissioning

Go into the world in the power of the Spirit. Pursue justice, faith, love, fortitude and humility. For to this you were called.

1 Timothy 6.11-12

Contrary to the biblical citation, it is only the second line which is based on the Timothy passage. The closest translation is the New English Version: "pursue justice, piety, fidelity, love, fortitude, and gentleness. . . . For to this you were called." The first sentence is from the Commissioning in the previous order and was added upon suggestion that the passage was too introspective on its own.[209]

(*The candidates shall say in unison*)

Help me, Lord, to accept my calling and to live my faith in every part of life.

This simple unison prayer is based on the corresponding prayer in the previous order. The content is greatly reduced and the "Amen" omitted.[210]

The Response

Offertory Prayer

We bring our gifts to you, O God.
Here is the labour of our hands.
Here is the love our hearts.
Accept them and use them;
through Christ our Lord.
Amen.

This Offertory Prayer is a contemporary version of one found in the "Material for Services of Worship" of the *Service Book*: "Unto thee, O Lord, do we offer the gift of our hands and the loyalty of our hearts. Accept us with our gifts, we pray, in Jesus' name. Amen."[211] This is reminiscent of some traditional Presbyterian prayers.[212]

Prayer of Thanksgiving

God of the heavens and the Earth,
with joy we praise you,
we thank you, we honour You.

Because you have made us
like yourself,
made us to be creative in your world,
we praise you.

Because you have given Jesus
to set us free,
given us courage to be,
we thank you.

Because your Spirit is
present with us,
present to guide and renew,
we honour you.

God of the heavens and the earth,
with joy we praise you,
we thank you, we honour
you for ever.

The Prayer of Thanksgiving combines the style of that of the second Order for the Baptism of Children with the content of that of the first Order for Adult Baptism and Confirmation. Its opening lines bear some resemblance to its berakah roots, in particular the beginning of the eucharistic prayer in the first Order for the Celebration of the Lord's Supper.[213]

Stylistically, the use and repetition of "we praise you," "we thank you," "we honour you," is effective, as is the trinitarian content and structure.[214]

(Prayers of intercession including a prayer for those who have been confirmed and concluding with a remembrance of the dead shall be said.)

The rubrics invite intercessions, in keeping with the previous order.

Lord's Prayer

Our Father in heaven:
holy be your name,
your kingdom come,
your will be done,
on earth as in heaven.
Give us today our daily bread.
Forgive us our sins
as we forgive those who
sin against us.
Save us in time of trial,
and deliver us from evil.
For yours is the kingdom,
and the power,
and the glory forever. Amen.

As with the second Order for the Baptism of Children, the version of the Lord's Prayer is the Consultation on Church Union text.[215]

Hymn

Blessing

The grace of the Lord Jesus Christ, and the love of God, and fellowship of the Holy Spirit, be with you all. **Amen.**

The service closes in the same manner as both orders for the Baptism of Children, rather than with both the Grace and the Aaronic Blessing, as in the previous order.[216]

Notes

1. Grant, *The Church in the Canadian Era*, 203. See also John G. Stackhouse, "The Protestant Experience in Canada Since 1945," in *The Canadian Protestant Experience*, 198-252.

2. Grant, 160-161.

3. Grant, 161; Stackhouse, 200-201.

4. *Year Book* (1993), 156.

5. "Boom Still Booms!" *Observer* (15 April 1962): 7.

6. Stackhouse, 206, 209.

7. *Year Book*, 156-157.

8. Grant, 184-204.

9. Harding, "The Development and Liturgical Resources," 234-270.

10. E.g., *Observer* articles: Francis Stevens, "In Plain English," (15 April 1962): 18, 22; Anonymous, "'Let's God!' Whatever May Be Said of the Christian Church—We Are on the Move" (1 January 1967): 9, 29; Harvey Shepherd, "Faith on the Free, Frantic Campus," (15 November 1967): 12-15; Clarke W. MacDonald, "Sunday 11:00 a.m. What's It All About?" (1 September 1969): 24-25; Patricia Clarke, "Is Anybody Here Celebrating?" (1 October 1969): 6; Barbara Bagnell, "Would You Call This Worship?" (April 1971): 14-17.

11. Stackhouse, 211.

12. *ROP* (1958), 90, 119. Among the members of the Committee were Richard H. N. Davidson (Chair), G. Campbell Wadsworth (Secretary), Ron Atkinson, Harriet Christie, John Webster Grant, D. S. Henderson, G. D. Kilpatrick, W. Morrison Kelly, Stanley Osborne, R. G. Oliver. The work was divided among subcommittees in Hamilton, Kingston, Montreal, St. Thomas-London, Toronto. UCA, Committee on Church Worship and Ritual Records, Revision of the Book of Common Order. For the purposes of this study, note especially: Box 6, Vol. 208; Box 8, Vols. 9-10; Box 9, Vols. 12-14. For the "Minutes" referred to in this part of the study, see Box 6, Vol. 3, Section 2 and Vol. 4, Sections 2-3.

13. Cf. *ROP* (1962), 560; *ROP* (1964), 437.

14. *ROP* (1966), 552.

15. "Minutes" of 25 September 1967: 1-3; 18 December 1967: 1.

16. "Minutes" of 23 September 1968: 2. By this time, the name of the Committee had been changed to The Committee on Church Worship. Significantly, "Ritual" had been dropped. The change was requested in 1965 but it was 1968 before the Sub-Executive of General Council acted on the request. See also "Minutes" of 27 April 1965: 3.

17. "Minutes" of 28 April 1969: 2.

18. *ROP* (1966), 552.

19. "News-Letter," November 69: 4.

20. *ROP* (1972), 274.

21. "Minutes" of 20 March 1972: 2; 25 September 1972: 1; 6-8 June 1973: 2.

22. Atkinson, an active proponent of experimental worship, was director of the University of Toronto International Students' Centre and served on the Committee. See Harding, "The Development of Liturgical Resources," 251-256.

23. E.g., Bagnell, "Would You Call This Worship?" 14-17.

24. *Catalogue of Resources, Celebration: A Centre of Contemporary Worship* (Toronto, 1969-1974); *Celebrate . . . what's happening*, Celebration Advisory/Resource Committee (Toronto: The United Church of Canada, 1976-1978). See also UCA, Records of the Celebration Advisory/Resource Committee.

25. *ROP* (1971), 364; *ROP* (1972), 274.

26. *ROP* (1971), 68; See the *Observer* article on Ambrose's work: Patricia Clarke, "Lift up your hearts," *Observer* (May 1975), 13. Cf. Harding, "The Development of Liturgical Resources," 260-264.

27. *Getting It All Together: A Packet for Worship Planners*, The Celebration Centre, The Committee on Worship, The Division of Mission in Canada (Toronto: The United Church of Canada, 1974-1983).

28. *Service Book for use in Church Courts* (Toronto: The United Church Publishing House, 1977).

29. Harding, "The Development of Liturgical Resources," 264-267.

30. *ROP* (1962), 560.

31. This allowed the Committee to examine publication design and layout. This was particularly important given the change in style of the texts in comparison with those of *The Book of Common Order*. As will be evident in the commentaries to follow, the *Service Book* used boldface type and sense line design in many unison prayers and responses.

32. An exception was Committee member, D. S. Henderson's article: "New Service of Baptism," *Observer* (1 February 1966), 29. Se also "Minutes" of 28 October 1963: 2; 15-16 June 1964: 6-7.

33. *SB* (1969), unnumbered pp. 3-5.

34. *SB* (1969), unnumbered p. 3.

35. *SB* (1969), unnumbered p. 3.

36. *SB* (1969), unnumbered p. 3.

37. *SB* (1969), unnumbered p. 4.

38. *Service Book for the use of the people*, The Committee on Worship, The United Church of Canada (Toronto: The Ryerson Press, 1969).

39. *Service Book for the use of the people*, unnumbered p. 5.

40. Grant identifies the thought of a variety of theologians as particularly influential at this time. Among them: Dietrich Bonhoeffer and his "religionless" Christianity; Harvey Cox and his "celebration of the secular city"; A. N. Whitehead's "process " philosophy; Paul Tillich's view of God as "the ground of all being"; Tielhard de Chardin's "evolutionary theology"; John Robinson's reconstructive theology after the "death of God." Grant, *The Church in the Canadian Era*, 198-199.

41. *SB* (1969), 39-48.

42. *The Order for the Ministration of the Sacrament of Baptism to the Children*, Draft, Lent 1965 (Toronto: The United Church of Canada, 1965), 7. [*MSBC* (1965)]. This draft was circulated to all ministers of The United Church for "trial use" in the hope of "further helpful observations and useful opinions" (p. 1). With respect to its title, many argued that the use of the indefinite article "an" rather than the definite article "the" was more in keeping with the liberal liturgical ethos of the United Church ("Minutes" of 2

February 24, 1964: 2-4). The only contemporary use of the term *ministration* was in the Canadian Prayer Book. See *The Book of Common Prayer and administration of the rites and ceremonies of the Church according to the use of The Anglican Church of Canada* (Toronto: Anglican Book Centre, 1969), 522.

43. *BCO* (1932), 9-12, 75-83. These orders became the governing structure of all the major *SB* (1969) rites. This will be discussed further in the following chapter under structural considerations.

44. "Many Christians have tended to think of the Church primarily as a human organization, dependent on the activity of those who voluntarily joined it. Today, we place more emphasis on God's initiative in calling men and women into his Church. . . . This change has led many Churches to re-think their concept of Baptism and to revise their services accordingly. . . .Baptism is the sacrament by which, dying and rising again with Christ into newness of life, one becomes a member of the covenant community which is the Church." *MSBC* (1965), 1-2.

45. Cf. *SB* (1969), 39 and 98.

46. John Huxtable, John Marsh, Romilly Micklem, and James Todd, *A Book of Public Worship; compiled for the Use of Congregationalists.* 2nd ed. (London: Oxford University Press, 1949), 85. [*BPW* (1949)].

47. *BCP* (1962), 729.

48. *Hymnary*, 820; *BC0* (1932), 75, 91. Because the third "Order for the Celebration of the Lord's Supper" in the *Service Book* is based on the *BCO* (1932) orders, the prayer can be found there as well. *SB* (1969), 25-26.

49. Cf. *SB* (1969), 3-4, 14-15, 78.

50. *BCP* (1552), 681, 683; *BCP* (1662), 681, 683.

51. *SS*, 128; *BCP* (1962), 77.

52. The assurance of pardon in the draft order was: "Now let us be comforted and be glad, and hear the good tidings of the Gospel: God so loved the world that he gave his only Son, that whoever believes in him should not perish but have eternal life." Cf. *MSBC* (1965), 8; *BCO* (1932), 77; *BPW* (1949), 94.

53. Cf. *SB* 1969), 40, 4, 15, which use the RSV in the first and then the NEB in the third. The NEB is used often where there is "an attempt to express the thought and language of the first order in a colloquial idiom." *SB* (1969), 1.

54. *MSBC* (1965), 8.

55. Cf. *SB* (1969), 4-5, 16, 79, with *BCO* (1932), 9, 76.

56. *BCO* (1932), 1. Cf. *BCO* (1932), 76 and 9. A common United Church practice was simply two readings, one from each of the Old and New Testaments.

57. *BCO* (1969), 1-8.

58. *Service Book for the use of the people* (1969), 46.

59. *SB* (1969), 131-133.

60. "Minutes" of 23 September 1963: 4.

61. *BCO* (1932), 46; *The Book of Common Order of the Church of Scotland*, The Committee on Public Worship and Aids to Devotion (London: Oxford University Press, 1940), 308 [*BCO* (1940)]; *The Book of Common Worship* (Philadelphia: The Board of Christian Education of the Presbyterian Church in the United States of America, 1946), 347 [*BCW* (1946)]; *BPW* (1949), 147; *The Book of Common Order of the Presbyterian Church in Canada* (Toronto: Presbyterian Publications, 1964), 320 [*BCO* (1964)].

62. *BCO* (1940), 28.

63. As noted in the discussion of the *Hymnary* in part 2, there were few baptismal hymns to choose from.

64. There is no mention of elders in *BCO* (1932), 97, 104.

65. The Matthew 28 text is also used in: *BCO* (1940), 90; *BPW* (1949), 159; *The Book of Common Worship*, The Church of South India (London: Oxford University Press, 1962), 114 [*BCW* (1962)]; *BCO* (1964), 80; Anthony Coates, John Gregory, Caryl Micklem (eds.), William Sewell, David Stapleton, Roger Tomes, and Brian Wren, *Contemporary Prayers for Public Worship* (London: SCM Press), 94.

66. *MSBC* (1965), 10-11

67. *SB* (1969), 38.

68. *MSBC* (1965), 11.

69. Cf. *BCO* (1932), 98. Note also some similarities with *BCO* (1964), 81. As discussed earlier, its *BCO* (1932) roots owe much to the *BCO* (1922) and the *BCP* (1928).

70. A collection of drafts can be found in UCA, Box 9, Vol. 12, Section 6-8 ["Draft" dated. . . .]. "Draft" dated 26 February 1967 and 24 April 1967 show that three versions were under consideration.

71. Atkinson first submitted this version to Davidson in a letter in May of 1967. By January of the following year it had been revised by the Committee to its final form. See Box 9, Vol. 12, Section 6, letter dated 24 May 1967; "Minutes" of 24 May 1967: 2; 26-27 June 1967: 6-7; 23 October 1967: 2.

72. *BCO* (1932), 97.

73. Cf. *MSBC* (1965), 11, and *BCO* (1932), 101.

74. *BCO* (1932), 101.

75. *BCW* (1962), 119.

76. *MSBC* (1965), 11.

77. This will be dealt with in more detail in the analysis in the next chapter.

78. This will be discussed further in the following chapter.

79. Cf. *BCO* (1940), 91; *BCO* (1964), 84. In these Presbyterian orders this vow was to be used as an alternate to the Apostles' Creed. In earlier Presbyterian sources, the first order in the *Forms*, and the 1949 Congregationalist order, the first two vows were combined into one. E.g., *Euchologion*, 307, *BCO* (1922), 119, *Forms*, 22, *BPW* (1949), 160.

80. *MSBC* (1965), 11.

81. Cf. *MSBC* (1965), 11-12; *BCW* (1962), 118.

82. *BCO* (1964), 118.

83. *BCW* (1962), 118.

84. *BCW* (1962), 118.

85. While it was used in the subtitle of the *BCO* (1932) order for Reception to Full Communion, it was not used in anything other than rubrical form in any of the earlier liturgies themselves.

86. Cf. *BCW* (1962), 118; *BCO* (1964), 82; *BCO* (1940), 91; *BCO* (1922), 119.

87. The opening lines of the first Appendix prayer include "Almighty, everlasting God, whose most dearly beloved Son Jesus Christ, . . .gave commandment to his disciples, that they should to teach all nations, and baptize them In the name of the Father, and of the Son, and of the Holy Ghost. . . ." *BCO* (1932), 103. The closing lines of the "Grant, O Lord" prayer are "sanctify with they Spirit this child now to be baptized according to thy Word; through Jesus Christ our Lord. Amen." *BCO* (1932), 99.

88. Cf. *MSBC* (1965), 12; *BCO* (1940), 91-92; *BCO* (1964), 82-83; *Euchologion*, 308.

89. Cf. *BCO* (1932), 99.

90. Cf. *MSBC* (1965), 12; *BCO* (1932), 99.

91. *BCO* (1932), 99.

92. *Contemporary Prayers*, 96. *BPW* (1949), 161, also uses "in the name of the Lord Jesus Christ" in its declaration.

93. *BCO* (1940), 92.

94. *BCO* (1932), 99.

95. *MSBC* (1965), 13-14

96. "Drafts" dated 11 January 1961.

97. "Minutes" of 18 June 1962: 3. The quotation is taken from "Draft" dated 23 February 1964: 7, and is based on *BCO* (1932), 79.

98. Cf. "Minutes" of 24 February 1964 and 23 March 1964 with the actual responses of ministers and presbyteries contained in Vol. 8, Section 3-4.

99. "Minutes" 24 February 1964: 3. A motion that the form of a "eucharistic prayer" not be used was carried by a vote of six to three. "Minutes" of 27 April 1964: 3.

100. "Draft" dated October 1968.

101. An adaptation of Chrysostom's litany had been incorporated into the first order for the Lord's Supper in *BCO* (1932). Harding, "The Major Orders," 77-78. A different version, more in line with the original, was later added to the "Treasury of Prayers" in the second edition of 1950. Cf. *BCO* (1932), 75; *BCO* (1932), 2nd ed., 1950, 31-33. The use of litanies of intercession after the sermon is recorded in draft as early as 1961 ("Draft" dated 11 January 1961). In 1962 the Chrysostom source was suggested as a model. (See "Minutes" of 26 February 1962). The "Explanatory Note" on the draft order refers simply to its *BCO* roots and describes it as follows: "It is a bidding prayer, an ancient form in the Christian tradition, which gives opportunity for the congregation to participate audibly, and the minister to introduce such intercessions as arise from the needs of the people." *MSBC* (1965), 2-3. The Committee's enthusiasm for the form is communicated by Davidson to Bonnell Spencer, Chairman of the Standing Liturgical Commission's Committee on Christian Initiation, in a letter dated 15 May 1968. (Box 9, Vol. 12, Section 8: 1).

102. Cf. *MSBC* (1965), 9-10; *BCO* (1932), 2nd ed., 1950, 31-33.

103. "Minutes" of 25 March 1968: 1.

104. "Minutes" of 1 April 1968: 1.

105. E.g., *BCO* (1940), 93; *BCO* (1964), 86; *BPW* (1949), 162; *Contemporary Prayers*, 96-97.

106. *BCO* (1932), 101; *BCO* (1940), 94; *BCO* (1946), 124-125; *BCO* (1964), 86.

107. *SB* (1969), 49-54.

108. *ROP* (1968), 66.

109. "Draft" dated 28 October 1968; "Minutes" of 23 September 1968 to 27 January 1969.

110. Today's English Version [TEV] is used throughout this order.

111. *Contemporary Prayers*, 23.

112. *Contemporary Prayers*, 36.

113. *Contemporary Prayers*, 36-37, 41.

114. *Contemporary Prayers*, 42.

115. "Minutes" of 22 November 1965: 3.

116. *Contemporary Prayers*, 48, 51.

117. *Contemporary Prayers*, 66-72.

118. The lack of discussion recorded in the minutes surrounding their addition may suggest that the practice was not entirely novel. "Minutes" of 27 January 1969: 2.

119. The first draft included the following: "In baptism we rejoice that God's love surrounds and upholds *this child*, the same love that was revealed in Jesus Christ. In love God receives *this child*, into his church. In faith we dedicate *him* to God, trusting in his unfailing goodness." "Draft" dated October 1968: 2.

120. *Contemporary Prayers*, 94, 95.

121. "Minutes" of 27 January 1969: 2.

122. *Contemporary Prayers*, 95.

123. *Contemporary Prayers*, 94.
124. "Minutes" of 23 December 1968: 2. [Parenthesis mine].
125. One draft included a question of intent: "Do you want your child to receive baptism?" "Draft" dated December 1968: 3.
126. "Minutes" of 23 December 1068: 2.
127. *SB* (1969), 71-72.
128. Cf. *SB* (1969), 43; *Contemporary Prayers*, 95.
129. *BCW* (1962), 110. In the South Indian rite, however, there is a fully articulated baptismal epiclesis following silent prayer.
130. Cf. *SB* (1969), 45. Note that the Committee considered giving the naming more emphasis with use of a question: "What name are you giving this child?" "Draft" dated December 1968: 3.
131. Cf. *SB* (1969), 45.
132. Cf. "Minutes" of 27 January 1969: 2; *Contemporary Prayers*, 25, 96-97.
133. *BCO* (1932), 97, 102.
134. "Minutes" of 27 January 1969: 2.
135. "Minutes" of 27 January 1969: 3.
136. Cf. *SB* (1969), 47-48.
137. *SB* (1969), 57-67.
138. *The Order for Confirmation with Provision for the Baptism of Persons Able to Answer for Themselves*, Draft, August 1966 (Toronto: The United Church of Canada, 1966). [*CPB* (1966)]. This draft was "made available to the ministers of the Church for experimental use and for further assessment." "Explanatory Note," *CPB* (1966), unnumbered p. 1. This order was the product of a similar process as that for the Order for the Baptism of Children. Presbyteries received copies of a draft in April of 1964. Subsequent to feedback and comments, a revised draft was prepared for publication and distribution to all ministers in August of 1966. A study of the drafts and minutes show that there was less struggle in getting this order into its final form than in the case of the Order for the Baptism of Children.
139. "Minutes" of 26-27 June 1967: 3.
140. The 1940 Church of Scotland rite kept them separate. *BCO* (1940), 95-104. The 1946 American Presbyterian rite kept them separate but provided for some (confusing) rubrical adaptations directed toward combination. *BCW* (1946), 126-133. The Canadian Presbyterian book provided four orders of various combinations: "Order for the Baptism of an Adult and Admission to the Lord's Table;" "Order for the Confirmation of Baptized Persons and for their Admission to the Lord's Table;" "Order for the Confirmation of Baptized Persons and for their Admission to the Lord's Supper;" "Order for Confirmation of those Baptized in Infancy and Baptism and Confirmation of Adults." *BCO* (1964), 87-104.
141. Cf. *BCO* (1932), 104-112.
142. E.g. *BCP* (1962), 199.
143. *BCP* (1962), 533.
144. *SB* (1969), 3-4, and *CPB* (1966), unnumbered p. 3.
145. *CPB* (1966), unnumbered p. 7.
146. "Minutes" of 22 October 1962: 4; 7 November 1966: 1.
147. *BCO* (1932), 92. See also Harding, "The Major Orders," 79-80.
148. Cf. *MSBC* (1965), 8; *SB* (1969), 40.
149. *CPB* (1966), 7.
150. *BCO* (1940), 41.
151. *BPW* (1949), 142.
152. *SB* (1969), 41.

153. *SB* (1969), 134; *BCO* (1932), 43-44. It is common to most such collections, often the first one listed; see, for example, *BCO* (1940), 309; *BCW* (1946), 347; *BPW* (1949), 146; *BCO* (1964), 320.

154. Cf. *BCO* (1940), 95; *BCW* (1946), 126-127; *BPW* (1949), 163-164; *BCP* (1959), 533-534; *BCW* (1962), 105; *BCO* (1964), 99-100; *Contemporary Prayers*, 94-95.

155. Cf. *BCO* (1940), 95; *BCW* (1946), 126; *BPW* (1949), 163; *BCW* (1962), 105.

156. Cf. *BCO* (1940), 100-101; *BCW* (1946), 131-132; *BPW* (1949), 167-168; *BCP* (1959), 557-558; *BCW* (1962), 125-126; *BCO* (1964), 94-95, 99-100; *Contemporary Prayers*, 98-99.

157. *BCP* (1962), 557-558. The Canadian *BCP* was the first book in the Anglican tradition to use this text, which, of course, has nothing to do with confirmation *per se*.

158. The 1966 draft order contained a version of this statement which shows more readily its reliance on both the 1932 Confirmation Statement and the closing rubrics to the 1932 Order for the Baptism of Children. It is interesting to not that the South Indian order contains a statement, the opening lines of which are also influenced by the 1932 United Church order. *BCO* (1932), 102, 104; *BCW* (1962), 124.

159. "Minutes" of 27 January 1969: 2.

160. *SB* (1969), 43.

161. *BCO* (1964), 89, 95.

162. Cf. *BCO* (1940), 97, 101; *BCO* (1964), 90. 96.

163. *BCW* (1962), 127.

164. The question in *CPB* (1966), 11, began with the *BCO* (1932), 105, phrasing: "Will you seek earnestly the peace and welfare of the Church of God."

165. The question in *CPB* (1966), 11, began with the *BCO* (1932), 105, phrasing: "Will you endeavour to do God's holy will." The American and Scottish Presbyterian rites included reference to "the service of Christ and His kingdom throughout the world." *BCW* (1946), 132; *BCO* (1940), 103.

166. "Minutes" of 27 December 1965: 2

167. *BCW* (1962), 108, 119, 128.

168. *BCO* (1932), 110. Early drafts proposed a version of the Prayer Book's Isaiah-based confirmation prayer, as in the 1932 confirmation order [(*BCO*) (1932), 105, 111], though it was soon dropped in favor of this more general prayer. "Minutes," 24 February 1964: 2.

169. Cf. *SB* (1969), 45.

170. Cf. *SB* (1969), 45.

171. Cf. *BCO* (1932), 105, 111.

172. "Minutes" of 10 May 1965: 3; 26-27 June 1967: 4.

173. "Defend, O Lord, this thy child (*or* servant) with thy heavenly grace, that he may continue thine for ever; and daily increase in thy Holy Spirit more and more, until he come unto thy everlasting kingdom." *BCO* (1932), 105, 111.

174. "Minutes" of 27 December 1965: 2; 24 January 1966: 1; 28 March 1966: 1.

175. *BCO* (1932), 99.

176. Such structural inconsistencies will be considered in the analysis in the following chapter.

177. E.g., "accept, we beseech thee, the offerings which thy people here present with willing and thankful hearts" and "grant that these offerings which we bring to thee may be used for thy glory: through Jesus Christ our Lord. Amen." *BPW* (1949), 144-145.

178. Cf. *SB* (1969), 45-46.

179. Cf. *SB* (1969), 45-46.

180. Cf. *SB* (1969), 46-47

181. Cf. *SB* (1969), 45.

182. *SB* (1969), 68-74
183. Cf. *SB* (1969), 49-54.
184. Cf. *SB* (1969), 57.
185. *SB* (1969), 57.
186. Cf. *SB* (2969), 49-50.
187. Cf. *SB* (1969), 39-40, 49-50.
188. Cf. *SB* (1969), 58.
189. The issue was raised, but not resolved, by the Committee. "Minutes" of 25 November 1968: 2.
190. Cf. *SB* (1969), 50.
191. Cf. *SB* (1969), 59.
192. Cf. *SB* (1969), 60-61. Note, however, that the passage from John should be cited as verses 21 and 22.
193. Cf. *SB* (1969), 60-61.
194. *SB* (1969), 56.
195. Cf. *SB* (1969), 61.
196. Cf. *SB* (1969), 43.
197. "Minutes" of 1 April 1968: 2. To this end, "A New Creed" (published with the authority of the 1968 General Council), "A Statement of Faith" (United Church of Christ, U.S.A.), the Nicene Creed, and the Apostles' Creed were printed on the inside covers of *SB* (1969). See also *Creeds: A Report of The Committee on Christian Faith* (Toronto: The Ryerson Press, 1969). This report and its relation to the role of the Creed in liturgy will be considered in the chapter to follow.
198. Cf. *SB* (1969), 51.
199. Cf. *SB* (1969), 62.
200. The first three questions for each order were worked out with a view to their being used in each. "Minutes" of 11 November 1968: 2.
201. Cf. *SB* (1969), 62.
202. Cf. *SB* (1969), 62.
203. Cf. *SB* (1969), 62.
204. Cf. *SB* (1969), 44, 52, 62.
205. Cf. *SB* (1969), 53, 62.
206. Cf. *SB* (1969), 63.
207. Cf. *SB* (1969), 53, 63.
208. Cf. *SB* (1969), 63. "Strengthen" also replaces "confirm" in the South Indian order. *BCW* (1962), 128.
209. "Minutes" of 25 November 1968: 3.
210. Cf. *SB* (1969), 64.
211. *SB* (1969), 137.
212. The phrase "love of our hearts" is common to some Presbyterian offertory prayers. E.g., *BCO* (1940), 307; *BCW* (1946), 345.
213. *SB* (1969), 9. This is a revision of the *BCO* (1932) eucharistic prayer, *BCO* (1932), 79-80.
214. Cf. *SB* (1969), 53-54, 64-65.
215. Cf. *SB* (1969), 54.
216. Cf. *SB* (1969), 47, 54, 67.

Chapter 5
Liturgical Reform in Turbulent Times

As with the analysis of the baptismal liturgies of *The Book of Common Order* in part II, the commentary on the *Service Book* orders prompts further consideration and analysis. The areas of structure, scripture, pneumatology and ecclesiology will again be examined, in addition to other issues generated by the texts and the context of their development. This can be seen as a study in United Church liturgical reform during particularly challenging and turbulent times.

Structure

One of the first decisions made by the Committee regarding the orders for baptism was to provide a full order of service centered around the sacrament itself. Their intention was to frame the celebration of baptism within an integrated liturgical whole rather than as a separate rite placed in Sunday worship. The movement and dynamic of the whole rite was to build toward the sacrament of baptism. There was no known precedent for such an approach and the Committee took pride in arguing that this idea would be "the one unique contribution to the new book of Common Order."[1]

This decision is appropriately placed within the context of the vision of the *Service Book* as a whole. In the *Service Book* the first and second orders for Public Worship are the reverse of those of *The Book of Common Order*, giving priority to the structure of the Lord's Supper as "normative." The introduction to the *Service Book* sums up the approach as follows:

> One concern is to emphasize the unity of word and sacrament. Implicit here is acceptance of the sacrament of the Lord's Supper as the basic Christian service and as such normative for Christian worship. No indication is given as to how often the sacrament of the Lord's Supper should be celebrated, although it is acknowledged that the early church did so weekly. It should be observed, how-

> ever, that the first order for public worship is based on the pattern of the Lord's Supper. This is also the shape of the orders for confirmation, marriage and, to some extent, burial.[2]

As mentioned earlier, this understanding marks an important development in United Church worship, signaling the shift from the Morning Prayer and *Westminster Directory* structures in public worship to the "Approach-Word-Response" structures that are now so common.

In the introduction the compilers go on to point out the implications of this vision for baptism: "The emphasis on the unity of word and sacrament has also meant that the sacrament of baptism is given as a complete order rather than an insert in an abbreviated order for Sunday worship. Baptism is administered after the word has been read and proclaimed."[3]

In the Committee's view, the custom of placing the sacrament of baptism in an order for public worship in an often arbitrary and *ad hoc* manner undermined the principle of the unity of word and sacrament. A full order would give the sacrament the same degree of liturgical attention as the Lord's Supper. In the words of the Explanatory Note to the 1965 draft: "This new structure for Baptism, the Committee believes, will help to give it the weight and importance it ought to have. No longer is it an insert that interrupts the usual Sunday order."[4]

The force of this vision persisted in spite of "an almost overwhelming objection" on the part of the presbyteries. In contrast to the Committee's liturgical and theological concerns, the concerns of the presbyteries were pragmatic and centered on the inconvenience of making infants and parents wait through a long service of Approach, Word (and sermon) before the baptism. In spite of the large volume of such criticisms, the Committee simply decided that they knew better; they would not compromise the structure of the rites.[5]

In retrospect, this was a bold step, intended to advance the liturgical understanding of baptism in the United Church. But its foundations seem confused and its premises doubtful. While the vision of the unity of word and sacrament was commendable, a closer look reveals the two flawed presuppositions with which the Committee was also working.

The original options considered by the Committee were in the form of two orders (see Table 5.1). Order I replaced the sermon with baptism and included communion. Order II included the sermon but replaced communion with baptism. The first, it was suggested, would work for the baptism of adults but not for the baptism of children, since "unconfirmed" children did not participate in the Lord's Supper. As one member put it, "communion would be often omitted," creating a "bastard form" of the order.[6] Thus, the second order became the basic working structure and was developed in conjunction with the *Service Book*'s First Order for the Lord's Supper and the Second Directory for Public Worship. To this end, the 1965 draft for the baptism of children was organized under the headings "The Approach," "The Word of God," and "The Action,"[7] corresponding to the three-fold Approach-Word-Response structure of Public Worship and the Lord's Supper.

Table 5.1
A Structural Comparison of Two Draft Orders of Service
Incorporating Baptism

Order I	Order II
Call to Worship	Call to Worship
Prayer of Invocation	Prayer of Invocation
Hymn	Hymn
Prayers of Confession, Pardon & Supplication	Prayers of Confession, Pardon & Supplication
Baptism	Word
Hymn	Sermon
Holy Communion	Baptism
Benediction	Benediction

Source: UCA, "Draft" dated 20 March 1961.

These origins reveal the two presuppositions which haunted the Committee's deliberations from this point onward and were manifested in the structural ambiguities of the rites themselves. First, the Committee did not see it as normative that the Lord's Supper and baptism take place in the same rite. Second, on the other hand, they did see it as normative that the word and sacrament structure of Christian worship meant that Baptism and the Lord's Supper shared an identical relationship to the Word. That is to say, Baptism and the Lord's Supper were seen as parallel sacraments, liturgically interchangeable and structurally equivalent, occupying the same place in the service as a response to the Word. In a sense, these presuppositions are two sides of the same coin. Together, they worked to ensure that the practice of restricting participation in the Lord's Supper to "confirmed" members was maintained. While this was consistent with the recently affirmed church polity of the time,[8] it nevertheless went unchallenged in spite of the subsequent structural inconsistencies which arose in the orders themselves. Ironically, in their efforts to give baptism "the weight and importance it ought to have," they skewed its relationship to both Public Worship and the Lord's Supper.

Such failings are evident in the final form of the rites, when compared with their structural counterparts. Table 5.2 shows the headings of the main *Service Book* orders.

According to the Committee's stated intentions, the Action of baptism was meant to correspond to, and hence replace, The Word of God Enacted in the Lord's Supper and the Response in Public Worship. The consistency of this plan began to break down, however, when the Committee decided to create a separate Response section in the baptismal rites for the combined Prayers of Thanksgiving and Intercession.[9] Failing to see baptism itself as a response to the Word, they ended up with a four-fold structure rather than their intended three-fold structure. The Approach-Word-Response structure became an Approach-Word-Action-Response structure in baptism.

Table 5.2
A Structural Comparison of
the Main *Service Book* Orders

An Outline for The Celebration of The Lord's Supper (abbreviated)	First Order for Public Worship (abbreviated)	An Outline for The Baptism of Children (abbreviated)	An Outline for Adult Baptism and Confirmation (abbreviated)
The Approach	The Approach	The Approach	The Approach
The Word of God Proclaimed & Acknowledged	The Word of God	The Word	The Word
The Word of God Enacted	The Word of God Enacted	Action	Action
		The Response	The Response

Source: *SB* (1969).

Such structural ambiguities become especially evident in the closing rubrics in both baptismal orders, which clearly imply that the celebration of the Lord's Supper with Baptism would be unusual.[10] Indeed, as one of the Committee members made clear in a review of the service, the rubrical provision for the celebration of the Lord's Supper with Baptism was included with a view to those "many student and lay supply charges" where "the supervising minister comes to celebrate both sacraments on the same Sunday."[11]

Even if one could grant the logic of all such features within the context of the time, the rubrics also betray a lack of clarity about the place and function of the Offering in relation to baptism. In the Order for the Baptism of Children, the Offering is placed at the beginning of the Action, but in Adult Baptism and Confirmation it is placed after the Action in the Response section.

As the commentary has shown, other inconsistencies are also present: differing forms for Confession; an anomalous Prayer for Illumination in the Order for the Baptism of Children; nearly twice as many questions in the contemporary Order for Adult Baptism and Confirmation as in other orders. Taken together, such inconsistencies reveal a lack of liturgical and theological clarity.

Some progress was made in the *Service Book* toward a greater unification of baptismal rites in the United Church. *The Book of Common Order* contained three orders (infant baptism, confirmation, and adult baptism), where the *Service Book* contains essentially two (infant baptism and adult baptism). With the integration of the orders for adult baptism and confirmation into one service, there is a sense in which the unification of the rite to be achieved in 1986 advanced one step closer.

However, this step toward liturgical integration is only partially successful and comes at a price. Rubrical provisions allow for the omission of various components pertaining to adult baptism "if there are no candidates." While this might allow for its convenient use as a confirmation service only, the result is that the order is essentially one for confirmation "with provision for" adult baptism included. The title of the 1966 draft is telling: "The Order for Confirmation with Provision for the Baptism of Persons Able to Answer for Themselves."[12] Its "Explanatory Note" also reveals a dismissive and subordinate view of baptism: "More often than not, some of those to be confirmed will also need to be baptized. Therefore, provision is made for joining the Sacrament of Baptism with Confirmation."[13]

There is no articulation of the theological reasons for this development in the records of the Committee, *per se*, no suggestion that it might be unusual. It suggests a degree of historical ignorance on the part of the Committee.

It also reflects the experience of the United Church in the fifties and sixties when growth was great and the "baby boomer" generation was coming to the "age of discretion." In this context, confirmation could be pressed into service to respond to the need to initiate large numbers of adolescents into "full membership." With so many confirmations taking place and so few adult baptisms in comparison, the primacy of confirmation in the order makes a certain kind of sense; albeit for reasons that have more to do with a demography than liturgical theology.[14]

Whatever convenience this order may have offered, the result was a liturgical experience still known in many United Churches today—namely, that adult baptism is experienced as an embarrassing infantile moment inserted into an otherwise mature confirmation service. Thus, in the context of confirmation, baptism had become simply another "liturgical insert"—the very thing the Committee was seeking to avoid. These results are indeed ironic when one considers that the intent of the new structure in these orders was to give baptism "the weight and importance it ought to have."

Scripture

The Committee also sought to make substantial changes to the use of scripture in United Church baptismal rites, again meeting with mixed success. Their work on this subject shows their struggle with the function and meaning of a scriptural warrant in baptism.

Early drafts of the Order for the Baptism of Children demonstrated a desire to end *The Book of Common Order*'s sole reliance on Mark 10 (Jesus' blessing of the children) and expand the use of scripture in the rite. Various texts move in and out of use in the early drafts, including: Matthew 18:107 ("unless you become like children"); Matthew 28:18-20 (the risen Christ's command to the disciples to baptize); Mark 1:6-11 (Jesus' baptism by John); Acts 2:38-39 (Peter's sermon at Pentecost: "Repent and be baptized"); 1 Corinthians 12:13 ("all members, though many are one body") and even Isaiah 40:11 ("he will gather the lambs in his arms").[15]

The draft sent to presbyteries contained Mark 1:9-11, Matthew 28:18-20, and Acts 2:38-39. This selection provoked much response, the influences of twentieth century historical-critical biblical scholarship being evident in the discussion. Some presbyteries, for example, questioned whether the story of Jesus' baptism was a valid model for Christian baptism in general and infant baptism in particular. Similarly, the historical authenticity of Matthew's "Great Commission" was questioned. On the other hand, the same hermeneutical methods did not seem to apply to Mark 10. Nearly all presbyteries objected strongly to its absence. Some granted that the subject of the text was not baptism *per se* but defended it nevertheless on the grounds of "tradition."[16]

For the purposes of the 1965 draft, the Committee held to their original choice of scripture. As the "Explanatory Note" put it: The scripture passages "relate the Sacrament of Baptism to the full Gospel. The first passage reminds us that Jesus Christ was baptized, identifying himself with all men. The second reminds us that Jesus Christ commissioned his Church to baptize the nations. The third reminds us of the gift of the Spirit, which is the promise of Pentecost."[17]

Thus, the notion of the "dominical institution" of the sacrament is actually preserved, if interpreted more loosely. The historical-critical questions raised by the Presbyteries found some sympathy in the Committee but, there being no consensus, it was decided to test these texts on the church.[18]

One concession which was made to the presbyteries at this point was the inclusion of an allusion to Mark 10 in the prayer before baptism. The "Explanatory Note" attempted to address these concerns with the remarks: "In the light of comments received from the Presbyteries, the prayer immediately preceding the baptism has been rewritten. It is derived from Prayer II, in *The Book of Common Order* page 148, and is associated with the cherished recollection of our Lord's blessing of the little children (Mark 10.13)."[19]

True, the address and relative clause of the prayer in question were altered to read "Almighty and everlasting Father, whose beloved Son Jesus Christ took the little children in his arms and blessed them,"[20] but real "comments" from presbyteries concerning this prayer were not in relation to its address and relative clause or Mark 10, but the blessing of water. The majority of presbyteries wanted both to include Mark 10 in the scripture passages and alter the prayer before baptism to exclude any notion of the blessing of water. The objections to such a practice had not changed since the days of *The Book of Common Order*. The Committee, on the other hand, wanted the opposite. To this end, the 1965 draft employs what must be seen as a clever political strategy disguised as a liturgical compromise. Mark 10 is included, but in the prayer before baptism; the prayer is altered, but the blessing of water remains. Mark 10 is tied to the blessing of water in the hope that the latter can be salvaged and the former can be kept out of the scripture passages.

The ploy did not work. The lack of any further mention of the subject in the minutes suggests that the consensus regarding the final decision was easy, given the responses from the church.[21] Matthew 28 was kept, Mark 10 was included, Mark 1 and Acts were deleted. In the "contemporary" order only Matthew 28 was used. The final result was similar to *The Book of Common Order*'s use of scripture after all.[22]

In the Order for Adult Baptism and Confirmation, the situation was very different. The 1966 draft of Adult Baptism and Confirmation provoked little criticism from presbyteries, ministers, and sessions, and remained largely unchanged until its final *Service Book* form. The scripture selections of Mark 1:9-11, Matthew 28:18-20, John 20:21-22, and Acts 8:14-17 survived the entire drafting process without strong objections. From one perspective, the use of these texts represents something of a more broad use of scripture in comparison to the orders in *The Book of Common Order*. In the 1932 texts the emphasis in adult baptism was strictly on dominical institution (Matthew 28) and repentance (Acts 2). In the *Service Book* order scripture is provided for both the context of adult baptism and confirmation. John 20 and Acts 8 are to be read for confirmation and Mark 1 and Matthew 28 for adult baptism.

However, the resulting theological losses outweigh the scriptural gains. Because the John 20 and Acts 8 are read for confirmation, it is presented as a pneumatic event. Moreover, even if one could grant that there were scriptural texts which could constitute a biblical warrant for confirmation, none of the baptismal texts are to read at confirmation in this order. Adults to be baptized and confirmed hear scriptural texts concerning baptism and the descent of the Holy Spirit, while those previously baptized hear about the Holy Spirit only. This further obscures the relation of the Spirit to baptism, setting confirmation apart as a separate quasi-sacrament of the Holy Spirit. The subtle pneumatological emphasis begun in *The Book of Common Order* has been taken to greater extremes.

What is significant about the Committee's struggle with the role and place of scripture in the *Service Book* orders is that they appeared to sense something was wrong with the medieval and Reformed notions of "dominical institution" and "scriptural warrant" but could not, in the end, break free of these hermeneutical and liturgical restraints. Some degree of sensitivity to historical-critical biblical scholarship allowed them to appreciate some critiques of the passages in question, but it did not prompt them to examine the more substantial question of the liturgical function of scripture. The desire for a scriptural warrant remained; it was simply a different kind of warrant. The medieval warrant became that twentieth-century warrant; literal proof-texting became liberal proof-texting.

Paul DeClerck has spoken to this question at a conference on the Bible and liturgy. A portion of his remarks can serve as an instructive summary of the issues at stake:

> [One] reason for giving importance to the relationship of liturgy and Bible is that it permits us to express in new terms the old quarrel between Catholics and Christians from the Reformation on the *institution of the sacraments and on their number*. While setting the number of sacraments at seven in the twelfth

> century was based on the liturgical practice of that period (which led them, for example, to count baptism and confirmation as two distinct sacraments), denominational polemics turned further toward scripture, asking it to point out when Christ instituted the sacraments and how many. Today biblical studies help us discover that the New Testament itself has been "instituted," if we could so speak, by the liturgical and sacramental celebrations as much as the New Testament itself institutes the sacraments. Baptism was celebrated before Paul wrote about its theology in his letter to the Romans. Here again we see the priority of liturgical practice, from which we have not yet drawn all the lessons for the discussion on the sacraments among the churches.[23]

Without such an understanding of the relationship between scripture and liturgy and the function of scripture in liturgy, churches of the Reformed tradition will tend to be locked in a never-ending search for the perfect scriptural warrant.[24]

Pneumatology

The role of the Holy Spirit in the *Service Book* orders for baptism can be examined from a variety of perspectives. The issues of epiclesis, regeneration, and again, confirmation stand out as in need of further comment.

As already mentioned, efforts to include an explicit invocation of the Holy Spirit on the baptismal water met with strong opposition. Any prayers to "set apart this water" or "bless this water" brought a consistent chorus of objections to the production of anything which could be construed as "holy water."[25] Again, the precise reasons for these objections were never clearly articulated. One can assume that a combination of Puritan-like sensibilities and loyalty to established United Church liturgical traditions was at work.

Even the attempt in the 1965 draft to use a prayer derived from the Scottish Presbyterian tradition did not satisfy concerns.[26] No precedent could convince United Church persons that the blessing of water was appropriate. While the Committee considered such objections "invalid," they nevertheless acted on them. Once again, as with their predecessors who worked on *The Book of Common Order*, the Committee's desire to use a more classic form of baptismal epiclesis was abandoned. The main orders invoke the Spirit on the candidates only and the contemporary orders invite a general silent prayer for the "gifts of God's Spirit."

United Church anxieties about the relationship between the Holy Spirit and the water also extended to the subject of baptismal regeneration. Here, concern was expressed over the notion that one is "born again" in baptism, as suggested by the same 1965 draft prayer before baptism.[27] In spite of the omission of the offending text, the services continue to contain regenerative connotations. The language of the "new beginning" in baptism is present in all the orders. In infant baptism it is found in the opening sentences and is reinforced by the opening prayer and statement in the contemporary order.[28] "In baptism we celebrate a new beginning," proclaims the first line of the Teaching Statement in the contemporary Order for Adult Baptism and Confirmation.

However, the precise meaning of this "new beginning" in the texts is varied. The exhortations identify it as God's salvific action in Jesus Christ, adoption into God's family, the beginning of the work of the Spirit, union with Christ as a "new creation," and God's "Yes" to us (as distinct from our "Yes" to God in confirmation). Is this new beginning our response to God's prevenient grace, or a Divine salvific act in baptism itself, or some combination of both? Regardless, one is left with the distinct impression that the idea of baptismal regeneration so carefully avoided in *The Book of Common Order* rites, has been reintroduced in the *Service Book* orders, albeit under this decidedly contemporary liberal heading, "new beginning."

While this concept is not identical to the classic concept of baptismal regeneration, neither is it unrelated. Part of what they both share is a focus on God's initiative in baptism. This was one of the most important goals of these *Service Book* orders, namely, to emphasize Divine, rather than human, initiative. The Explanatory Note to the 1965 draft of the Order for the Baptism of Children makes this clear:

> The Committee has been aware that it is working in a theological climate greatly altered in recent years. Many Christian have tended to think of the Church primarily as a human organization, dependent on the activity of those who voluntarily joined it. Today, we place more emphasis on God's initiative in calling men and women into his Church, feeding them at this table, and sending them out on his mission into the world. The change has led many Churches to re-think their concept of Baptism and to revise their services accordingly.[29]

This explanation goes on to present the only explicit articulation of the Committee's theology of baptism.[30]

> Despite this theological rediscovery, certain views inconsistent with the teaching of the Bible are still current. To avoid this the Committee has endeavored to express the doctrine of Baptism more clearly. Children are dedicated with this sacrament, but it is not primarily a service of dedication. Parents profess their faith, but this sacrament is not primarily for that purpose. Baptism is the sacrament by which, dying and rising again with Christ into newness of life, one becomes a member of the covenant community which is the Church. Like the Lord's Supper, it is a sacrament of the fatherhood and love of God as revealed in the redeeming work of Jesus Christ and the activity of the Holy Spirit. Through it we celebrate and proclaim God's initiative in the salvation of men. Baptism involves the fellowship of the whole Church.[31]

By far the most significant issue relating to the Spirit is the liturgical theology of confirmation presented in the rites. At the risk of repetition, a further synthesis of the situation presented in the orders is appropriate within this consideration of pneumatology.

The Book of Common Order introduced the term "Confirmation" into the subtitle of the order for the Reception to Full Communion. It has been shown that this was a signal of the beginning of a significant shift in the United Church liturgical theology. The Reformed emphasis of the founding traditions on profession of faith for reception into "full" communicant membership began to be supplemented by an increasing pneumatological theme: confirmation as "strengthening" by the Holy Spirit.

The commentary and previous remarks has shown that this shift is no longer subtle in the *Service Book* orders. The term *confirmation* appears not simply in the subtitle of an order, but in its main title and, for the first time in United Church history, in the texts of the liturgies themselves—from the questions to the parents in the baptism of children, to the exhortation-style statements in adult baptism and confirmation and in most of the prayers associated with the laying on of hands.

This development is all the more remarkable in light of the pneumatological meaning given to confirmation. Confirmation is not taken as simply synonymous with profession of faith, reception to full communion, or admission to full membership. In the readings, exhortations, questions, promises, and prayers it is defined as reception of the Holy Spirit and strengthening by the Holy Spirit. The Explanatory Note to the 1966 draft makes this clear: "Confirmation is the work of the Holy Spirit. It has been called the ordination of the laity and is accompanied by the laying on of hands. Those who have been baptized are enjoined to go forth in the power of the Spirit to fulfill their high calling as servants of Christ in the world."[32]

In the *Service Book*'s introduction to the Services of Initiation, however, only profession of faith is emphasized: "When the baptized child has come to years of discretion it is expected that he will stand before the church and make a responsible profession of his own faith. This implies that he has been carefully instructed."[33]

With this, the introduction seems to describe a very different rite than the one which follows. It is not surprising therefore that so much ambiguity and confusion surrounding the role and meaning of confirmation still abounds in the United Church, given the inconsistencies within the *Service Book* itself.

On the other hand, even if the 1966 pneumatological definition were to have been clearly presented in the *Service Book*, the problem would not have been solved. The very existence of confirmation, let alone any interpretation rendering it a quasi-sacrament of the Holy Spirit, has its own historical and theological problems, the significance of which the Committee did not seem to fully grasp.[34] For example, their view of confirmation as "the ordination of the laity" was, of course, mistaken. If the term applies to anything it is to baptism itself.

If there is to be any sympathy for the Committee's work on confirmation, it is that they may have been pushed into this theological and liturgical corner by the 1962 General Council which declared "that the traditional order of Baptism, Confirmation, First Communion" was the "accepted order of initiation into the United Church of Canada."[35] With official authorization of the existence and practice of confirmation, the Committee had little choice but to provide some order for its celebration.

There is evidence to suggest that at least few members of the Committee were uncomfortable with the church's position on the subject. One wonders, for example, if they were not aware of some historical, theological, and liturgical inconsistencies given their synopsis of the issue in the Explanatory Note to the 1966 draft order. Three paragraphs are worth quoting in full:

> In the preparation of the Order for Confirmation, serious attention has been given to the work of the Committee on the Christian Faith entitled "Church Membership." The Twentieth General Council gave general approval to this document, which asserts that by Baptism we are initiated into and made members of the Church; but we enter into "full membership" when we come to years of discretion and answer for ourselves. It is pointed out that the New Testament is not unambiguous about the Confirmation or the laying on of hands following Baptism.
>
> In the history of the Church different practices have developed. The Orthodox Churches baptise infants, confirm them using oil, and give them first communion in the same service. In the Western Churches Confirmation has come to be separated from Infant Baptism. In the Roman Catholic Church, Confirmation is a sacrament, administered by the Bishop, who anoints with oil and lays on hands. The Church of England and the Reformation not only rejected Confirmation as a sacrament but also abandoned the practice of anointing with oil. However, it kept the laying of hands by the Bishop and associated Confirmation with first Communion.
>
> Calvin repudiated Confirmation as a sacrament and rejected the practice of laying on of hands. He felt there was a place for a simple service which would give young people the opportunity to profess their faith, although in his Form of Prayers he does not provide such a Service. Many Protestants following Calvin have made no provision for the laying on of hands. In place of Confirmation they have had a Service of Reception at which those who made a responsible and public profession of their faith are received into membership and admitted to the Lord's Table. In popular speech this has been known as "joining the Church," but the phrase is not accurate, since strictly speaking, we become members of the Church in Baptism (Basis of Union, Article 15). The Committee on the Christian Faith decided that there was a value in restoring the word "Confirmation" and the Twentieth General Council declared as normative the sequence "Baptism-Confirmation-First Communion." (The Manual, 6a).[36]

The passive descriptive voice of this passage almost seems to be an attempt to distance the Committee from General Council on the matter.

Discussion on the preparation of this very text in April of 1966 reveals that some members had difficulty with the insistence that first communion follow confirmation, that the church had "come down too hard" on the subject. Said one member, "It leads to intellectual commitment too soon and full participation in worship too late." But even here, it appears that it was the order of the initiation sequence that was in question, not the practice or meaning of confirmation *per se*. The minutes record the conclusion of the discussion on a note of consensus: "However, all agreed that our Committee does not formulate the policy of the Church."[37]

While the formulation of policy was not the mandate of the Committee, the crafting of liturgical texts was. Considering the large number of confirmations and the heavy focus on confirmation classes and their related resources in this period, these resulting orders probably did more to institutionalize confirmation, with all of its ambiguities and inconsistencies, than any General Council policy could have done.

Ecclesiology

Also institutionalized as a result of the *Service Book* orders were a variety of features which enhanced the ecclesiological dimensions of baptism in the United Church. In spite of the problems already discussed, one must acknowledge that the orders made real progress in placing baptism more firmly in the context of public worship and opposing any notion of private baptism.[38] To this end, the rites encourage greater active participation on the part of the congregation through unison prayers, bidding prayers, responses, psalmody, and litanies. The roles of elders or the Clerk of Session and Session is given greater attention than in any previous orders.[39] The explicit role of the congregation in the vows is also part of this framework: "The congregation stands for the vows, since they also sponsor the child and assume with the parents the responsibility for his Christian education and spiritual growth. The entire congregation fulfills the role of those who in some communions are designated as godparents."[40]

This is reminiscent of the clarification approved by the 1954 General Council:

> The term godparents has no official standing in The United Church of Canada. As a courtesy persons may be so designated and be present at the Sacrament but may not take the vows in the place of parents or sponsors. Sponsors are admitted in the case of orphaned children or children being presented for infant baptism in special cases by those other than their parents. Sponsors must be professing Christians.[41]

In view of this growing ecclesiological consciousness, it is both surprising and unfortunate that the General Council approved baptismal orders which only include a congregational vow in the baptism of children. Surely the church is also responsible for the spiritual nurture and support of adults. Certainly adults also require such support.

A significant development which relates to the issue of ecclesiology, but is not immediately evident in the orders themselves, is the subsequent publication of the *Service Book for the use of the people*.[42] The Committee had originally assumed that worship materials would also be included in the soon-to-be-revised hymnary. As the work on the hymn book evolved into a joint Anglican-United project, this material was no longer appropriate to that text and a "people's book" was proposed.[43] Published the same year as the *Service Book for the use of ministers*, it contained a selection of the major orders (including those for infant and adult baptism), psalm selections arranged for responsive reading, and the "Material for Services of Worship" section from the minister's book. This meant that congregations could participate fully in the unison prayers, litanies, and psalms, thus enhancing the ecclesiological dimensions of the rites through an increased level of active participation. At its best, it meant that baptism could be even more "public" than had previously been experienced in the United Church.

Along with the ecclesiological dimensions of liturgical participation, the Committee was also concerned about the larger issue of the catholicity of baptism. Of all the various attempts to recover more catholic liturgical forms in the orders, the most explicit example lies in the role of the Apostles' Creed. As mentioned in the commentary, while the Committee agreed on the fact that the Apostle's Creed was integral to the catholic integrity of the orders, there was considerable discussion with regard to its form and location during the drafting process, particularly with respect to the Order for the Baptism of Children. A survey of early drafts shows it printed out in full in some, mentioned only the rubrics in others, before the vows in some and after the vows in others.[44] Initially, it had been placed before the vows and those who preferred this location defended it on the grounds that it expressed the historic faith "with which the child is surrounded"[45] or "into which the parent comes bringing the child."[46] But some members, and many presbyteries, argued that it would be best placed after the vows, allowing individuals to "confess" their personal faith, after which this would be "gathered up in the faith of the congregation."[47] The former argument eventually prevailed, this position being the one in the 1965 draft. The Explanatory Note alluded both to the logic of its location and the catholicity of its use: "The Apostles' Creed has been associated with the Sacrament of Baptism throughout Christian history. It took its form from the questions put to candidates for Baptism in the early Church. It is used here as a symbol of the faith of the Holy Catholic Church into which the child is baptized."[48]

The most serious and significant challenge to the role and place of the Creed in the orders was to come from the Committee on Christian Faith. The Committee on Church Worship and Ritual had invited that committee to examine and respond to the 1965 draft. They, in turn, expressed "some doubts" about the rubric, "The Apostles' Creed shall be said by all," and suggested that "there was need in the Church for a modern statement of faith which might be used as an alternative to the Apostles' Creed."[49] By the time the 1966 draft of Adult Baptism and Confirmation had been published, the corresponding rubric had been changed to "the people may stand and say the Apostles' Creed."[50] The Explanatory Note explained: "The Apostles' Creed has held a distinctive place in the service of Baptism and Confirmation in the Church. However, there are those who feel that it does not convey to the present generation what it is meant to say. Therefore, its use has been made permissive. When used it is recited by the Congregation before the Candidates are questioned."[51]

In the meantime, the Committee on Christian Faith had sought and obtained the permission of the Sub-Executive of the General Council "to attempt to draft a brief profession of faith, suitable for liturgical use, as a possible alternative to the use of the Apostles' Creed, especially in the new order for the administration of the sacrament of baptism."[52]

The Sub-Executive soon added to this mandate the larger tasks of examining "the status and authority of the classical creeds in The United Church of Canada today," and collecting and examining "representative modern statements of faith."[53] The resulting "Report on Creeds" was presented and adopted by the 1968 General Council and "A New Creed" was given "general approval . . . for use in congregations" by the Executive of General Council a few months later. Both were later published by Ryerson Press in the study booklet *Creeds*.

In *Creeds* the Committee on Christian Faith identified the following "consensus":

1. The use of creeds, whether ancient or modern, will not of itself guarantee theological vitality or faithfulness to the gospel.
2. Creeds, whether ancient or modern, will continue to be useful in the Church.
3. The classical creeds . . . will continue to be useful especially for instruction and as ecumenical instruments.
4. The responsible use of the classical creeds implies preparatory instruction.
5. Appropriate introductory formulae should be provided for use with the classical creeds in public services.
6. In addition to the classical creeds, modern creeds should be made available to the Church for possible use.
7. Modern creeds usually begin by being local and experimental and most of them no doubt will be short-lived; but only through experience will acceptable new creeds be developed.[54]

Out of this came four recommendations:

1. We recommend that in the service books soon to be published there be included at least the Apostles' Creed, the Nicene Creed, the Statement of Faith by the United Church of Christ in the U.S.A., and the new creed prepared by this Committee.
2. We recommend the following words of introduction for the use with these creeds in public worship; for the Apostles' and Nicene Creeds: "Let us repeat together the historic expression of Christian faith known as the Apostles' (Nicene) Creed." For the Statement of Faith and the Committee's new creed, the recommended words of introduction are: "Let us repeat together a contemporary expression of Christian faith."
3. In order that the classical creeds will have their rightful place in our faith and life, and that we shall be properly prepared to use them in public worship, we recommend that greater effort be made to instruct United Church congregations in the meaning and significance of the classical creeds.
4. We recommend that in services of baptism and confirmation, if a creed be used, it be said by the congregation as a whole.[55]

The "New Creed" prepared by the Committee of Christian Faith was:

Man is not alone, he lives in God's world.
We believe in God:

Who has come in the true Man, Jesus,
to reconcile and make new
who works in us and others by the Spirit.
We trust Him.
He calls us to be his church:
to celebrate his presence
to love and serve others,
to seek justice and resist evil,
to proclaim Jesus, Crucified and risen,
our judge and our hope.
In life, in death, in life beyond death, God is with us.
We are not alone.
Thanks be to God.[56]

Creeds provides the context within which the use of the Apostles' Creed in the baptismal orders must be placed. One can, for example, detect an interesting response to the report's recommendations in the *Service Book* and its baptismal orders. The minutes of the Committee on Worship and Ritual record that the Committee strongly disliked the words of introduction in the second recommendation, arguing that the use of "repeat" "emasculated" the nature of belief, profession, and confession.[57] The fact that no such introductory words and only rubrical direction appears in the final orders shows that, while the Committee deleted its original wording ("Let us profess the faith of the Church as it is declared in the Apostles' Creed"[58]), it ignored the recommendations of the Committee on Christian Faith and, therein, the General Council—at least with respect to the liturgical texts. The concession was that the creeds and statements of faith referred to in the first recommendation were printed on the inside covers of both service books with the introductory words given in the second recommendation.

The interpretative context provided by *Creeds* is also one which contains a range of attitudes toward the historic creeds—a mixture of patristic witness, Puritan rejection, liberal suspicion, and ecumenical appreciation.[59] There is a sense in which this range of views reflects the United Church ethos as a whole and can be seen within the baptismal liturgies themselves. In the orders for the Baptism of Children there is corporate use of the Apostles' Creed, but it is permissive. In the first Order for Adult Baptism and Confirmation the rubrics imply that the candidates do not say the Creed. In the second Order for Adult Baptism and Confirmation the rubric is simply "A Creed (optional)" thus allowing for the use of other modern affirmations of faith, including the New Creed, and leaving unclear whether or not the candidates say the Creed with the congregation. These inconsistencies may be due in part to the timeline of the process of liturgical revision; i.e., the last liturgy to be drafted, the second order for Adult Baptism and Confirmation, takes into account *Creeds*, while the other previously completed orders do not. The result is that, with the approval of the texts by General Council, the treatment of the Apostles' Creed in the orders shows both the lack of consensus between the Committee on Christian Faith and the Committee on Church Worship and Ritual regarding their use, and the range of attitudes toward the Creeds in the United Church. Once again, it is an example of how a more conservative liturgical vision was modified by the liturgical liberalism of the United Church context.

Other Issues

As with the analysis of *The Book of Common Order* texts in part II of this study, a number of other considerations beyond structure, scripture, pneumatology, and ecclesiology will be noted to help clarify the context of study and evaluation.

Language

One of the issues of contemporary concern which came before the compilers of the *Service Book* was the style of liturgical language. Before its publication, many clergy had been modernizing the language of worship and joining in the call for the same in the revised rites.[60] "Some people," wrote one columnist in the *Observer*, "find Sunday services a drag. They really don't dig what goes on."[61] The sixties were, to say the least, unpredictable.

Early in the process of revision the Committee spent much time struggling with the tension between the use of "Thou" and "You," especially in relation to the orders for Communion. This led to larger discussion on the style of liturgical language in general.[62] Atkinson presented a well-received paper on the principles for liturgical revision in a contemporary idiom, and put forward the McLuhanesque argument that, at a time "when the Guttenburg world [was] dying and the electronic world [was] already with us," the time was right for the development of a "truly secular, liturgical language."[63] The Committee was aware of the trend: "about half the ministers in Western Canada," "younger ministers," and "half the students of Emmanuel College" were addressing God with "you."[64] They settled on a "compromise motion" that "our services consistently use 'thee' and 'thou' but that in the Treasury there be a proportion of prayers in the modern idiom using 'you.'"[65]

However, the tide could not be held back. Presbyteries continued to press for modernization and, as already noted, the General Council eventually demanded it. In the case of the orders for baptism, the Committee's discovery of such resources as *Contemporary Prayers* and its use of new biblical translations allowed for a process of quick modernization.[66] In the end, the result can only be seen as a slight concession, grudgingly given and hastily executed: traditional usage was continued in reference to God in all the major orders; it was eliminated altogether from the contemporary versions of the orders; examples of both were provided in the resources in the "Materials for Services of Worship." Often exhortative statements seem thoroughly modern while much of the scripture and some of the prayers sound more traditional. At best, it represents a cautious step forward, a desire to balance the much-loved cadences of the Prayer Book, as cherished in *The Book of Common Order*, with the demands of the contemporary context. One Committee member tried to put a good face on it by calling it a "liturgical amphibian," able to survive in both environments, traditional and contemporary.[67]

In actual fact, traditional language quickly faded from use, due, in no small part, to the implied permission of the *Service Book*. The more traditional prayers and orders tended to be modernized *in situ*, with the contemporary orders dominating sacramental practice. Still today, one often experiences United Church baptismal celebrations with various components taken from the 1969 contemporary orders. All the efforts on the part of the Committee to hold on to some degree of traditional liturgical language were pointless. In addition, it was not long after the publication of the *Service Book* before concerns around inclusive language began to arise—an area of liturgical language the members of the Committee did not and could not have anticipated. Such issues contributed to the book seeming out of date just as it was published. One cannot help but wonder if the same Committee member who had hoped for a "liturgical amphibian" was more accurate in his fear of a "stillborn enterprise."[68]

In this sense, some of the Committee members were correct in their anxiety about producing any book at all during a time of such rapid change. It was argued in relation to the *Service Book for the use of the people*, for example, that "Gestetner can do all we need for our congregations. This is a throw away time that requires throw-away material."[69] Such opinions also relate to discussions about the book-medium itself. As the Committee anticipated the response of General Council to their work, some expressed doubt about the relevance of the medium in the contemporary context. "Loose-leaf" formats were considered and discussed. "Certain practical advantages in the adding and removal of material" were cited, and the view that such a format would make an important statement "about the nature of worship itself" was attractive. In the end, considerations of appearance, cost, and durability ruled these options out. The argument that "it is never a good time" to produce a worship book settled the differences of opinion of these matters.[70]

Action

The *Service Book* orders also exhibit other significant developments in other forms of liturgical language for the United Church. The baptismal orders show growing attention to the role of posture and gesture. The congregation stands for their vows of support and profession of the faith using the Creed (if done). In the first Order for Adult Baptism and Confirmation, the candidates for confirmation stand when called upon by the Clerk of Session or Elder. The drama is further enhanced when, after the questions, the congregation is seated, the candidates remain standing and are called forward individually to kneel for the laying on of hands. The result is the highlighting of the laying on of hands in these rites as never before. Following this, they rise for individual commissioning and the Elder or Clerk of Session extends the "right hand of fellowship." More attention is given to such details in the rubrics for confirmation than in the other orders.

Other liturgical and symbolic actions remain minimal, however. An early draft contained both the ancient practice of meeting the candidates at the door and processing into the church as well as a renunciation.[71] When the subject of renunciation was discussed in reference to its use in the much-admired South Indian rite, it was concluded that it was only appropriate to those countries in which Christianity was threatened by pagan gods and idolatry![72] While, in keeping with the founding principles of the United Church, provision is made in the notes for baptism by immersion, "sprinkling and pouring are the usual methods."[73] The rationalist and didactic bias of the rites is betrayed by the continued reliance on exhortation and teaching statements. In particular, the ease with which the Committee accepted most of the Congregationalist Statement from *Contemporary Prayers* in the contemporary Order for the Baptism of Children is noteworthy. One line from this source has become something of a classic in many United Church liturgies: "Although, in our tradition, people are seldom baptized by going down under the water, the meaning is the same."[74] Suspicion of the symbolic is not far beneath the surface here, the emphasis clearly being laid on (rational) meaning over (liturgical) symbol.

In short, as in *The Book of Common Order*, the water of baptism is virtually invisible, mentioned only in rubrics or didactic exhortation, if at all. Much of the same sacramental minimalism as in *The Book of Common Order* prevails.

Liturgical Space

One area in which a measure of success can be discerned was in the area of liturgical space. One sees the beginnings of sensitivity to the placement of the font in the publications and work of the Committee on Church Architecture and in articles in the *Observer*.[75] Nevertheless, the font itself remained small and no connection was made between the symbol of water and its conspicuous lack in fonts of such size.

The choir-inspired "divided chancel" established itself as the preferred arrangement in this period.[76] The neo-Gothic plan supplanted the Reformed plan in most new structures. The central pulpit was replaced by the central communion table with a lectern and pulpit on either side of the chancel. The gothic-inspired "A-frame" building became synonymous with the United Church in suburbia, replacing both the solid historic lines of Presbyterian structures and the curved Akron Plan of North American Methodism. One such new building, for example, was held up as "Canada's most significant new United Church." It was, the minister of the church claimed,

> designed for Christian worship in a United Church congregation in the reformed tradition. The core of such worship is the Word and the Sacrament. We have tried to underline the centrality of them by placing the Bible, the communion table, and the baptismal font in a central position in the Church. . . . [the font] deserves a central place that suggests that baptism is the mark of initiation into the fellowship, culminating at the Lord's Table.[77]

This "central place" for the font was the end of the aisle at the foot of the chancel steps. It is significant that the author chose to speak of "liturgical center" rather than "chancel," the latter having, in his words, "no relevance in this structure."[78]

In the same period Richard Davidson wrote of the growing "functional approach" to church architecture, one rooted in a careful study of the worship to take place in a given space. His comments on baptism link the *Service Book* orders for baptism with spatial considerations.

> Baptism should take place in a significant place. The congregation as well as the parents are involved. Two reasons among others why the Sacrament of Baptism has failed to command the attention it deserves are, first, the apparent inconsequential nature of the service, inserted in Sunday worship at any point which meets the whim of the individual minister, and second, the architectural significance of the font and its location. The placing of the font and the importance of the Baptismal Service must both receive more consideration and emphasis.[79]

The discussion of such perspectives in such a forum as the *Observer* marks an important development in the understanding of United Church architecture and its relation to the service of baptism.

Calendar and Lectionary

The *Service Book* also advanced the cause of calendar and lectionary in United Church worship, though not without mixed results. It has already been suggested that, while there was a "Table of Lessons" with "Prayers for Grace" included in *The Book of Common Order*, its use was minimal, due in no small measure to the lack of any real sense of the Christian calendar in weekly worship. It was not that there was no *de facto* calendar for the United Church, but that it had little relation to the classic Christian seasons and festivals. Throughout the history of the United Church there evolved a number of "special" Sundays, climaxing in the period of the sixties and seventies: from the rise of the now-familiar "Week of Prayer" and "World Wide Communion" Sundays, to the Sunday celebration of "secular" holidays (Dominion Day, Labor Day, Remembrance Day, Mother's Day), Sundays with an educational or moral aim (Rural Life Sunday, Christian Family Sunday, Rally Day, Youth Sunday, Christian Education Sunday, Temperance Sunday), and other more creative inventions ("Fill the Pew Sunday").[80] One critic responded to this growth by suggesting: "I am wondering if the time has not come to call a halt to these ever-growing Special Days? . . . I fear that the Church in its desire to keep up with the times may have to set apart a Gospel Sunday."[81]

This is the context within which the Committee agreed, early on, that a more traditional three-year lectionary based on the Christian year be constructed, consisting of three lessons for each Sunday (Old Testament, Epistle, and Gospel) and a corresponding psalm.[82] Little was accomplished on the task until, a few years later, an initial proposal for a four-season calendar (Creation, Christmas, Easter, Pentecost) based on A. Allan McArthur's work was well received by the Committee.[83] Difficulties arose as the Committee tried to agree on the principles for the selection of texts to be fit into this calendar. One member expressed concern about the proposed procedure of simply "picking the four-hundred best passages from the Bible" and placing them in the appropriate season on the best Sunday. Another raised the question of the relationship of the Old Testament lesson to the New Testament passages and the assumed priority of the gospel lesson in the light of modern biblical scholarship.[84] In time, the whole idea of a lectionary began to come under question within the Committee itself. What were the relative values of topical preaching and textual preaching? Was it to be curriculum-driven or calendar-driven? Was its intention proscriptive of permissive; was it a directive or a directory? Enthusiasm waned. By 1966 some "did not feel that a lectionary was too useful" and were "reluctant to expend a great deal of energy on it." Perhaps it was too "binding" during an age of "the happening."[85] Atkinson's comment was to be the most prophetic: "the moment is not timely. This is a period of reconsideration and the lectionary that is going to make its way will be produced under broader sponsorship than that of one denomination."[86]

To this end, Grant, now chair of the "Lectionary Committee," wrote to Weibe Vos of *Studia Liturgica* to inquire about ecumenical work on the subject. Upon learning that little was happening (in retrospect, an astounding response given the development which shall be referred to below), work proceeded. The completed work was presented and accepted in June of 1968.[87]

The result was a distinctively United Church innovation. The Introduction to the Table of Lessons in the *Service Book* summarizes its structure and intentions:

> The lectionary consists of three complete series of readings, each of which forms a unit in itself. They correspond roughly with the cycle of the New Curriculum and will be used most effectively in conjunction with it. In Year 1, God's Purpose, attention is concentrated upon the mighty acts of God. In Year 2, God's Way, aspects of Christian living predominate. Year 3, God's People, contains a fair amount of historical and biographical material. . . .
>
> For reasons both of logic and of practicality, the structure does not correspond precisely with that of the traditional Christian Year. Its logical order, as suggested by Dr. A. A. McArthur, is that of the Apostles' Creed. The season of Creation, an innovation proposed by Dr. McArthur, marks the activities of God the Father and emphasizes his role in the natural order. The seasons taking their name from Christmas and Easter trace the career of the Son from the first anticipation of his coming to his exaltation and continual intercession for us. During Pentecost and the Sundays following it our attention is turned to the Holy Spirit, the church and the Christian hope.
>
> Practical considerations have also been kept in mind. The year beings, as it effectively does in most congregations, on the Sunday after Labour Day. It reaches a climax in June, when most people are still worshipping in their home churches. Provision is made, so far as possible, for such commonly observed occasions as World-wide Communion Sunday and the Week of Prayer for Christian Unity. . . .
>
> Before the reading of the Gospel a selection from one of the Psalms is provided. . . .
>
> The table is intended to be suggestive, not restrictive. When the calendar or local usage raise complications, or when circumstances suggest the use of

other readings, the best criterion for selection will be the judgement of the minister.[88]

In addition to the thematic thrust of each year, the set of readings for each Sunday had its own heading, "intended to convey at a glance a major theme of each day's readings."[89]

Like McArthur's proposal, the system was intended to "serve as a vehicle for teaching and preaching."[90] Herein lies the key to its shortcomings. The methodology was primarily pedagogical, derived from a combination of the structure of the Apostles' Creed, the themes of the New Curriculum, and weekly topics selected by the Committee. This convergence of educational "themes" for each year, seasons, and Sunday, ran the risk of imposing a heavy *a priori* hermeneutical bias on the texts. The lectionary principle of *lectio continua* was totally abandoned in favor of a pedagogical agenda specific to The United Church of Canada. Furthermore, the catholicity of the Christian calendar was also compromised and, with it, its paschal-based roots in the Christian *cultus*.[91] This meant that, in the case of baptism, for example, any awareness of the festivals and seasons traditionally associated with this sacrament, its preparation and celebration, were muted. Thus, the sacramental and liturgical efforts of the Committee in the *Service Book* orders were undermined by a lectionary and calendar system hostile to liturgical celebration in general and sacramental celebration in particular.

While, in one sense, the Table of Lessons may have advanced the cause of integrating education and worship in the United Church, its pedagogical hermeneutics ("a vehicle for teaching and preaching") betray a largely didactic and narrowly homiletical concept of worship.[92] Indeed, the Committee may have unwittingly promoted the problematic United Church syllogism: worship equals preaching and preaching equals education, therefore worship equals education. In the language of liturgical theology, the classic relationship of *lex orandi, lex credendi*, was reversed. As one set of critics put it: "In retrospect, we might ask: Should doctrine and education dictate worship or should they follow from worship? The order in 1969 was backwards. Education comes out of liturgy and leads back to liturgy, not the other way around. It is worship that is at the center of our experience together."[93]

In addition, because the Table of Lessons was so tied to the New Curriculum, it fell from what little use it enjoyed as the Curriculum faded from use.[94]

There was an even more practical (and somewhat embarrassing) reason for its failure than either of those relating to liturgical theology or curricula. In spite of the information given to the Committee regarding the lack of ecumenical work in this area, the Roman Catholic *Ordo Lectionum Missae*[95] was published to wide acclaim in the same year as the *Service Book*. This is yet another example of the bad timing which plagued the Committee. The Roman Lectionary quickly gathered enthusiastic ecumenical attention in North America and immediately became the basis for several other lectionary systems. Eventually the convergence of interest around an ecumenical lectionary allowed the Consultation on Common Texts to produce the "Common Lectionary."[96] Ironically, these external developments were to have a far greater influence on United Church worship and curricula than the uniquely United Church 1969 Table of Lessons. Atkinson's prediction, three years earlier, that success would belong to a lectionary "produced under broader sponsorship" could not have been more accurate.

The Hymn Book and United-Anglican Union

An area in which broader sponsorship was at work was *The Hymn Book.*[97] Its production has been recounted in detail in other studies.[98] For purposes of this study, the important features to be emphasized are its joint sponsorship and its liturgical emphasis.

In spite of the esteem in which *The Hymnary* was held, calls for a new hymn book were coming from various conferences by 1962.[99] With the authority of General Council, the Committee on Church Worship and Ritual struck a subcommittee to begin the task of revision.[100] At the same time, separate negotiations directed toward the union of the Anglican Church of Canada and The United Church of Canada were proceeding, under the direction of two "Committees of Ten."[101] They were quick to respond positively to the suggestion by the subcommittee that a "common hymn book" be produced.[102]

By 1965 the General Synod of the Anglican Church gave authority to its Hymnal Committee to work with its United Church counterpart toward this end. The resulting joint committee labored for five years, wading through over one hundred hymnals, including detailed studies of *The Hymnary*, the Anglican *Book of Common Praise*, and thousands of original contributions. Along the way it also provided the *Observer* with many columns of passionate and entertaining copy.[103]

By the time it was authorized by the General Council of The United Church of Canada and the General Synod of the Anglican Church of Canada in February of 1971, a cloud of suspicion had formed over the book; one which was to remain throughout its lifetime. For many United Church persons the changes to texts, tunes, and harmonies, the exclusion of many "old favorites" and the inclusion of chants, plainsong, and other liturgical material was too much of a compromise—a concession to the Anglicans—bought at the price of the traditions of *The Hymnary.*[104] For many Anglicans, there was not enough plainsong, a lack of material for the liturgical year, and too many "cheap music-hall tunes." Even some on the Committee on Church Worship and Ritual began to think of it as "purist" and "high-brow." The Anglican General Synod saw one of its most bitter debates over the motion to approve it.[105] Finally, the demise of union negotiations in 1975 served only to support the perception that the book was a failure.[106]

That *The Hymn Book* failed to take deep root in United Church liturgical soil also served to undermine much of the vision of the *Service Book* and its baptismal rites. Where United Church persons focused on the Anglican content of the book (i.e., the "Liturgical Appendix" and the "festivals" of the "Christian Year") and the loss of the traditional United Church responses (i.e., *The Hymnary*'s Gloria Patri, Lord's Prayer, Aaronic Benediction, and the three-fold

Amen), they also overlooked significant *Service Book* influences. The bulk of the contents of *The Hymn Book* are arranged according to the Approach-Word-Response structure of the *Service Book* orders. While over one hundred hymns are grouped according to the traditional headings of the "Christian Year" as used by the Anglicans,[107] this section is prefaced by a listing of hymns appropriate for the season of "Creation"—the first season of the *Service Book's* Table of Lessons. Finally, *The Hymn Book* places more baptismal hymns before United Church congregations than ever before in its history (though there are still very few), in keeping with the sacrament's higher profile in the *Service Book*. Unfortunately, most of them can be called upon to support the *Service Book*'s assumption that baptism is a sacrament for children and confirmation functions as a sacrament of the Holy Spirit.[108]

An important question to be asked coming out of these and other previous observations is: Were the *Service Book* baptismal rites driven by the Committee's desire for church union? On the one hand, it has been shown that early drafts of the orders favored various liturgical forms more familiar to Anglicans (i.e., litany and berakah structures, the Sursum Corda, canticles). The *BCP* language of "the ministration of baptism" in the earlier drafts and the rise in the profile of confirmation also suggests Anglican influence. In particular, the decision to exclude the laity from the laying on of hands in confirmation turned on the point of its implications for union.

In addition, several influential members of the Committee were also on *The Hymn Book's* Joint Committee and one was on the United Church's Committee of Ten working toward union.[109] In some United Church minds, this was tantamount to conspiracy. One congregation's response to an early draft of the baptismal service was representative of this opinion, if more tactful than most. (It is amazing in its similarity to that letter cited with reference to *The Book of Common Order* texts): "One of the elders asked if this service was an attempt to bridge the gap with the 'impending union of the Anglican and United Church in mind.'"[110] If so, he continued, it should be clearly stated that this is the case.

On the other hand, Committee records suggest that they spoke very little of union in their deliberations. The bulk of the evidence indicates that their aim was not so much Anglican-United amalgamation as catholic liturgical content. This agenda was neither hostile nor conspiratorial with respect to union. At most, it was both compatible and complementary. But even on this question the Committee had to back away from many of its catholic forms, "liberalizing" them for a United Church constituency and resulting in uniquely United Church baptismal rites in a uniquely United Church book. This is in marked contrast to the largely Prayer Book-based orders of *The Book of Common Order*.

A particularly revealing discussion took place in the Committee in 1965. With the recent publication of the "Principles of Union" by the Committees of Ten, Grant (a member also of both the Committee of Ten and the Joint Committee of *The Hymn Book*) raised the question of the relevance of their work given the possibility of union. The discussion makes clear that even Grant understood their work to have been, at least to date, distinctly United Church in ethos. He began by suggesting the advisability of a soft-covered book, so as to give it less authority and therein pose less potential problems for union negotiations.

> "[I]t should be printed so that it cannot be ignored but not between hard covers so that it would appear codified." Mr. Oliver disagreed. "We should look upon our work as a contribution to the Holy Catholic Church and the contribution should be so bound so that it would be permanent." As the Committee was reminded by Professor Boyce, we have no alternative but to fulfill the commission laid upon us by the General Council and make our revisions. Any future action will have to be determined by the Council.[111]

The discussion concluded with agreement on several related points: that it would be a number of years before any such union would take place; that in any union worship would be permitted to continue in the congregation of the newly constituted church according to the traditions and practices of their respective founding communions for some time to come; that, therefore, United Church worship should and must continue to proceed and develop; that the new *Service Book* would be an important component of the United Church's contribution to any union. The same perspective was later expressed on at least two occasions in the Committee's reports to General Council: "the United Church cannot afford to mark time. . . . Worship in the United Church has its own characteristics."[112] "This new *Service Book* may well be one of our more precious gifts to church union."[113]

The documents of the General Commission on Church Union also suggest that Union discussions did not have as much influence on the *Service Book* baptismal orders as one might expect.[114] A paper on the essential elements in baptism and confirmation by the United Church representatives cited the *Service Book* orders as a faithful expression of United Church theology and worship, with the additional recommendation that, in spite of the *Service Book* orders, Holy Communion would best be included in adult baptism and confirmation.[115] Furthermore, the consensus statement of the Commission identified renunciation in baptism and the role of the bishop in confirmation as essential. It even downplayed the three-stage view of Christian initiation by asserting the primacy of baptism over confirmation: "The commission wishes to emphasize that Christian initiation is baptism. The Service of Confirmation is seen as an effective means whereby the meaning of our baptism is given personal expression."[116]

With Richard Davidson as co-chair of the Liturgical Commission and John Webster Grant on the Committee of Ten, the details of such discussions would have been well known to the Committee on Church Worship and Ritual. Yet such liturgical directions did not find expression in the *Service Book* orders.[117]

Such evidence demonstrates that, while some "Anglican" sensibilities may have been present in the liturgical tastes of some Committee members, unlike *The Hymn Book* (and even *The Book of Common Order*), the *Service Book* baptismal orders show little significant influence by the movement for union.

United Church Publications

This period in the life of the United Church was marked by a flood of official publications ranging from pamphlets, policy statements, and reports to curricula, devotional material, and books. From among the wealth of material I will mention only two sources as a brief illustration of the role and place of baptism in United Church understanding.

The New Curriculum was one of the most ambitious and controversial undertakings in United Church history. It was an effort to communicate the latest and best in theological and biblical scholarship to people of all ages in the church through the most advanced methods of pedagogy. For the purposes of this study, what is notable about much of the material is the lack of attention given to baptism. In the early stages of the formation of the New Curriculum the need for more intentional "plans for participation in worship" was identified as a major concern and goal. However, this was not related in any significant degree to theological foundations rooted in an understanding of baptism or Christian initiation.[118] The "heritage resources" for the curriculum were identified as the Bible, not liturgical practice or worship traditions.[119] In spite of an emphasis on such topics as covenant, fellowship, family, church, world, Christian witness, and "child of God," things liturgical or baptismal were absent.[120] The foundational material clearly relied heavily on the theological scholarship of twentieth-century Protestant liberalism, in which liturgical concerns did not figure prominently. Work on the development of this material took place separate from the Committee on Church Worship and Ritual. Worship seemed to be only one venue, among many, for education.

Perhaps the most significant piece of material in the New Curriculum was Donald M. Mathers' *The Word and The Way*.[121] In many respects a masterful example of popular theological writing, it was the adult resource, introduced first, and on which other volumes in the series were dependent. While creative and nuanced on many matters of contemporary theology and biblical scholarship, the sacraments, prayer, and worship were treated in a matter of lines. They were together defined as "a means of grace, the proven ways by which the life of the believer is built up and nourished." The sacraments in particular were defined as the "actions" of the "word," thus dependent on the Bible, the primary means of grace.[122] This reflects the pedagogical bias of the material in the New Curriculum. "Christianity is after all an educated religion,"[123] wrote Mathers. Conceptual aspects of faith and theology were emphasized rather than the liturgical.

This lack of liturgical and/or baptismal piety and its implications in polity was reflected also in the title and conclusions of the major study *Church Membership*.[124] This was indeed a misnomer, for the document itself contained, for its time, the best examination of the historic and theological dimensions of baptism in a United Church publication. However, because its prime mandate was to make recommendations to General Council dealing with the polity and discipline of church membership, most of the subtleties of the document got lost (or undermined) in its problematic conclusions and recommendations.

The title also reflected the increased concern about the meaning of membership in a time of increased church growth. This focus tended to shift the spotlight from strategy to tactics,[125] from meaning to methods, from liturgy to polity. In other words, it represented a shift away from the meaning of baptism in relation to its liturgical celebration to the meaning of membership in relation to its oversight and discipline. Juridical and polity concerns were emphasized at the expense of liturgical and theological concerns.

The cornerstone of this thrust was found in the affirmation of the "traditional order" of "Baptism Confirmation, and First Communion" as the official "order of Initiation into The United Church of Canada."[126] Thus, "Confirmation" was embraced as a means to clarify and manage membership through its focus on education for "full membership."

This official pronouncement supports what has been found in the details of the liturgical rites themselves. It suggests what I would call a "confirmation-based" paradigm of initiation. In such a paradigm confirmation takes on an increasingly sacramental significance at the expense of the primacy of baptism. In addition, confirmation resources and classes become the focus of much pastoral energy, adult baptism all but fades from view, Holy Communion becomes the privilege of "full members," the fragmentation of initiation becomes entrenched, and the occasional orders for restoration and transfer of membership take on an increased profile. While this was by no means the intended outcome of such a well-written study as *Church Membership*, it was, for all intents and purposes, the product of its recommendations and its pastoral result.

Conclusions

The process of revision and compilation of the *Service Book* baptismal orders is, again, instructive about United Church sensibilities regarding worship and its efforts to respond to the contemporary context. The analysis of this process can also be meaningfully related to the genetic makeup of the United Church tradition and the practices of the founding traditions.

Puritan-like sensibilities continued to the extent that both liturgical simplicity and freedom were demanded by most of the church and surprisingly little attention was paid to the project of producing a book of orders as a whole. Indeed, the liturgical "experts" again encountered resistance to their desire for more classic forms than the church could countenance at any given time.

The didacticism of many historic Presbyterian orders was recast in the language of liberalism and its tendency to see worship as an educational opportunity (e.g., Teaching Statements).

The covenant ecclesiology of Congregationalism and Presbyterianism continued to be present, though again communicated in the liberal and often vague language of "new beginning." Surprisingly, a theology of "adoption" found its way back into the orders after being omitted from *The Book of Common Order* rites. Anglican influence, while not as great as one might expect in the context of Anglican-United dialogue, was marginally present. If the Methodist ambiguities observed in part I surrounding confirmation, reception, and profession of faith were seeds which had only just begun to sprout in *The Book of Common Order*, they reached full flower in the *Service Book.*

If there is one major issue which emerges from this study of the baptismal orders of the *Service Book* it is the growing status of confirmation in United Church worship and practice, and the rise of a "confirmation-based" paradigm of Christian initiation. It is surprising that the Committee and the church were so willing to overthrow the traditional Reformation position on this subject and give the rite a pneumatic character.

The significant liturgical and theological gains of the Approach-Word-Response structure of the rites were seriously compromised by the ambiguities and inconsistencies of many of the details of the form and content in the orders. Efforts to avoid the problem of treating baptism as an event "inserted" into public worship ended up making it a rite interpolated into confirmation.

The use of scripture was somewhat broadened, though not as much as the Committee would have liked, but the hermeneutical framework was still tied to the basic notion of a sacramental warrant (albeit more liberally interpreted). In particular, in the context of confirmation, the function of such a view only reinforced its character as a pneumatic event. Ironically, all this took place in the face of the Committee's failed efforts to suggest that water could be "blessed" in baptism. While they carefully guarded the sacramental minimalism of baptism, an over-sacramentalization crept into confirmation.

The strengths of the orders are in keeping with the Committee's general vision behind the *Service Book* as a whole. Out of such turbulent times emerged significant features which subsequently came to be characteristic of United Church worship. For example, further steps were taken toward the unity of word and sacrament in worship. The ecclesiological dimensions of worship were strengthened by an increase in the level of active congregational participation. In addition, the first official steps were taken toward the realization of a variety of other goals which would continue to be important in the years to come: the firm commitment to the context of public worship for baptism; sensitivies surrounding liturgical language; a growing consciousness of calendar and lectionary; the recovery of some classic liturgical forms "new" to United Church experience (litanies, berakah forms of prayer, creedal confession, etc.); and signs of the beginning of an appreciation of architectural concerns related to baptismal space. While these steps were often tentative, they were significant developments which both built upon past themes and anticipated future directions.

Notes

1. "Minutes" of 31 October 1960: 2.
2. *SB* (1969), unnumbered p. 3.
3. *SB* (1969), unnumbered p. 3.
4. *MSBC* (1965), 2.
5. "Minutes" of 24 February 1964: 2-3
6. "Minutes" of 27 February 1961: 3.

7. *MSBC*, (1965), 5.

8. The 1965 General Council had affirmed "that the practice of admitting children to the Table of the Lord be discouraged with a view to reserving it ultimately for members who have been received into full communion with the Church." *Church Membership: Doctrine and Practice in The United Church of Canada*, Committee on Christian Faith (The Board of Evangelism and Social Service and The Board of Christian Education, 1963), 7.

9. Cf. *MSBC* (1965), 5.

10. *SB* (1969), 47-48, 67.

11. Donald Henderson, "The New Service of Baptism," *Observer* (1 February 1966): 29.

12. That the 1966 draft was viewed as essentially a confirmation service is also evident in the headings of the order: "The Approach," "The Word of God," "The Laying on of Hands," and "The Response of the People." *CPB* (1966), 5.

13. *CPB* (1966), 3.

14. Articles in the *Observer* from this period testify to the large educational emphasis on confirmation in congregations. E.g., 15 April 1963: "Editorial: The Confirmation Class," 10; A. C. Forrest, "Confirmation: What does it mean?" 2, 12, 13; "One Minister's Unique Approach to Confirmation," 14. The last article notes that 97 boys were confirmed on Palm Sunday at Islington United Church in Toronto in 1962. In 1963 the number was 80 girls. The confirmation classes involved 14 hours of meetings beginning after Christmas.

15. "Drafts" dated from 11 January 1961 to January 1968.

16. "Minutes" of 24 February 1964: 2-3.

17. *MSBC* (1965), 3. The third passage also alludes to the covenant promise "to you and your children."

18. "Considerable uneasiness" had been expressed, for example, about the appropriateness of Jesus' baptism by John, especially in the light of Cullmann's recently published work, *Baptism in the New Testament*. "Minutes" of 23 March 1964: 2.

19. *MSBC* (1965), 2.

20. *MSBC* (1965), 12.

21. Nothing is recorded regarding any decision about the final selection of scripture, save the various general approvals of drafts after 1965 and the final form of the orders. Mark 10 was back in the working draft by October of 1966. "Minutes" of 24 October 1966: 1. The final versions were approved in January of 1969. "Minutes" of 27 January 1969: 2.

22. The exception being that in the contemporary order the Mark 10 text was not included, leaving only the Matthew 28 text.

23. Paul DeClerck, "In the beginning was the Word: Presidential Address," *Studia Liturgica* 22 (1992): 1-16. The papers in this volume were given at the 1991 Toronto Congress on Bible and Liturgy. All of them are relevant to this discussion. DeClerck's is an helpful overview of the issues.

24. There is, of course, other scriptural content in the baptismal rites, from the opening scripture sentences and lectionary texts chosen in accordance with the Christian Year to a few biblical allusions in some of the prayers. Yet most of these are optional and are experienced as secondary to the passages read in association with the action of baptism. The opening sentences do anticipate particular interpretations of baptism to be elaborated upon in the warrants and exhortations. In infant baptism the opening sentences highlight covenant theology and the concept of "new beginning." In adult baptism and confirmation they focus mostly on "strengthening."

25. E.g., "Minutes" of 24 February 1964: 4.

26. The offending line was "Bless this water for use in thy holy sacrament." *MSBC* (1965), 12.

27. *MSBC* (1965), 12. One cannot help but wonder if the issue was as much a liberal discomfort with the contemporary "evangelical" connotations of "born again" as a concern over sacramental regeneration.

28. At least one Committee member is on record as expressing some discomfort with this emphasis, especially in relation to the contemporary order: "We have selected particular interpretation of baptism—the new beginning—which I do not find very suitable for infants." "Minutes" of 23 December 1968: 2.

29. *MSBC* (1965), 1.

30. The Explanatory Note for the 1966 draft of adult baptism and confirmation did not contain any elaboration of a theology of baptism *per se*, but focused only on confirmation. The Introduction to the Services of Initiation in the *Service Book* makes no substantial theological comments.

31. *MSBC* (1965), 2.

32. *CPB* (1966), 1.

33. *SB* (1969), 37.

34. This will become more explicit in the context of the studies on Christian initiation associated with *BRBF* (1986), to be discussed in part IV below.

35. *Church Membership*, 5.

36. *CPB* (1966), 1-2.

37. "Minutes" of 25 April 1966: 2.

38. The 1956 General Council upheld and approved the policy "that baptism should normally be administered in the presence of the congregation to which the parents or sponsors of the child are attached, or in the case of adult baptism to which the candidate is attached." *Church Membership*, 7.

39. This also reflects the spirit of several earlier studies and recommendations by the General Council on the eldership and related issues of discipline, polity, and doctrine. E.g., *Doctrine and Practice*, 7-9; *Church Membership*, 5-6.; *The Eldership: The Report of the Committee on Christian Faith* (Toronto: The Ryerson Press, 1966), 20. All emphasize the fact that in United Church polity it is the Session which has pastoral and administrative oversight of baptism and the preparation of candidates and/or parents for baptism.

40. *SB* (1969), 37.

41. *Doctrine and Practice*, 9.

42. Its formation is recounted in Harding, "The Development of Liturgical Resources," 102-106, 110-116, 117.

43. "Minutes" of 24 May 1967: 1.

44. Eg., "Drafts" dated December 1961, May 1962; April 1964; June 1964.

45. Daniel C. Matheson, "Baptism Service Sent to Presbyteries," *News-Letter* (October 1962): 13.

46. "Minutes" of 23 March 1964: 2-3.

47. "Minutes" of 24 February 1964: 2; 23 March 1964: 2-3.

48. *MSBC* (1965), 3.

49. *Creeds*, 5.

50. *CPB* (1966), unnumbered p. 11.

51. *CPB* (1966), unnumbered p. 3.

52. *Creeds*, 5.

53. *Creeds*, 5.

54. *Creeds*, 6.

55. *Creeds*, 22.

56. *Creeds*, 22. In its original form it was also noted that the first line could "be used as a versicle, with the rest as a response." This form has seldom been observed in practice.

57. "Minutes" of 1 April 1968: 2; 8 April 1968: 1-2.

58. *MSBC* (1966), 11; *CPB* (1966), 11.

59. *Creeds* 7, 9-16. Mathers, the chair of the Committee on Christian Faith, reporting to the Committee on Church Worship and Ritual on the findings of their report, spoke of the struggle within his Committee between "liberals" who "disliked all creeds" and "conservatives" who "wanted preservation of the historical faith." "Minutes" of 8 April 1968: 1-2.

60. E.g., Francis Stevens, "A plea for the use of modern language in church liturgy: In Plan English," *Observer* (15 April 1962): 18, 22; Editorial, "Vulgarity: Let us Use More Vulgar, More Earthly Language in Our Common Prayers!" *Observer* (1 May 1963): 7.

61. Clarke M. MacDonald, "Sunday 11:00 a.m. What's It All About?" *Observer* (1 September 1969): 24.

62. For a more detailed account of the Committee's discussion of this issue with particular reference to the orders for the Lord's Supper, see Harding, "The Development of Liturgical Resources," 94-102.

63. "Minutes" of 22 November 1965: 3.

64. "Minutes" of 11 March 1968: 2; 19 December 1966: 2.

65. "Minutes" of 19 December 1966: 2.

66. The Introduction to *Contemporary Prayers* contains an instructive reflection on the issue of liturgical language from this period. It would appear that the Committee was convinced of this perspective for the purposes of its contemporary orders, if its heavy reliance on both the liturgical material and poetic sense-line style of this source is any indication.

67. "Minutes" of 25 September 1967: 2.

68. "Minutes" of 25 September 1967: 1-2.

69. "Minutes" of 25 September 1967: 1-2.

70. "Minutes" of 7-8 June 1966: 1.

71. "Draft" dated 11 June 1961: 1-2.

72. "Minutes" of 8 February 1961: 1.

73. *SB* (1969), 37.

74. *SB* (1969), 52.

75. See, for example, publications of The Committee on Church Architecture: *Design For Worship* (1952); *So You Have a Church Building Program* (1952); *Building Your Church* (1958); *Building the Smaller Church* (1959); *Design for Worship* (1962). Most devote at least a few lines to the placement of the font at the "chancel entrance" in "full view of the congregation." Though admittedly often brief, even this is a significant development. Several articles appeared in the architecture issue of the *Observer* on 15 August 15, 1964. Also: Orville P. Hossie, "Your Church Building—Focus on Church Life" (15 August 1954): 3; Donald A. Amos, in "Canada's Most Significant New United Church" (1 April 1963): 12; "The Church You Built" (1 April 1963): 14-16; Richard H. N. Davidson, "How to Build a Church for Worship" (1 April 1963): 19, 45.

76. See especially, Victor Fiddes, *The Architectural Requirement of Protestant Worship* (Toronto: Ryerson Press, 1961), 77-93. The UCA Records of the Committee on Church Architecture show the dominance of the "divided chancel" in the building plans of the period.

77. Donald Amos, "Canada's Most Significant New United Church," *Observer* (1 April 1963): 12.

78. Amos, "Canada's Most Significant New United Church," 12.

79. Davidson, "How to Build a Church for Worship," 19. Ironically, other pictures of other new churches in the same issue do not show a font.

80. See also, Harding, "The Development of Liturgical Resources," 39-44. Early *Observer* articles illustrate the ongoing tension between the rise of "special" Sundays and the desire to recover the traditional festivals of the Christian Year. E.g., "Church to Observe Youth Sunday" (1 May 1939): 11; "Magna Carta Sunday" (1 June 1939): 19; W. G. Onions, "We Should Celebrate the Great Christian Festivals" (1 February 1940): 16; Victor Fiddes, "The Observance of the Church Year" (1 September 1961): 13; T. E. Hollings, "The Rationale of Lent" (15 February 1952): 5.

81. "Roman Collar," *Observer* (15 June 1944): 15.

82. "Minutes" of 12 June 1961: 3.

83. "Minutes" of 14-15 June, 1964: 3.

84. "Minutes" of 27 September 1965: 2.

85. "Minutes" of 7-8 June 1988: 4-5.

86. "Minutes" of 7-8 June 1966: 5.

87. "Minutes" of 26 September 1966; p. 1; 10-11 June 1968: 5.

88. *SB* (1969), 254-255. The Sundays of Advent are called Sundays before Christmas; the Sundays of Lent are called Sundays before Easter.

89. *SB* (1969), 254.

90. *SB* (1969), 254.

91. For a discussion on these principles see: "Introduction," in *Common Lectionary: The Lectionary Proposed by the Consultation on Common Texts* (New York: The Church Hymnal Corporation, 1983), 10-23.

92. In addition, while the coordination of the readings and themes of worship with those of curricula help in such integration, it can only meet with limited success when children are absent from most of the Sunday liturgy while in Sunday school. For comments on the rise of the Sunday school and the exclusion of children from worship, see Harding, "The Development of Liturgical Resources," 44-48.

93. Barthel, et al. *A Guide to Sunday Worship*, 118.

94. "Now that the *New Curriculum* is rarely used, the Table of Lessons is of diminished value." Barthel, et al., *A Guide to Sunday Worship*, 118.

95. *Ordo Lectionum Missae* (Vatican City: typis Polyglottis Vaticanis, 1969).

96. *Common Lectionary*. See "Introduction," 7-10 for an account of the process. Other background information and evaluation can be found in *The Revised Common Lectionary: The Consultation on Common Texts* (Winfield: Wood Lake Books, 1992), and papers devoted to the subject in two special issues of *Studia Liturgica*, Vols. 21-22, no 1. (1991-1992).

97. *The Hymn Book of the Anglican Church of Canada and the United Church of Canada* (Toronto: The Anglican Church of Canada and the United Church of Canada, 1971).

98. Harding, "The Development of Liturgical Resources," 198-228; Kervin, "The Three Hymn Books."

99. *ROP* (1962), 560, 119.

100. "Preface," in *The Hymn Book*, unnumbered p. 1.

101. Union discussions had in fact begun in 1943, but encountered difficulties over the mutual recognition of ministries. Efforts were renewed in 1963. "Principles of Union" were approved by 1966. The Christian Church (Disciples of Christ) joined the discussion in 1969, but did not participate in the production of *The Hymn Book*. Douglas F. Campbell, "The Anglican and United Churches in Church Union Dialogue, 1943-75," *Studies in Religion*, XVII, 3 (1988): 303-314. See also *Plan of Union By-Laws*, The Anglican

Church of Canada, Christian Church (Disciples of Christ) in Canada, The United Church of Canada (Toronto: The General Commission on Church Union, 1972).

102. "Preface," *Hymn Book*, unnumbered p. 1.

103. For a sample of *Observer* articles see: A. C. Forrest, "A New Hymnary" (1 May 1964): 8-10, 26; Richard H. N. Davidson, "Which Bible for the New Hymnary?" (15 October 1964): 18; Editorial, "New Hymnary not needed" (15 April 1965): 10; Editorial, "One Hymnary" (August 1965): 8; Patricia Clarke, "Hymning and Hawing in Smoke-filled Room" (15 March 1970): 8; "The New Hymnary: What's In, What's Out, What's What" (15 March 1970): 12-15; "Battlefront Report on the New Hymnbook" (August 1970): 8; and letters to the editor, including those of 1 May 1970: 3; August 1970: 2.

104. Semple has observed that "The present *Hymn Book* is, in fact, less 'Anglican' than the old *Hymnary*. The back of each book contains the specifically liturgical materials. The *Hymn Book* gives five percent of its space to that material whereas the Hymnary gives nine percent – and that includes prose psalms pointed for Anglican chant, no less." Stuart Semple, "*The Hymn Book* Revisited," *Touchstone* 4, no. 1 (January 1986): 43.

105. Harding, "The Development of Liturgical Resources," 206-209, 209 (n. 41), 215-223, 225-227.

106. The *Observer* reported the verdict of Anglican General Synod in June of 1975 with the title of its editorial, "Now it's final" (August 1975): 9.

107. Advent, Epiphany, and Lent are not called The Sundays Before Christmas, The Sundays After Christmas, The Sundays Before Easter, as in the *Service Book* Table of Lessons.

108. Nine hymns appear in the section organized for baptismal hymns, with an additional thirteen listed in cross reference. Only two of nine are suitable for adult baptism. (In *The Hymnary* only four are given in the section on baptism. While twenty-seven general hymns are cross referenced as "suitable" for infant and adult baptism and confirmation, only two or three could be construed as explicitly baptismal). In *The Hymn Book* two appear in the section organized with confirmation in mind, one pneumatological in focus, the other confessional. An additional twenty-seven more general hymns are listed in cross reference.

109. Ron Atkinson, Richard Davidson, and Don Henderson were on *The Hymn Book* Joint Committee; John Grant was on it and the United Church's Committee of Ten Union Committee.

110. Letter to Davidson, dated 13 June 1967, from The Rev. A. A. Cross on behalf of the Broadway United Church Session, Regina, Sask. Box 8, Vol. 11, Section 2: 2.

111. "Minutes" of 14-15 June 1965: 2.

112. *ROP* (1966), 552.

113. *ROP* (1966), 358.

114. UCA, Union Negotiations Collection, General Commission on Church Union, 1967-1972.

115. Byron F. Howlett and John B. Corston, "Essential Elements in Baptism/Confirmation," 1-2. Union Negotiations Collection, Liturgical Commission, Box 33. This paper also defines confirmation in the United Church as the "confirming of baptismal vows," in contrast to the pneumatological focus in the *Service Book* rites themselves.

116. "Essential Elements of Initiation," 1. Union Negotiations Collection, Liturgical Commission, Box 34.

117. When the Disciples of Christ joined the discussion in 1969 the commission also began to discuss such issues as: replacing the term *confirmation* with "service of affirmation of faith and commissioning for Christian service"; the laying on of hands by laity in the consecration of bishops, ordination of presbyters and confirmation; a Service of

Thanksgiving for the Birth of a Child. A range of particular liturgical issues had yet to be worked out, therefore the Doctrinal Commission chose to simply affirm the general theological principles already articulated, leaving the liturgical and doctrinal details "with confidence to the new church itself." The discussion with the Disciples, however, began too late in the process to have any effect on the *Service Book.* See Drafts to "Declaration of Faith," Joint Consultation on Doctrine, Box 29, File 6, 17-19 September 1971: 10. See also: Box 30, Files 18, 19, 23, and "Membership," Doctrinal Commission Papers, Box 30, File 19: 2.

118. *Presuppositions for the Development of a curriculum for the Sunday Church Schools of the United Church of Canada: A statement from the Board of Christian Education and the Board of Publications of the United Church of Canada* (Toronto: The United Church of Canada, 1958), 5, 34.

119. *Presuppositions*, 18.

120. *Presuppositions*, 18-30. Year Three, "The Church and the World," did propose to give some attention to worship in general.

121. Donald M. Mathers, *The World and The Way* (Toronto: United Church Publishing House, 1962).

122. Mathers, 205-209.

123. Mathers, 223.

124. Mathers was the primary author of *Church Membership* as well. As chair of the Committee on Christian Faith he also was the primary author of *Creeds.*

125. Aidan Kavanagh, "Christian Initiation: Tactics and Strategies," in *Made, Not Born New Perspectives on Christian Initiation and the Catechumenate*, The Murphy Center for Liturgical Research (Notre Dame: University of Notre Dame Press, 1976), 1-6.

126. *Church Membership*, 5.

Part IV
Ecumenical Convergence in Christian Initiation

Chapter 6
Baptism in *Baptism and Renewal of Baptismal Faith*

Baptism and Renewal of Baptismal Faith

With the creation of the Committee on Liturgy within the Division of Mission in Canada in 1980, the liturgical life of the United Church was ready to respond to another turbulent time. Where the *Service Book* was largely a product of the United Church context of the fifties and sixties, the next generation of liturgies would be conceived within the context of broader ecumenical developments.

This is not to suggest that the *Service Book* orders were totally uninfluenced by some of the general principles common to ecumenical liturgical renewal. The Word and sacrament structure of the liturgy, the increased participation of the laity, and the use of vernacular (which in the United Church meant the modernization of English) can all be meaningfully related to the first principles which began to flow from the Second Vatican Council and *Sacrosanctum Concilium* (The Constitution of the Sacred Liturgy).[1] But the timing of the publication of the *Service Book* left it just out of step with the sweeping developments which were to overtake all of the major western Christian liturgical traditions.

In 1981 Fred McNally, successor to John Ambrose as Special Assistant—Worship presented his view of what "directions for worship" the United Church should focus on in the "early eighties" to the Division of Mission in Canada.[2] There were eight "thrusts:" 1. "more biblically centered worship," with a particular focus on the use of the "Ecumenical Lectionary" (based on *Ordo Lectionum Missae*); 2. "a fuller sacramental life," including the provision of new communion liturgies and the encouragement of more frequent celebration of communion;[3] 3. a more intentional process of churchwide education in the history and theology of liturgy; 4. worship that was more sensitive to social justice concerns; 5. more incarnational worship—that is, more holistic with respect to the body and all its senses; 6. the use of forms which provide enough flexibility and possibility for the "spontaneous intervention of the Holy Spirit"; 7. worship that was more "corporate and communal," more participatory and inclusive of people of all ages and abilities; 8. worship that was more "sensitive" to the "spiritual, emotional and intellectual needs" of the worshippers.

On most of these points the popular publication *Getting It All Together*, renamed *Gathering* in 1983,[4] was enlisted as the main vehicle of communication and education. The ecumenical lectionary and calendar became the guiding structure of the resource and the continued use of study papers, reviews, and columns on a variety of topics supported the educational and liturgical aims of the Committee on Liturgy. The Committee supported workshops, seminars, and a host of congregational and presbytery gatherings on liturgical renewal.

By 1982 the Committee was experiencing frustration because of their location within the structure of the Division of Mission in Canada. As a Committee of the Working Unit on Evangelism and Worship, they were finding that a disproportionate amount of time was being given to concerns other than their own. Upon request, they were granted independent status as the Working Unit on Worship and Liturgy, with direct budgeting and accountability to the Division of Mission in Canada.[5] Their articulated purpose was:

> Recognizing the interdependence of the worship life of the United Church and the need to maintain continuing contact with local congregations and Conference Worship Committees, we provide assistance and offer direction for worship in the life of The United Church of Canada so that:
>
> worship is informed by the liturgical heritage and current practice of the United Church in particular, and of the ecumenical church in general;
>
> worship is related to the milieu of our time, including the social, economic, political, and cultural factors which are shaping our society;
>
> worship's true character is found in a balance of Word and Table, and in an integrated use of words, music, movement, gesture, dance, architecture and art.[6]

In 1981 two subcommittees of the Committee on Liturgy (later to become the Working Unit) began work on services of communion and baptism. Gradually, other regional subcommittees were assigned the work on marriage, funeral, and other pastoral liturgies.[7] Each of the new texts in this new generation of liturgies was published in booklet form bearing the common subtitle, "for optional use in The United Church of Canada." As such, they were not subject to the same process of consultation and response by presbyteries and congregations of the church, nor were they officially authorized by the General Council. In the context of the new structure of the Division of Mission in Canada, they were publications carried out simply under the authority of that division. They were *A Sunday Liturgy* (1984), *The Celebration of Marriage* (1985), *Baptism and Renewal of Baptismal Faith* (1986), *Services for Death and Burial* (1987), and *Pastoral Liturgies and Prayers for Special Occasions* (1990).

A Sunday Liturgy established the basic Service of the Word/Service of the Table structure within which all the other remaining texts would be placed. This framework was common to all the major contemporary ecumenical work on the eucharist and was a hallmark of the emerging ecumenical liturgical convergence.[8] While the primary sources were the drafts of the Canadian Anglican *Book of Alternative Services*, its liturgical roots are common to *The Roman Missal* of Paul VI, the *Lutheran Book of Worship*, *The Alternative Service Book of the Church of England*, the United Methodist *The Book of Services*, the *Book of Worship: United Church of Christ*, and the Canadian Presbyterian *Word and Sacraments*.[9] David Newman, the professor of worship at Emmanuel College, was the guiding force behind the production of this text. The work of this small group has been recounted elsewhere and the sources identified.[10]

The subcommittee which produced *Baptism and Renewal of Baptismal Faith* was twice as large as that of *A Sunday Liturgy*, its process at least twice as complicated.[11] It had to work not only within the context of active ecumenical liturgical scholarship, but also within emerging concerns about Christian initiation in the United Church. On the one hand, there was an acknowledged revolution in ecumenical liturgical scholarship taking place, precipitated by the failure of traditional patterns of confirmation and catalyzed by the publication of the Roman Catholic *Ordo Initiationis Christianae Adultorum*.[12] On the other hand, a unique United Church-generated process was emerging which was to lead to the whole-scale reexamination of Christian initiation within that denomination. What began in the United Church as a request from congregations for "confirmation resources" in 1972 developed into a full-scale churchwide study of Christian initiation which was to last over two decades. A Task Force on Confirmation led to The Task Force on Christian Initiation, The Project Group on Christian Initiation, and two churchwide remits on the subject. *Baptism and Renewal of Baptismal Faith* emerges out of this complex context.

Because the complexities of these circumstances are significant for the purposes of this study, I will depart from the procedure established in the previous two parts and turn directly to the commentary on the liturgical text, *Baptism and Renewal of Baptismal Faith*, without further background or elaboration. This will allow for a more straightforward treatment of the formation of the liturgy, followed by a detailed treatment of the United Church work on Christian initiation as part of the analysis in chapter 7.

A Commentary on the Texts

BAPTISM AND RENEWAL OF BAPTISMAL FAITH

The title of the first draft of this liturgy was "Service of Baptism, Profession of Faith, Re-Affirmation of Faith."[13] The difference in titles is the first clue to two important developments rooted in the United Church studies on Christian initiation: first, a movement away from the concept of "confirmation;" second, toward a single integrated rite

This rite follows the sermon as a response to the Word.

INTRODUCTION

All occasions
The presider shall move to the font and introduce the act of baptism and/or renewal of baptismal faith with appropriate scripture passages (e.g., Galatians 3:27-28; Romans 6:3-4; I Corinthians 12:13; Matthew 28:18-20) or the following.

Presider
Brothers and sisters, we gather now to celebrate the gift of grace that is given to us in the sacrament of baptism.

People
We are one body and one spirit.
We have one hope in God's call to us.

Presider
There is one Lord, one faith, one bap-

for the baptism of both children and adults.[14]

The final form of all the rubrics in this order underwent considerable editing by David Newman, then professor of worship at Emmanuel College. Newman argued that they should "be spare" and that the accompanying "Guidelines" should elaborate on the details and possible variations.[15]

The location of the rite is defined in terms of structure of *A Sunday Liturgy*. While this follows the precedent of the *Service Book* in placing it after the Word, it abandons the efforts to provide a full order of worship, returning to the *Book of Common Order*-like format of an insert into the Sunday service.[16]

Early drafts attempted to take into account the fact that many United Church congregations place baptism at the beginning of Sunday worship. Thus, an alternative opening was suggested with provision for scriptural "warrants" to be used "in procession." In the final version, one sees barely a trace of this flexibility. Instead, the preferred location after the Word is emphasized with the possibility for "appropriate scripture" to be added.[17]

The high profile given to scripture continues, recast here in the form of a litany based on Ephesians 4:4-7. The change of "Father" to "Creator" is an early example in official United Church liturgies of editorial changes tism, one God and Creator of us all.

People
Out of the water of baptism we rise with new life,
forgiven of sin and one with Christ,
members of Christ's body.

being made to scripture for reasons of inclusive language in reference to God.[18]

The introduction and its function was the subject of considerable struggle and revision on the part of the committee, as evidenced by the range of headings in different drafts: "Introduction," "Preparation," "Words of Welcome," "Invitation," "Teaching Statement."[19] The first draft, for example, contained a statement of the meaning of baptism and profession of faith based upon the introduction to the United Methodist text.[20] Later versions also included statements based on the Order for the Baptism of Adults in the *Service Book* as well as reference to the baptism of children and the desire for their subsequent profession of faith.[21]

The committee's decision to make a "major shift" away from such "teaching statements" towards a "liturgical act which would do its own teaching" was inspired by a variety of sources, including the United Church of Christ text, the draft of the Anglican *Book of Alternate Services* rite, a local United Church source, and comments included in a paper for the Consultation on Common Texts. In addition, the larger Working Unit on Worship and Liturgy advised the committee to consider such a move.[22]

Earlier forms of the litany also included John 3:3, 5 and Romans 6:3-4. While the passages were eventually dropped, simplifying the litany to its final form, an "Opportunity for a Teaching Statement" lingered on through several drafts.[23]

Note that the phrase "out of the water" suggests immersion, a mode unlikely in United Church practice.

PRESENTATION OF CANDIDATES FOR BAPTISM

Baptism: children and adults

The candidates, parents, and sponsors shall gather at the font.

Sponsor(s)
I/we present N____ for initiation into the body of Christ through baptism.

A similar process of simplification and progressive elimination of didacticism led to the final form of the presentations. What began as a three-fold presentation of candidates for "admission into the body of Christ through baptism," "profession of faith," and "renewal of their baptismal covenant by re-affirmation of faith," followed by teaching, became (in the second draft) a single presentation of all involved (though still followed by some teaching).[24] Discussion about the logistics of presentation soon gave rise to the recognition that, in order to allow for circumstances in which not all such categories of candidates would be present at each celebration, it needed to be in at least two parts: one presentation for (adult and infant) candidates for baptism; one for the renewal of the "baptismal covenant" by "profession of faith."[25]

Baptism: adults

Leader to *adult candidates for baptism*
Do you desire to be baptized?

Adult candidates(s) for baptism
I do, by the grace of God.

Baptism: children

Leader *to parents presenting their children for baptism*
Do you desire to have your child baptized?

Parents
I do, by the grace of God.

The use of questions of intent ("Do you desire. . . ?") follow general United Church custom. Yet the first draft contained no such questions, dependent as it was on the United Methodist text. An early decision that "the Anglican Order" be followed on this point was lost in subsequent drafts. When the questions of intent did finally appear, they were placed at the beginning of the Renunciation (as in the United Church of Christ order), before finally being moved to this location.[26]

Leader
Will you accept the responsibility of acting and speaking on your child's behalf?

Parents
I will, God being my helper.

Similarly, the need for a specific question regarding parental responsibilities was also decided early on but appeared only months later at the beginning of the renunciation (again following United Church of Christ form). The first version began with the *Service Book* phrasing: "Since infants cannot understand what is being done, will you. . . ?" While this was eventually left out, the problematic notion of a vicarious profession of faith remains.[27]

Leader
Will you endeavour to show your child the Christian life and to grow with him/her in faith?

Parents
I will, God being my helper.

The second question is a greatly simplified version of that found in a draft adapted from the United Church of Christ order:

> Do you promise to show these children a Christian life, grow with these children in the Christian faith, guide these children in a life of prayer and offer them the nurture of the Christian church?[28]

The placement of the questions of parental responsibility together with those of intent in the presentation reveals a combination of United Church of Christ content and Anglican structure.

PRESENTATION OF THOSE RENEWING THEIR BAPTISMAL FAITH

Renewal

Persons renewing their baptismal faith shall gather at the font.

Sponsor(s)
I/we present N____ who seek to renew their baptismal faith.

The use of a simple heading referring to all "those renewing their baptismal faith" further shows that earlier notions of "confirmation," "profession of faith," and "re-affirmation of faith" have been combined into one liturgical action. Furthermore, as the rubrics point out, this action includes the parents of the children to be baptized, assuming therefore that the baptism of their children involves a renewal of their faith as well.

Renewal & baptism of children.

Leader to *all renewing their baptismal faith, including parents of child candidates for baptism*
I ask you now, are you prepared to renew your baptismal faith?

Those renewing their faith.
I am.

Such matters were of course, a subject of considerable discussion and debate within the Committee. Again, the variety of titles entertained reveal the struggle for liturgical and theological clarity and the desire to move away from problematic notions of confirmation: "Renewal of Baptism," "Renewal of the Baptismal Covenant," "Commissioning into Discipleship," "Induction into Lay Ministry," "Induction into Responsibility," "A Service of Christian Adulthood."[29]

When appropriate, those renewing their baptismal faith may testify individually, or through one person.

Finally, the rubrical provision for testimonials is an interesting evangelical innovation consistent with the suggestion included in the Response to the Word of *A Sunday Liturgy*.[30]

RENUNCIATION AND DECLARATION AND CONGREGATIONAL PROFESSION OF FAITH

All occasions

Leader to *adult candidates for baptism, parents of child candidates for baptism, and those renewing their baptismal faith*

The convergence resulting from the integration of the presentations and their questions also occurs here with the questions of renunciation and declaration. The questions are to be put to all parents and adult candidates for baptism and renewal.[31]

Desiring the freedom of new life in Christ, do you turn away from the forces of evil and renounce their power?

Candidates/Parents and those renewing faith
I do, by the grace of God.

Leader
Do you turn to Jesus Christ and accept him as Saviour and Lord?

The Renunciation was one of the most debated issues in the work of the committee, second only to that of confirmation. Reminiscent of earlier attempts to introduce it into United Church practice, the question was asked, "Is it appropriate, anyway (given our tradition)?"[32]

The first draft contained, in effect, two renunciations, following closely the United Methodist rite, but broken into two distinct sections: a "Renunciation of Sin" and a "Declaration of Commitment."

Candidates/Parents and those renewing faith
I do, by the grace of God.

The draft Renunciation of Sin was as follows:

> New life in Christ is a life of faith which makes itself known through turning from sin and turning to righteousness. Therefore on behalf of the whole church, the body of Christ, I ask you: Do you reject the bondage of sin and the pressures of culture and accept the liberty which God gives you to live a new life in Christ?

This was followed immediately by the Declaration of Commitment:

> Will you resist evil, injustice, and oppression in whatever guises they present themselves (and assist those whom you sponsor to recognize and resist them?)[33]

The second draft contained no renunciation and returned to a form of questions based upon those of the *Service Book* order for adult baptism and confirmation. However, further discussion resulted in a consensus that "the rite needs some act of repentance indicating a turning."[34] To this end, different variations were entertained over the next several months, including a "Declaration of Repentance," and a "Renunciation of the Forces of Darkness and Declaration of Allegiance." The final version of these questions is a simple rendering of those in the United Church of Christ order for adult baptism (with the metaphor of "turning" made more explicit).[35]

Leader
Do you commit yourself to the mission and ministry of Christ's church?

This question developed throughout the drafting process along with those of renunciation and declaration. What began as a longer question based upon the United Methodist rite was gradu-

Candidates/Parents
and those renewing faith.

I do, by the grace of God.

ally simplified under the influence of the more familiar *Service Book* vocabulary of "mission" and "ministry."[36]

It is also interesting to note that an early decision "that faith statements should be trinitarian in form" was lost, there being no explicit reflection of this in the form and structure of later drafts and the final version.[37]

The people stand.

Leader *to the people*
As a baptized and baptizing church, do you commit yourselves to support and nurture these persons within a community which worships God, resists evil and seeks justice?

People
We do.

The question to the congregation appears to be an original composition of the committee, though it is reminiscent of the United Church of Christ's "Congregational Assent."[38] The final phrases, "within a community which worships God, resists evil and seeks justice," anticipate the lines in the United Church "New Creed" below.

Leader *addressing all*
Let us with the whole church confess our faith.

I believe in God,
the Father almighty,
maker of heaven and earth;
and in Jesus Christ his only
Son our Lord,
who was conceived by the
Holy Spirit,
born of the Virgin Mary,
suffered under Pontius Pilate,
was crucified, dead and buried.
He descended into hell;
the third day he rose again
from the dead;
he ascended into heaven,
and sitteth on the right hand of God
the Father Almighty;
from thence he shall come
to judge the quick and the dead.

The questions to the parents, candidates, and congregation climax in the corporate profession of faith using the Apostles' Creed or the United Church's "New Creed." The first draft placed these, along with the provision for "any recognized historic creed for the Church," as the final act of the entire rite. The "Notes" appended to this draft also suggested other classic uses of the Apostles' Creed, including a three part interrogation to replace the questions to the candidates, or serve as a corporate profession following the Prayer of Thanksgiving.[39]

Variations in the placement of the Creed appear to have been inspired by the variety in the various sources before the committee. Their review of the first draft resulted in the decision that it be placed before the baptism

He descended into hell;
the third day he rose again
from the dead;
he ascended into heaven,
and sitteth on the right hand of God
the Father almighty;
from thence he shall come
to judge the quick and the dead.
I believe in the holy Spirit;
the holy catholic church;
the communion of saints;
the forgiveness of sins'
the resurrection of the body;
And the life everlasting.
Amen.

itself. However, its precise location moved around in subsequent drafts, including after the presentation (before the questions to the candidates), after the prayer over the water (immediately before the baptism), and eventually this final location after the questions to the candidates (before the prayer over the water).[40]

or

Let us join in a statement of our communal faith.

We are not alone,
we live in God's world.
We believe in God:
who has created and is creating,
who has come in Jesus,
the Word made flesh,
to reconcile and make new,
who works in us and others
by the Spirit.
We trust in God.
We are called to be the Church:
to celebrate God's presence,
to love and serve others,
to seek justice and resist evil,
to proclaim Jesus,
crucified and risen,
our judge and our hope.
In life, in death,
in life beyond death,
God is with us.
We are not alone.
Thanks be to God.

The people are seated.

The option of using the Apostles' Creed or a contemporary statement of faith builds on the *Service Book* precedent and follows the spirit of the United Church of Christ order.[41] For several drafts, the United Church "Creed" was placed before the Apostles' Creed on the page. It was later decided that they should appear side by side, each with their own introduction.[42] In the final version the Apostles' Creed comes first, suggesting its historic precedence.

Note also that this version of the United Church "Creed" is that altered by the 1980 General Council for reasons of inclusive language. Thus, "Man is not alone, he lives in God's world" is now "We are not alone, we live in God's world;" "the true Man, Jesus" is rendered "Jesus, the Word made flesh;" and other constructions have been similarly altered with a view to the elimination of masculine pronouns for God.[43]

PRAYER OF THANKSGIVING AND POURING OF WATER

All occasions
Presider
The Lord be with you.

People
And also with you.

Presider
Lift up your hearts.

People
We lift them to the Lord.

Presider
Let us give thanks to the Lord our God.

People
It is right to give God thanks and praise.

With the Prayer of Thanksgiving the United Church finally succeeds in placing a prayer over the waters in its service of baptism after two generations of effort on the part of its worship committees.

While passing note was made to the potential "danger in referring to blessing of water,"[44] it did not seem to be as pressing a theological concern in this committee as in previous ones. Indeed, a prayer of this form and function was present from the first draft.

The use of the Sursum Corda is also a first in United Church baptismal liturgies. It did not, however, appear in the text until very late in the drafting process. Earlier versions contained simply the greeting "The Lord be with you." Discussion at one point entertained the idea of using simply "Let us pray."[45] For a time, concern about repetition resulted in the use of a rubric suggesting its omission "if the Lord's Supper is to follow in the same service."[46] The final version, however, calls for its use on "all occasions," thus recognizing its function as a general call to thanksgiving, rather than an exclusive association with the eucharist.

Water is poured visibly and audibly into the font.

The intentional prominence given to the use of the water is in stark contrast to the minimalism of previous United Church orders and a direct reflection of one of the "Recommendations" of *The Report on Christian Initiation.*[47]

Consideration of this rubric alone gave rise to interesting issues in the deliberations of the committee, including the use of processionals and the participation of children. It had been suggested in an early draft that the water be both carried in procession and poured by a child (three times during the prayer).[48] For some, this was an important effort to involve children more fully in the liturgical action and a response to increasing calls in the United Church for "inter-generational" worship. For others it was "childrenizing the service" and falling into the very trap that a unified rite for adults and infants sought to avoid. The outcome was mixed. The reference to processing with the water was eventually dropped on the grounds that it was "not analogous to the bread and wine of the eucharist" and thus not deserving of such prominence.[49] The reference to a three-fold pouring was also dropped, but the possibility of those other than the presider pouring the water was suggested in the Guidelines.[50]

Presider
Blessed are you, our God,
Ruler of the universe,
Maker of heaven and earth,
  keeper of sky and sea.
In your goodness
  you give us the sign of the water.
At the beginning
  your Spirit was at work,
  brooding over the waters
  of creation's birth,
  breaking the waters
  with the word of power,
  bringing forth life in all its fullness.
Over and over again
  you have shown your grace to us
  as water—
cleansing the earth at the flood,
parting for the exodus at the Red Sea,
flowing from the rock
in the wilderness.

People
Blessed are you, our God.

The prayer itself is the work of Sylvia Dunstan, United Church minister and hymn writer. The committee, unsatisfied with their own attempt to revise the more didactic versions of the United Methodist and United Church of Christ prayers, asked Dunstan to apply her poetic talent to the task.[51]

The opening lines show some evidence of influence from the United Church of Christ's "Prayer of Baptism."[52] Dunstan's original version used the refrain from the Anglican source, "Blessed be God forever." The committee changed it to the rather awkward sounding "Blessed are you, our God" to express continuity with the opening line of the prayer and allow refrains to more directly address God.[53] The committee also sought further changes from Dunstan, however she never did provide them.[54] In the end, they simply went ahead with a few minor editorial changes on their

Presider
In Jesus you promised that all who
thirst could come to the living water.
He who was baptized
in the water of repentance
becomes for us
the never-failing spring,
welling up to eternal life.

As he suffered for us,
the piercing of his side
brought forth blood and water,
sign of the death we all die in him
so that we may also rise with him.

People
Blessed are you, our God.

Presider
Therefore, eternal and present God,
we bless you for the water
with which you bless us.
We pray that those who are given to
the waters of life
will live in your grace,
knowing the death and
resurrection of Jesus.
Send, O God, your Holy Spirit
upon us and upon this water,
that all who are gathered under
this sign, being one in Christ,
may be nurtured by the bread of life.

All
Now to God be given
all glory, praise, honour and might
Blessed be God forever. Amen.

own. The final phrase "may be nurtured by the bread of life" was added to provide a link to the eucharist. The unison doxology, reminiscent of the style of the United Methodist rite, was also added.[55]

It is a significant improvement over the prayer in the United Methodist rite, which was the model of choice in early drafts of this liturgy before Dunstan became involved. The first draft had even separated the epiclesis from the body of the prayer, providing for a "Dedication of the Water" before the "Thanksgiving Over the Water." From the second draft onward, however, the fuller berakah form of the prayer was restored in an effort to be true to a "trinitarian shape" and "thankful" tone.[56]

While the epiclesis is an invocation of the Spirit "upon us and this water," anxieties over the "blessing of water" may have also been helped by the use of the word "bless" only in association with human blessing of God and God's blessing of human beings (albeit via the sign of water). A survey of the sources available to the committee suggests that this is a somewhat original formulation.[57]

Where there are no candidates for baptism, the service continues with the Renewal of Baptismal Faith.

The rubric immediately following the unison doxology shows that the Prayer of Thanksgiving was intended for use even "where there are no candidates for baptism." This again emphasized the high profile given to the symbol of water and therein the liturgical and theological grounding of renewal of baptismal faith in baptism itself (a fact arguably absent in previous United Church orders for confirmation.)

ACTION OF BAPTISM

Baptism: children & adults

Candidates for baptism shall come or be brought to the font in turn for all baptismal actions.

The presider pours or sprinkles water generously and visibly three times on the candidate's head or immerses the candidate three times.

The Guidelines elaborate on these rubrics:

> In the Action of Baptism, the *entire sequence* of actions—baptism with water, signing with the cross (if used), the laying on of hands, and such other symbolic actions as may be used—should be administered to each person individually before repeating the sequence with the next person. The water should be administered "generously and visibly" three times, once with the naming of each Person of the Trinity.[58]

The mention of pouring, sprinkling, or immersing is a return to the rubrics of *The Book of Common Order*,[59] though the accompanying intentional visibility of water is, of course, a contemporary development.

Presider
N____, I baptize you in the name
of the Father,
and of the Son,
and of the Holy Spirit.

People
Amen

The use of the traditional trinitarian formula was again affirmed by the *Report on Christian Initiation* and the 1984 General Council. However, its use in this text was not without controversy and discussion in relation to the issue of inclusive language. The Introduction to the liturgy notes:

> Both in the United Church and in other churches the use of this formula is the subject of discussion and debate. But for the time being it remains the officially acceptable (and in the eyes of some churches, the only valid) formula for baptism.[60]

The presiding or diaconal minister may mark the newly baptized person's

The issue of "clericalism" was also discussed in relation to the roles of *forehead with the sign of the cross, with or without oil.*

Baptism: children & adults.

Leader
N____, with the sign of the cross, you are marked as Christ's forever.

People
Amen

ordained, diaconal, and lay liturgical leaders, particularly with respect to chrismation. The distinctions among these roles also become evident in the Introduction, Prayer of Thanksgiving, and Blessing.[61]

Early drafts experimented with different variations of signation/chrismation, laying on of hands and their order of administration. The question was raised, "is it practical in the face of our community's spirituality?" The Committee did not spend long on this question however, and moved quickly to the assumption that it be included in some form.

Some believed that signing with the cross and chrismation should be separate actions; others that, whatever the form of signing, it should be as normative as the laying on of hands (that is, administered to every candidate). The accompanying words are based on that of the Anglican rite, as is the order of the action as a whole.[62]

The hands of the presiding and diaconal ministers and sponsor shall rest on the head of the newly baptized person.

Presider
N___, the power of the Holy Spirit work within you, that being born of water and the Spirit, you may be a faithful witness of Jesus Christ.

People
Amen

This use of the laying of hands was an explicit Recommendation of the *Report on Christian Initiation* and essential to the Committee's vision of a reunified rite.[63] Unlike in the *Service Book* orders, the Committee did not hesitate in allowing the laity to participate in this action. The wording of the prayer for the Spirit was from the first draft of the United Methodist rites.[64]

Other symbolic acts may be performed: dressing in a white garment; lighting of candles from the paschal candle; presenting of Bibles and/or Certificates; a handshake; presentation of the newly baptized to the congregation.

This rubric also reflects the Recommendation regarding "Other Symbolic Acts" in the *Report on Christian Initiation.*[65] The drafting process entertained a wider variety of suggestions, including "additional symbolic actions that are appropriate to the traditions of the congregation and/or the candidates and their families," "acts of community fellowship such as a handshake, hug, etc.," presentation of flowers, presentation of infants to the congregation, etc.[66]

The Guidelines of the liturgy elaborate on the biblical symbolism of the actions suggested here and suggest some words to accompany the acts. For clothing in a white garment: "N___, you have become a new creation, and are being clothed in Christ." For the giving of a lighted candle: "Receive the light of Christ" or "N___, be as one who lives in the light of Christ."[67]

ACTION OF RENEWAL OF BAPTISMAL FAITH

Renewal

Addressing those persons renewing their baptismal faith, the presider may, with cupped hand, lift water from the font and let it fall back into it or may sprinkle water towards them or omit all symbolic action.

The structural revolution of this rite is again evident with respect to the placement and function of the Action of Renewal of Baptismal Faith. While this will be discussed again below, it is worth keeping in mind that the first draft separated the actions of baptism, first profession of faith, laying on of hands, individual renewal of baptismal faith (with asperges), and corporate renewal of baptismal faith (a creedal profession). The evolution toward integration begins with the second draft.[68]

Presider
Remember your baptism and be thankful.

People
Amen

The asperges was another "innovation" to be introduced into a United Church liturgy. While it was present from the first draft (based, as it was, upon the United Methodist text), it disappeared from the next several, to reappear in the appendix almost a year later. The discussion which accompanied it raised questions about its meaning (was it a simple "remembrance" or a "renewal"?) and its appropriateness (is it a "violation" of the unbaptized when directed toward the congregation?).[69] The optional status of this action seems to have satisfied all concerned. The Guidelines provide further comment:

> This sprinkling ritual, known as *asperges*, has long been connected with baptism, as a sign of a renewal of its grace. The possibility is open for the sprinkling to be administered to the whole congregation, assuming common consent to this.[70]

Those who are renewing their baptismal faith shall come forward in turn to receive the laying of hands, with prayer for the Spirit.

Presider
N____, the power of the Holy Spirit work within you, that being born of water and the Spirit, you may continue to be a faithful witness of Jesus Christ.

People
Amen.

The prayer for the Spirit is the same as the earlier one, with "continue to" inserted for the purposes of the context of renewal (again, as in the United Methodist rite).[71] Noteworthy is the departure from the traditional confirmation prayers ("Strengthen/Defend, O Lord, your servant.").[72]

Persons transferring their membership from other congregations may be welcomed at this time.

Relatively late in the drafting process the United Church of Christ order was noted for its incorporation of the transfer and welcoming of baptized members from other congregations and/or denominations. With this in mind, a traditional United Church-sounding presentation was incorporated into the liturgy at this location, later to be reduced to this rubrical form.[73]

BLESSING

All occasions

Presider *addressing those who have participated in baptism or the renewal of baptism faith*
All who join in this baptismal covenant are the body of Christ in the world. Go in peace.

or

The grace of Christ attend you, the love of God surround you, the Holy Sprit keep you.

People
Amen

Participants return to their places in the congregation.

The service continues with the prayers of the people, in which the newly baptized, the families, and those who have renewed their baptismal faith are particularly mentioned; and then with the sacrament of the Lord's Supper. (See A Sunday Liturgy).

A variety of closing acts were suggested and entertained by the Committee, including no blessing at all (as in the United Methodist rite), a sung Aaronic benediction (a United Church tradition), and the *Service Book* commissioning used in the Order for the Welcoming of Members from Other Churches ("As God has called you."). The final choice is actually a dismissal and blessing. The former is based on that of the third draft, with the popular benediction from the *Service Book* added later.[74]

The final rubric is a significant development in that it presupposes the eucharistic context of *A Sunday Liturgy*.[75]

Notes

1. In translation see "Sacrosanctum Concilium: The Constitution on the Sacred Liturgy," in *Vatican Council II: The Conciliar and Post Conciliar Documents*, ed. and trans. Austin Flannery, O.P. (Collegeville: The Liturgical Press, 1975), 1-37.

2. Published later as Fred McNally, "Directions for Worship in the Early Eighties," *Getting It All Together* (Advent/Christmas 1981): Study Papers, 1-5.

3. To this end, the booklet by David Newman was published, *As Often As You Do This Toward More Frequent Celebration of the Lord's Supper in The United Church of Canada*. National Committee on Liturgy, Division of Mission in Canada (Toronto: The United Church of Canada, 1981).

4. *Gathering: A Packet for Worship Planners*. Unit for Worship Mission and Evangelism, Division of Mission in Canada (Toronto: The United Church of Canada, 1983-2003).

5. UCA, Division of Mission in Canada Records, Committee on Liturgy/Working Unit on Worship and Liturgy, "Minutes" of 27-29 March 1981: 12.

6. "Minutes" of 1-4 March 1984: 8.

7. "Minutes" of 5 October 1981: 1; 6-8 November 1981: 4; 12-14 November 1982: 5; 15-17 April 1983: 5; 17 September 1983: 1; 11-13 November 1983: 2; 1 December 1984: 4; 7-9 March 1984: 1.

8. For an articulation of some of the features of this convergence, see James F. White, "A Protestant Manifesto," *The Christian Century* 99 (27 January 1982): 82-86.

9. *Roman Missal*, Revised by Decree of the Second Vatican Ecumenical Council and published by authority of Pope Paul VI (Ottawa: Canadian Catholic Conference, 1974); *Lutheran Book of Worship* (Minneapolis: Augsburg Publishing House, 1978); *The Book of Alternative Services of the Anglican Church of Canada* (Toronto: Anglican Book Center, 1985); *Book of Worship: United Church of Christ* (New York: Office for Church Life and Leadership, 1986). Note also the particular influence of *Word and Table: A Basic Pattern of Sunday Worship for United Methodists* (Nashville: Abingdon, 1976).

10. The other members of the subcommittee were Douglas Bacon, Fred McNally, Miriam Tees. See also, Harding, "The Development of Liturgical Sources," 295-320.

11. The members were John Ambrose, Jim Dowden, Keith Knill, Fred McNally, David Newman, Joan Robertson, Jim Taylor, Laurie White. UCA, Division of Mission in Canada Records, Christian Initiation Task Group, 1984-1986, "Minutes," Box 1, No. 2, File 1. "Drafts" contained in File 2. "Minutes" of 19 November 1984: 1.

12. The Canadian text is *Rite of Christian initiation of adults* (Ottawa: Canadian Conference of Catholic Bishops, 1987).

13. The first draft was based largely upon the United Methodist text, *A Service of Baptism, Confirmation, and Renewal: Alternate Text, 1976*, Supplemental Worship Resources 2, The United Methodist Church (Nashville: The United Methodist Publishing House, 1976) [*BCR* (1976)] with the integration of some favored *Service Book* passages. "Draft" dated December 1984; "Minutes" of 19 November 1984, and 7 January 1985.

14. This will be discussed in more detail in chapter 7.

15. "Minutes" of 24-25 June 1985: 2; "Drafts" dated 7 March 1982: 8; 1 May 1986; August 1986. The sparse style of rubrics is also evident in *ASL* (1984), of which Newman was, for all intents and purposes, the primary author. The Guidelines to *BRBF* (1986) were written by Newman and McNally, then consultant on Congregational Worship for the United Church. "Drafts" dated 7 March 1985, 1 May 1986, and August 1985.

16. The rubric in *ASL* (1984) describing the content of possible Responses to the Word includes baptism and reaffirmations of faith. Cf. *ASL* (1984), 9; *SB* (1969), 38, 56; *BCO* (1932), 97, 104, 109. The Guidelines to *ASL* (1984) also point out: "Baptism or Christian Initiation appropriately takes place within the Eucharist as a response to the proclaimed Word. It is especially appropriate at some times such as the Easter Vigil, the Day of Pentecost, the Sunday after All Saint's Day and the First Sunday after Epiphany (the Feast of the Baptism of our Lord)." *ASL* (1984), 42.

17. Other suggested passages included Matthew 28: 18-20, John 20: 21-22, and Acts 8: 14-17. "Draft" dated 24 March 1985: 1-2.

18. Cf. Ephesians 4: 4-7 (RSV): "There is one body and one Spirit, just as you were called to the one hope that belongs to your call, one Lord, one faith, one baptism, one God and Father of us all, who is above all and through all and in all."

19. E.g., "Drafts" dated 4 February 1984; 24 May 1985; 24 June 1985; 13 September 1985.

20. Cf. "Draft" dated December 1984: 2 and *BCR* (1976), iii.

21. E.g., "Draft" dated 24 March 1985: 1-2 .

22. "Minutes" of 7 January 1985: 1 and 4 March 1985; "draft of United Church of Christ order, adapted, 1 [*UCC* (adapted)] (see its final form in *Book of Worship*, 133-136 [*BW* (1986)]; "draft of *Book of Alternative Services* order, 2 [*BAS* (draft)]. The paper, "A Collation of Baptismal Orders," by Dainel Meeter (dated November 1, 1984) for the Consultation of Common Texts compared orders from various communions and noted the tendency of some toward the didactic explanation of liturgical action (pp. 2-3). This paper was appended to the "Minutes" of 4 February 1985. The first draft (December 1984) also appended a similar litany from Birtle-Miniota Pastoral Charge, Manitoba (see "Draft" dated December 1984: 9). A summary of a critique of the "Draft" dated 15 October 1985 by the Working Unit on Worship and Liturgy was attached to the "Minutes" of 29 November 1985, where the majority spoke against the need for a teaching statement.

23. Cf. "Draft" dated 24 June 1985: 1; "Minutes" of 25 June: 4; *SB* (1969), 43.

24. Cf. "Draft" dated December 1984: 2; *BCR* (1976), iii. The presentation in the second draft reads: "Sisters and Brothers in Christ, I/we present (names) for admission into the body of Christ through baptism and (names) who seek to renew their baptismal covenant by making a profession of faith." "Draft" dated 4 February 1984: 2. The "Brothers and Sisters" phrase was much liked and though later eliminated from the presentations was eventually added to the beginning of the introduction.

25. "Minutes" of 4 March 1985. Cf. "Drafts" dated 4 March 1985: 2; 1 April 1985: 2; 24 May 1985: 2.

26. Cf. "Draft" dated December 1985: 1; *BCR* (1976), iii, iv; *BAS* (draft), 4; *UCC* (adapted), iii, iv; "Draft" dated 24 June 1985, pp. 1-2; "Draft" dated 13 September 1985: 1-2. See also "Minutes" of 7 January 1985: 5.

27. Cf. *SB* (1969), 52. The decision that such a question was needed was noted in both February and April but did not appear until the June draft. See "Minutes" of 4 February 1985: 1; 1 April 1985: 1; "Draft" dated 24 June 1985: 3. On the subject of a vicarious profession of faith, one must question how parents can speak for their child's faith in the act of baptism. They are able, however, to profess their own faith and that of the church, the faith within which children are included and nurtured.

28. *UCC* (adapted), iv.

29. "Minutes" of 22 May 1985: 1.

30. *ASL* (1984), 9.

31. This principle was agreed upon at the June meeting of the Committee. "Minutes" of 24-25 June 1985: 2.

32. The most substantial and interesting discussion is recorded in the "Minutes" of 4 February 1985: 1, and 24-25 June 1985: 2. See also "Minutes" of 7 January 1985: 1.

33. Cf. "Draft" dated December 1984: 23, and *BCR* (1976), iii-iv. A note appended to the draft (p. 10) reveals a possible reason for the repetition: "sometimes these [i.e., renunciation, declaration, and congregational commitment] cannot be fully separated."

34. Cf. "Draft" dated 4 February 1985: 4, and *SB* (1969), 62. The changes suggested included replacing "heavenly father" with "heavenly parent," another example of the growing consciousness regarding inclusive language in reference to God. A version of these questions also appeared in the first draft at the "Profession of Faith (for those who have been baptized previously)" later in the service. "Draft" dated December 1985: 5. For the discussion about "turning" see "Minutes" of 4 February 1985: 1, and "Draft" dated 4 February 1985: 3.

35. The "Declaration of Repentance" in the "Draft" dated 4 March 1985: 2, was "Leader: In whom do you put your trust? Candidates: Jesus is Lord. Leader: Do you repent of your sins? Candidates: We repent of all that separates us from the love of God."

The "Renunciation of the Forces of Darkness and Declaration of Allegiance" in the "Draft" dated 24 June 1985: 3 was "Presider: Do you renounce the authority in your life of those powers and principalities which rob us of compassion for our neighbour, which come between us and God, and which transcend our best intentions. Candidates: We do, God being our helper. Presider: Do you intend to run from darkness to light, from sin to salvation from death to life? Do you accept Jesus as Lord? Candidate: We do."

The United Church of Christ questions for adult baptism were "Do you renounce the powers of evil and desire the freedom of new life in Christ?" and "Do you profess Jesus Christ as Lord and Saviour." Cf. *UCC* (adapted), iii; "Draft" dated 15 October 1985: 3; "Minutes" of 15 October 1985: 3. The final version of the second question is also very close to that of the Anglican rite. *BAS* (draft), 5.

36. The United Methodist question was "According to the grace given to you, do you promise to lead a Christian life, always to remain faithful to Christ's holy church, and to serve as Christ's representatives in the world [and by word and example teach these whom you sponsor to do the same]?" Cf. *BCR* (1976), iv; *SB* (1969), 62; "Drafts" dated December 1984: 3; 4 February 1985: 3.

37. "Minutes" of 4 February 1985: 2.

38. *UCC* (adapted), v.

39. "Draft" dated December 1984: 6, 8.

40. The United Methodist order used an optional interrogative form (to be used corporately) following the questions to the candidates. *BCR* (1976), iv. The United Church of Christ draft called for a similar act following the "Congregational Assent." *UCC* (adapted), v. The Anglican rite placed the three-fold corporate interrogation after the Thanksgiving Over the Water as a renewal of the baptismal covenant." *BAS* (draft), 9; *BAS* (1985), 158-159. An experimental order in use at Eden United Church [EUC] placed the United Church "New Creed" in the same location. EUC, 5. Cf. also "Minutes" of 7 January 1985: 3; "Drafts" dated 4 February 1985 (the location after the presentation was called "The Congregational Basis for Baptism"); 4 March 1985; 4 May 1985; 24 June 1985. At the June meeting of the Committee it was agreed that "the renunciation, declaration and creed *precede* the water, prayer and action." "Minutes" of 24-25 June 1985: 2.

41. Cf. *UCC* (adapted): v; *BW* (1986), 140; *SB* (1969), 71.

42. "Minutes" of 24-25 June 1985: 5; 13 September 1985: 2. The introductions are not those approved by the Committee on Christian Faith. Cf. *SB* (1969), inside covers.

43. This prompted some discussion in the pages of the *Observer*: "The Church" (January 1981): 15; "Letters," (March 1981): 4.

44. "Minutes" of 7 January 1985: 1.

45. "Minutes" of 17 January 1986: 1.

46. "Drafts" dated December 1984: 4, and March 1985: 4.

47. *ROP* (1982), 193. This report and its related issues will be dealt with more extensively in the following chapter.

48. "Draft" dated 4 February 1985: 5.

49. "Minutes" of 24-25 June 1985: 2; Cf. "Drafts" dated 4 May 1985 and 24 June 1965.

50. The Guidelines state: "A person who has been involved in the preparation of the candidates such as a sponsor or a diaconal minister might do the pouring. Another option is that prior to the opening dialogue members of the congregation, including children, may be invited to pour the water." *BRBF* (1986), 18.

51. "Minutes" of 24, 25 June: 5. Dunstan's hymn "Crashing Waters at Creation" was written to accompany this prayer. *In Search of Hope and Grace* (Chicago: GIA Publishers, 1991), 66-67; *VU*, 449.

52. The opening lines of the United Church of Christ prayer are "We thank you, God, for the gift of creation called forth by your saving Word. Before the world had shape or form, your Spirit moved over the waters. You formed the firmaments from the waters of the deeps, and brought forth the earth to sustain all life." *UCC* (adapted), vi.

53. Cf. "Minutes" of 29 November 1985: 1 and 17 January 1986: 6.

54. The Committee asked Dunstan to give it a more "eschatological" and "expectant" tone. "Minutes" of 13 September 1985: 3; 17 January 1986: 1.

55. See "Draft" dated 14 March 1985: 7, and *BCR* (1976), vi.

56. "Draft" dated December 1984: 4; "Minutes" of 7 January 1985: 1.

57. The three main sources in use by the Committee use the phrase "bless. . . this water. . . ." See *BCR* (1976), vi; *UCC* (adapted), vii; *EUC*, 5. The Anglican rite prays "sanctify this water. . . ." *BAS* (draft), 8, 9.

58. *BRBF* (1986), 18.

59. *BCO* (1932), 99, 110.

60. *BRBF* (1986), 6. In addition, the form of the formula (i.e., "I baptize," and "You are baptized,") was briefly considered. "Minutes" of 17 January 1986: 2. Note that the United Church of Christ order contained the passive form from *UCC* (adapted), viii.

61. *BRBF* (1986), 5-6. The Committee decided to "identify what *has* to be done by the presider, and in the rubrics keep suggesting that others have a role." "Minutes" of 17 January, 1986: 2.

62. "Minutes" of 15 October, 1985: 1; 13 September 1985: 3; 15 October 1985: 1. While the signation/chrismation is optional in the final United Church rite, the "with or without oil" provision is reminiscent of the Anglican text. The final wording is a passive form of the Anglican version. Cf. *BAS* (draft), 10; "Minutes" of 24-25 June 1985: 2.

63. *ROP* (1982), 195-196.

64. Cf. "Draft" dated December 1984: 6; *BCR* (1976), vi.

65. *ROP* (1982), 195.

66. E.g., "Drafts" dated March 1986 and April 1986. The United Church of Christ order contained a rubric suggesting "the sponsors or others may walk through the congregation with the newly baptized and introduce them as a sign of entry and incorporation into the living community of faith." *UCC* (adapted), ix. If the present-day popularity of this "tradition" is any indication, this practice was fast becoming very popular even though The United Church of Canada did not include it.

67. *BRBF* (1986), 19.

68. Cf. "Drafts" dated December 1984 and 4 February 1985 and "Minutes" of 7 January 1985: 1.

69. "Minutes" of 15 October 1985: 1; "Draft" dated 15 October 1985: 6-7; "Minutes" of 17 January 1986: 1.

70. *BRBF* (1986), 20.

71. *BCR* (1976), vii.

72. Cf. *BCO* (1932), 152; *SB* (1969), 63.

73. Cf. "Drafts" dated December 1984: 7; 4 March 1985: 5; 13 September 1985: 7; *SB* (1969), 188, 233.

74. Cf. "Drafts" dated December 1984: 7; 4 March 1985: 5; 13 September 1985: 7; *SB* (1969), 188, 233.

75. *ASL* (1984), 9-11.

Chapter 7
Liturgical Reform in an Ecumenical Context

Baptism and Renewal of Baptismal Faith has raised both familiar and new themes with respect to United Church baptismal liturgies. Among the familiar themes observed in the previous generations of texts: the tendency toward structural integration and simplicity; the liberal borrowing from other traditions; the continued movement toward the recovery of more classic liturgical forms; the continuing struggle to clarify the role and meaning of profession of faith and confirmation; and increased attention to the participation of the congregation in the celebration.

Yet these very themes, while they can be viewed as being in developmental continuity with the texts of previous generations, also gave rise to significant "new" developments in United Church practice, among them: the movement away from a "Reformed" style of exhortation and proclamation toward a more "catholic" liturgical style of celebration; the use of "sponsors" in baptism; several liturgical elements new to United Church experience such as the renunciation of evil, the prayer over the water, renewal of baptismal faith, anointing with oil, and other symbolic actions; more attention given to the issue of preparation and catechesis. These developments also represent the United Church response to the context of ecumenical developments in Christian initiation at the time.

As in previous chapters in this study, these and other issues will now be reviewed from a variety of perspectives, beginning with structural considerations. However, unlike the case with previous orders, *Baptism and Renewal of Baptismal Faith* arose out of a much more dynamic process than that of the compilers' work in the committee alone. This is process of churchwide study led by the Task Group on Confirmation, the Task Force on Christian Initiation, the Project Group on Christian Initiation, and the resulting remits on Christian Initiation. Because this work is essential to an understanding of *Baptism and Renewal of Baptismal Faith*, this analysis must begin with an overview of this important background. Moreover, it is, in its own right, an important chapter in United Church history in general, the story of which has not been told in any systematic way. It is significant not only because it relates to Christian initiation in the United Church but also to the extent that it sheds some light on its developing United Church liturgical tradition.

Background

The Task Group on Confirmation

Within three years after the publication of the *Service Book*, the General Council began to receive petitions reflecting a renewed concern about the place and theology of infant baptism and the meaning of confirmation.[1] This fact alone suggests that, for all the *Service Book* liturgies attempted, they did not resolve the confusion. Indeed, they may well have contributed to it by giving confirmation such prominence and, by turning the spotlight on it, begging the question of its meaning and purpose.

This discussion began to gain momentum during a time of declining numbers in church membership. United Church membership, which had steadily climbed to an all-time high in 1965, fell back below the one million mark in 1972 for the first time in a decade. The number of adults and infants baptized and those "Received on Profession of Faith" began to drop at the end of the fifties. Membership in Sunday schools began to show a similar decline in the early sixties.[2] Petitions spoke of the failure of parents "to take their vows made at the baptisms of their infants seriously," the "disturbing decrease in the number of adults being received into full communion," the need for "adequate preparation for Confirmation," and the "abundant and increasing confusion . . . concerning the doctrine and practice of baptism, confirmation and church membership."[3]

The 1977 General Council established a Task Group on Confirmation Resources, believing that this was the most pressing concern and that clarification here might address the larger issues. As one person was to put it a few years later, after several major studies on Christian initiation, "This all grew out of a request for new filmstrips!"[4] The findings of the Task Group on Confirmation, gleaned largely through a churchwide survey, showed that while clergy-led confirmation classes of a few weeks in length had become the norm, there was a shortage of resources, a wide range of opinion about the meaning of confirmation, and little confidence that the process was actually initiating youth and young adults into active membership in the church.[5] On the question of meaning, the group noted that the "majority of replies" to the survey defined confirmation as "joining the church," "becoming a full member," or "admission to membership in the United Church." This, they argued, was "a vitiation of the historic meaning of baptism" and "called for a study of 'Christian Initiation' generally, rather than 'confirmation' alone."[6] Thus, to use Kavanagh's language, the discussion shifted from the "tactical" question of confirmation policy and polity to the "strategic" question of theology and meaning.[7] In early 1978 the Task Group received, at their own request, a large mandate from the Executive of General Council and began their expanded work as the Task Force on Christian Initiation.[8]

The Task Force on Christian Initiation

The work of this Task Force began with a study of various theological works, church documents, and liturgies. The United Methodist, Lutheran, and Episcopal orders for baptism were reviewed. The classic debates of Barth and Cullman on infant baptism were studied.

The question of confirmation continued to be a helpful starting point for the Task Force, being as it was the practical expression of the difficulties in United Church practice and theology. Their study of the United Church's 1962 document, *Church Membership*, proved to be critical to their interpretation of the development of confirmation in the United Church. "Confirmation," they concluded, "came into more common use in the United Church with the report on *Church Membership*, not with the Anglican-United Church talks." Moreover, a consensus emerged within the group that "confirmation as we now practice it is not the rite of entry to communion."[9] These working presuppositions guided much of their future work.

The bulk of this work was spent producing the study document *Christian Initiation: The Quest for Renewal* and monitoring the response of congregations to this study.[10] An overview of the contents of *The Quest for Renewal* provides a revealing summary of the group's understanding of the issues at stake and the possible options for the future.

The Quest for Renewal began with a description of the present circumstances of initiation in the United Church as one of "crisis." It described an "uneasiness about the faithfulness of our baptismal practices," a "malaise around confirmation, experienced by both clergy and candidates," and a growing ecumenical consensus around the reintegration of the separated rites of baptism, confirmation, and first communion.[11]

The Quest for Renewal also spoke of the "ever deepening dilemma" with respect to the administration of baptism and provided a descriptive litany of several symptoms. Among them: the frequent requests for the baptism of infants by those who have little or no relationship to the church (thus "undermining" its "essential meaning"); the continued perception that baptism is needed to secure the "future well-being of the child"; concerns surrounding adequate preparation for baptism; increasing doubts about the "defensibility of infant baptism on biblical and theological grounds"; the expressed desire for liturgies for "infant dedication" or "thanksgiving for the birth of a child"; a "mounting dissatisfaction" with the liturgical form of baptism, its didacticism, and "negligible use of symbolic action"; the perceived inconsistencies of initiation structures which imply a distinction in status between (baptized) membership and (confirmed) "full membership"; the exclusion of children from the sacrament of the Lord's Supper.[12]

A similar crisis in confirmation was described with reference to such concerns as "the decline in the number of young people presenting themselves for confirmation"; the increase in the number of young people "leaving the church after conformation"; the popular perception that confirmation is "of greater significance than baptism"; and, again, a "growing uneasiness" with respect to the historical, biblical, and theological defensibility of confirmation.[13] The document also suggested that the postchristendom context of the contemporary church implied that confirmation could no longer be though of simply as a "rite of passage" into adulthood in Christian society (if this ever was appropriate!). Christian initiation is not about the affirmation of the status quo but the process of conversion.[14]

Next, an historical overview set the stage for a consideration of future options. Various historical glimpses were provided to give the reader a sense of what was both missing and possible in Christian initiation. The rich variety of biblical metaphors for baptism were summarized; a brief picture of the early Church catechumenate was painted; the gradual breakdown of the process and rite of initiation from the eighth to fifteenth centuries and the attendant rise of the "norm" of infant baptism was outlined; the response of the Reformers to the circumstances they inherited was critiqued. The present circumstances were identified as owing much to the context to the Reformers. The Reformed and Free churches, it was argued, inherited a baptismal liturgy stripped to the barest essentials of a water rite. They eliminated all other symbolic action for primarily two reasons: there was, they claimed, no biblical warrant; they objected to the susceptibility to abuse and superstition. Confirmation thus became a public profession of faith and admission to the Lord's Supper. Yet with infant baptism remaining as the norm in the Reformed model, confirmation gradually attracted other features:

> It became a pre-condition for communion in some churches; it was viewed as an opportunity to renew baptismal vows when one had reached an age of discretion; it became the occasion for making a personal affirmation of faith. In most instances, confirmation came to be something added, a separate and independent rite, no longer part of Christian initiation, but almost a rite of passage to Christian adulthood.[15]

On the basis of this interpretation of the issues at stake, *The Quest for Renewal* presented three options for future consideration and study on the part of the whole church: 1. continue with the present practice; 2. provide an expanded and integrated form for full initiation in one rite; 3. "phase down—though not necessarily out—" infant baptism in favor of a stronger emphasis on adult initiation.[16]

The first option, it was noted, would pose few theological problems in the case of adult baptism, since baptism, confirmation, and admission to communion were already present in the Order for Adult Baptism and Confirmation. The real challenge, however, concerned infant baptism, where the present practice invited "serious questions about the adequacy of the United Church's theology of baptism and confirmation."[17] The second option would provide for the desired unification of the rite, though questions of infant and child participation in communion would have to be worked out in practice. An expanded and integrated rite could provide for complete initiation in one liturgical act (with the use of such traditional signs as the laying on of hands and signing with oil), and an opportunity for "renewal of baptismal vows" in later youth or adult life could be prefaced by a thorough program of instruction. The third option would signal a shift toward believer's baptism and could be accompanied with the development of a liturgy of dedication or thanksgiving for the birth or adoption of a child. All of these options, it was suggested, needed to be accompanied by increased attention to the congregational renewal of baptismal vows, programs of instruction and preparation, and sensitivity to the liturgical opportunities provided for by structure of the liturgical year. Finally, *The Quest for Renewal* concluded with a questionnaire for congregations to assist themselves and the larger church in the process of study.[18]

It is interesting to note that the Task Force's *The Quest for Renewal* presented the issues in a much more conciliatory style than did the original paper by Bruce Underhill on which it was based. In the case of the latter, the "grave inconsistencies" of *Church Membership*, and therein United Church policy and practice, were openly criticized.[19] In *Quest* criticism was only implied. For Underhill, the "emerging ecumenical consensus" was that "a radical reintegration" of the rite was an "urgent necessity." The final document, on the other hand, presented the various options being "considered by different churches" in an almost value-free style conducive to the spirit of a study document and inviting the participation of the wider church into the discussion. Nevertheless, John Ambrose, the primary author/editor of *The Quest for Renewal*, had also expressed his personal preference in a revealing note to the Task Force listing the desired outcome of the study: 1. the "recovery of a complete and integrated rite of initiation embracing baptism, giving of the Holy Spirit and eucharist;" 2. the restoration of adult baptism as the liturgical and theological norm; 3. a rite rich in liturgical expression; 4. greater congregational involvement in the whole process of preparation and liturgical celebration; 5. a general movement toward fuller integration between education and liturgy.[20]

The Quest for Renewal gives the first glimpse of the essential features of the context out of which *Baptism and Renewal of Baptismal Faith* grew and in which it is best located and understood. Not only was this context that of the United Church, it was also that of the wider ecumenical community. The similarities between this and, for example, similar studies taking place at the time in the Anglican Church in Canada is no mere coincidence. The Canadian Liturgical Society's Conference on Christian initiation held in Toronto in 1977 was followed with great interest by the members of the Task Force. The influence of other conferences, papers, and publications is evident in the deliberations of the Task Force and in *The Quest for Renewal.*[21]

While the document genuinely invited discussion and input, it was also an exercise in "testing the water" for reform. Thus, it was not only a case of education *about* Christian initiation, but also education *for* its reform. The results of the general questionnaire provided the Task Force with the data to document their view that there was genuine confusion in both the theory and practice of Christian initiation and that the need for continued study was necessary.[22] With this confidence, the Task Force was able to move ahead and present the church with a series of "Theological Affirmations" for doctrine and "Recommendations" for practice.

The Theological Affirmations were "received and approved" by the 1980 General Council. These signal an important development in the theology of Christian initiation in The United Church of Canada. They were, in a sense, the first such foundational statement since the Basis of Union. While, as has been shown, *Church Membership*, the *Statement of Faith,* and the *Catechism* were significant in their time, each of these was based upon the doctrinal principles of the Basis of Union and accepted it as the foundation. The 1980 Theological Affirmations, on the other hand, chose a different starting point, namely, that of the early church as seen through the eyes of a developing ecumenical consensus around Christian initiation. Thus, they represent the first rethinking of initiation theology in the United Church since union. For this reason, it is important that they be cited in their entirety:

> 1. We affirm that the Sacrament of Baptism with water in the Triune Name of God is the visible sign and seal of the covenant love of God, of incorporation into Christ and of entry into membership in the Christian Church.
>
> 2. We affirm that Baptism is the single rite of initiation bringing one to full membership in the Church. While it requires no further ritual to make it complete, we recognize it as the initial step in an ongoing process of Christian maturity. It grants admission to the Sacrament of the Lord's Supper and introduces the recipient into a life of witness, priesthood and ministry.
>
> 3. We affirm that there is one baptism as the rite of initiation into the Christian Church whatever the age at which it is administered. The baptizing of people at varying stages of maturation variously reflects both divine gift and human appropriation, of corporate and individual response, of child-like trust and mature responsibility.
>
> 4. We affirm the theological validity within the church of rites which acknowledge that the response to God's grace set forth in Baptism will be, to the end of the Christian's pilgrimage, an ongoing, developing response, varying with the time and place in which Christian disciples find themselves in their life's journey.
>
> 5. We affirm that, while the sacrament of Baptism is a visible sign that sets forth the reality of God's love, all persons are within the scope of God's saving love and power, whether baptized or not.[23]

The use of the phrase "the Triune Name of God" haunted the work of the Task Force. It was to become a flash point for controversy, perceived by many as a downplaying of the traditional trinitarian formula in baptism, a kind of "notice of motion" that the formula was on its way out and a controversial concession to concerns around inclusive language. Otherwise, the first Affirmation was reminiscent of the first lines of Article XVI of the Basis of Union: "Baptism with water into the name of the Father and of the Son and of the Holy Spirit is the sacrament by which are signified and sealed our union to Christ and participation in the blessings of the new covenant."[24]

The second Affirmation reflected the desire on the part of the Task Force for a reunified rite rooted in an understanding of baptism as the beginning of a lifelong process. In practical terms, it implied the redundancy of confirmation, the admission of all the baptized to the Lord's Supper and a correction of the contradictory distinctions between "membership" and "full membership." In short, it was a shift from the baptism-confirmation-first communion model of initiation to a baptism-eucharist model which would be reflected in the liturgy itself. Such a shift would require church-wide remits requesting the appropriate changes to the Basis of Union.

The third Affirmation reasserted the dynamic value of both infant and adult baptism and the possibility of their coexistence. The fourth prepared the way for the development of the broad category of Renewal of Baptismal Faith within the process of Christian growth and nurture. The final Affirmation placed all this in the context of God's "saving love and power," the scope of which is greater than the "visible sign and seal" of baptism. Thus, it countered the equation in popular piety between baptism and salvation.

Interestingly enough, while these Theological Affirmations were "received and approved" by the 1980 General Council in Halifax, the practical and liturgical Recommendations which accompanied them proved more controversial and were not. These Recommendations, which will be treated in greater detail below, involved issues under three headings: "Preparation for Baptism: (dealing with the preparation of candidates, congregation and the role of sponsors); "Celebration of Baptism" (the liturgical components to be included); and "Sequel to Baptism" (the admission of all baptized to the Lord's Supper, the importance of ongoing "Christian nurture and education," and the relation of baptism to individual profession of faith as well as individual and corporate "reaffirmation of faith").[25]

The General Council judged the content of these Recommendations to be too far reaching for approval without further study. Thus, it requested that they be presented to the church for comment and response. With this, the Task Force was given a new and more focused mandate: "to refine the recommendations" and to "prepare a comprehensive study document for comment and reaction by pastoral charges, presbyteries and conferences."[26] While the Task Force had achieved the significant accomplishment of convincing the General Council of the wisdom of committing considerable resources to a large-scale study of Christian initiation, the real work had only just begun.

The Project Group on Christian Initiation

The remandated Task Force now became the Project Group on Christian Initiation. *The Report on Christian Initiation* was published and circulated to each pastoral charge in April of 1981.[27] Like *A Quest for Renewal*, it too was a study document and covered much of the same ground. But, unlike it, it did more than seek to present the state of the question and suggest possible options. It pushed the information presented in *A Quest for Renewal* to the next level, proposing the particular Recommendations themselves and inviting the church's specific response. By April of 1982, submissions representing nearly 4,000 persons had been received.[28] In addition, another "random sampling" of 128 pastoral charges was conducted by the Research Office on the subject of present baptismal practice. Together these surveys provide an important summary of baptismal practice and the receptiveness to the Recommendations.

The survey of present practice consisted of seven questions covering the frequency of baptismal celebrations, its congregational context, its liturgical form, and the use of baptismal symbols.[29] The results included the following statistics: 60 percent of congregations surveyed conducted baptism "whenever there was a need" without designating baptismal days according to the classic liturgical calendar; 90 percent celebrated the sacrament in the context of public worship; 82 percent continued to place the sacrament early in the liturgy, in spite of its *Service Book* location after the Word; nevertheless, 68 percent used the *Service Book* orders "all the time" (23 percent "part of the time").[30] The survey also showed openness to a variety of other "new" liturgical components in spite of their absence in the *Service Book* orders. The question was asked: "Which of the following symbols might you use regularly?" While only one congregation (of 123) was open to the use of oil "regularly," other baptismal actions and symbols were received more positively: sponsors, 51 percent; laying on of hands, 14 percent. It would appear that resources and sources from other traditions were already making their presence felt alongside the preferred *Service Book* orders. The recovery of some of the classic symbols and actions of baptism was evident.

The results of the *Report*'s questionnaire also reinforced some of these trends with particular reference to the Recommendations. Table 7.1 shows where the Project Group found its mandate to proceed with their Recommendations. No more than 10 percent of respondents found any of the six suggestions "undesirable" or "unacceptable"; the majority viewed most of them as "desirable" or "optional."[31]

However, within this overall pattern some other features were evident.[32] The idea of sponsorship, whether desirable or optional, was certainly not deemed essential by most congregations. The general content of the comments on this subject were characterized as "lukewarm," with concerns about its "workability" often expressed.[33] The belief that baptism should take place in the congregation of participating parent(s) or guardian(s) revealed a dramatic division between rural and urban congregations. "The rural churches are up in arms over this question," wrote one member of the Project Group.[34] Most rural congregations spoke of the need to preserve the right of parents to "return to their home congregation for the baptism of their children." While most appeared to support the statement that "all baptized persons should have access to the Lord's Table," a number of the respondents also added the comment "except children." Others were concerned that the statement was too restrictive and limited participation only to the baptized. A strong majority felt that a Profession of Faith should be expected of all baptized persons and remained puzzled about the desire of the Project Group to downplay confirmation.

These surveys revealed much about United Church practice and belief at the time and affirmed many of the directions of the Project Group's work and Recommendations. However, they also pointed to potential problems with respect to their pastoral and liturgical implementation. In particular, the issues of sponsorship, admission to the table, Profession of Faith/confirmation and the use of "new" baptismal symbols would continue to be a challenge for the work of the Project Group and influence the reception of the liturgy.

Table 7.1
Responses to the
Report on Christian Initiation Questionnaire

	Essential	Desirable	Optional	Undesirable	Unacceptable
Sponsors?	16%	40%	36%	6%	2%
Celebrated in congregation of active parents / guardians?	31%	57%	10%	1%	1%
Laying on of hands?	18%	34%	38%	8%	2%
Admission to table?	33%	33%	38%	8%	2%
Later Profession of Faith required?	60%	34%	5%	1%	0%
Thanksgiving after birth / adoption?	8%	35%	48%	6%	3%

Source: UCA, General Council Standing Committee Records, Project Group on Christian Initiation, "Christian Initiation: An Update from the Project Group on Christian Initiation," Box 63, File 1.

In order to provide the church with still more time to respond to and digest the contents of the *Report*'s Recommendations, deadlines on the survey were extended and the Project Group presented an "Interim Report" to the 1982 General Council. The Interim Report resulted in two significant actions. First, the General Council approved "a trial period permitting implementation of the Recommendations." Second, the Council instructed its Executive "to proceed with remits to Presbyteries and Pastoral Charges, dealing with the changes in the Basis of Union as required by the adoption of the . . . Affirmations."[35] Specifically, the second Affirmation (affirming baptism as the sole rite of initiation into full membership and admission to the sacrament of the Lord's Supper), necessitated changes to the Basis of Union, a task which, under United Church polity, could only be accomplished by the process of a remit.

Before turning to a consideration of the remits, it is also important to examine briefly the Recommendations themselves. It will be immediately evident, in light of the previous liturgical commentary, that they provide the practical foundation on which the liturgical text itself was based.

> Preparation for Baptism
>
> 1a) Preparation of Parents/Guardians when Children are to be Baptized.
> We recommend that the congregation, through the session or its equivalent, be responsible for ensuring that parents/guardians requesting baptism for their children are appropriately aware of the meaning of baptism, that they recognize the necessity for the baptized child to be nurtured and guided in the Christian Faith, and that at least one of the parents/guardians be a participating member of the church.
>
> b) Preparation of Candidates who Present Themselves for Baptism.
> We recommend that the congregation, through the session or its equivalent, be responsible for ensuring that persons seeking baptism are appropriately aware of the meaning of baptism and that they recognize the necessity for the baptized person to grow in faith.[36]

These two Recommendations were well received in the process of congregational study and trial implementation and required no amendments. They seemed to speak to many of the pastoral concerns articulated in *A Quest for Renewal* and addressed the perceptions of many congregations that such signs of corporate sponsorship and individual responsibility were lacking in baptismal practice, undermining its essential meaning. The requirement that "at least one of the parents/guardians be a participating member of the church" was in keeping with previous General Council policy statements on infant baptism.[37] In commenting on the meaning of "participating membership" the Project Group noted that in the United Church this has traditionally meant "any person who has been baptized, made an individual profession of faith . . . and who, barring exceptional circumstances, is in the habit of regular attendance at public worship."[38] It was acknowledged, however, that the Session (or its equivalent) had the authority to define "participating member" in another way or allow exceptions to the rule on a case-by-case basis. The overall framework of these two Recommendations is, like that of the Theological Affirmations, an understanding of baptism as the beginning of a lifelong journey of faith. With this in mind, the Project Group acknowledged the responsibility of the church to provide assistance through the production of resources and, to this end, had already set about doing so.[39] Behind this was the Project Group's vision of a baptismal praxis rooted in the ancient example of the catechumenate and even the function of renunciation:

> It is important that the candidate come to understand that to be baptized means to be placed on the firing-line of the forces against evil. This time of prepara-

> tion is thus first of all a time for socialization and conscientization of the candidate which aims at his/her recognition and acceptance of the strangeness of the Christian community in a non-Christian society. As was the practice in the early church, one needs to start with the experience of life in the faith community and only later move into the doctrine and mysteries of the faith.[40]

The second Recommendation concerned the congregation's preparation: "We recommend that the congregation, as corporate sponsor, be adequately prepared to participate meaningfully in the role that it is called to play in the preparation, nurture and guidance of the newly baptized." [41] With this Recommendation the Project Group was trying to move beyond the simple provision of instruction and a program of Christian Education toward greater congregational responsibility for the celebration of baptism. The remaining Recommendations suggested some of the forms this could take, including program of sponsors, programs of preparation for renewal of baptismal faith, and individual and corporate liturgical acts of baptismal remembrance and renewal. An intentional observance of particular times and seasons of baptismal preparation in the liturgical year was also part of the context of this issue.[42]

The third Recommendation concerned the role of sponsors: "We recommend that individual sponsor(s) may be named by the Session or its equivalent to support the person(s) to be baptized (and/or the parents/guardians) and to make specific and personal the corporate sponsorship of the congregation."[43]

This provoked the "greatest misunderstanding and resistance."[44] In spite of the Project Group's attempts to model this on the practice of the early church and commend its practice in a contemporary context, only a minority of congregations reported success during trial implementation and testing. Most struggled with its practical implementation. The *Report* suggested many possibilities, including a process of appointment by the Session, Pastoral Care Committee, or Worship Committee, a program of prebaptism pastoral visits, lay-lead preparation sessions, and liturgical leadership in baptism. Confusion continued, however, and the distinction between godparents and sponsors seemed impossible to clarify on the practical level.[45]

Recommendations concerning the celebration of baptism itself were also included, the first being: "We recommend that baptism be celebrated during corporate worship and normally in the congregation in which the parents/guardians are participating members or with which the candidate is affiliated."[46] Popular practice allowed for ready support for this affirmation of the corporate celebration of the sacrament.[47] This also permitted the Project Group once again to reinforce the value of a more catholic vision of the seasonal celebration of baptism. The real challenge came in attempting to put an end to what some clergy called "visit baptism: (i.e., the baptism of nonresident candidates. The insertion of the word "normally" in this Recommendation allowed for the provision of exceptions to the norm,[48] and the reluctant acknowledgment that "visit baptisms" would continue, especially in the rural church.

The use of the traditional tinitarian formula was also affirmed: "We recommend that the candidate be baptized with water into the name of the Father, and of the Son, and of the Holy Spirit."[49] The issue of inclusive language prompted emotional debate over the use and significance of this wording. The Project Group favored its use for reasons of ecumenical consensus and recognition and argued that "it behooves individuals and congregations to move with great caution" in using other formulations.[50] However, in an effort to mediate conflict over this issue the 1984 wording of this Recommendation replaced the formula with the phrase "the Holy Trinity." But, as with similar attempts to speak of "the Triune Name" and "the Holy Trinity" in the remits, this prompted response from many that the "scripturally-mandated and ecumenically received" formula was being compromised. Further study of the question was referred to the Theology of Faith Committee and, in the meantime, the traditional formula was returned to the Recommendation.[51]

The third Recommendation under "Celebration of Baptism" concerned use of water. "We recommend that in the celebration of baptism there be a generous and visible use of water."[52] This was a clear critique of the "virtually dry events" and "sacramental minimalism"[53] of most United Church baptisms. It found perhaps the most explicit expression of all the Recommendations in *Baptism and Renewal of Baptismal Faith*. The *Report* emphasized the role of a prayer of thanksgiving over the water and the need for larger fonts and more attention to baptismal space in architectural planning and renovations. "A more copious and visible use of water," it was noted, "could contribute significantly to the impact and understanding of that event."[54] Most testing congregations reported benefiting from "a greater stress on the water, its generous use, its importance as a symbol, pouring during the service, etc."[55] This was a major liturgical development in the United Church experience of baptism.

On the subject of laying on of hands, it was recommended "that the laying on of hands with prayer for the Holy Sprit be incorporated into the liturgy of baptism."[56] Again, appeal to early church precedent was at the source of this Recommendation and its efforts to achieve a unified rite of initiation. Commenting on this, the Project Group followed Underhill's earlier lead and cited the *Church Membership* report as the origin of the present United Church emphasis on confirmation.[57] But this Recommendation needs to be considered in conjunction with that on "Profession of Faith by Individuals" below. Together they attempted to ensure that hand laying with baptism at the expense of confirmation did not nullify the importance of a public profession of faith by those baptized as infants.

"Other Symbolic Acts" were also considered: "We recommend that consideration be given to the inclusion within the liturgy of baptism of such traditional symbolic actions as: anointing with oil, signing with the cross, dressing in a new garment and lighting a candle."[58] Like the two previous Recommendations, this was also aimed at enriching the symbolic dimensions of baptismal celebrations in order to "provide a means of conveying the rich variety of meanings implicit in the sacrament." Commenting further on this, the Project Group noted "a growing feeling that our worship has been made unnecessarily barren by too great a dependence on the spoken word."[59] In spite of efforts to explain and comment on the biblical and historical roots of the various symbolic actions suggested, this Recommendation continued to evoke many comments that they were "foreign to our tradition," would "take away" from the centrality of the symbol of water, or could give rise to "superstitious or magic connotations."[60]

A series of recommendations were also grouped under the heading "Sequel to Baptism," the first concerning "Baptism and the Lord's Supper": We recommend that all baptized persons be encouraged to participate in the Lord's Supper."[61] As the process of study and trial implementation continued, it became increasingly clear that there were many reasons why people had objections to this recommendation, though often it was for very different reasons. For some, it was the issue of a perceived need for an adult profession of faith, or its conflict with the "Reformed" tradition as reflected in the Basis of Union's requirement of a "credible profession of faith" before admission to communion.[62] For others, it was not so much the admission of baptized children to the table (about 25 percent of congregations reported already admitting children to communion) but the exclusion of the nonbaptized. Efforts to explain that the notion of an "open table" came from "a time when it was simply assumed that everyone in the community was baptized," and that even the Basis of Union considered communion to be the meal of the baptized, did not address the popular perception that all should be welcome regardless of baptismal status. A few others were cautious about what "a truly 'open table' would do to our relations with other churches in the ecumenical community."[63] The compromise, for the time being (at least while the remit process proceeded), was to change the previous wording of this Recommendation from "be granted access to the Lord's table" to "be encouraged to participate in the Lord's Supper."[64] The spirit of this solution was also reflected in the fifth Theological Affirmation discussed earlier.

A Recommendation under the heading "Renewed Attention to Christian Nurture and Education" read: "We recommend that the church address itself anew to the matter of Christian nurture and education of persons of all ages, with particular attention being given to children and their participation in worship, the Lord's Supper, and the life and mission of the church."[65] This followed, in a sense, from those principles established with respect to preparation for baptism. In the words of the Project Group, it called for "an integrated approach of worship and education for children and adults, that is, the whole community of faith."[66] This was a subject of considerable discussion and work in the Task Force and Project Group and was reflected in their work on educational resources. The Working Unit on Worship and Liturgy and the Task Group/committee which produced the liturgy itself also devoted considerable study and work to educational resources which would be supportive of the liturgy. This momentum eventually helped fuel the large-scale discussion on the role and place of children in the church, leading eventually to the publication of the major report *A Place for You*.[67] Thus, this Recommendation represented a vision, the effects of which extended far beyond the work on Christian initiation to the church as a whole. Its effects continue to be felt today on issues from intergenerational worship to the participation of youth and young adults in the courts of the church. Indeed, there is an important sense in which this Recommendation, while easily overlooked or underemphasized in comparison to those dealing with preparation or celebration, was in fact the focus of the vision of

Christian initiation in the work of the Task Force, the Project Group, and the liturgy. As McNally put it in his paper to the committee, "the starting point [for a Christian Education program] is the rite of Christian initiation . . . the program must be built both explicitly and implicitly on that base." Or, in Newman's words: "Christian formation and nurture begins [*sic*] in baptism."[68] This perspective is very much in line with what was being considered ecumenically and was prompted, in particular, by the Roman Catholic *Rite of Christian Initiation of Adults*. Within this framework, the renewal of baptismal practice and theology is a key to the renewal of Christian nurture, education, life, and mission.[69]

Under "Profession of Faith by Individuals," it was recommended that, "within the context of congregational worship, an individual profession of faith and personal commitment to the life and mission of the church be expected of those baptized as children."[70] As the Project Group reported, "the response from the church on this Recommendation was unequivocal. A majority considered that a personal profession of faith and commitment was essential. . . . Less than 1 percent had any reservations."[71]

What was not clear, however, was whether or not respondents had confirmation in mind as the only valid form of profession of faith. Similarly, it was not clear if the liturgy's notion of "renewal of baptismal faith" would effectively address these concerns.

The final two Recommendations also showed the Project Group's attempt to think broadly in this respect:

> 4. Reaffirmation of Faith on Various Occasions
> We recommend that there be opportunities for all baptized persons to reaffirm their faith on a variety of occasions and in relation to different life experiences.
> 5. Corporate Reaffirmation of Faith
> We recommend that there be special opportunities for a reaffirmation of the baptismal covenant by the whole community of faith.[72]

Once again, the resistance to this on the part of congregations during the trial period of implementation revolved mostly around questions of practicality and implementation. The efforts of the Project Group to explain the potential personal (life cycle) and corporate (seasonal) opportunities for reaffirmation can only be viewed as a tentative beginning to a process of education which still had far to go.[73] Ironically, the one opportunity of this sort affirmed by the majority of congregations—the desire for a liturgy of Thanksgiving for the Birth or Adoption of a Child—was not taken up by the Project Group.[74]

In summary, the Recommendations as "approved in principle" by the 1984 General Council, clearly constitute the framework out of which *Baptism and Renewal of Baptismal Faith* emerged. This was a dynamic process aimed at the renewal of the United Church Christian initiation theology and practice as a whole. The ecumenical influence on the process is clear, though the United Church context transposed the discussion into a uniquely United Church key. Issues such as the use of sponsors, the trinitarian formula, liturgical/symbolic actions, admission to the Lord's Supper, profession of faith, reaffirmation of faith, Christian nurture and education, and the role of children in worship came clearly to the fore as the United Church struggled in its quest for the renewal of Christian initiation.

In proposing the approval of these Recommendations to General Council, the Project Group reported that, like the Theological Affirmations, they were "strongly supported" by the majority of congregations. Any criticism or resistance was cast in a positive light and characterized as "an exciting range of theological and educational insights."[75] Had this been the sum total of the process, the United Church would have been well on its way to a broadly-based revolution in its theology and practice of Christian initiation. Indeed, the process of study, response, and trial implementation was impressive, well-executed, and involved a high degree of participation within the church. However, the remit controversy was to bring the whole process to a halt, at least on the level of polity and doctrine. The remits on Christian initiation are the final components of this background to *Baptism and Renewal of Baptismal Faith.*

The Remits on Christian Initiation

In addition to the theological and liturgical process of study, survey, report, and recommendation, there emerged a parallel judicial process of remits addressing questions of doctrine and polity. At stake was the question of whether or not the Theological Affirmations as approved by the 1980 General Council were in conflict with the Basis of Union of the United Church. This question was referred to the Judicial Committee, which in turn ruled that Affirmations 2 and 3 were indeed in conflict with Articles XV, XVI (2) of the Doctrine section, and II B II(a) of the polity section.[76] Under United Church polity, any changes to the Basis of Union must be passed by a remit, a unique form of churchwide referendum.

The process of the remit is important to understand in order to interpret the subtleties of the outcome. The normal procedure is to solicit the agreement or disagreement of presbyteries (each presbytery having one vote) regarding the proposed changes. A simple majority of presbyteries (50 percent plus one) carries the decision. This particular remit was significant because its scope was expanded to include Sessions (or their equivalent). Thus each pastoral charge also had one vote. A simple majority of *both* presbyteries and pastoral charges was required before the General Council could accept the proposed changes. This remit was the first to include Sessions since the United Church's formation in 1925. The desire to ensure the direct involvement of all congregations underscored its perceived importance in the life of the church at the time.

In mathematical terms it meant that, given the number of presbyteries and pastoral charges in the United Church in 1982, a simple majority of presbyteries would be forty-seven; a simple majority of Sessions would be 1197. An important factor which was to become significant was that these figures were absolute, regardless of the number of responses received. That is to say, it was not a percentage of the responses received which was to carry the decision, but an absolute majority of both (actual) presbyteries and (actual) sessions in the United Church. To complicate the matter further, presbyteries and sessions which did not respond were to be counted as votes against the proposed changes. Finally, while four changes to the Basis of Union were proposed, they were not to be voted on separately but as one entire package. As the covering letter to the proposed changes put it: "It is ONE question and each Presbytery or Pastoral Charge has ONE vote."[77]

The remit as sent to presbyteries and pastoral charges proposed changes to the Articles in question with a view to establishing baptism as the sole rite of initiation into the Christian Church. This meant that children would be admitted to the Lord's Supper without a profession of faith. Great pains were taken in the supporting material to point out that this was not meant to imply that a profession of faith was not longer expected or desired, but simply that it was not necessary for admission to the communion. The proposed changes were essentially the Theological Affirmations written in the form and style of the Articles of Faith of the Basis of Union.

Given that the Theological Affirmations had already been approved easily by the General Council and that they seemed to have garnered a significant base of support within the church, the success of the remit appeared, at first glance, to be a foregone conclusion. To the surprise of many, however, it was soundly defeated. Of the ninety-two presbyteries, the vote was thirty in favor and sixty against. Of the 2,406 pastoral charges, it was 557 in favor and 1,849 against.

Upon closer examination, however, several complicating factors allowed the issue to be kept alive instead of bringing the question to an end. First was the question of the fairness of the rules of remits. In this case, of the 1,849 pastoral charges recorded as voting against the remit, 801 of these did not in fact cast any vote but, under the rules described above, had been counted as negative votes. The fact that the "real" vote against was actually 1,048 (not a majority) was not lost on the supporters of the remit. The General Council Executive was asked to review remit procedures with a view to assessing their fairness.

Another issue was the content of the remit itself. While the question was intended as one, the popular issues turned out to be many. In spite of the Project Group's protestations to the contrary, many in the church interpreted the net effect of the changes as undermining the importance of profession of faith and the loss of the popularly valued rite of confirmation. On the level of polity, such developments were viewed as particularly confusing. Without the criteria of profession of faith or confirmation as a rite of "full membership," how were congregations to categorize people in the management of church records and membership rolls? Who was to have voting and office holding privileges? While the Project Group tried to assure the church that such issues could be resolved and made several specific recommendations to this effect in their 1984 report, this seemed to fall on deaf ears.[78]

On the question of admission to the Lord's Supper, the ground seemed to shift under the feet of the Project Group. The reaction of the church to such proposed phrases as "[Baptism] grants admission to the sacrament of the Lord's Supper" and "all who by baptism are members of the Church may be admitted to the Lord's Supper" showed that, in practice, the "open table" of the United Church had become more open than the compilers of the Basis of Union ever could have imagined. No amount of logical analysis of the proposed phrasing seemed to be able to convince congregations that they were not exclusive in intent. Thus, the issue became not so much the admission of children to the Lord's Supper, but its restriction to the baptized alone.

Finally, the first line of the proposed changes to Article XVI (1) changed "Baptism with water into the name of the Father and of the Son and of the Holy Spirit" to "Baptism with water in the triune name of God." In addition, "brotherhood" was changed to "family of faith" and "community of faith" in other sections. Thus, for many the argument became focused on the issue of inclusive language and the essential goals of the remit became increasingly blurred.[79]

Given all of these factors, it would be unwise to suggest any single reason for the defeat of the remit. It was, at the very least, a combination and convergence of several factors with widespread confusion being the final result. Kenneth Gallinger, the writer of the popular "Question Box" in the *Observer*, expressed it bluntly some time later. The remit was lost, he wrote, "partly because the wording was so confusing that most of us didn't know whether 'yes' meant 'no' or vice versa."[80]

The Project Group seemed painfully aware of the confusion and immediately set about redrafting for another attempt. Word of this was immediately met with protests charging that due democratic process and church polity was being subverted and ignored.[81] In response to this criticism, the case for a second remit was argued by the now-chair of the Project Group, Richard Moffat. In a letter to the *Observer* he wrote:

> [T]he theological affirmations passed by General Council in 1980 are still on the books and . . . results from the trial implementation of the recommendations authorized by the 29th Council have yet to be reported. Widespread opinion expressed through many letters and workshops is that, despite a bad process and some bad wording, the direction and intention of the remit was good and should be continued. The vote count simply didn't accurately reflect the mind of the church on the whole issue of Christian initiation. There still remains a great deal of unfinished business.[82]

In spite of reports of 150 "unsolicited letters" expressing support for the direction of the remit and the growing positive response from the seventy-five testing congregations, reports in the *Observer* continued to communicate a rather cynical view on the subject, as if to predict another failure.[83]

The report to the 1984 General Council attempted to address the concerns of the congregations and to explain the problematic complexities of the remit process.[84] The reworded remit was more in line with the language and style of the Basis of Union and clearly acknowledged the expectation of a public profession of faith from those baptized in infancy. Conceding that "language about the table" needed to speak "in a more positive, welcoming, less offensive way" than in the first remit, "while still holding us within the ecumenical community,"[85] a revised wording relating to admission to the Lord's Supper was presented: "All members of the Church [i.e., all the baptized] are expected and encouraged to come to the Lord's Table. The nature of grace and Christian hospitality dictate that no one who comes to the table sincerely desiring to receive God's blessing, whether member or not, shall be turned away."[86]

In addition, the Division of Mission in Canada, attempting to balance traditional, ecumenical, and feminist interests, advised replacing the controversial phrase "the triune name of God" with "the Holy Trinity." Admitting the tension around the issue, it was acknowledged that "such a change in the language of the Basis of Union may continue to cause an uneasiness across the church that is not likely to be resolved until The General Council directs an explicit study of the biblical, theological, liturgical and ecumenical implication of language referring to God."[87] Such a study was directed by the 1984 General Council and results were reported in 1986.[88] But before that report was heard, the second remit also failed.

The *Observer* reported that John Ambrose, the former chair of the Project Group, was "dumbfounded."[89] All early indications were that it would be successful. The first responses from the presbyteries were "overwhelmingly" positive.[90] But the process seemed doomed. One hundred mailings were lost. The deadline had to be extended. Confusion about the process continued. In the end the issues remained the same. Letters to the *Observer* confirm that most of the objections remained unchanged, in spite of whatever clarifications the reworded remit had attempted. It was characterized variously as "a move away from the Reformed tradition" and its emphasis on profession of faith; a "trivialization" of the responsibilities of church membership (by considering infants full members); a "fencing of the table" excluding faithful believers; and a sacrifice of the centrality of the trinitarian formula in baptism.[91]

But again, the actual results of the remit revealed a more complex picture. A "vast majority" of presbyteries and congregations had in fact voted in its favor, but, once more, not the "absolute majority" needed under the rules of procedure. To add insult to injury, it was learned that it would have passed under the new rules which were soon to be introduced (requiring only a majority of those votes cast), but these were not to come into effect until after the next General Council.[92]

If there was any remaining consolation in all of this, it was that a large percentage of congregations had engaged in a closer look at their initiation theology and practices, and that many could not now turn back from the course of renewal precipitated by, if nothing else, the discussion itself. Matters of baptismal policy were again left with the Session of each congregation. With any luck, perhaps the resources resulting from the work of the Task Force and Project Group would serve as a guide into the future.

As Patricia Clarke of the *Observer* had pointed out after the failure of the first remit, the church was again left in something of an ironic situation. "The verdict leaves the church with a theological statement about baptism which has been approved by two General Councils, a constitutional change based on that statement which has been rejected, existing affirmations about baptism and membership which are inconsistent or ambiguous, and a bewildering range of beliefs and practices around a fundamental doctrine of the church."[93]

The background to *Baptism and Renewal of Baptismal Faith* is a complex combination of ecumenical scholarship and denominational politics. The process of study and dialogue on Christian initiation in the United Church was intended to provide the soil in which a renewed practice of Christian initiation could take root and grow. Indeed, it was even hoped that it would be the critical factor leading to a renewal of liturgy and Christian formation in the United Church as a whole. While it could be argued that some of the results of this became evident on the level of practice (to the extent that the study and dialogue did take place), their absence on the level of officially approved doctrine and institutionally supported polity compromised the integrity of the resulting liturgy and its hopes for broadly based pastoral use. The result was, at best, a rather anticlimatic stalemate; at worst, a pastoral vacuum—both of which were bound to affect the life of the liturgy itself. With this background as a complement to the liturgical commentary, a brief analysis of the liturgy can now proceed.

Structure

At each critical point in the foregoing commentary and background discussion, considerations of structure have begged questions of liturgical function and theological meaning. The desire for the reunification of confirmation and baptism is, from a liturgical perspective, primarily a structural issue. The question it prompts is: if baptism is the sole rite of Christian initiation, how is this celebrated liturgically? *Baptism and Renewal of Baptismal Faith* is an attempt to provide an answer to this question.

The first meeting of the Committee whose task it was to draft a new liturgy began with an examination and critique of the United Methodist's *Alternate Text, A Service of Baptism, Confirmation, and Renewal.* This exercise proved to be an important step in helping the committee clarify its liturgical goals. The United Methodists, they concluded, had "knuckled under" to the "confirmation industry" in their rite, perpetuating the very theology of confirmation and subsequent dichotomy of membership that this Committee wanted to avoid. This text was judged to be ambiguous about the relation between baptism, confirmation, renewal, and profession of faith.[94] Interestingly enough, however, as the commentary has shown, the first drafts of the United Church order were based on the United Methodist text, albeit with adjustments and revisions aimed at overcoming some of these problems. Upon reviewing the first draft (which attempted a separation between profession of faith and reaffirmation of faith from baptism), the Committee agreed on its basic liturgical goals: "We need a service that combines profession of faith by parents, adult candidates for baptism and baptized adults making their first profession."[95] This was later expressed as a desire for an "omnibus rite" in "modular" form[96]—that is that is to say, an order which held together all the rites of the baptismal covenant and did so in such a way as to allow for use in a variety of pastoral circumstances (i.e., the baptism of adults and/or children and/or first profession of faith and/or subsequent reaffirmations of faith). The challenge for a modular omnibus rite was to do all of this while still pointing to the unity of all the action within a unified paradigm of Christian initiation. Table 7.2 shows the significant stages in the drafting process which illustrate the efforts to achieve this goal.

Table 7.2
Selected Stages in the Drafting Process Leading to
Baptism and Renewal of Baptismal Faith

First Draft (Dec. 1984)	Second Draft (Feb. 4. 1985)	Fifth Draft (June 24, 1985)	Final Draft (Mar. 1985)
Introduction to the Service *Statement*	Introduction to the Service *Statement*	Words of Welcome and Invitation *Litany* (Eph. 4:4-6) *Opportunity for a Teaching Statement*	Introduction *(Scriptural warrants suggested in rubrics)* *Litany* (Eph. 4:4-6)
Presentation of Candidates *(for baptism, profession of faith, reaffirmation of faith)*	Presentation of Candidates *(for baptism and profession of faith)* *Statement*	Presentation of Candidates, Parents, and Sponsors *(for baptism and renewal of baptismal covenant)*	Presentation of Candidates for Baptism Presentation of Those Renewing Their Baptismal Faith
Renunciation of Sin	The Congregational Basis for Baptism	Renunciation of the Forces of Darkness and Declaration of Allegiance	Renunciation and Declaration and Congregational Profession of Faith
Declaration of Commitment	Declaration of Commitment		
Promises of the Congregation		A Congregational Affirm. of Faith	
Dedication of the Water			
Thanksgiving Over the Water	A Prayer of Thanksgiving	Prayer of Thanksgiving, Pouring of Water	Prayer of Thanksgiving and Pouring of Water
Baptism by Water	The Signing and Sealing of the Baptismal Covenant	Signing, sealing, and Affirmation of the Baptismal Covenant: A. Water	Action of Baptism
The Signing of the Cross	*(Signing of the Cross)*	B. Signing with the Cross	Signing with the Cross

	(Laying on of Hands) *(rubrical provision for Other Symbolic Acts)*	C. Laying on of Hands D. Other Symbolic Acts	Laying on of Hands *(rubrical provision-for Other Symbolic Acts)*
Profession of Faith *(for those who have been baptized previously)*			
Baptism in the Holy Spirit, by the Laying on of Hands *(for those just baptized and those who have just professed their faith)*			Action of Renewal of Baptismal Faith *Asperges* *Laying on of Hands* *(rubrical provision transfer of membership)*
Reaffirmation of Faith/Renewal of Baptismal Covenant *(for others)* *Asperges* *Laying on of Hands*		Commissioning	Blessing
Corporate Renewal of Covenant			

Source: UCA, Division of Mission in Canada Records, Task Force on Chistian Initiation, Drafts, "Minutes," 1984-1985.

The successive convergence and consolidation of the Presentation and the baptismal action in the first three columns shows the development of the omnibus character of the rite. A comparison of the Presentation and baptismal action in the last two columns highlights the development of the modular character of the rite—that is, explicit identification of different groups of candidates requiring distinct action and response. The result is an order which reunites and integrates the variety of candidates and actions into one service and gathers all the action around common baptismal symbols (i.e., Renunciation and Declaration and Congregational Profession of Faith; the Prayer of Thanksgiving and Pouring of Water; the symbolic use of water and laying on of hands with prayer for the Spirit). Thus, the common roots of all the action in baptism itself are emphasized.

Ironically, as Table 7.3 shows, the final result is in fact more of a return to the original United Methodist rite than perhaps the process of drafting would indicate. Thus, the United Church text owes most of its omnibus and modular structure to the United Methodist source, though the modular potential is enhanced by such features as the distinctions in presentation, symbolic actions and, most significantly, the elimination of any reference to confirmation.

Table 7.3
A Structural Comparison of
A Service of Baptism, Confirmation and Renewal and
Baptism and Renewal of Baptismal Faith

A Service of Baptism, Confirmation and Renewal (United Methodist, 1976)	*Baptism and Renewal of Baptismal Faith* (United Church of Canada, 1986)
Introduction to the Service	Introduction
Presentation of the Candidates *for baptism, confirmation, and renewal of the baptismal covenant*	Presentation of Candidates for Baptism, Presentation of Those Renewing Their Baptismal Faith
Declaration of Repentance, Commitment, Affirmation of Faith	Renunciation and Declaration, Congregational Profession of Faith
Thanksgiving over the Water	Prayer of Thanksgiving, Pouring of Water
Administration of Water Baptism and Laying on of Hands	Action of Baptism, Signing of the Cross, Laying on of Hands
Declaration	*rubrical Provision for Other Symbolic Acts*
Confirmation and Other Renewal of Baptismal Covenant	Action of Renewal of Baptismal Faith
Professional or Renewal of Full Membership in the United Methodist Church	*rubrical provision for transfer of membership*
Commendation and Welcome	Blessing

Source: *BCR* (1976), *BRBF* (1986).

Scripture

Significant developments are found in this order with respect to the role of scripture. It signals a departure from the traditional Reformed and United Church use of scripture as a warrant for sacramental action. Gone is the sole reliance of *The Book of Common Order* and the *Service Book* on Matthew 28 and Mark 10. Where scripture is present as an opening to the liturgy, it is reduced to a rubrical option. But even here the texts suggested expand the scope of scriptural reference. The introduction, in its use of a litany-like form based on Ephesians 4:4-7, builds on the tradition of beginning with scripture but, by casting it in a new form, has the advantage of avoiding both the proof-texting connotations of a warrant and the didacticism of teaching statements and exhortations, while inviting a greater degree of participation on the part of the congregation. This "major shift," as the Committee called it, from a "teaching statement" toward a more "liturgical act" is a movement away from a didactic style of proclamation to a more celebrative style of liturgical action. This shift is evident throughout the liturgy and becomes explicit in the use of such acts as anointing, laying on of hands, asperges, and other symbolic actions. It is most evident in the Prayer of Thanksgiving, where the imagery presented in berakah form expands the biblical richness of the liturgy in ways that the previous use of warrants and exhortations did not.[97]

The Prayer of Thanksgiving, however, is not without potential theological problems. The poetic strength of such an approach is also its hermeneutical weakness. It is selective in its use and exegesis of the various biblical metaphors of water. As a result, one is tempted to conclude from it that scripture presents water as the primary focus or means of salvation. This could easily be mistaken for a new theology of baptismal regeneration if care is not taken to emphasize the Christological foundations of the prayer. In addition, it is important to keep in mind that, while the liturgy is a *locus theologicus*, it is not a work of systematic theology. What is at work here is not so much a systematically consistent theology of baptism, or one bent on avoiding potential magical or superstitious tendencies, as a liturgical celebration of rich scriptural mystery and even ambiguity.[98] It is on this level that this liturgy, when placed in its United Church context, makes significant strides. The Prayer of Thanksgiving, together with the symbolic action of the liturgy as a whole, expands the scriptural horizon of the United Church experience of baptism.

Pneumatology

The most important pneumatological development in *Baptism and Renewal of Baptismal Faith* is the reunification of baptism and confirmation in one act of initiation. This is ritualized liturgically by the laying on of hands with every baptism, in keeping with the specific Recommendation of the *Report on Christian Initiation*. This effort to show more fully the unity of "the water and the spirit" in baptism is also visible in the overall language of the rite, especially at several points, including the Introduction, the Prayer of Thanksgiving, and the prayer for the Spirit at the hand laying itself. As a result, the language of the Spirit is present in the language of baptism to a much greater degree in this liturgy than that of any other United Church baptismal text. With *Baptism and Renewal of Baptismal Faith*, the Spirit and baptism are inseparable.

However, this liturgy also attempts to go further than mere structural reunification. It actually seeks to dispense with the notion of "confirmation" altogether, replacing it with the notion of Renewal of Baptismal Faith. Renewal of Baptismal Faith is intended to be a liturgical action celebrating the renewal of the baptismal covenant by any number of participants in varying circumstances. As the final form of the Introduction points out:

> About the "renewal of baptismal faith" component: *The Report on Christian Initiation* recommends that ". . . within the context of congregational worship, an individual profession of faith and personal commitment to the life and mission of the church be expected of those baptized as children . . ." and further that ". . . there be opportunities for all baptized persons to reaffirm their faith on a variety of occasions and in relation to different life experience." This service is intended to function for both the initial profession of faith and subsequent reaffirmations. (One of the "life experiences" is the presentation of one's child for baptism. Hence the parents of child candidates join in one profession of faith with those making their first adult profession, with adult candidates for baptism and with any other reaffirming their faith.)[99]

This represents a shift from the confirmation paradigm of the *Service Book* to an initiation paradigm in *Baptism and Renewal of Baptismal Faith.* The former tended to blur the distinctions between the sacramental and juridical views of confirmation. The sacramental view took confirmation to be a kind of sacrament of the Spirit, or at least a sacrament of belief (profession of faith), the significance of which seemed more important in the *Service Book* than baptism itself. The juridical view took confirmation to be admission to communion, a rite of passage into the responsibilities and privileges of adult membership. The language of "full membership" confused the sacramental and juridical dimensions even further. This was the very confusion that the Task Force on Confirmation faced, with no clear answer to be found in United Church policy and practice. *Baptism and Renewal of Baptismal Faith*, by returning to the classic early church initiation paradigm of baptism, seeks to clarify this confusion by asserting that baptism is of water *and* the Spirit and as such is the sole rite of initiation into the Body of Christ, the church—a right of which is admission to the table and a consequence of which is the continued life in the Spirit.

This initiation paradigm is more a process than a liturgy. In this respect, the liturgy takes as its primary source the *Rite of the Christian Initiation of Adults.*[100] It presupposes the preparation of individuals and communities, the celebration of initiation into the full corporate life of the church, and the expectation and opportunity for individual and corporate reaffirmation of faith at various times during the ongoing life of faith. This was reflected in the mandate of the Committee, which from the beginning saw their role as one of producing "liturgical and educational resources consistent with the Recommendations of the Report on Christian Initiation."[101] Thus, the work of drafting a liturgy was conducted parallel to and simultaneously with the work of producing the resources for preparation and education. While this study has focused primarily on the liturgical texts, it is important to keep in mind that they are but a portion of what was conceived as part of a larger picture: the renewal of the whole process of Christian initiation. The question that this raises is whether the resulting liturgical text is consistent with the development and content of the process as a whole. A complete answer would involve a detailed study of the supporting educational materials. For the purposes of this study, however, I would argue that, in light of the discussion of the background to the liturgy, the educational process was seriously compromised by the failure of the remits on Christian initiation. The doctrine of the Basis of Union still speaks of profession of faith as necessary for admission to communion. The polity of the church continues to assert that the process of Christian initiation is one of baptism, confirmation, and first communion. The General Council has approved Theological Affirmations affirming baptism as the sole rite of initiation into the church and Recommendations identifying the specific importance of a first profession of faith for those baptized as children. The liturgical texts presuppose the demise of the confirmation paradigm, the advent of the initiation paradigm, and prefer to speak simply of renewal of baptismal faith. The supporting educational material must contend with this state of confusion. A prime example of this is evident in the very title of Part II of the series, *Preparing Young People for Profession of Faith—A Confirmation Resource*. One can only conclude that, given the outcome of the remits (which the committee could not have foreseen) and the call from the church for a service of first profession of faith (as distinct from subsequent reaffirmations of faith),[102] the liturgy fails on this count. It does not sufficiently differentiate between such a profession of faith and subsequent reaffirmations of faith within its notion of renewal of baptismal faith. While, on its own terms, the liturgy makes a valiant attempt to clarify some of the pneumatological confusion, the failure to take into account the pastoral and political realities of the United Church context seriously compromises its pastoral effectiveness and use. Even a good liturgy has little hope of renewing liturgical practice when it remains unused.

Finally, a related pneumatological issue involved the renunciation. This may be one of the greatest stumbling blocks for may United Church persons encountering *Baptism and Renewal of Baptismal Faith.*[103] This popular resistance is reminiscent of that demonstrated in the other United Church texts, where efforts at including a renunciation were often proposed but never survived the drafting and consultative process. In the contemporary context, it is interesting to note that while the popular "United Church Creed" includes the call to "seek justice and resist evil," its ritualization in baptism seems more problematic.

Several questions tend to arise in United Church circles with respect to the renunciation. First, it has been asked, is a personal renunciation necessary if it is going to take place in corporate form in the Congregational Profession of Faith? Second, is it enough to speak simply of turning away "from the forces of evil and renouncing their power" without naming this evil and being more specific about the powers we must renounce? In other words, is this too easy or in risk of trivial moralization? (To be sure, the same could be argued of any question or vow taken in baptism or any other liturgical act). Third, one could ask, does this question, and for that matter all questions of individual profession of faith in baptism, set up a dynamic of "conditional" baptism built on doctrinal assent, thus undermining the prevenient grace of God? Similarly, do individual questions, as distinct from a corporate profession of faith, push baptism in a dangerously individualistic direction? These are some of the questions which the renunciation in *Baptism and Renewal of Baptismal Faith* raised and which would continue to be considered in the process of revision for the next generation of baptismal liturgies.

Ecclesiology

Baptism and Renewal of Baptismal Faith makes important efforts to expand the ecclesiological dimensions of baptism in the United Church. From the perspective of liturgical action, there is a greater degree of congregational participation in word, action, and gesture than ever before. This liturgical character of the rite allows the congregation to bear more dynamic witness to the church as the "priesthood of all believers" and the Body of Christ.

The celebration of the rite in the context of the liturgical year has the capacity to more fully manifest the catholic dimensions of Christian initiation (insofar as certain times and seasons in the church provide a classic context for baptism). The explicit placement of the rite as a response to the Word, and thus solidly in the context of public worship, frames the whole action as "initiation" into the Body of Christ. The explicit use of the questions and responses of the congregation and the congregational profession of faith reinforce this corporate dimension of baptism. That the text of the Apostles' Creed is included in the rite itself is as important a link to the historic baptismal faith of the whole church.[104] In spite of the controversy caused at the time, the trinitarian formula is retained in baptism for the sake of doctrinal orthodoxy and out of ecumenical concern. Finally the celebration of the sacrament of the Lord's Supper is assumed, to show the full initiatory implications of the rite.[105] Together these features point to a surprisingly orthodox and classic ecclesiology of the church as the Body of Christ in the world, a Body into which and in the context of which candidates must be "initiated." Christians are made, not born. While United Church baptismal liturgies have always been understood as initiation into the holy Catholic church, this rite expresses this with the most force of any.

The continued insistence of the Committee on the use of sponsors in the liturgy was intended to reinforce this collective ecclesiology of baptism, but it met with only marginal success. Liturgically, sponsors can be involved in a variety of forms of leadership: presentation, pouring of water, laying on of hands, lighting a baptismal candle, etc. Theologically, the intentional and careful identification of sponsors can be an important symbol of the congregation's corporate commitment to the nurture and support of candidates. Practically, the continued confusion of sponsors with godparents is something the liturgy could never seem to overcome in spite of much effort and explanation. The importance of sponsors in a post-Christendom context was noted by the Project Group as an important factor in the long-term success of renewed patterns of Christian initiation.[106] In those few testing congregations where the use of sponsors was embraced, it was welcomed as a concrete expression of the community's commitment to pastoral care and Christian nurture. This was especially the case where they were involved with the candidates in baptismal preparation and ongoing pastoral care. In the end, however, a consciousness of the ecclesiological significance and pastoral potential of sponsorship remains rare in United Church circles. On this point the *Report*'s Recommendations and the *Baptism and Renewal of Baptismal Faith* fell well short of its mark.

Another aspect of the liturgy with ecclesiological implications is the use, for the first time in a United Church rite, of the term *presider* and its distinction from *leader*. This distinction between the liturgical functions of ordained and lay ministries (and later ordained, diaconal, and lay ministries) was always implicit United Church practice, but seldom explicit in a liturgical text. The intent is outlined in the Introduction.

> While it is assumed that as an ordained minister the presider in the sacramental action functions as the voice and hands of the congregation (as well as of the wider church), provision is made for diaconal ministers and members of the congregation to take on leadership roles, too. Hence, in the service the term "presider" is used only where it is deemed appropriate for the ordained persons to speak or act. Elsewhere "leader" is indicated.[107]

In the context of increasingly blurred lines of ordered authority in the United Church, such distinctions are not without controversy.[108] Many continue to argue that the use of the term *presider* is an example of a move in the direction of a "priestly" liturgical style of leadership, as distinct from a theology of the "priesthood of all believers." Thus it is viewed as a betrayal of the Reformed roots of United Church worship and polity and points to a problematic ecclesiology which legitimates hierarchical and patriarchal models of leadership and clericalism rather than celebrating and embodying the freedom and liberation of the gospel. For others (and this would include the members of the Committee, as the above quotation illustrates), it is intended as a distinction appropriate to those aspects of designated liturgical leadership which are exercised on behalf of the congregation and the whole church.

At the very least, the use of the term *presider* in this rite represents a significant development: a theology of ordained ministry rooted in the liturgy. This is a new perspective for the United Church. To root a theology of ministry and its implied ecclesiology in the liturgical life of the church is not something most United Church persons would contemplate. Nevertheless, the foundational papers on Christian initiation which informed the background study of the Task Force, the Project Group, and the Committee all share this vision. To the extent that the United Church has always had an ordered ministry in which persons are ordained to a ministry of "Word, sacrament and pastoral care,"[109] the use of the term *presider* may in fact be helpful in pressing the United Church to further examine its own theology of ministry and therein its implied ecclesiology. *Baptism and Renewal of Baptismal Faith*, when taken seriously within a United Church context, certainly begs such questions and invites reflection on a liturgical theology of ministry.

Conclusions

Baptism and Renewal of Baptismal Faith serves as a fascinating case study in the development of baptismal liturgies in The United Church of Canada. While this study has been able to treat only some of the issues raised, it has demonstrated a continued movement toward classic liturgical forms under the influence of ecumenical developments, all framed within a United Church context.

Some of the liturgical forms made familiar by the use of the *Service Book* continue to be expanded, utilized, and reinforced in *Baptism and Renewal of Baptismal Faith*. Litany forms, unison prayers, and sense-line style statements are now the norm rather than the exception. The liturgy also points to the fact that the contemporary "United Church Creed" is gaining the status of a baptismal symbol (even overtaking the Apostles' Creed in popular appeal). The Sursum Corda and berakah form of prayer, previously limited to Holy Communion and some "new" prayers of thanksgiving in the *Service Book*, are here introduced in the prayer over the water. The *Service Book* compilers, like those of *The Book of Common Order*, were forced to avoid any connotations of blessing water and even used silent prayer as a way of avoiding potential problems with respect to epiclesis. In light of this history, the Prayer of Thanksgiving and Pouring of Water in *Baptism and Renewal of Baptismal Faith* was a development of major significance. And yet, such "new" forms as the Prayer of Thanksgiving and renunciation were, in fact, recoveries of classic forms. The same can be said of the recovery of such optional baptismal symbols as anointing, dressing in a white garment, the lighting of a candle, and asperges.

Structurally, it is important to point out that *Baptism and Renewal of Baptismal Faith* continued the process of evolution begun with *The Book of Common Order* and carried on in the *Service Book*. This was an evolution toward an "omnibus" (unified) and "modular" (integrated) rite. *The Book of Common Order* began this movement by intentionally adding its order for Reception to Full Communion and Confirmation to the Order for Adult Baptism. With this it simplified the structures common in many of the sources available to the Committee at the time, resulting in one order each for the baptism of children, reception to communion, and the baptism of adults. The *Service Book* reduced these three orders to two, one for children and one for adults, with a modular provision in the latter for the celebration of confirmation alone. This trend toward structural simplification and integration reached its climax in *Baptism and Renewal of Baptismal Faith* with one order of service for the entire complex of initiation rites.

Subsequent pastoral experience revealed that the lack of detailed rubrics and the length of the rite were perhaps the most common structural criticisms.[110] The spare rubrics were intended to allow simple and straightforward use, however for many of those unaccustomed to its "new" features they seemed to raise more questions than answers. The assumption that presiders and worship committees would turn to the accompanying Introduction and Guidelines was optimistic. There is very little tradition of careful liturgical study and preparation in the United Church. Thus, structurally speaking, the sophistication of *Baptism and*

Renewal of Baptismal Faith was both its strength and its weakness. While it achieved the omnibus and modular form true to the theology of a reunified and integrated rite of Christian initiation, it proved confusing and complicated in the hands of most United Church clergy.

Similar problems were also associated with its length. Popular United Church practice tends to continue to think of baptism as an ad hoc liturgical insert into the service of worship. As such, it must be brief, immediately accessible, and easily wedged between more common and/or "important" matters. The notion that the celebration of Christian initiation would come only at certain specific times and liturgical seasons after individual and collective preparation, and thus warrant a rich and perhaps more lengthy celebration (with the possibility of liturgical adjustments elsewhere in the service to accommodate it) continues to be largely foreign to many in the United Church. These attitudes were reflected in the most common popular responses of clergy to *Baptism and Renewal of Baptismal Faith*: liturgically, "it's too complicated"; practically, "it's too long."[111]

The presentation of the rite as an "insert" is worth noting from another perspective. There is a sense in which *Baptism and Renewal of Baptismal Faith* was a return to a *Book of Common Order* style, with the important exception that it is to be placed after the sermon as a response to the Word, as in the *Service Book*. The *Service Book* provided full orders of service for baptism with the hope of placing the sacrament more intentionally within the context of a full service of worship. In practice, however, as demonstrated in the surveys of the Task Force, ministers and congregations continued to excerpt the baptismal "Action" and place it in other locations, most often at or near the beginning of the service in the "Approach" section. *Baptism and Renewal of Baptismal Faith* affirms the *Service Book* location but chooses *The Book of Common Order* style of an insert. In practice, however, these changes did not prevent ministers and congregations from placing the rite wherever they willed.

Overall, *Baptism and Renewal of Baptismal Faith* was perhaps the most radical (literally, in the sense of a return to roots) of the three generations of baptismal liturgies. With it the Committee was able to do much of what earlier committees and compilers had tried and failed to do—namely, recover the classic liturgical forms, symbols, and practices of Christian initiation and place them within a fuller process of Christian initiation supported by integrated educational resources rooted in the liturgy itself. Had the remits on Christian initiation passed, the success of this achievement would have been greatly enhanced by the support of institutional polity. As it was, the Committee had to be content with reflecting in its liturgy all the Theological Affirmations and most of the Recommendations of the Task Force. As such, it was the first such liturgy in the United Church history to be the product of such a comprehensive churchwide process. Both its strengths and its shortcomings cannot be separated from this context. To ask again the question asked earlier: did *Baptism and Renewal of Baptismal Faith* achieve the desired reunification of baptism and confirmation within a reunified paradigm of Christian initiation? On the basis of this analysis one can only conclude: structurally, yes; pastorally, no.

In closing, however, one must be reminded that *Baptism and Renewal of Baptismal Faith* was a "draft liturgy," "for optional use," even if it was available and in circulation for over a decade.[112] However, with the loss of funding for the Working Group on Worship and Liturgy, it circulated as a kind of *de facto* authorized text with no further work being done on it until in recent years. However, as has been shown, its significance is far beyond that of any draft in United Church history and, as shall be suggested below, its influence continued to be felt into the future. When placed in the context of the studies and remits on Christian initiation, it clearly must be taken seriously as a major development in United Church baptismal theology and practice. Finally, as the conclusion to this study will argue, it also serves as an important case study in the development of United Church worship as a whole.

Notes

1. *ROP* (1972), 92-93.

2. Church membership in 1965 was 1,063,951 and has dropped every year since. In 1972 it was recorded at 993,190. The highest number recorded for persons under pastoral care was that of 1964 at 2,654,375. The number of those "Received on Profession of Faith" (it is interesting that this is the term which continues to be used in all church statistics, thus including mostly "confirmations," but not exclusively so) peaked in 1958 at 41,713, as did the number of "Baptisms (Adults and Children)" at 67,217. The "Membership of Sunday Schools" peaked in 1961 at 757,338. *Year Book* (1993), 156-157.

3. *ROP* (1972), 92-93; *ROP* (1977), 106-107.

4. Patricia Clarke, "Now what's happening to baptism?" *Observer* (March 1980): 12.

5. UCA, Division of Mission in Canada Records, Task Force on Christian Initiation, Task Group on Confirmation Resources, 1976-1977, Box 57, File 1, "Minutes" of 25, 26 October 1977.

6. UCA, Division of Mission in Canada Records, Task Force on Christian Initiation, 1978-1979, Box 57, File 2, Minutes, "Report to the Executive," 13-16 November 1977: 18.

7. Kavanagh, "Christian Initiation: Tactics and Strategy," 1-6.

8. *Christian Initiation: The Quest for Renewal*, 2-3. [*Quest*].

9. Task Force on Christian Initiation, "Minutes" of 11-12 September 1978: 1, 4.

10. The document was prepared largely by John Ambrose, chair of the Task Force. Some of the text was based on a paper by Bruce Underhill, then chair of the Committee on Worship. Cf. Underhill, "Putting Humpty Dumpty Together Again: Christian Initiation in The United Church of Canada from a Liturgical Perspective," *Getting It All Together* (Advent-Christmas, 1978), Studies in Worship.

11. *Quest*, 5.

12. *Quest*, 6-8.

13. *Quest*, 8-9. Underhill's paper cites specific English and American studies and surveys. Both *Quest* and Underhill refer to the Church of England report, *Christian Initiation: Birth and Growth in the Christian Society*, Report of the Commission on Christian Initiation (Oxford: The Church Army Press, 1971). Cf. *Quest*, 10; Underhill, 3-5.

14. *Quest*, 13.

15. *Quest*, 21.

16. *Quest*, 23-27.

17. *Quest*, 24.

18. *Quest*, 28-30.

19. "If baptism is truly the universal gateway into the Christian Church, (and few would deny that it is), on what basis do you immediately excommunicate that infant by denying him or her the nurture of the eucharist? As fine a document as it is, I find a grave inconsistency in our 1962 statement which claims that baptism is 'complete in itself' and then goes on to say that confirmation 'is the completion of the process of Christian initiation.' One becomes a member of the Christian church at baptism. Period! There is no need to complete it. No matter what the age!" Underhill, 8.

20. Task Force on Christian Initiation, Box 57, File 5. Document, dated October 1978.

21. Cf. *Christian Initiation: Towards A Renewed Understanding of Christian Initiation*, Canadian Anglican Liturgical Series, No. 1 (Toronto: The Anglican Book Centre, 1974); *Christian Initiation, Membership: Its Meaning and Expression*, Canadian Anglican Liturgical Series, No. 2 (Toronto: The Anglican Book Centre, 1975); *The Rite of Christian Initiation of Adults* (Study Edition), The Canadian Conference of Catholic Bishops (Ottawa, Canadian Catholic Conference, 1974); *A Service of Baptism, Confirmation and Renewal: An Alternate Text 1976*, Supplemental Worship Resources 2, The United Methodist Church (Nashville: Abingdon Press, 1976); M. Perry, *Crisis for Confirmation* (London: SCM, 1967). These and several other studies of United Methodist and Episcopal origin are cited in the "Bibliography" of *Quest* (31-32) and the Minutes of the Task Force. The papers of the Canadian Liturgical Society's conference, published as James Schmeiser, ed., *Initiation Theology* (Toronto: The Anglican Book Centre, 1978), were also closely studied. "Minutes" of 13-17 November 1977: 13; 14-15 December 1978.

22. Task Force on Christian Initiation, Box 62, Files 5, 7-10.

23. This version of the Affirmations is from "The Report of the Project Group on Christian Initiation" contained in *ROP* (1982), 188-189, and takes into account the amendments. *ROP* (1982), 58-59.

24. *Manual* (2001), 16.

25. *ROP* (1982), 189-200.

26. *ROP* (1982), 187.

27. *The Report on Christian Initiation*, Division of Mission in Canada, The Project Group on Christian Initiation (Toronto: The United Church of Canada, 1981). It is a slightly edited version of the "Report" found in *ROP* (1982), 187-206.

28. *ROP* (1982), 187.

29. UCA, Division of Mission in Canada Records, (late accessions) Box 1. "A Survey of Baptismal Practice" dated February 1982; "A Summary of Baptismal Practice" dated Spring 1982.

30. A previous survey in Halton Presbytery showed that 82 percent of congregations used the *Service Book* orders. (Task Force on Christian Initiation, Box 57, File 3). Nevertheless, the *Service Book* goal of providing a full order of worship for baptism in order to avoid ad hoc insertion was clearly not successful. The majority appeared to simply excerpt the Action section of the order and insert it earlier in the service; 56 percent placed it in the Approach section, according to the survey of the Project Group.

31. Table 7.1 shows the responses to the questions, expressed to the nearest percentage point of the total number of responses. The questions were in the form of statements which respondents were invited to rank on a scale from "essential" to "unacceptable." For presentation in this Table the statements have been abbreviated as questions. The original statements were: "1. Sponsors should be designated for all persons being baptized. 2.

Baptism should take place in the congregations where the parents/guardians are participants. 3. The laying on of hands should be part of the sacrament of baptism whenever administered. 4. All baptized persons should have access to the Lord's Table. 5. Those persons baptized as children should make a later profession of faith. 6. A liturgy of thanksgiving after the birth or adoption of a child should be celebrated." Project Group on Christian Initiation, Box 63, File 1, "Christian Initiation: An Update from the Project Group on Christian Initiation," letter to pastoral charges and presbyteries from John Ambrose, dated January 1982.

32. Project Group on Christian Initiation, Box 63, File 1, "Summary of Responses to Christian Initiation Report for Study," 1-3 provides some subtlety, if not skepticism, to the analysis. The anonymous writer for this summary interpreted the results as "widely divergent" and suggested that "it is obvious that whatever direction we move in there will be hurts left across the country" (1).

33. "Summary of Responses to Christian Initiation Report for Study," 1.

34. "Summary of Responses to Christian Initiation Report for Study," 1.

35. *ROP* (1982), 59, 206. In addition, the Division of Mission in Canada was instructed to "oversee the development of suitable pastoral resources (including audio-visuals) to aid in the interpretation and trial implementation of the Recommendations, to receive responses from congregations and presbyteries and to prepare a report for the 20th General Council." *ROP* (1982), 206.

36. The version of the Recommendations quoted in the following pages is that of the final version, as amended and approved "in principle" by the 1984 General Council. Cf. *ROP* (1982), 189-206; "Christian Initiation," *ROP* (1984), 336-337; *The Report of the Project Group on Christian Initiation* (Toronto: The United Church of Canada, 1983); *BRBF* (1986), 21-23. See also the relevant Minutes of the 1982 and 1984 General Councils: *ROP* (1982), 58-61, 88-89, 445, 482, 483; *ROP* (1984), 79-80, 114-116.

37. E.g., *Doctrine and Practice*, 9; *Church Membership*, 6.

38. *ROP* (1982), 190.

39. The filmstrip and cassette set *Beginning the Faith Journey* was, by this time, in the process of production, later to be made available from the Audio-Visual Education Library (AVEL). Similarly, a series of booklets for preparation for baptism were also being developed. See n. 67 below.

40. *ROP* (1982), 190.

41. The version of the Recommendations quoted in the following pages is that of the final version, as amended and approved "in principle" by the 1984 General Council. Cf. *ROP* (1982), 189-206; "Christian Initiation," *ROP* (1984), 336-337; *The Report of the Project Group on Christian Initiation* (Toronto: The United Church of Canada, 1983); *BRBF* (1986), 21-23. See also the relevant Minutes of the 1982 and 1984 General Councils: *ROP* (1982), 58-61, 88-89, 445, 482, 483; *ROP* (1984), 79-80, 114-116.

42. *ROP* (1982), 192; *BRBF* (1986), 6.

43. *BRBF* (1986), 21.

44. *ROP* (1984), 335.

45. *ROP* (1982), 200-201.

46. *BRBF* (1986), 22.

47. The Project Group also argued that: "the service should be carefully integrated into worship "so that it does not appear to be an intrusion or appendage"; "candidates and sponsors should be present for the entire worship service"; the Lord's Supper "might occasionally be celebrated in conjunction with baptism to reinforce . . . the important connection" between the two; the presence of children should be encouraged." *ROP* (1982), 193.

48. In this regard, the Project Group suggested that "when a child is to be baptized in a congregation other than where the family would normally attend, consultation should take place between the two congregations and some form of approval be given." *ROP* (1982), 193. This also related to the recommendation regarding corporate worship above.

49. *BRBF* (1986), 22.

50. *ROP* (1982), 193. The Project Group was following the progress of the World Council of Churches Faith and Order study which eventually resulted in the publication of *Baptism Eucharist and Ministry*.

51. *ROP* (1982), 193; *ROP* (1984), 332, 336; *ROP* (1984), 114.

52. *BRBF* (1986), 22.

53. *ROP* (1982), 193.

54. *ROP* (1982), 194.

55. *ROP* (1984), 335.

56. *BRBF* (1986), 22.

57. [Public profession of faith] . . . before participating in the Lord's Supper or having voting or office-holding privileges . . . was not commonly called confirmation, nor was the practice of laying-on hands widespread until the action of the General Council in 1962." *ROP* (1982), 194.

58. *BRBF* (1986), 22.

59. *ROP* (1982), 195.

60. *ROP* (1984), 335.

61. *BRBF* (1986), 22.

62. *Manual* (2001), 17.

63. *ROP* (1986), 332.

64. Cf. *ROP* (1982), 196.

65. *BRBF* (1986), 22.

66. *ROP* (1982), 203. Note also that the original language in this Recommendation was changed from "Christian formation and nurture" to the more "Protestant" vocabulary of "Christian nurture and education." Cf. *ROP* (1982), 197.

67. Two papers on educational theory rooted in the classic models of baptismal catechesis were given by Newman and McNally in the Task Group. Newman, "An Integrated Model for Worship, Pastoral Care and Outreach," and McNally, "Baptism and Christian Nurture: A Position Paper," are found in Christian Initiation Task Group, Box 1, No. 2, File 1. Three preparation resources eventually resulted from the work of the Task Group: Margaret Spencer, *Preparation for Baptism and Renewal of Baptismal Faith*, Part I: Preparing Parents for Baptism of Their Children (Toronto: The United Church of Canada, 1989); *Preparation for Baptism and Renewal of Baptismal Faith*, Part II: Preparing Young People for a Profession of Faith (Toronto: The United Church of Canada, 1990); Gail Hopkirk and Janice MacLean, *Preparation for Baptism and Renewal of Baptismal Faith*, Part III: Adult Baptism or Faith Renewal (Toronto: The United Church of Canada, 1990). Review articles by Louis Pellissier on these resources can be found in *Touchstone* 7, no. 3 (September 1989): 48-51; 9, no. 2 (May 1991): 46-49; and 9, no. 3 (September 1990): 49-53, respectively. Several of the proposals in *A Place For You* are rooted in the affirmation of baptism as the sole rite of membership in the church admission to the Lord's Supper. *A Place For You: The Integration of Children Into the Life of the Church*, A Report to the 31st General Council with Appended Study Guide. A Report from the Ministry With Children Working Unit, Division of Mission in Canada (Toronto: The United Church of Canada, 1986). See also two reviews of this document in *Touchstone* by Daphne Anderson and Rose Ferries, in 5, no. 3 (September 1987): 49-52.

68. McNally, "Baptism and Christian Nurture: A Position Paper," 3; Newman "An Integrated Model for Worship, Pastoral Care and Outreach," 3.

69. The opening lines of *Quest* state: "In recent years a wave of renewal has been set in motion across the Church. The centre of that renewal is Christian initiation." *Quest,* 2.

70. *BRBF* (1986), 23.

71. *ROP* (1982), 204.

72. *BRBF* (1986), 23.

73. *ROP* (1982), 205-206. The report's comments in this regard are very much in keeping with the spirit of a variety of popular works of the time, some of them being cited in the work of the Task Force. See, for example, *Ritual in a New Day: An Invitation.* Alternate Rituals Project, Section on Worship, Board of Discipleship of the United Methodist Church (Nashville: Abingdon, 1976); *From Ashes to Fire*, Services of Worship for the Seasons of Lent and Easter with Introduction and Commentary, Section on Worship, Board of Discipleship of The United Methodist Church, Supplemental Worship Resources 8 (Nashville: Abingdon, 1979); Gwen Kennedy Neville and John H. Westerhoff, III, *Learning through Liturgy* (New York: The Seabury Press, 1978); John H. Westerhoff, III and William H. Willimon, *Liturgy & Learning through the Life Cycle* (New York: The Seabury Press, 1980).

74. The Project Group cited "widespread confusion" on this subject and decided to drop the matter. *ROP* (1982), 200.

75. *ROP* (1984), 334-335.

76. Cf. *Manual* (2001), 16-17, 20. The new numbering system designates them 2.15, 2.16.2, and 5.8.1, respectively. Article XVI (2) "Of the Sacraments" requires admission to the Lord's Supper upon "credible profession of their faith in the Lord Jesus." Article XV "Of the Church" similarly identifies the Church as "consisting of those who profess faith in Jesus Christ and obedience to Him." Section II B I (a) speaks of "full membership" as those who have made a "profession of faith." The following summary of the remit process and related issues is taken from the primary source documents: *ROP* (1982), 59, 61, 88; *ROP* (1984), 79, 80, 330-334; General Council Standing Committee Records, Task Force on Christian Initiation, "Remit on Christian Initiation," Box 63, File 1, 1-6. [Remit].

77. Remit, 2.

78. *ROP* (1984), 337-338.

79. Remit, 3. In addition to inclusive language, other controversial issues were occupying much of the church's agenda at this time. In particular, that of sexuality and homosexuality was getting national attention in the press. The change in wording with respect to the Trinity may well have been the proverbial straw that broke the camel's back, resulting in a kind of backlash directed at all things "radical," "feminist," and "Toronto-generated."

80. Kenneth Gallinger, "Question Box," *Observer* (August 1989): 17.

81. E.g., Letters to the editor in *Observer* (March 1984): 5, (June 1984): 3-4; (August 1984): 6-7, spoke of "abandoning the spirit of democracy," the church's failing "institutional health," questioning "the legitimacy of its decision-making process," and its lack of sensitivity to the "people at the grassroots."

82. Richard H. Moffat, "More on Christian Initiation," *Observer* (June 84): 3.

83. E.g., Patricia Clarke, "Church votes against baptism change," *Observer* (January 198): 10-11; Mike Milne, "Christian Initiation: play it again," *Observer* (October 1984): 16.

84. *ROP* (1984), 330-338.

85. *ROP* (1984), 332.

86. *ROP* (1984), 333-334. Parenthesis added.

87. *ROP* (1984), 333.

88. "The Biblical, Theological, Liturgical, and Ecumenical Implications of the Use of Inclusive Language With Reference to God," *ROP* 1986, 337-342. "Inclusive Language in the History of General Council," *ROP* 1986, 343-345. The end result of this report was the passing of Resolution 91, which allows the continued use of the trinitarian formula in baptism but "affirms an inclusive language for God in church documents, worship and liturgy" and seeks to "engage its members and . . . ecumenical partners" in the further exploration of the issue, especially in reference to the trinitarian formula. *ROP* (9184), 346.

89. "Christian Initiation Remit Fails," *Observer* (August 1990): 10.

90. Bob Bettson, Murial Duncan, "Christian Initiation Remit," *Observer* (May 1990): 10.

91. "When is a Member a Member?" *Observer* (November 1989): 6-10; Rev. Lorne O'Neill, "Fencing the Table," *Observer* (January 1990): 5; Rev. Alex Taylor, "Who's in, who's out," *Observer* (February 1990): 4; Mary Fraser, "Who makes the rules," *Observer* (March 1990): 5.

92. "Christian Initiation Remit Fails," 10.

93. Patricia Clarke, "Church votes against baptism change," *Observer* (January 1984): 10.

94. "Minutes" of 19 November 1984: 2.

95. Christian Initiation Task Group, "Minutes" of 7 January 1985: 10

96. "Minutes" of 4 March 1985 and 24-25 June 1985: 1.

97. Dunstan's poetic text has been ecumenically recognized, finding its way into the Consultation on Common Texts' *A Celebration of Baptism*, 115. Note, however, that in the CCT's adaptation of the text the feminine metaphor of "breaking waters" was omitted.

98. From the beginning of the United Church studies, a variety of biblical imagery and meanings for baptism was explored and encouraged rather than the tendency to settle on any single metaphor or meaning. This prayer seems to follow in this spirit. Cf. *Quest*, 15-16.

99. *BRBF* (1986), 4.

100. *Rite of Christian initiation of adults*, 14. This process is one of four "periods" of initiation, each mediated by a "step" entailing catechetical and liturgical action, potentially lasting, in total, several years.

101. "Minutes" of 19 November 1984: 1.

102. *ROP* (1982), 198-199, 204-205.

103. UCA, Consultants Reports, 1993-94, Baptism, Hymn-Worship Resource Project, Liturgy Sub-Committee, Division of Mission in Canada, [HWRP]. As work began on the new hymn and worship resource, *Voices United*, feedback on *BRBF* (1986), and preliminary drafts of the next generation of baptismal liturgies was received. This information confirmed, among other things, the continued discomfort of United Church persons with the renunciation. This was also confirmed by the author's personal experience in workshops and local and national gatherings on worship in the United Church.

104. Such usage is in keeping with the Task Force Recommendations. Note that, while the United Church "Creed" was provided as an optional baptismal symbol, for the Task Group, unlike the previous committees, the issue was not if the Apostles' Creed should be used, but where it should be placed.

105. *BRBF* (1986), 15, assumes the celebration of the Lord's Supper with baptism; though in United Church practice this is observed more in the exception than the norm. Cf. *ROP* (1982), 196; *ROP* (1984), 336.

106. *ROP* (1982), 192, 200-201.

107. *BRBF* (1986), 5-6.

108. E.g., *Project Ministry*, The Report of the Task Force on Ministry, Division of Mission in Canada (Toronto: The United Church of Canada, 1984).

109. *Manual* (2001), 17.

110. HWRP (n. 103 above).

111. HWRP (n. 103 above).

112. *BRBF* (1986) and the other related liturgies of the Working Group were finally out of print in 2002.

Part V
The Language of Baptism and the Language of Worship

Chapter 8
Liturgical Reform through Recovery and Renewal

Toward the Recovery of Classic Liturgical Forms

This study of four generations of baptismal liturgies in The United Church of Canada has demonstrated a process of liturgical reform through both recovery and renewal. A progressive movement toward the use of classic liturgical forms has been evident. To be sure, in each generation the meaning of "classic" has varied somewhat.[1] In addition, particular contextual appropriation has marked the renewal that accompanied such recovery.

In *Forms of Service*, the first service book *in* The United Church of Canada, the language of baptism favored the vocabulary of Calvin and Knox (i.e., Presbyterianism) over that of Congregationalism and Methodism. Methodist and Congregationalist anxieties about certain theological aspects of this vocabulary prompted some "revision by omission," but a significant amount of the language of the Reformers remained and was carried forward into the new United Church. The ambiguities and confusion around reception to communion and profession of faith were inherited through a combination of Methodist and Presbyterian orders. Such features proved to be a precursor of problems yet to come in this area.

In *The Book of Common Order*, the first service book *of* The United Church of Canada, the language of baptism turned again to the Reformers through Presbyterianism, but even more so towards the *Book of Common Prayer* for its classic Cranmerian turns of phrase and liturgical structures. The compilers saw themselves as recovering "lines marked out by Apostolic practice and hallowed by the general usage of Christendom."[2] Limited efforts were made to incorporate practices from the founding traditions. More effort was made to smooth the path toward potential union with the Anglican church. The laying on of hands was introduced. This was also accompanied by the beginning of a movement away from the Reformers' notion of profession of faith toward more pneumatic connotations within orders for Reception to Full Communion. Some progress was made toward a greater ecclesiological depth in the orders through the more explicit consciousness of the role of the congregation in baptism and the context of public worship.

In the *Service Book*, the book born in the "seething sixties," a variety of features implied in the previous generations of liturgies became explicit. Overall congregational participation in the forms of prayer increased significantly. A greater consciousness of calendar and lectionary was evident. More evidence of the unity of word and sacrament was present in the structure of the rites. Litanies, a hesitant use of berakah-forms, the laying on of hands, and the occasional use of the Apostles' Creed were all introduced. However, the intimations of the pneumatic confirmation structures which began in *The Book of Common Order* became full-blown in the *Service Book.* A departure from the Reformed tradition on this question was the presenting symptom of a confirmation-based paradigm of baptism.

Baptism and Renewal of Baptismal Faith arose out of a combination of ecumenical convergence and denominational turmoil. In this liturgy the recovery of classic forms extended to liturgical features reminiscent of initiation in the early church. An "omnibus" and "modular" rite permitted the reunification of baptism and confirmation as the sole rite of initiation into the church. To this end, the laying on of hands was linked to baptism rather than to confirmation. The "sacramental minimalism" of United Church baptismal liturgies was countered by a variety of features including a "generous and visible use of water" and the possibility for a variety of other symbolic actions (e.g., anointing with oil, the giving of candles, clothing in a white garment, asperges). The baptismal significance of the Apostles' Creed was affirmed and other ecclesiological dimensions of baptism were emphasized both by the participatory character of the rite and the supporting educational materials arising out of the liturgy itself. After over fifty years of effort, a renunciation and berakah-style prayer over the waters were finally placed in the hands of United Church presiders by its official worship committee. In the end, however, the vision of initiation presented by this liturgy was compromised by the failure of the remits on Christian initiation and its lack of pastoral use.

What model best expresses the development of United Church baptismal liturgies? This study suggests one that is more evolutionary than perhaps might have been expected. With each successive stage of liturgical development different features have been experienced as "new," often cited as a "departure" from "United Church tradition." However, the evidence shows that the process has been relatively constant over the long term. This process of recovery and retrieval operates parallel to efforts at renewal that are decidedly contemporary and contextual.

However, this evolutionary model of development needs to be qualified in light of the details described in this study. A dialectical process would also seem to be at work. First, the compilers of each successive generation of liturgies sought to recover several classic liturgical forms. Second, in reaction to this the initial proposals were resisted by the presbyteries and congregations of the church on a wide variety of grounds—including length, liturgical style, and theology. Finally, the compilers compromised, allowing some proposals to be abandoned and others to be kept or modified. The original "thesis" of the compilers was also conditioned by the scholarly and historical context of the time. That is to say, they were both aware of what was happening in liturgical renewal and were influenced by the historical circumstances of the church in that period. The "antithesis" was often expressed in terms of popular suspicion (e.g., the liturgies are "not United Church" or "too Anglican," etc.), or theological objection (e.g., the liturgies contain elements contrary to the "Reformed tradition" of worship). The resulting "synthesis" was the product of both pastoral sensitivity and political expedience. While this compromise meant that there were some losses in the search for liturgical roots in classical forms, there were also major advances in the process of recovery which renewed and enriched the liturgical life of the church.

On the other hand, perhaps a more simple and circumstantial model makes as much sense. One might suggest a less intentional process of development, simply contingent on the particular context of each era. This might explain many of the curious liturgical compromises made along the way and would contain insights not gleaned from this study's more cursory treatment of the historical context of the liturgies. On the other hand, such a view would run the risk of not taking seriously enough the intentionally catholic vision of each generation of compilers, who clearly saw themselves as United Church persons operating within the wider ecumenical liturgical tradition.

Still another model might suggest that, until recently, United Church baptismal liturgies were solidly within the Reformed tradition of worship and have taken a "sacramental" turn since the emergence of the ecumenical liturgical movement. This, however, does not stand up to scrutiny in the face of the evidence. The Reformed tradition of baptismal liturgies, at least as inherited by the United Church from the founding traditions, was fraught with significant liturgical ambiguities and inconsistencies. In particular, the growing status of confirmation and its emerging pneumatic character in *The Book of Common Order* and the *Service Book* contradicts such claims. United Church baptismal liturgies have never unambiguously reflected the purity of the Reformation ethos, if there ever was such a thing.

Thus, a model which tries to take into account a dialectical process seems to be the most helpful. It has the capacity to make sense of many tensions which have been evident in this study, among them: the catholic vision of the compilers on the one hand and the liberal sensibilities of the congregations, on the other; the gradual recovery of classic liturgical forms and the inconsistencies which often accompanied them.

From United Church Baptismal Liturgies to United Church Worship

Can this model of the development of United Church baptismal liturgies help one understand the history and development of United Church worship as a whole? Thomas Harding, in the only other detailed study of United Church worship, has argued that

> the history of worship in The United Church of Canada falls rather naturally into three distinct periods: the classical period (1925 through to the early 1960s), the "time of unrest" (the 1960s and early 70s), and the emerging "ecumenical convergence" (the late 1970s to the present). These three periods were marked by the creation of three sets of worship resources: the *Hymnary* (1930) and *The Book of Common Order*, the *Service Book* (1969) and the Anglican United Church *Hymn Book* (1971), and *Sunday Liturgy* (1984) and its various attendant liturgies "for optional use."[3]

This study has built upon Harding's foundational work. However, its findings suggest that Harding's organization of the development of United Church worship into three periods fails to take serious account of the first service book of the United Church, *Forms of Service*. By his own admission, *The Book of Common Order* did not come of age until the post war period.[4] This study has shown, further, that until during and after the Second World War, the liturgical ethos embodied in *Forms* prevailed. Thus, there is cause for skepticism about the existence of any "classical period" of worship in the United Church. Indeed, I would argue that the first period of United Church worship was characterized by *Forms*, not *The Book of Common Order*.

On the other hand, Harding's description of the history of United Church worship as "a search for an order we can live with" is particularly helpful.[5] United Church worship can be seen as a search for that particular blend of "order" and "liberty" appropriate to each era. Furthermore, the correct "mix" or synthesis will be contingent even upon the particular congregation in question. United Church polity permits, encourages, and protects this degree of contextualization. Such variety makes United Church worship both challenging and difficult for systematic study by liturgical scholars. As the scholarship on United Church worship develops, ways must be found to take this into account for a more accurate reflection of actual liturgical praxis.

Additional observations are in order if this study of baptismal liturgies of the United Church is to serve as a case study for United Church worship as a whole. From this study it seems clear that the development of United Church worship is more complex than a simple battle between the forces for order and those for liberty. Taking into account the significance of *Forms*, it could be argued that the history of United Church worship from 1925-1995 can be grouped into four periods characterized by *Forms*, *The Book of Common Order*, the *Service Book*, and the "optional liturgies" of the eighties.[6] One might be tempted to suggest that each period tends toward either liberty or order in worship: *Forms* was a study in the liturgical liberty of the founding traditions; *The Book of Common Order*, a study in the order of the Prayer Book; the *Service Book*, a case of the demand for contemporary liberty in the sixties; and the "optional liturgies" an expression of renewed order through ecumenical liturgical convergence. In this schema, the history of United Church worship appears as a pendulum, swinging between liberty and order, between Puritan and catholic sensibilities, a continual repetition of action and reaction.

The pendulum model has much to commend it. However, while it is helpful in explaining the overall context of United Church worship in the four eras in question, it creates too facile a dichotomy between freedom and order. It does not satisfactorily explain some of the subtleties of congregational life or the findings of this study. For example, it would be difficult to find a United Church congregation that does not desire both order and liberty in its worship. In addition, this study has shown that there is an important sense in which the recovery of classic liturgical forms has been a consistent and recurring theme, as has the adaptation and appropriation of such forms in the context of the church at the time. The search for "an order we can live with" is not simply a two-dimensional tug-of-war but a three-dimensional process of evolution. Thus, the pendulum model is insufficient. One needs to think in more dynamic and dialectical terms. Perhaps the "hermeneutical circle" has something to offer here as well, as it does in so many contemporary branches of theology.[7] What needs to be emphasized is that certain familiar themes, including both order and liberty, have been revisited in each era of the development of United Church worship. However, this always takes place on a new level and in a new context, having benefited from and built upon the momentum of what has gone before.

This process can, however, play itself out with both positive and less than positive results. This use of an evolutionary model is not meant to imply success, or progress in a value-laden sense, but only to help describe developments. In the case of the baptismal liturgies, the increasing emphasis on the pneumatic character of confirmation, for example, was a theologically and liturgically problematic outcome. On the other hand, the emergence of greater congregational participation within the context of a Word and table structure was a theologically and liturgically positive development. Both can be described in terms of an evolutionary and dialectical model. This thesis has yet to be tested to determine the extent to which it can be of help in further study.

From *Baptism and Renewal of Baptismal Faith* to *Celebrate God's Presence* and Beyond

In closing, and by way of looking toward the future, a brief comment on continuing developments in the evolution of United Church worship is in order.

The 1990 General Council committed the church to "a process leading to the testing and production of worship and hymn resources in format [*sic*] as practical, economical, and accessible as possible."[8] This resulted in the formation of the Hymn and Worship Resource Project and a Hymn and Worship Resource Committee (HWRC) of twenty-five persons drawn from across the church. John Ambrose was given the job of managing editor.[9]

The work of the HWRC began with a review of *The Hymnary*, *The Hymn Book*, and *Songs for a Gospel People*,[10] as well as a host of hymnals published within the last two decades. Subcommittees on texts, tunes, psalms, service music, liturgies, production, education, and computer technology took on related work. Testing packets of hymn material were sent to one hundred congregations in October of 1992. A hymn sampler was published and distributed to the whole church in May of 1993.[11] An additional sampler was presented to the 1994 General Council under the title *Voices United: The Hymn and Worship Book of The United Church of Canada.*[12]

As the subtitle of the book implies, the intention was that *Voices United* would be more than a hymn book—and indeed it is. However, it was also to include liturgies for Holy Communion, baptism, and others. It is interesting to note that in the process of consulting with a variety of committees of the church some were quick to suggest that it was not a "good time" to produce liturgical resources for the United Church, given the widespread lack of consensus about the form and content of such orders. It was further suggested by some that the *Service Book* would suffice for the time being, albeit with a few minor adjustments. Such arguments are reminiscent of those advanced at every significant point of liturgical evolution in the United Church. As the compilers of the *Service Book* noted, it is never a "good time" to produce liturgical resources.

The desire to include liturgies in the work would have finally realized what the compilers of the *Service Book* had hoped for but were unable to achieve due to the joint sponsorship of *The Hymn Book*. In the end, however, after a heated debate at the 1994 General Council, it was decided that major liturgical resources be prepared and published separately. In this the United Church's Puritan and Congregationalist sensibilities, so evident in the spirit of union in 1925, continue to be in evidence as an important aspect of its liturgical ethos. *Voices United* was published to wide acclaim in 1996. *Services for Trial Use, 1996-1997* was published in 1996 as a liturgical sampler, leading to the publication of the mammoth three-ring worship resource, *Celebrate God's Presence: A Book of Services for The United Church of Canada* in 2000.[13] The structure and content of both *Voices United* and *Celebrate God's Presence* continue many features already prefigured in previous resources and examined in this study.[14]

The context of the United Church in the nineties brought with it substantial pressures from a variety of constituencies. While the HWRC was on record from the beginning as committed to resources that would "embrace all God's people, with particular sensitivity to age, race, gender, physical abilities, and reflect a wide range of images of God,"[15] achieving this was one of its greatest challenges. The most high-profile example had to do with concerns around inclusive language with respect to God. Strong objections were made from some committees of General Council to the use of the Apostles' Creed and the traditional trinitarian formula for baptism.[16] While *Services for Trial Use* offered other formulations (for discussion only), a ruling from the General Council's Judicial Committee legislated the use of the traditional wording, noting that any such change would require a church wide remit to change the Basis of Union.[17] Once again, many of the issues at stake in the *Report on Christian Initiation* almost twenty years earlier were being revisited in a new context.

Overall, initial responses to the preliminary drafts of the baptismal liturgies themselves suggested that certain basic presuppositions had to be reevaluated.[18] For example, the subcommittee on baptism had to readjust its perception of the starting point for revision. When work began, the assumption was that the next generation of baptismal liturgies would be a revision of *Baptism and Renewal of Baptismal Faith* and thus built solely upon that text. As the work progressed, it became clear that this liturgy was not as widely used as had been assumed. While, as has been shown, many of its liturgical elements and features were welcomed (e.g., the more visible use of water and the use of a wider range of biblical imagery and symbolic action), this turned out to be practiced more in the form of an adaptation of the *Service Book* texts than an adoption of *Baptism and Renewal of Baptismal Faith, per se*. Thus, one can most helpfully locate the new liturgies of "The Covenant of Baptism," in *Celebrate God's Presence* somewhere "between" the *Service Book* and *Baptism and Renewal of Baptismal Faith.*[19] To the extent that *Baptism and Renewal of Baptismal Faith* can be viewed as a "draft" (and insofar as it was not "authorized" by General Council, it is), one can see some of the same dialectical dynamics of reform through recovery and renewal as we have observed in the earlier generations of baptismal liturgies.

More detailed analysis to substantiate this claim needs to be undertaken with respect to the present generation of liturgies and is beyond the scope of this study. However, these cursory indications remain suggestive. The evolutionary and dialectical model of the development of United Church baptismal liturgies suggested by the findings of this study helps to explain these unfolding dynamics. By offering a concrete case study in reform in the complex liturgical environment of The United Church of Canada, it also allows application to worship in general, a means of extrapolating from the language of baptism to the language of worship.

United Church liturgical reform seems to continue to enjoy a net gain through historic recovery in the context of contemporary renewal. This is its way of discerning "an order it can live with," one which, in the words of *The Book of Common Order*, seeks to honor "the experience of the ages" while being "flexible enough for the many-sided life of a growing Church."[20]

Notes

1. My use of the term *classic* is not meant to imply the existence of a single patristic liturgy of baptism to which one should appeal. Indeed, recent work has demonstrated the diversity of early church liturgical practice. See, for example, Paul Bradshaw, *The Search for the Origins of Christian Worship: Sources and Methods for the Study of Early Liturgy*. 2nd ed. (London: SPCK, 2002).

2. *BCO* (1932), iii.

3. Harding, "The Development of Liturgical Resources," 4.

4. Harding, "The Development of Liturgical Resources," 21-22, 56-57, 63, 84-85, 353.

5. Harding, "The Development of Liturgical Resources," 357.

6. Harding's more recent study of United Church marriage liturgies implies a revision of his "three periods" thesis to four. "The Marriage Services of the United Church of Canada," 169-195.

7. E.g., Gustavo Gutiérrez, *A Theology of Liberation*. 15th Anniversary Edition with a new introduction by the Author (New York: Orbis Books, 1988), xxiii.

8. *ROP* (1990), 185.

9. I was a consultant to the project (see *VU*, xiii); my views presented here are partially rooted in that experience.

10. *Songs for a Gospel People: A Supplement to the Hymn Book (1971)* (Winfield: Wood Lake Books, 1987). This hymn book gained wide popularity and served as a *de facto* draft for *Voices United*. In its hymn selections were evident a growing consciousness of baptismal piety in the life of the church. E.g., 62, "Now there is no male or female," 78, "Out of deep unordered water," 122, "You have put on Christ."

11. *Voices United: A Sampler for Congregations*. This also included two new baptismal hymns: 7, "Child of Blessing, Child of Promise," 42, "We Know That Christ."

12. The title was drawn from the final verse of the hymn "We Praise You, O God," *VU*, 218.

13. *Services for Trial Use 1996-1997*, Hymn and Worship Resource Committee. Toronto: United Church of Canada, 1996; *CGP*.

14. For an analysis of these resources, see: John Ambrose, "*Voices United:* A Balanced Collection," *Touchstone* 15:1 (January 1997): 3-6; Alan Barthel, "*Voices United:* The Hymn and Worship Book of The United Church of Canada," *The Hymn*, 50, no. 2 (April 1999): 8-11; Bruce Harding, "Singing Our Faith: The Music of *Voices United*," *Touchstone*, 15:1 (January 1997): 26-37; Kervin, "Celebrate God's Presence, Part III: A Service Book vs. A Book of Services," *Gathering* (Summer-Autumn 2000/2001): 52-54; "Celebrate God's Presence, Part II: 'But Is It United Church Tradition?'" *Gathering* (Lent-Easter-Pentecost 2001): 38-39; "Celebrate God's Presence, Part I: 'It's not a good time to publish a service book,'" *Gathering* (Advent-Christmas-Epiphany 2000/2001): 34-36; Mac Watts, "*Voices United*: A Warm-Hearted Book," *Touchstone* 15:1 (January, 1997): 7-25.

15. *Voices United: A Sampler for Congregations*, 84.

16. E.g., HWRP, "Consultants reports"; Letter of 26 October 1993 to Fred Graham from the barb janes [*sic*], General Council Standing Committee on Sexism.

17. Cf. *Services for Trial Use*, 59, and *CGP*, 322-323. Works related to the theological and liturgical background of these discussions include: Marjorie Procter-Smith, *In Her Own Rite: Constructing Feminist Liturgical Tradition* (Nashville: Abingdon, 1990); Ruth C. Duck, *Gender and the Name of God: The Trinitarian Baptismal Formula* (New York: The Pilgrim Press, 1991). Duck's proposal for an alternative to the trinitarian baptismal formula is drawn from David R. Holeton, "The Liturgical Implications of Feminist Proposals to Change the Trinitarian Baptismal Formula," *Ecumenical Trends* 17:5 (1988): 69-72. For a discussion in a United Church context see Harold Wells, "The Trinity and The Good News (Part I)," *Touchstone* 8:2 (May 1990): 4-13; "The Trinity and The Good News (Part I)," *Touchstone* 8:3 (September 1990): 6-16.

18. HWRC, "Consultants reports." Some of these perceptions are offered as one who served on the committee for *CGP* (see CGP, xv).

19. *CGP*, 319-374.

20. *BCO* (1932), iii.

Bibliography

Liturgies, Service Books, and Hymn Books

Aids for Social Worship: Being Short Services of Prayer and Praise for the use of Christians. Prepared by a Special Committee under the Authority of the General Assembly of the Presbyterian Church in Canada. Toronto: Westminister Press, 1900.

Baptism and Renewal of Baptismal Faith for optional use in The United Church of Canada. The Task Group on Christian Initiation, The Working Unit of Worship and Liturgy, The Division of Mission in Canada. Toronto: The United Church of Canada, 1986.

The Book of Alternative Services of The Anglican Church of Canada. Toronto: Anglican Book Centre, 1985.

Book of Common Order for use in Church Services and Offices. Toronto: Oxford University Press, 1922.

The Book of Common Order of the Church of Scotland. The Committee on Public Worship and Aids to Devotion. London: Oxford University Press, 1940.

The Book of Common Order of the Presbyterian Church in Canada. Toronto: Presbyterian Publications, 1964.

The Book of Common Order of the United Church of Canada. Toronto: The United Church Publishing House, 1932; revised and reset, 1950.

The Book of Common Prayer and administration of the rites and ceremonies of the Church according to the use of The Anglican Church of Canada. Toronto: Anglican Book Centre, 1969.

The Book of Common Prayer and administration of the Sacraments and other rites and ceremonies of the Church according to the use of The Anglican Church of Canada. Toronto: The Anglican Book Centre, 1959.

The Book of Common Prayer and Administration of the Sacraments and other rites and ceremonies of the Church according to the use of The Church of England in the Dominion of Canada. Toronto: Oxford University Press, 1918.

The Book of Common Prayer and Administration of the Sacraments and Other Rites and Ceremonies of the Church. According to the use of The Episcopal Church. New York: Church Hymnal Corporation, 1979.

The Book of Common Prayer and Administration of the Sacraments and Other Rites and Ceremonies of the Church. According to the use of The Episcopal Church in the United States of America. New York: Thomas Nelson & Sons, 1892.

The Book of Common Prayer with Additions and Deviations Proposed in 1928. London: Cambridge University Press, 1928.

The Book of Common Worship. The Church of South India. London: Oxford University Press, 1962.

The Book of Common Worship. Philadelphia: The Board of Christian Education of the Presbyterian Church in the United States of America, 1946.

The Book of Common Worship. Philadelphia: Presbyterian Board of Publication and Sabbath School Work, 1906.

The Book of Common Worship. Philadelphia: Presbyterian Board of Publication and Sabbath School Work, 1928.

The Book of Common Worship. Provisional Services. Philadelphia: The Westminster Press, 1966.

Book of Congregational Worship. Congregational Union of England and Wales. London: Memorial Hall, 1920.

The Book of Praise. Authorised by The General Assembly of The Presbyterian Church in Canada. London: Oxford University Press, 1918.

The Book of Services. Nashville: United Methodist Publishing House, 1985.

Book of Worship: United Church of Christ. New York: Office for Church Life and Leadership, 1986.

Bucer, Martin. *Censura.* In *Martin Bucer and The Book of Common Prayer,* ed. by E. C. Whitaker. Essex: Mayhew-McCrimmon, 1974.

Calvin, John. *La Forme des prières et chants écclesiastiques. Genève 1542: facsimilé de l'édition originale.* Kassel: Barenreiter, 1959.

——. *The Form of Prayers and Ecclesiastical Chants with the Manner of Administering the Sacraments and solemnizing Marriage According to the Custom of the Ancient Church. 1542.* In *Christian Initiation: The Reformation Period. Some Early Reformed Rites of Baptism and Confirmation and Other Contemporary Documents,* ed. J. D. C. Fisher. London: S.P.C.K., 1970.

Celebrate God's Presence: A Book of Services for The United Church of Canada. Toronto: The United Church Publishing House, 2000.

A Celebration of Baptism: An Ecumenical Liturgy. The Consultation on Common Texts. Nashville: Abingdon Press, 1988.

The Celebration of Marriage for optional use in The United Church of Canada. The Working Unit on Worship and Liturgy, Division of Mission in Canada. Toronto: The United Church of Canada, 1985.

Coates, Anthony, John Gregory, Caryl Micklem (eds.), William Sewell, David Stapleton, Roger Tomes, and Brian Wren. *Contemporary Prayers for Public Worship.* London: SCM Press, 1967.

Confession of Faith, Larger Catechism, Shorter Catechism, Directory of Public Worship. Toronto: Presbyterian Publications, 1900.

Dexter, Henry Martyn. *A Hand-Book of Congregationalism.* Boston: Congregational Publishers, 1880.

The Doctrine and Discipline of the Methodist Church, 1902. Toronto: William Briggs, 1902.

The Doctrine and Discipline of the Methodist Church, Canada, 1922. Toronto: Methodist Book and Publishing House, 1923.

The Doctrines and Discipline of the Methodist Church of Canada, 1874. Toronto: Samuel Rose, 1874.

Dunstan, Sylvia G. *In Search of Hope and Grace: 40 Hymns and Gospel Songs.* Chicago: GIA Publications, 1991.

Euchologion. Book of Common Order. Being Forms of Prayer, and Administration of the Sacraments, and Other Ordinances of the Church. Church Service Society. Seventh Edition. Edinburgh: William Blackwood and Sons, 1896.

Forms of Service for the Offices of the Church. Toronto: The United Church Publishing House, 1926.

Hunter, John. *Devotional Services for Public Worship.* Eighth Ed. London: Dent & Sons, 1903.

Huxtable, John, John Marsh, Romilly Micklem, and James Todd, eds. *A Book of Public Worship compiled for the use of Congregationalists.* Second Ed. London: Oxford University Press, 1949.

The Hymn Book of the Anglican Church of Canada and the United Church of Canada. Toronto: The Anglican Church of Canada and the United Church of Canada, 1971.

The Hymnary of The United Church of Canada. Toronto: The United Church Publishing House, 1930.

Jackson, Samuel N. *A Hand-Book of Congregationalism.* Toronto: Congregational Publishing Company, 1894.

Knox, John. "The Order of Baptism." In *John Knox's Genevan Service Book 1556.* The Liturgical Portions of the Genevan Service Book used by John Knox while a minister of the English Congregation of Marian Exiles of Geneva, 1556-1559. Trans. by W. D. Maxwell. Edinburgh: Oliver and Boyd, 1931.

Luther, Martin. "Dass tauff buchlin verdeutscht." In *D. Martin Luthers Werke.* Vol. 19. Weimer: H. Bohlau, 1883-1914.

——. "The Order of Baptism Newly Revised." In *Luther's Works.* Vol. 53. Trans. Paul Zeller Strodach and Ulrich S. Leupold. Ed. Helmut T. Lehman. Philadelphia: Fortress Press, 1965.

——. "The Order of Baptism." In *Luther's Works.* Vol. 53. Trans. Paul Zeller Strodach and Ulrich S. Leupold. Ed. Helmut T. Lehman. Philadelphia: Fortress Press, 1965.

Lutheran Book of Worship. Minneapolis: Augsburg Publishing House, 1978.

Ordo Initiationis Christianae Adultorum. Vatican City: Typis Polyglottis Vaticanis, 1972.

Pastoral Liturgies and Prayers for Special Occasions for optional use in The United Church of Canada. The Working Unit on Worship and Liturgy, Division of Mission in Canada. Toronto: The United Church of Canada, 1990.

Rite of Christian Initiation of Adults. Ottawa: Canadian Conference of Catholic Bishops, 1987.

Roman Missal. Revised by Decree of the Second Vatican Ecumenical Council and published by the authority of Pope Paul VI. Ottawa: Canadian Catholic Conference, 1974.

"The Sarum Rite: The Order for the Making of a Catechumen, the Blessing of the Font, Baptism and Confirmation (1543)." In *Documents of the Baptismal Liturgy.* Trans. J. D. C. Fisher. Ed. E. C. Whitaker. London: S. P. C. K., 1960.

A Service of Baptism, Confirmation and Renewal: An Alternate Text 1976. Supplemental Worship Resources 2. The United Methodist Church. Nashville: Abingdon Press, 1976.

Service Book for use in Church Courts. Toronto: The United Church Publishing House, 1977.

Service Book for the use of ministers conducting public worship. Toronto: The United Church Publishing House, 1969.

Service Book for the use of the people. Toronto: The Ryerson Press, 1969.

Services of Death and Burial for optional use in The United Church of Canada. The Working Unit on Worship and Liturgy, Division of Mission in Canada. Toronto: The United Church of Canada, 1987.

Songs for a Gospel People: A Supplement to The Hymn Book (1971). Winfield: Wood Lake Books, 1987.

Songs from the Psalter. Toronto: The United Church Publishing House, 1928.

A Sunday Liturgy for optional use in The United Church of Canada. The Working Unit on Worship and Liturgy, Division of Mission in Canada. Toronto: The United Church of Canada, 1984.

Voices United: The Hymn and Worship Book of The United Church of Canada. Toronto: The United Church Publishing House, 1996.

Voices United: A Sampler for Congregations. Toronto: The United Church Publishing House, 1993.

Wesley, John. *John Wesley's Sunday Service of the Methodists in North America.* With an Introduction by James F. White. Methodist Bicentennial Commemorative Reprint. Nashville: The United Methodist Publishing House, 1984.

——. *Wesley's Doctrinal Standards: Part I. The Sermons.* Edited by N. Burwash. Toronto: William Briggs, 1881.

Word and Table: A Basic Pattern of Sunday Worship for United Methodists. Supplemental Worship Resources 3. The United Methodist Church. Nashville: Abingdon Press, 1976.

Zwingli, Ulrich. "The Second Revision of the Zurich Order of Baptism." In *Christian Initiation: The Reformation Period.* Trans. and ed. J. D. C. Fisher. London: SPCK, 1970.

——. "A Short and Public Form for the Tender in Faith for the Baptism of Children." In *Christian Initiation: The Reformation Period.* Trans. and ed. J. D. C. Fisher. London: SPCK, 1970.

——. "Works." In *Corpus Reformatorum.* Vols. 91, 93. Ed. C. G. Bretschneider. Lasis Sax: Schwetschke, 1834-1860.

Archival Materials

(The United Church of Canada/Victoria University Archives, Toronto, Ontario)

Board of Christian Education Records. "The New Curriculum."

Church Union Collection. "Union Negotiations, General Commission on Church Union," 1967-1972.

The Committee on Church Architecture.

The Committee on Church Worship and Ritual. "Old Files," 1925-1958.

The Committee on Church Worship and Ritual. "Revision of *The Book of Common Order.*" (1958-1968).

The Committee on Worship (1968-1969).

Davidson, Richard. Personal Papers.

Division of Mission in Canada. Committees and Councils, Records of the Celebration Advisory/Resource Committee, 1976-1978.

Division of Mission in Canada. Department of Christian Development, Records of the Special Assistant on Worship and the Arts, 1973-1976.

Division of Mission in Canada. Task Group on Confirmation Resources, 1976-1977; Task Force on Christian Initiation, 1977-1980; Working Unit on Worship and Liturgy, 1981-1987; Project Group on Christian Initiation, 1981-1982; Christian Initiation Task Group, 1984-1986.

Joint Committee for the Preparation of the Hymnal.

Matheson, Hugh. Personal Papers.

Books, Articles, Periodicals, and Pamphlets

Abba, Raymond. *Principles of Christian Worship.* London: Oxford University Press, 1957.

Abbott, Walter M., and Joseph Gallagher, eds. *The Documents of Vatican II.* New York: Guild Press, 1966.

Airhart, Phyllis D. "Ordering a New Nation and Reordering Protestantism, 1867-1914." 98-138 in *The Canadian Protestant Experience: 1760-1990,* edited by George A. Rawlyk. Burlington: Welch, 1990.

——. *Serving the Present Age: Revivalism, Progressivism, and the Methodist Tradition in Canada.* Montreal & Kingston: McGill-Queen's University Press, 1992.

Aland, Kurt. *Did the Early Church Baptize Infants?* Translated by G. R. Beasley-Murray. Philadelphia: Westminster Press, 1963.

Allen, Richard. "Salem Bland and the Spirituality of the Social Gospel: Winnipeg and the West, 1903-1913." In *Prairie Spirit: Perspectives on the Heritage of the United Church of Canada in the West.* Edited by Dennis L. Butcher, et al. Winnipeg: University of Manitoba Press, 1985.

——. *The Social Passion: Religion and Social Reform in Canada 1914-1928.* Toronto: University of Toronto Press, 1973.

Ambrose, John. "*Voices United:* A Balanced Collection," *Touchstone* 15, no. 1 (January 1997): 3-6.

Amos, Donald A. "Canada's Most Significant New United Church." *The United Church Observer* (1 April 1963): 12.

Anderson, Daphne. 'Review of *A Place for You. The Integration of Children Into the Life of the Church.' A Report to the 31st General Council with Appended Study Guide. Touchstone* 5, no. 3 (September 1987): 49-50.

Anonymous. "Boom Still Booms!" *The United Church Observer* (15 April 1962): 7.

——. "Canada: The Hymn Book." *Studia Liturgica* 6, no. 1 (1969): 58.

——. "Christian Initiation Remit Fails." *The United Church Observer* (August 1990): 10.

——. "Church to Observe Youth Sunday." *The United Church Observer* (1 May 1939): 11.

——. "Editorial: The Confirmation Class." *The United Church Observer* (5 April 1963): 10.

——. "Editorial: New Hymnary Not Needed." *The United Church Observer* (15 April 1965): 10.

——. "Editorial: One Hymnary." *The United Church Observer* (August 1965): 8.

——. "Editorial: Vulgarity: Let us Use More Vulgar, More Earthy Language in Our Common Prayers!" *The United Church Observer* (1 May 1963): 7.

——. "Let's God! Whatever May be Said of the Christian Church—We Are on the Move." *The United Church Observer* (1 January 1967): 9, 29.

——. "Liturgical Revision in the United Church of Canada." *Studia Liturgica* 3, no. 3 (1964): 189-190.

——. "Magna Carta Sunday." *The United Church Observer* (1 June 1939): 19.

——. "Metropolitan Church: Symbol of Reunion." *The New Outlook* (26 February 1930): 198-199.

——. "Now It's Final." *The United Church Observer* (August 1975): 9.

——. "Our Reader's Forum: The Book of Common Order." *The New Outlook* (6 June 1934): 430.

——. "When Is a Member a Member?" *The United Church Observer* (November 1989): 6-10.

Atkinson, Ron. "Factors in the Preparation of a 'Contemporary' Liturgy." *Studia Liturgica* 4, no. 3 (1965): 187-188.

Bacon, D.A. "The Impact of a Study of Christian Worship (with Special Reference to the Sacrament of the Lord's Supper) on a Congregation of The United Church of Canada." D. Min. project report, Drew University, 1982.

Badertscher, John. "As Others Saw Us." In *Prairie Spirit: Perspectives on the Heritage of the United Church of Canada in the West.* Edited by Dennis L. Butcher, et al. Winnipeg: University of Manitoba Press, 1985.

Bagnell, Barbara. "Would You Call This Worship?" *The United Church Observer* (April 1971): 14-17.

Baker, Frank. "The Trans-Atlantic Triangle: Relations between British, Canadian, and American Methodism during Wesley's Lifetime." *Bulletin of The United Church Archives* 28 (1979).

Baptism, Eucharist, and Ministry. World Council of Churches Faith and Order Paper No. 111. Geneva: World Council of Churches, 1982; First Canadian Edition. Toronto: The Anglican Book Centre, 1983.

Barkley, John M. "Baptism: Reformed." In *A New Dictionary of Liturgy and Worship*. Edited by J. G. Davies. London: SCM, 1986.

——. *The Worship of the Reformed Church*. London: Lutterworth Press, 1966.

Barth, Karl. *The Teaching of the Church Regarding Baptism*. Translated by E. Payne. London: SCM Press, 1948.

Barthel, Alan. "*Voices United:* The Hymn and Worship Book of The United Church of Canada." *The Hymn* 50, no. 2 (April 1999): 8-11.

Barthel, Alan, David R. Newman, and Paul Scott Wilson. *A Guide to Sunday Worship in The United Church of Canada*. Toronto: The United Church Publishing House, 1988.

Bedell, Kenneth B. *Worship in the Methodist Tradition*. Nashville: Discipleship Resources, 1976.

Beginning the Faith Journey. A Filmstrip with Cassette. Audio-Visual Education Library, Toronto.

Berry, W. G. *Schools for Elders: A Manual for Elders Outlining Their Duties and the Responsibility of Sessions in the Local Church*. Toronto: The Board of Evangelism and Social Service, The United Church of Canada, 1953.

Bettson, Bob, Murial Duncan. "Christian Initiation Remit." *The United Church Observer* (May 1990): 10.

Birks, W. N. *The Chancel Before and After*. Toronto: The United Church Publishing House, 1947.

Bouyer, Louis. *Christian Initiation*. Translated by J. R. Foster. New York: Macmillan and Co. Ltd, 1960.

——. *Liturgical Piety*. Indiana: Notre Dame Press, 1955.

Bradshaw, Paul F. *The Search for the Origins of Christian Worship: Sources and Methods for the Study of Early Liturgy*. Second Edition. London: SPCK, 2002.

Brightman, F. E. *The English Rite: Being a Synopsis of the Sources and Revisions of the Book of Common Prayer*. Vol. II. Second Edition Revised. London: Revinstons, 1921.

Building the Smaller Church. The Committee on Church Architecture. Toronto: The United Church of Canada, [1959].

Building Your Church. The Committee on Church Architecture. Toronto: The United Church of Canada, 1958.

Butcher, Dennis L. et al., eds. *Prairie Spirit: Perspectives on the Heritage of The United Church of Canada in the West*. Winnipeg: University of Manitoba Press, 1985.

Campbell, Douglas F. "The Anglican and United Churches in Church Union Dialogue, 1943-75." *Studies in Religion* 17, no. 3 (1988): 303-314.

Cardwell, Edward. *A History of Conferences and Other Proceedings Connected with the Revision of the Book of Common Prayer: from the Year 1558 to the Year 1690*. Third Edition. Oxford: Oxford University Press, 1849.

Caron, Charlotte. *Eager for Worship: Theologies, Practices, and Perspectives on Worship in The United Church of Canada*. The McGeachy Papers, VII. Toronto: Division of Ministry Personnel and Education, United Church of Canada, 2000.

Carson, George S. *A Primary Catechism for religious instruction in the home and Sunday School.* First Edition, 1904. Toronto: The United Church Publishing House, 1931.

Catalogue of Resources. Celebration: A Centre of Contemporary Worship. Toronto: The United Church of Canada, 1969-1976.

Catechism. The Commission on Christian Faith. Toronto: The Board of Evangelism and Social Service, The United Church of Canada, 1942.

Celebrate...what's happening. Celebration Advisory/Resource Committee. Toronto: The United Church of Canada, 1976-1978.

Chalmers, Randolph Carleton. *Our Living Faith: An Interpretation of the Faith of The United Church of Canada.* Toronto: The United Church Publishing House, 1949.

——. *See The Christ Stand! A Study in Doctrine in The United Church of Canada.* Toronto: The Ryerson Press, 1945.

Christian Initiation. Task Force on Christian Initiation, The Anglican Church of Canada. Toronto: The Anglican Book Centre, 1974.

Christian Initiation: Birth and Growth in the Christian Society. Commission on Christian Initiation, Church of England. London: The General Synod of the Church of England, 1971.

Christian Initiation, Membership: Its Meaning and Expression. Canadian Anglican Liturgical Series. No. 2. Toronto: The Anglican Book Centre, 1975.

Christian Initiation: The Quest for Renewal. Division of Mission in Canada, The Task Force on Christian Initiation. Toronto: The United Church of Canada, 1979.

Christian Initiation: Towards a Renewed Understanding of Christian Initiation. Canadian Anglican Liturgical Series. No. 1. Toronto: The Anglican Book Centre, 1974.

Christianizing the Social Order. The Board of Evangelism and Social Service. Toronto: The United Church of Canada, 1934.

Christie, Nancy. "In these Times of Democratic Rage and Delusion: Popular Religion and The Challenge to the Established Order." In *The Canadian Protestant Experience: 1760-1990.* Edited by George A. Rawlyk. Burlington: Welch, 1990.

Church and Manse. The Committee on Architecture. Toronto: The United Church of Canada, 1964.

Church Membership: Doctrine and Practice in The United Church of Canada. Committee on Christian Faith. Toronto: The Board of Evangelism and Social Service and The Board of Christian Education, 1963.

Clarke, Patricia. "Battlefront Report on the New Hymnbook." *The United Church Observer* (August 1970): 8.

——. "Church Votes Against Baptism Change." *The United Church Observer* (January 1984): 10-11.

——. "Hymning and Hawing in Smoke-filled Room." *The United Church Observer* (15 March 1970): 8.

——. "Is Anybody Here Celebrating?" *The United Church Observer* (1 October 1969): 6.

——. "Lift Up your Hearts." *The United Church Observer* (May 1975): 13.

——. "The New Hymnary: What's In, What's Out, What's What." *The United Church Observer* (15 March 1970): 12-15

——. "Now What's Happening to Baptism?" *The United Church Observer* (March 1980): 12.

Clifford, N. Keith. "No Easy Process: Alexander Macmillan and the Birth of 'The Hymnary.'" *Touchstone* 8, no. 1 (January 1990): 30-43.

——. *The Resistance to Church Union in Canada: 1904-1939.* Vancouver: University of British Columbia Press, 1985.

Common Lectionary: The Lectionary Proposed by the Consultation on Common Texts. New York: The Church Hymnal Corporation, 1983.

Creeds: A Report of The Committee on Christian Faith. The Committee on Christian Faith. Toronto: The Ryerson Press, 1969.

Cullmann, Oscar. *Baptism in the New Testament.* Translated by J. K. S. Reid. London: SCM Press, 1950.

Davidson, Richard. "The Book of Common Order and The Book of Common Prayer." *Cap and Gown Magazine* (April 1937): 13-16.

——. "The Lord's Supper as the Norm of Common Worship." *Christendom* 5 (1940): 560-568.

——. *The Meaning of Baptism.* Toronto: The Board of Evangelism and Social Service, The United Church of Canada, 1943.

——. "Purposes of the New United Church Catechism." *Saturday Night* (15 April 1944): 22.

Davidson, Richard H. N. "How to Build a Church for Worship." *The United Church Observer* (1 April 1963): 19, 45.

——. "Which Bible for the New Hymnary?" *The United Church Observer* (15 October 1964): 18.

Davies, Horton. "Baptism: Congregationalist." In *A New Dictionary of Liturgy and Worship.* Edited by J. G. Davies. London: SCM, 1986.

——. *The Worship of the English Puritans.* Westminster: Dacre Press, 1948.

Davies, J. G. *The Architectural Setting of Baptism.* London: Barrie and Rockliff, 1962.

——. "Baptistery." In *A New Dictionary of Liturgy and Worship.* Edited by J. G. Davies. London: SCM, 1986.

——. "The Disintegration of the Christian Initiation Rites." *Theology* 50 (1947): 407-412.

——, ed. *A New Dictionary of Liturgy & Worship.* London: SCM, 1986.

De Clerck, Paul. "In the Beginning was the Word: Presidential Address." *Studia Liturgica* 22 (1922): 1-16.

Design for Worship. The Committee on Church Architecture. First Edition, 1952. Toronto: The United Church of Canada, 1962.

Dingham, W. S. "The Making of the Hymnary." *The New Outlook* (3 June 1931): 517, 518.

Dix, Gregory. *The Theology of Confirmation in Relation to Baptism.* London: Dacre Press, 1946.

The Doctrine and Practice of Infant Baptism. The Commission on the Christian Faith. Toronto: The Board of Evangelism and Social Service, The Board of Christian Education, The United Church of Canada, 1954.

Documents on the Liturgy, 1963-1970: Conciliar, Papal, and Curial Texts. International Commission on English in the Liturgy. Collegeville: Liturgical Press, 1982.

Donnelly, Ralph. "Editorial: Spectators at a Revolution." *Touchstone* 1, no. 2 (May 1983): 4-5.

Dow, John. "Richard Davidson: Churchman." *The Living Church.* Edited by Harold W. Vaughan. Toronto: The United Church Publishing House, 1949.

———. *This Is Our Faith: An Exposition of the Statement of Faith of The United Church of Canada.* Toronto: The Board of Evangelism and Social Service, The United Church of Canada, 1943.

Duck, Ruth C. *Gender and the Name of God: The Trinitarian Baptismal Formula.* New York: The Pilgrim Press, 1991.

Dunstan, Sylvia. Review of *A Sunday Liturgy. Touchstone* 3, no. 2 (May 1985): 55-56.

Eddy, Earl B. "The Congregational Tradition in Canada." In *The Churches and the Canadian Experience.* Edited by John Webster Grant. Toronto: Ryerson Press, 1963.

The Eldership: The Report of The Committee on Christian Faith. Toronto: The United Church of Canada, 1966.

Ferries, Rose. "Review: *A Place For You: The Integration of Children Into the Life of the Church.*" *Touchstone* 5, no. 3 (September 1987): 50-52.

Fiddes, Victor. *The Architectural Requirements of Protestant Worship.* Toronto: The Ryerson Press, 1961.

———. "The Observance of the Church Year." *The United Church Observer* (1 September 1961): 13.

Fink, Peter E., ed. *The New Dictionary of Sacramental Worship.* Collegeville: The Liturgical Press, 1990.

Fisher, J. D. C. *Christian Initiation. Baptism in the Medieval West. A Study in the Disintegration of the Primitive Rite of Initiation.* London: SPCK, 1965.

———. *Christian Initiation. The Reformation Period. Some Early Reformed Rites of Baptism and Confirmation and Other Contemporary Documents.* London: SPCK, 1970.

———. "Lutheran, Anglican, and Reformed Rites." In *The Study of Liturgy.* Cheslyn Jones, Geoffrey Wainwright, Edward Yarnold, S.J., eds. London: SPCK, 1978.

Forrest, A. C. "Confirmation: What Does It Mean?" *The United Church Observer* (5 April 1963): 2, 12, 13.

———. "A New Hymnary." *The United Church Observer* (1 May 1964): 8-10, 26.

Fraser, Mary. "Who Makes the Rules." *The United Church Observer* (March 1990): 5.

French, Goldwin. *Parson & Politics: The Role of the Wesleyan Methodists in Upper Canada and the Maritimes from 1780-1855.* Toronto: The Ryerson Press, 1962.

———. "The People Called Methodists in Canada." In *The Churches and the Canadian Experience.* Edited by John Webster Grant. Toronto: Ryerson Press, 1963..

From Ashes to Fire. Services of Worship for the Seasons of Lent and Easter with Introduction and Commentary, Section on Worship, Board of Discipleship of The United Methodist Church. Supplemental Worship Resources 8. Nashville: Abingdon, 1979.

Fullerton, Aubrey. "The Oughtness of Traditions." *The New Outlook* (10 January 1934): 23.

Gallinger, Kenneth. "Question Box." *The United Church Observer* (August 1989): 17.

Gathering: A Packet for Worship Planners. (three times a year) The Working Unit on Worship and Liturgy, The Division of Mission in Canada. Toronto: The United Church of Canada, 1983-2003.

Getting It All Together: A Packet For Worship Planners. The Celebration Centre, The Committee on Worship, The Division of Mission in Canada. Toronto: The United Church of Canada, 1974-1983.

Grant, John Webster. "Blending Traditions: The United Church of Canada." In *The Churches and the Canadian Experience.* Edited by John Webster Grant. Toronto: Ryerson Press, 1963.

——. *The Canadian Experience of Church Union.* London: Lutterworth Press, 1967.

——. *The Church in the Canadian Era.* First Edition, 1972. Burlington: Welch Publishing Company Inc., 1988.

——. *A Profusion of Spires: Religion in Nineteenth-Century Ontario.* Toronto: University of Toronto Press, 1988.

——. "The United Church and Its Heritage in Evangelism." *Touchstone* 1, no. 3 (October 1983): 6-13.

——, ed. *The Churches and the Canadian Experience.* Toronto: The Ryerson Press, 1963.

Growth in Understanding: A Study Guide on Church Union. The Committee on Christian Unity and the Church Universal of The Anglican Church of Canada and The Commission on Union of The United Church of Canada. Toronto: The Anglican Church of Canada, The United Church of Canada, 1960.

Gutiérrez, Gustavo. *A Theology of Liberation.* 15th Anniversary Edition with a new introduction by the Author. New York: Orbis Books, 1988.

Harding, Bruce. "Singing Our Faith: The Music of *Voices United.*" *Touchstone* 15, no. 1 (January 1997): 26-37.

Harding, Thomas Reginald. "The Development of Liturgical Resources in The United Church of Canada, 1930-1986." Th.D. diss., Trinity College, Toronto School of Theology, 1990.

——. "Do Away with Confirmation!" *Practice of Ministry in Canada* 2, no. 4 (Winter 1985): 9-10.

——. "The Major Orders of *The Book of Common Order of the United Church of Canada* (1932): Sources and Development." Th.M. thesis, Vancouver School of Theology, 1986.

——. "The Marriage Services of the United Church of Canada: Stages on a Liturgical Journey." *Toronto Journal of Theology* 7, no. 2 (1991): 169-195.

——. "The Reformed Tradition." *The Practice of Ministry in Canada* 4, no. 5 (January 1988): 9-10.

——. *Presbyterian, Methodist, and Congregational Worship in Canada Prior to 1925.* Toronto: Evensong, 1995.

——. Review of *Baptism and Renewal of Baptismal Faith.* In *Touchstone* 6, no. 3 (September 1988): 49-50.

Harding, Thomas R., Bruce Harding. *Patterns of Worship in The United Church of Canada, 1925-1997.* Toronto: Evensong, 1996.

Hatchet, Marion J. *Commentary on the American Prayer Book.* New York: Seabury, 1981.

Henderson, Donald. "The New Service of Baptism" *The United Church Observer* (1 February 1966): 29.

Highways of the Heart: A Devotional Book Based on "The Statement of Faith." The Commission on Christian Faith. Toronto: The United Church Publishing House, 1941.

Hill, John W. B. *Making Disciples: Serving Those Who Are Entering the Christian Life.* Toronto: The Hoskin Group, 1991.

——. *Thinking about Baptism.* Toronto: Anglican Book Centre, 1982.

Hoffman, Lawrence A. *Beyond the Text: A Holistic Approach to Liturgy.* Bloomington and Indianapolis: Indiana University Press, 1987.

Hogman, John. "Christian Initiation." *Touchstone* 1, no. 2 (May 1983): 30-35.

Holeton, David R., ed. *Growing in Newness of Life: Christian Initiation in Anglicanism Today.* Papers from the Fourth International Anglican Liturgical Consultation. Toronto: Anglican Book Centre, 1993.

——. "The Liturgical Implications of Feminist Proposals to Change the Trinitarian Baptismal Formula." *Ecumenical Trends* 17, no. 5 (1988): 69-72.

——. "Liturgical Space and Christian Formation." *Consensus: A Canadian Lutheran Journal of Theology* 17, no. 2 (1991): 135-154.

Holland, Bernard G. *Baptism in Early Methodism.* London: Epworth Press, 1970.

Hollings, T. E. "The Rationale of Lent." *The United Church Observer* (15 February 1952): 5.

Hopkirk, Gail, and Janice MacLean. *Preparation for Baptism and Renewal of Baptismal Faith.* Part III: Adult Baptism or Faith Renewal. Toronto: The United Church of Canada, 1990.

Hossie, Orville P. "Your Church Building—Focus on Church Life." *The United Church Observer* (15 August 1954): 3.

Hutchinson, Gerald. "British Methodists and the Hudson's Bay Company, 1840-1854." In *Prairie Spirit: Perspectives on the Heritage of the United Church of Canada in the West.* Edited by Dennis L. Butcher, et al. Winnipeg: University of Manitoba Press, 1985.

Irwin, Wayne. Review of *A Guide to Sunday Worship in The United Church of Canada*, by Alan Barthel, David R. Newman, Paul Scott Wilson. In *Touchstone* 7, no. 2 (May 1989): 55.

Jagger, Peter John. *Christian initiation, 1552-1969: Rites of Baptism and Confirmation since the Reformation Period.* London: SPCK, 1970.

Jones, Cheslyn, Geoffrey Wainwright, and Edward Yarnold, S.J., eds. *The Study of Liturgy.* London: SPCK, 1978.

Kavanagh, Aidan. "Christian Initiation: Tactics and Strategies." *Made, Not Born: New Perspectives on Christian Initiation and the Catechumenate.* The Murphy Center for Liturgical Research. Notre Dame: University of Notre Dame Press, 1976.

——. "Confirmation: A Suggestion from Structure." *Worship* 58 (1984): 386-395.

——. *Confirmation: Origins and Reform.* New York: Pueblo Publishing Company, 1988.

——. "How Rite Develops: Some Laws Intrinsic to Liturgical Evolution." *Worship* 41, no. 6 (1967): 334-347.

——. *On Liturgical Theology*. New York: Pueblo Publishing Company, 1984.

——. *The Shape of Baptism: The Rite of Christian Initiation.* New York: Pueblo Publishing Company, 1978.

Kelly, J. N. D. *Early Christian Creeds.* Third Edition. New York: Longman, 1991.

Kelly, W. Morrison. "Fifty Years of Worship in the United Church." *Gathering: A Packet for Worship Planners.* Advent/Christmas/Epiphany (1985), Study Papers: 1-6.

——. "Liturgical Trends in The United Church of Canada." *Anglican Dialogue* Autumn (1967): 17-22.

——. "Preaching from the Lectionary." *Getting It All Together* Lent/Easter (1976), Studies in Worship: 1-4.

Kervin, William S. "Celebrate God's Presence, Part I: 'It's not a good time to publish a service book.'" *Gathering* (Advent-Christmas-Epiphany 2000/2001): 34-36.

——. "Celebrate God's Presence, Part II: 'But Is It United Church Tradition?'" *Gathering* (Lent-Easter-Pentecost 2001): 38-39.

——. "Celebrate God's Presence, Part III: A Service Book vs. A Book of Services." *Gathering* (Summer-Autumn 2000/2001): 52-54.

——. "*Forms of Service (1926):* A Study in the Liturgical Ethos of The United Church of Canada," *Toronto Journal of Theology* 17, no. 2 (Fall 2001): 315-229.

——. "The Language of Baptism: A Study of the Authorized Baptismal Liturgies of The United Church of Canada." Th.D. diss., Emmanuel College, Toronto School of Theology, 1994.

——. "The Three Hymn Books of The United Church of Canada: The Dialectic of a New Song." *Touchstone* 19, no. 2 (May 2001): 6-21.

Kilpatrick, Thomas Buchanan. *Our Common Faith.* Toronto: The Ryerson Press, 1928.

The Liturgy Constitution. New York: Paulist Press, 1964.

Lockhead, Arthur W. *A Companion to the Catechism.* Toronto: The United Church Publishing House, 1945.

MacDonald, Clarke W. "Sunday 11:00 a.m. What's It All About?" *The United Church Observer* (1 September 1969): 24-25.

MacMillan, Alexander. "Church Praise in The United Church of Canada." *The New Outlook* (24 June 1925): 4.

——. *Hymns of the Church: A Companion to The Hymnary of The United Church of Canada.* Toronto: The United Church Publishing House, 1935.

——. "A New Musical Triad." *The New Outlook* (24 June 1925): 14.

Made, Not Born: New Perspectives on Christian Initiation and the Catechumenate. The Murphy Center for Liturgical Research. Notre Dame: University of Notre Dame Press, 1976.

The Manual. Toronto: The United Church Publishing House, 1929-1993.

The Manuel of The United Church of Canada: Constitution and Government. Issued Under the Authority of the General Council of 1926, by the Executive, Subject to Revision and Amendment by the Next General Council. Toronto: The United Church Publishing House, 1928.

Mathers, Donald M. *The Word and The Way.* Toronto: The United Church Publishing House, 1962.

Matheson, Daniel C. "New Baptism Service Sent to Presbyteries." *News-Letter* (October 1962): 13.

Matheson, Hugh. "The Interior Arrangement of a Church: Some Applications of the Principles of Public Worship to the Art of Church Building." *The New Outlook* (8 February 1928): 7, 8.

Maxwell, William D. *A History of Worship in the Church of Scotland.* London: Oxford University Press, 1955.

——. *John Knox's Genevan Service Book.* Edinburgh: Oliver and Boyd, 1931.

——. "On Observing the Christian Year." *The New Outlook* (28 March 1928): 4.

——. *An Outline of Christian Worship with Special Reference to the Free Churches.* Revised Edition. London: Oxford University Press, 1949.

McArthur, A. Allan. *The Christian Year and Lectionary Reform.* Toronto: The Ryerson Press, 1958.

McNally, Fred W. "Baptism and Christian Nurture: A Position Paper." TMs. The United Church of Canada/Victoria University Archives, Division of Mission in Canada, Christian Initiation Task Group, Minutes.

——. "Directions for Worship in the Early Eighties." *Getting It All Together* Advent/Christmas, Study Papers (1981): 1-5.

——. "Lord, Sometimes We Just Feel Like . . ." *Touchstone* 1, no. 2 (May 1983): 16-20.

McNeill, John Thomas. *The Presbyterian Church in Canada: 1875-1925.* Toronto: Presbyterian Church in Canada, 1925.

Membership: Its Meaning and Expression. The Doctrine and Worship Committee of the Anglican Church of Canada. Canadian Anglican Liturgical Series No. 2. Toronto: The Anglican Book Centre, 1975.

Mercer, Francis Dean. "The Liturgical and Sacramental Development of the Free Methodist Church in Canada, with Special Attention to the Rituals of Baptism and the Lord's Supper." Th.D. diss., Trinity College, Toronto School of Theology, 1991.

Milne, Mike. "Christian Initiation: Play It Again." *The United Church Observer* (October 1984): 16.

Moffat, Richard H. "More on Christian Initiation." *The United Church Observer* (June 84): 3.

Moir, John S., ed. *The Cross in Canada.* Toronto: The Ryerson Press, 1966.

——. *Enduring Witness: A History of the Presbyterian Church in Canada.* Toronto: Bryant Press, 1974.

Morris, John. "Sequence of Events in Christian Initiation." *Getting It All Together* Creation, Studies in Worship (1976): 1-2.

Newman, David. "An Integrated Model for Worship, Education, Pastoral Care, and Outreach." TMs. The United Church of Canada/Victoria University Archives, Division of Mission in Canada, Christian Initiation Task Group, "Minutes."

——. *As Often as You Do This: Toward More Frequent Celebration of the Lord's Supper in The United Church of Canada.* Toronto: The Division of Mission in Canada, the United Church of Canada, 1981.

——. "Ordination in The United Church of Canada: An Essay in Liturgical Theology." *Toronto Journal of Theology* 2, no. 1 (1986): 94-104.

———. "Worship in The United Church of Canada." *Worship* 53 (1979): 538-48.
"News-Letter." Committee on Church Worship and Ritual. November 1969.
Old, Hughes Oliphant. *Worship That Is Reformed According to Scripture.* Atlanta: John Knox, 1984.
O'Neill, Lorne. "Fencing the Table." *The United Church Observer* (January 1990): 5.
Onions, W. G. "We Should Celebrate the Great Christian Festivals." *The United Church Observer* (1 February 1940): 16.
Ordo Lectionum Missae. Vatican City: Typis Polyglottis Vaticanis, 1969.
Pellissier, Louis. "Review Article: *Preparation for Baptism and Renewal of Baptismal Faith.* Part I: Preparing Parents for Baptism of Their Children." *Touchstone* 9, no. 2 (May 1991): 46-49.
———. "Review Article: *Preparation for Baptism and Renewal of Baptismal Faith.* Part II: Preparing Young People for a Profession of Faith." *Touchstone* 8, no. 3 (September 1990): 49-53.
———. "Review Article: *Preparation for Baptism and Renewal of Baptismal Faith.* Part III: Adult Baptism or Faith Renewal." *Touchstone* 8, no. 3 (September 1990): 49-53.
Perry, M. *Crisis for Confirmation.* London: SCM, 1967.
A Place for You: The Integration of Children Into the Life of the Church. A Report to the 31st General Council with Appended Study Guide. A Report from The Ministry with Children Working Unit, Division of Mission in Canada. Toronto: The United Church of Canada, 1986.
Plan of Union and By-Laws. The Anglican Church of Canada, Christian Church (Disciples of Christ), The United Church of Canada. Toronto: The General Commission on Church Union, 1972.
Plato, William Russell. "Eucharistic Worship and The United Church of Canada." Ph.D. diss, St. Michael's College, Toronto, 1974.
———. "The United Church of Canada and Eucharistic Worship." *The Bulletin* 22 (1973): 16-20.
Preparation for Baptism and Renewal of Baptismal Faith. Part II: Preparing Young People for a Profession of Faith. Toronto: The United Church of Canada, 1990.
Presuppositions for the Development of a Curriculum for the Sunday Church Schools of The United Church of Canada. A statement from the Board of Christian Education and the Board of Publication of the United Church of Canada. Toronto: The United Church of Canada, 1958.
Principles, Criteria, Resources for Confirmation. Task Group on Confirmation Resources, Division of Mission in Canada. Toronto: The United Church of Canada, [1978].
The Principles of Union between the Anglican Church of Canada and The United Church of Canada. The Committee on Christian Unity and the Church Universal, The Anglican Church of Canada and the Committee on Union, The United Church of Canada. Toronto: The Anglican Church of Canada, The United Church of Canada, 1965.
Procter-Smith, Marjorie. *In Her Own Rite: Constructing Feminist Liturgical Tradition.* Nashville: Abingdon Press, 1990.
Project Ministry. The Report of the Task Force on Ministry, Division of Mission in Canada. Toronto: The United Church of Canada, 1984.

Prospectus: The New Curriculum. First Edition, 1961. Toronto: Board of Christian Education and Board of Publications, The United Church of Canada, 1963.

Rawlyk, George. *Ravished by the Spirit: Religious Revivals, Baptists, and Henry Alline.* Montreal & Kingston: McGill-Queen's University Press, 1984.

Ritual in a New Day: An Invitation. Alternate Rituals Project, Section on Worship, Board of Discipleship of The United Methodist Church. Nashville: Abingdon, 1976.

Record of Proceedings. Toronto: The United Church Publishing House, 1927, 1929-1993.

The Report on Christian Initiation. Division of Mission in Canada, The Project Group on Christian Initiation. Toronto: The United Church of Canada, 1983.

The Report of the Project Group on Christian Initiation. Division of Mission in Canada, The Project Group on Christian Initiation. Toronto: The United Church of Canada, 1983.

The Revised Common Lectionary: The Consultation on Common Texts. Winfield: Wood Lake Books, 1992.

Sacrosanctum Concilium: The Constitution on the Sacred Liturgy. 4 December 1963. In *Vatican Council II: The Conciliar and Post Conciliar Documents.* Edited and translated by Austin Flannery, O.P. (Collegeville: The Liturgical Press, 1975).

Saunders, J. Clark. "Congregationalism in Manitoba, 1879-1937." In *Prairie Spirit: Perspectives on the Heritage of the United Church of Canada in the West.* Edited by Dennis L. Butcher, et al. Winnipeg: University of Manitoba Press, 1985.

Schmeiser, James, ed. *Initiation Theology.* Toronto: The Anglican Book Centre, 1978.

Semple, Stuart. "The Hymn Book Revisited." *Touchstone* 4, no. 1 (January 1986): 40-44.

Senn, Frank. "Protestant Worship: Does It Exist?" *Worship* 64, no. 4 (1990): 322-330.

Sewell, William, David Stapleton, Roger Tomes, and Brian Wren. *Contemporary Prayers for Public Worship.* London: SCM Press, 1965.

Shepherd, Harvey. "Faith on the Free, Frantic Campus." *The United Church Observer* (15 November 1967): 12-15.

Silcox, C.E. *Church Union in Canada.* New York: Institute of Social and Religious Research, 1933.

Smith, Fred. "Spiritual Calisthenics." *The New Outlook* (26 October 1932): 1001.

Smith, Neil. G. "The Presbyterian Tradition in Canada." In *The Churches and the Canadian Experience.* Edited by John Webster Grant. Toronto: Ryerson Press, 1963.

Smith, Neil G., Allan L. Farris, and H. Keith Markell. *A Short History of the Presbyterian Church in Canada.* Toronto: Presbyterian Publications, 1967.

So You Have a Church Building Program. The Committee on Church Architecture. Toronto: The United Church of Canada, [1953].

Spencer, Margaret. *Preparation for Baptism and Renewal of Baptismal Faith.* Part I: Preparing Parents for Baptism of Their Children. Toronto: The United Church of Canada, 1989.

Spinks, Bryan D. *Freedom or Order? The Eucharistic Liturgy in English Congregationalism, 1645-1980.* Allison Park: Pickwick, 1984.

Stackhouse, John G. "The Protestant Experience in Canada Since 1945." In *The Canadian Protestant Experience: 1760-1990.* Edited by George A. Rawlyk. Burlington: Welch, 1990.

Statement of Faith. The Commission on Christian Faith. Toronto: The Board of Evangelism and Social Service, The United Church of Canada, 1940.

Stevens, Francis. "In Plain English." *The United Church Observer* (15 April 1962): 18, 22.

Stevens, Francis. "A Plea for the Use of Modern Language in Church Liturgy: In Plain English." *The United Church Observer* (15 April 1962): 18, 22.

Stewart, Gordon, and George Rawlyk. *A People Highly Favoured of God: The Nova Scotia Yankees and the American Revolution.* Toronto: Macmillan, 1972.

Studia Liturgica. Vol. 21-22, no. 1 (1991-1992).

A Suggested Plan for the Reunion of the United Church of Canada and the Anglican Church of Canada. (As submitted to the two Communions by a committee appointed by The London Conference of the United Church of Canada and The Anglican Diocese of Huron). London, On.: The London Conference of the United Church of Canada and the Anglican Diocese of Huron, [1964].

Sutherland, Alexander. *Methodism in Canada: Its Work and Its Story.* Toronto: Methodist Mission Rooms, 1904.

Taft, Robert F. *Beyond East and West: Problems in Liturgical Understanding.* Washington, D.C.: The Pastoral Press, 1984.

——. "The Structural Analysis of Liturgical Units: An Essay in Methodology." *Worship* 52 (1978): 314-329.

Taylor, Alex. "Who's In, Who's Out." *The United Church Observer* (February 1990): 4.

Thompson, Bard. *Liturgies of the Western Church.* Philadelphia: Fortress Press, 1961.

Toon, Peter. *Hyper-Calvinsim*. London: Orange Tree, 1967.

Towards a Renewed Understanding of Christian Initiation. The Doctrine and Worship Committee of the Anglican Church of Canada. Canadian Anglican Liturgical Series No. 1. Toronto: The Anglican Book Centre, 1974.

Underhill, Bruce. "Putting Humpty Dumpty Together Again: Christian Initiation in The United Church of Canada from a Liturgical Perspective." *Getting It All Together.* Advent-Christmas, Study Papers (1978): 3-14.

Unsworth, J. K. "Liturgical Forms of New Book Show Social Sympathy.' *Daily Colonist*, 4 December 1932, 10.

——. "Many Communions Contribute to New Volume of Liturgy." *Daily Colonist*, 27 November 1932, 12.

——. "United Church Has Liturgical Forms." *Daily Colonist*, 20 November 1932, 5.

Vatican Council II: The Conciliar and Post Conciliar Documents. Edited and translated by Austin Flannery, O. P. Collegville: The Liturgical Press, 1975.

Vaughan, Harold W., ed. *The Living Church*. A Book in Memory of the Life and Work of Rev. Richard Davidson, M.A., Ph.D., D.D., Principle of Emmanuel College, Toronto. Toronto: United Church Publishing House, 1949.

Wadsworth, G. Campbell. "Our Readers' Forum: The Book of Common Order." *The New Outlook* (14 February 1934): 109.

——. Title unknown. *Gazette*, 21 February 1959, 10.

——. "The United Church Communion Rite of 1932." *Canadian Journal of Theology* 22 (1966): 110-117.

Wainwright, Geoffrey. *Christian Initiation*. London: Lutterworth Press, 1969.

Watkins, Keith. "Protestant Worship: Many Traditions or One?" *Worship* 64, no. 4 (1990): 308-331.

Watson, David Lowes. "Methodist Spirituality." In *Protestant Spiritual Traditions*. Edited by Frank C. Senn. New York: Paulist Press, 1986.

Watts, Mac. "*Voices United*: A Warm-Hearted Book." *Touchstone* 15, no. 1 (January, 1997): 7-25.

Wells, Harold. "The Trinity and the Good News (Part I)." *Touchstone* 8, no. 2 (May 1990): 4-16.

——. "The Trinity and the Good News (Part II)." *Touchstone* 8, no. 3 (September 1990): 6-16.

Wesley, John. "The New Birth." In *Wesley's Doctrinal Standards: Part I. The Sermons*. Edited by N. Burwash. Toronto: William Briggs, 1881.

Westerhoff, John H. III, and William H. Willimon. *Liturgy and Learning through the Life Cycle*. New York: The Seabury Press, 1980.

Whitaker, E. C., ed. *Documents of the Baptismal Liturgy*. Second Edition. London: SPCK, 1970.

White, James F. "Baptism, Methodist." In *A New Dictionary of Liturgy and Worship*. Edited by J. G. Davies. London: SCM, 1986.

——. "A Protestant Manifesto." *The Christian Century* 99 (27 January 1982): 82-86.

——. *Protestant Worship and Church Architecture: Theological and Historical Considerations*. New York: Oxford University Press, 1964.

——. *Protestant Worship: Traditions in Transition*. Louisville: Westminster/John Knox Press, 1989.

The Whole People of God. A Curriculum for Church Schools published by Winfield: Wood Lake Books, 1987-2002.

Wright, Robert A. "The Canadian Protestant Tradition." In *The Canadian Protestant Experience: 1760-1990*. Edited by George A. Rawlyk. Burlington: Welch, 1990.

Year Book (& Directory). Toronto: The United Church Publishing House, 1927, 1929-1993.

Year Book and Record of Proceedings. Toronto: The United Church Publishing House, 1926, 1928.

Young, John H. "Sacred Cow or White Elephant? The Doctrine Section of the Basis of Union." *Touchstone* 16, no. 2 (May 1998): 29-46.

Young, W. Harold. "The New Hymnary." *The New Outlook* (30 July 1930): 731, 743.

Index

About the Author

William S. Kervin is Assistant Professor of Public Worship (The Old St. Andrew's Chair) at Emmanuel College of Victoria University and the Toronto School of Theology in the University of Toronto. An ordained minister of The United Church of Canada, he has served in rural, urban, and overseas ministries. He has also contributed to the development of the United Church's recent hymn and worship resources, *Voices United* and *Celebrate God's Presence.* Educated at Mount Allison University in New Brunswick (B.Sc.), Atlantic School of Theology in Nova Scotia (M.Div.), and Emmanuel College (Th.D.), he is a member of the North American Academy of Liturgy, The Hymn Society in the United States and Canada, and Societas Liturgica. The author of numerous articles on liturgy, he is a frequent preacher, presider, lecturer, and workshop leader.